Mac for Linux Geeks

Tony Steidler-Dennison

Apress®

Mac for Linux Geeks

ISBN-13 (pbk): 978-1-4302-1650-6

ISBN-13 (electronic): 978-1-4302-1651-3

Lead Editors: Frank Pohlmann and Michelle Lowman
Technical Reviewer: Peter O'Gorman
Editorial Board: Clay Andres, Steve Anglin, Mark Beckner, Ewan Buckingham, Tony Campbell, Gary Cornell, Jonathan Gennick, Michelle Lowman, Matthew Moodie, Jeffrey Pepper, Frank Pohlmann, Ben Renow-Clarke, Dominic Shakeshaft, Matt Wade, Tom Welsh
Project Manager: Sofia Marchant
Copy Editor: Marilyn Smith
Associate Production Director: Kari Brooks-Copony
Production Editor: Liz Berry
Compositor: Dina Quan
Proofreader: Lisa Hamilton
Indexer: Broccoli Information Management
Artist: April Milne
Cover Designer: Kurt Krames
Manufacturing Director: Tom Debolski

Distributed to the book trade worldwide by Springer-Verlag New York, Inc., 233 Spring Street, 6th Floor, New York, NY 10013. Phone 1-800-SPRINGER, fax 201-348-4505, e-mail orders-ny@springer-sbm.com, or visit http://www.springeronline.com.

For information on translations, please contact Apress directly at 2855 Telegraph Avenue, Suite 600, Berkeley, CA 94705. Phone 510-549-5930, fax 510-549-5939, e-mail info@apress.com, or visit http://www.apress.com.

Apress and friends of ED books may be purchased in bulk for academic, corporate, or promotional use. eBook versions and licenses are also available for most titles. For more information, reference our Special Bulk Sales–eBook Licensing web page at http://www.apress.com/info/bulksales.

As always, for my girls, Laurie and Mia

Contents at a Glance

Contents

About the Author

TONY STEIDLER-DENNISON is a longtime Linux user and a recent convert to the Mac. He has coauthored two books on Linux and has written frequently for *Linux Journal* and *LinuxWorld*. He is also the host and producer of The Roadhouse Podcast, a weekly hour of "the finest blues you've never heard," at `http://roadhousepodcast.com/`.

Tony is a systems engineer with Rockwell Collins, Inc., leveraging open source technologies in communication products for commercial aviation. He and his family make their home in Iowa City, Iowa.

About the Technical Reviewer

PETER O'GORMAN is a software engineer. He first used a Mac in 1988, when he was a student at the University of Limerick, Ireland. Although he still uses one today, he also uses Linux, Solaris, AIX, and HP-UX on a daily basis.

Peter has contributed to a number of open source projects, including Apple's Darwin, Fink, MacPorts, GNU libtool, GCC, and Autoconf. He continues to make contributions to these projects when time allows.

Originally from Ireland, Peter has traveled the world, living in the United Kingdom, Australia, Hong Kong, and Japan before moving to Winnipeg, Canada, where he shivers through winters with his wife and daughter.

About the Technical Reviewer

Preface

I didn't come to the Mac overnight, though it must have seemed that way to my friends and family. One day, I was extolling the virtues of Linux and open source; the next, I was talking about the Macintosh platform with nearly as much vigor.

My first computer was an Atari 1040ST, a stunning piece of machinery for 1986. It was available for less than $1,500 and came equipped with an entire megabyte of RAM. I hadn't been in the fledgling computer club in school during the 70s, and I really couldn't put my finger on why I had any interest at all in computers. In fact, I'm not sure I had even seen one before taking a sales job at a Federated electronics store. Computers were for geeks, after all (or, as we so mockingly called them in school, nerds). But from the first time I connected to CompuServe, computing had its hooks in me deeply. In just a few short weeks, I had made friends with a fellow computer enthusiast in our city of Arlington, Texas, and we managed to battle it out in mock dogfights online with a crude flight simulator for hours on end. Our families quickly tired of the sound of the modem when they called. According to my wife, I had clearly developed a substance-abuse problem. I had. The substance was silicon.

My strong affinity for computing continued, but by 1996, I had begun to tire of the install/reboot/blue screen sequence of the young Windows 95. I acquired a Toshiba Infinia, a reasonably stout machine for its time, and often lugged a thick, heavy Compaq laptop to and from work. But I felt constrained, limited by the roadblocks that seemed built into Windows.

One day at work, I commiserated with a friend who happened to work in our company's IT department. He nodded his agreement without saying much, pulled on his ponytail, and let me finish. Then, almost casually, he mentioned, "I've been playing with this new operating system. It's called Linux. Been out for a few years. It's not easy to get configured, but it's pretty powerful and interesting."

Challenging, powerful, and interesting—that description caught my attention. "Where can I get it?" I asked.

"Net. It's free."

It took just a few all-nighters at home to research this new operating system, find and download the install diskettes (the Infinia had no CD burner, and ISO images of the few Linux distributions were few and far between), and fail miserably at the first several installation attempts. With each failed installation, I would give up and reinstall Windows, adding yet more hours to the already painful process. But with each attempt, the challenge rose a bit higher, until I resolved that no simple computer was going to defeat me. I researched, learned, and researched some more. When I discovered a HOWTO on dual-booting Windows and Linux, the lights started to come on. Shortly after, I got my first good installation of Red Hat 4.0, dual-booting with Windows 95, and was off to the races. I made a commitment when that installation was complete that I would use Windows only when absolutely necessary, and that it wouldn't be necessary too often. And I found my powerful, flexible, challenging operating system of choice. In short, Linux revived my love of computing, making my wife once again a victim of my renewed substance-abuse problem.

Within a few short years, I had left a legal-field programming position with a large Iowa insurance company to pursue dreams of dot-com dollars. My writing experience and abilities got me in the door of the first startup, a company that was founded by Anton Olsen, my Linux friend and mentor from the previous company. The shop was entirely open source, and I reveled in the atmosphere of a small company where, in one minute, I could draft and send out press releases, while the next brought yet another learning experience in a room full of open source gurus. The company was short-lived, but the experience infused me with even more passion for Linux, for programming, and for the unbridled idealism of the open source philosophy.

Less than a year later, I began writing a daily Linux e-mail newsletter for Chris Pirillo, Lockergnome's Penguin Shell. For my day job, I took a position building and configuring Linux-based computers—not just any computers, but computers to control observatory-grade robotic telescopes built by a company in my hometown of Iowa City. I also helped assemble those telescopes and flew around the world to install them at dark locations around the planet. When that small company failed, I became a partner in another, building and repairing computers, with a special interest and expertise in Linux. Over the next four years, I chased Linux through a revival of the telescope company, a presidential campaign, online shopping, online real estate, online document scanning, and finally, into the world of commercial aviation, where I still work today. It's not always been the best living; Linux has, nonetheless, been very good to me.

During those Linux-chasing years, I was aware of the other computing platforms outside the open source realm. In fact, as the necessity of home computers grew, snaring friends with a new desire to discover the Web, I often recommended Macintosh machines as their first. Although I had barely even seen a Mac, I knew they had a reputation for user-friendliness and some serious brand loyalty. In return for the recommendation, those friends planted a very small seed in my mind. I watched as they became real computer enthusiasts and hard-core advocates for the Macintosh platform. I saw in them a dedication that I understood. It wasn't much different from the one I felt for Linux. Although they didn't have (or require) the hard-core skills I had picked up over the years, there was no doubt that they were enjoying their computing experiences. That was the feeling that had drawn me into the Linux world. I enjoyed seeing it in others, even on the Mac.

The real seed for the move to the Mac came in late 2003, when I joined the presidential campaign of General Wesley Clark in Little Rock, Arkansas. I was the second hire in the tech staff and gladly worked from my Fedora-installed Dell Inspiron laptop. As we filled the tech department to what eventually totaled 18 staff members, more and more of them arrived in Little Rock with MacBooks under their arms. And those small computers just worked. I watched coworkers switch effortlessly between a stunning GUI and the command line—whatever suited their needs for the particular task at hand. All the Linux commands that I used so frequently were available, and the hardware and desktop were beautifully designed. Much of the technical heavy lifting in that campaign was done on Macs, including all the web design, large chunks of the database design, and significant portions of the PHP development. I left Little Rock in February 2004, knowing that, at some point in the future, I would own a Mac.

While it took a few years, I did fulfill that promise to myself in December 2006. I purchased a Mac mini, one of the 1.83 GHz Intel Core Duo variety, with 2GB of RAM. At the time, I was nearly two years into the production of The Roadhouse Podcast, a weekly hour of "the finest blues you've never heard." Although I understood that Mac OS X was solidly designed and built around the BSD operating system, I had some concerns about moving the production of the podcast to the Mac. I had landed on a routine with the show that was working well, though large periods of time were spent waiting for my old 800 MHz P3 Linux box to churn through encoding and conversion tasks. I had landed on a set of open source tools that met all my needs for the show, both practical and esoteric, and had no desire or time to learn a new Mac tool set. In the first week with the Mac mini on my desktop, I downloaded and installed those tools, either from the Web or via the MacPorts utility. And, on that first Saturday, my production time was actually reduced by a full two hours. The open source tools worked equally well on the Mac, and the solid hardware took less than half the time to accomplish the most CPU-intensive processes involved in assembling the show. In short, I was hooked.

It was at that point that I began to evangelize with friends and fellow computing professionals about the power of the Mac OS X system. Those who knew me well understood that efficiency was always my primary goal. They knew that for many years, an acceptable level of efficiency and stability were possible only with Linux. And, while they may have scratched their heads at the suddenness of my conversion, that conversion really wasn't, as it appeared, a transient overnight revelation. It had been a long time coming and was capped by the BSD base of Mac OS X.

It was only after purchasing the Mac mini that I realized the two pieces of Macintosh history that made this easy transition possible. The first was the introduction of Mac OS X. It was the first version of the Macintosh operating system to fully utilize BSD at its core. While Apple has added much to BSD for its version of Mac OS X, the full functionality of the renowned UNIX operating system remains. The classic set of UNIX tools is readily accessible and is also fully extensible via the MacPorts and Fink utilities. These utilities are similar to the apt tool in Debian-based Linux distributions. The MacPorts repositories, in particular, continue to add new tools, both for the command line and the GUI desktop. It's possible to accomplish many tasks on the Mac with either "for-pay" tools created specifically for the Mac OS X platform or open source tools. And, with a known hardware profile, developers of either application type can focus on a single platform, removing most of the obstacles found in Windows development and eliminating the instability of unknown hardware and peripherals. (Many Mac users have made the case that Windows installations on Intel Macs are, in fact, the best Windows installations they have used.) In other words, Mac developers know what hardware will be used to run their applications. Unlike the ad hoc nature of Windows hardware, developers can make full use of the Mac hardware.

The other enabling event in the history of the Mac was the transition from Motorola to Intel processors in 2006. That transition brought to bear the full weight of the existing BSD codebase. It also unleashed the full power of BSD on the Macintosh platform. In combination, the powerful capabilities of BSD on a known and native hardware platform pushed Mac OS X and the Macintosh well into the mainstream for serious developers.

My transition to the Mac has been, for all intents and purposes, seamless. Much like the move from Windows to Linux in 1996, the change in platform has breathed new life into both my recreational and vocational computer experiences. I've come the closest yet to that long-time goal of complete computing efficiency. I didn't need to relearn tools I relied upon in my Linux work. While I did need small adjustments to the structure of Mac OS X, the core functionality of the tools was virtually the same as I had spent years learning and using in Linux. Nestled within the clean and friendly designs of both hardware and software, the common UNIX codebase of Mac OS X made it possible to move, overnight, from one platform to the other, and to enjoy an even higher level of efficiency.

If I've learned anything about the greater Linux community, it's that we are, as a group, extreme Tux loyalists. There's a sincere dedication on the part of many to the grandeur and idealism of the free and open source software (FOSS) philosophy as presented by Eric Raymond's seminal *The Cathedral and the Bazaar*. Longtime Linux users may find it difficult to make the mental shift from that idealism to an acceptance of a proprietary operating system—even one that relies so heavily on a FOSS core. In my own experience, I've been no less the loyal idealist.

But for many, there's a deeper issue at play. An evangelist's attitude regarding FOSS is only as good as the efficiency of the code itself. If FOSS applications are cranky, inefficient, and generally difficult to implement, those applications will never make it beyond the horizon of hard-core users. Despite a history approaching 15 years, for example, the Linux desktop has yet to find its way into the mainstream, where the underlying FOSS principles can reach full fruition. Making computing more affordable and accessible is a goal that, essentially, starts with the usability of the operating system and the user interface. In other words, the greater FOSS goals of spreading the power of computing without regard to economic circumstance are entirely reliant on making the entire computing platform—hardware and software— efficient and usable for all who choose it. If a computing system is so complex as to be accessible only to geeks, it's unlikely that those goals will ever be accomplished.

Almost without exception, I've found the Mac OS X experience to be rewarding. The tools work. The hardware is stable and robust. And, like the proverbial icing on the cake, the GUI is pretty, intuitive, and very functional. There's a reason Macs have gained their reputation in the world of multimedia. All those elements are critical in an operating system that will spend many, many hours churning out beautiful graphics, editing video, and making music. Not coincidentally, those uses tend to put a complete computing system to its full test. Processor-intensive applications shine on the Mac. That's a function of known hardware for which developers can write code with relative ease. Most certainly, that's one of many reasons why open source code runs so well and so easily on the Mac, too. It's also a function of a common set of development tools, included with every Mac OS X operating system disc. A well-executed operating system based on BSD, a known hardware platform, a view toward design and ease of use—these are the leading reasons for my personal migration to the Macintosh and Mac OS X, and the reasons I've chosen to present you with this book.

I'll say it right up front: Mac OS X just works. It has the power, the tools, and the stability to rival any operating system—Linux and UNIX included. If you're interested enough to have picked up this book, you're about to enter a new and thoroughly satisfying computer experience.

Mac for Linux Geeks is based on my own personal experience in the transition from Linux to the Mac. Those of us who have spent time in the Linux realm tend to view and use computers a bit differently than the rest of the world (as epitomized by the old joke: "What are the two best things to come out of Berkeley? UNIX and LSD."). Personally, I love the power and flexibility of the command line. Mac OS X has that. I love the ability to dash off a quick script to solve an immediate problem, and then finding that it works in other situations just as well. Mac OS X has that. I like to compile my own software with options to tailor it specifically for my use or my machine. Mac OS X has that. I'm almost cranky in my devotion to source control. Mac OS X has that. I want a nice visual representation of the hour-long audio files I knock out each week in The Roadhouse Podcast. Mac OS X has that. I want a filesystem layout that makes sense in light of my longtime Linux use. Mac OS X has that, too. I want complete control and flexibility in my operating system environment. Mac OS X certainly has that. In the pages that follow, we'll walk through these personal requirements and many others for the millions of Linux users around the world. But be aware that if you've purchased this book, it's more likely than not that your days with our old pal Linux are numbered.

■ ■ ■

## CHAPTER 1

The Backstory

The focus of this book is migrating from Linux-based systems to Mac OS X. To lay the foundation for the information to come, a little history is in order. This chapter provides a brief history of UNIX, BSD, and Mac OS X.

Of Macros and Manuals: UNIX

The creation of Mac OS X really starts with the creation of UNIX. That story is well known, especially among Linux geeks—a group that owes a great debt of gratitude to the work of Dennis Ritchie, Ken Thompson, and a team of Bell Labs engineers. In the summer and early fall of 1969, these engineers cobbled together a rough operating system based on the Multiplexed Information and Computing Service (MULTICS) operating system. MULTICS was a project taken on jointly in 1966 by Bell, General Electric, and Massachusetts Institute of Technology (MIT), but dropped in 1969. Although MULTICS would continue as a commercial venture until 2000, its life in the labs was limited. However, its contribution to the world of computing cannot be overestimated. It produced the team of engineers that, during those heady days of 1969, would create the UNIX operating system.

Like so many technical projects, work on the UNIX system began with an informal discussion. Ritchie, Thompson, and fellow Bell Labs engineer Rudd Canaday met to talk about the project in the summer of 1969. The notes from that brainstorming session were phoned to the Bell Labs dictation system, transcribed, and sent to the engineers. These informal notes would become the working concept of operations for the initial version of UNIX.

Over four months following that meeting, work on the UNIX system rolled forward. A rough filesystem was created on the PDP-7, a system that, at its creation, was state of the art. The engineers, primarily Thompson, created the operating system, shell, assembler, and editor in just four weeks. They also developed a set of tools that would be accessible to users on the system, including tools to copy, print, and delete files. This core tool set was created with the General Electric Comprehensive Operating System (GECOS)—a system still in limited use on servers and mainframes today. The tools were then transferred to the PDP-7 using paper tape. With the assembler—the final piece of the original system—successfully transferred to the PDP-7, the fledgling UNIX system was no longer reliant on GECOS. UNIX was completely self-contained, with the full capabilities to develop and build new tools for the system included as part of the system itself.

From Assembly to C

The year 1970 would prove to be one of high activity for the UNIX team at Bell Labs. Concurrent to the development of the early UNIX framework on the PDP-7, Bell Labs had acquired an upgrade to the PDP-7 system: the PDP-11. As components of the PDP-11 rolled into Bell Labs, the UNIX system was ported to this new platform, taking full advantage of its extended capabilities.

Originally written in assembly language, the new system was simultaneously ported to the word-based B language. It was quickly adopted by the Bell Labs patent department to process the reams of applications and research the office churned through each month. But the B language was limited in its use of data structures—code objects containing fields, items, members, and/or attributes that describe the operation of the code itself. These structures exist as abstractions of actual code operations, and they help to allow developers to work at an increasing distance from assembly language. In short, the creation and existence of data structures can dramatically reduce the time and the number of errors in developing subsequent code.

To further streamline the development process, Ritchie and Bell engineer Brian Kernighan developed a set of data structures to overlay on the B language. The resulting powerful language, C, bore little resemblance to its predecessor. To this day, C serves as the core of many operating systems and applications. It also serves as the basis for such widely used languages as C++, Perl, and Java. The scope and philosophy of C have been carried on in countless other languages and environments.

Macros and Pipes

Two more milestones in the development of UNIX were accomplished in the years between 1970 and 1975. The first was, in essence, another modernization of an older computing idea—the concept of macros. Like data structures at the code level, macros contained a set of actions and operations that could be executed by users and developers with minimal keystrokes. The overriding idea was to group these sets of tasks together in a series of operations initiated by a single keystroke. Also like data structures, these operations could be created and tested discretely, assuring error-free operations when combined.

Macros did not exist in the early iterations of the C language. Due to the growing complexity and power of that language, macros for it were more difficult to create, because that power and complexity demanded a similar level of power in macro-like operations. Ritchie and Kernighan approached this problem head on, creating a concept that would truly distinguish the UNIX operating system from others of its day and from most that followed.

Rather than creating new code for macros, Ritchie and Kernighan envisioned a concept that would allow the output of one existing command or tool to be passed as input to another. This concept efficiently leveraged the previous work of creating the individual system tools, eliminating duplicate effort. More important, it also created a seemingly infinite number of tool combinations. Any tool could perform its discrete operations, and then seamlessly pass the result of those operations as input to any other tool for further processing and output—perhaps to yet another tool, if necessary. In effect, the concept created system "glue" capable of tying many tools to many others as required. Ritchie and Kernighan called this glue *pipes*.

In practice, pipes were revolutionary. Pipes gave users power and flexibility that simply could not be achieved with mere macros. They also had an interesting side effect on subsequent UNIX development: they narrowed the scope of new tools to single tasks. What would become the hallmark philosophy of UNIX systems was born in that reduced scope: "Do one thing, and do it well." The implementation of pipes allowed developers to write programs that performed a single task well, and then to tie those applications, as necessary, to others created under the same philosophy. At the highest level, the use of pipes encouraged developers to create system and user tools that worked well together. Many would later make the case that this single concept was the genesis of the legendary flexibility, stability, and reliability of overall UNIX system performance.

User Manuals

One more significant internal milestone lay ahead in the steady progression of UNIX from esoterica to mainstream use. Engineer Doug McIlroy took on the task of creating a manual that would fully expose the operation of the system to those on the other side of the development and engineering fence—the users.

McIlroy appreciated the shortcomings of existing user manuals. For the most part, they didn't go far enough in explaining the operations and options of the systems. And they didn't present that minimal information in a way that was readily accessible to the end users. McIlroy believed Bell Labs could do a much better job with its user manual and would, by that effort, fully distinguish its operating system from other burgeoning operating systems. In some sense, McIlroy took on the creation and management of the UNIX manual with a unique mix of pride of ownership and commercial savvy.

The result opened the eyes of the computing world to an approach that seemed almost paradoxical. It was at once revolutionary yet born in pure common sense. For starters, the UNIX manual was incorporated into the operating system itself. It was fully accessible within the very environment in which questions about the system's use would arise. The man command, while strictly adhering to the philosophy of doing "one thing right," also put the full knowledge of the system's creators at the fingertips of its users. And that full knowledge was breathtaking in its scope. Every option for the use of every tool on the system was described. Examples were included where they might clarify a complex implementation. Tool descriptions included a brief summary of the relationship of a single tool to other system tools. And, in a revelation for system users, the limitations of individual tools were described, as well, including existing bugs.

The scope, accessibility, and practicality of the UNIX manual made it possible for near-novices to learn the system quickly. True to the business goal, UNIX adoption in business and academia sectors began to escalate at a rate unseen in previous UNIX versions or in rival operating systems.

By 1976, just seven short years removed from the ad hoc meeting that created its concept of operations, UNIX had become the operating system of choice for many companies and schools around the world. Licensing fees for the system reached an all-time high and continued to grow. Through constant revision, the system had reached a previously unsurpassed level of reliability—a key factor in its adoption by increasingly computing-intensive businesses and schools. And it also proved to be highly portable, allowing its adoption on a widening range of hardware platforms.

The Fork: BSD

In a sign of the broad acceptance of UNIX, engineer Ken Thompson was invited by University of California, Berkeley (UCB), to take a yearlong sabbatical from Bell Labs to teach computing at the school. It would serve as a much-needed break from the daily rigors of operating system development. Unknown to the principal players, that sabbatical would mark the beginning of another critical milestone in the history of UNIX. Indirectly, it would also serve as the first real seed for Apple's Mac OS X operating system.

1BSD to 4BSD

Thompson focused his teaching at UCB on UNIX. He found the students to be more than capable of making system improvements and upgrades. Interest in the system ran so high during Thompson's time at the school that students continued to develop the system after Thompson's departure. One, graduate student Bill Joy, took particular interest in the system. Shortly after the end of Thompson's sabbatical, Joy released the first Berkeley Software Distribution, or 1BSD. Rather than a complete system, 1BSD was an add-on to UNIX System 6, including a Pascal compiler and Joy's text editor, ex. Further upgrades and releases followed, including 2BSD, with the C shell and the vi text editor, in 1978.

In the meantime, UCB purchased and installed a Virtual Address eXtension (VAX) computer on the campus. Built by Digital Electronics Corporation (DEC), the VAX was a significant upgrade to the PDP-11 system, including a full step up from 16-bit to 32-bit memory addressing. In order to utilize the larger address space of the VAX, students began what would amount to a full rewrite of the UNIX code.

Incorporating rewritten kernel code, the 2BSD utilities, and other operating system tools, 3BSD was released in 1979. The release was a critical milestone in the development of Berkeley's UNIX-based operating system. It was the first to contain a complete kernel, rather than merely providing a set of add-on tools for UNIX. In reality, 3BSD was the first stand-alone BSD operating system and the first fork of UNIX.

3BSD also represented an important win for UCB. The Defense Advanced Research Projects Agency (DARPA) was so impressed with the 3BSD release that it agreed to fund efforts at UCB's Computer Systems Research Group (CSRG) to create a standard UNIX platform for future DARPA research projects.

BSD releases into the 1980s continued to refine and add new tools to the system. Major releases occurred in 1980 (4BSD) and 1981 (4.1BSD). The 4.2BSD version took two years to release in total, including several incremental releases during that period. Of significant interest, the 4.1a release included a complete rewrite of the Transmission Control Protocol/Internet Protocol (TCP/IP) stack originally developed by Cambridge, Massachusetts, acoustic analysis firm Bolt, Beranek and Newman (BBN). Again, one of the foundational pieces of BSD's success was the result of the efforts of Bill Joy. Reportedly disappointed by BBN's TCP/IP implementation, Joy completely rewrote the stack. Later, when questioned in a meeting with BBN about how he accomplished the mammoth rewrite, Joy reportedly responded that the task was simple. "You read the protocol and write the code."

Licensing Issues

By the time of the 4.2BSD release in 1983, significant portions of the BSD code had been completely rewritten or created from scratch. What remained was still licensed by Bell Labs, under the control of AT&T. In 1984, AT&T divested itself of Bell Labs, creating AT&T Computer Systems, with the primary goals of UNIX development and licensing.

Licensing fees for UNIX System V, which included code created at UCB, continued to increase. As a result, many began to push for and investigate the possibility of a BSD-like release that would be freely distributable, without the encumbrance of AT&T's licensing fees. This lead to the release of Networking Release 1 (Net/1) in 1989, which provided only the Berkeley-developed networking tools to those without licenses for the AT&T code.

Work then began in earnest on Net/2, a release that would completely rewrite the UNIX tools using non-AT&T-licensed code. That release, in 1991, spawned two new efforts focused on porting BSD to the Intel architecture: 386BSD, a free version of the operating system based on Net/2, and another version created by Berkeley Software Design (BSDi).

BSDi quickly became a legal target for AT&T's newly formed UNIX System Laboratory (USL) subsidiary. USL successfully pursued injunctive relief against BSDi, preventing the distribution of the system while further legal action determined whether BSDi had violated the USL-held copyright on UNIX System V and its trademark on UNIX. That action prevented the distribution of BSDi's version for nearly two years. It also prevented the further development of BSDi-derived systems, as rights to all BSDi code remained in question.

The USL action was settled in 1994. After two years of litigation, USL signed off on an agreement that would require only 3 of the 18,000 BSD files in the Net/2 system to be removed. An additional 70 files were targeted for modification to show USL copyright notices. Critically, the settlement also stipulated that no further legal action would be taken by USL against BSD developers, users, or distributors. With those minimal modifications, 4.4BSD was released in June 1994.

BSD had won a hard-fought freedom from the strictures of AT&T licensing, but that freedom did not come without a cost. The 1995 release of 4.4BSD-Lite Release 2 would mark the end of formal BSD development at UCB. The university closed the CSRG shortly after the release. But the freely distributable code created at CSRG remained in the public domain under the permissive BSD license. 4.4BSD-Lite Release 2 served as the basis for the BSD projects we recognize today: FreeBSD, NetBSD, and OpenBSD.

The Enthusiast and the Marketer: Apple Computer

In March 1975, as Dennis Ritchie and Ken Thompson worked toward a stable version of the C programming language, a group of electronics enthusiasts met for the first time in Palo Alto, California. While providing an opportunity to exchange information, to discuss the latest advances in electronics, and to swap electronic parts, the Homebrew Computer Club also had an informal mission of making computing affordable to individuals.

Homebrew Days

Meeting in what would later be referred to as the Silicon Valley, just 40 miles south of Berkeley, many of Homebrew's initial members were well aware of the advances in computing taking place on the UCB campus. At the time, the benefits of those advances were targeted at business and academia. The idea of personal computing was limited, for the most part, to technologists and amateur hobbyists like those who gathered to form the Homebrew Computer Club.

At the time of Homebrew's formation, Stephen "Woz" Wozniak had left the Electrical Engineering program at UCB without a degree. A 25-year-old introvert with the dual talents of hardware design and software programming, Wozniak found in the Homebrew club a group of peers with an enthusiasm for computing he might be able to share.

In 1970, Wozniak became friendly with a summer intern at Wozniak's employer, Silicon Valley stalwart Hewlett-Packard. The friend made an increasingly compelling case that a computer could be built and sold on a single circuit board; that such a computer could, in fact, be the basis of a company created specifically to sell computers to individuals, rather than to businesses. Though initially skeptical, Wozniak was eventually convinced that his friend, Stephen Jobs, might be onto something. After ending a brief college career of his own at Reed College in Portland, Oregon, Jobs returned to Palo Alto in 1974, taking a job as a technician at Atari. Jobs and Wozniak became regular attendees and contributors at the Homebrew meetings.

During their time in the Homebrew Computer Club, Wozniak and Jobs achieved several milestones that reinforced their shared view that computers could be built in a size that would fit on desktops. In the first, Jobs enlisted Wozniak's assistance in collecting a bonus initiated by his employer. Atari instituted a program to reduce the number of chips used in its game consoles, offering employees $100 per eliminated chip. Jobs turned to Wozniak for the hardware design, offering a 50/50 split of the bonus. Wozniak quickly reduced the number of chips in the system by 50. Though Atari later paid out only $600 for the reduction of 50 chips, the effort further honed Wozniak's uncanny ability to design for maximum power with minimal hardware resources.

The second was a purely personal milestone for Wozniak. In early 1975, Wozniak read an article in *Popular Mechanics* describing how to build a video computer terminal. At the time, video terminals were rare; most computers were paper-based teletypes. Following the concepts of that article, Wozniak designed and built a 24-line, 40-character-width video terminal from off-the-shelf parts. The terminal was capable of producing 60 characters per second, more than six times the number of printed characters from the existing teletype terminals. Later, to foster his growing reputation among his Homebrew peers, Wozniak built a microprocessor into the terminal, creating, in essence, a complete computer.

In 1976, MOS Technology introduced a new central processing unit (CPU). The $20 6502 chip was a close relative to Motorola's $170 6800, which was the chip Wozniak preferred in his computer designs. Wozniak modified an earlier 6800-based computer design to incorporate the 6502 chip, and took the machine to demonstrate to his peers in the Homebrew club.

Based on this design, Jobs convinced a local computer shop to purchase 50 of the machines. Jobs also managed to secure the necessary parts on credit, paying on net-30 terms when the machines were delivered on time. Eventually, 200 of these machines, dubbed the Apple I, would be built. With the considerable profits on that initial sale, Jobs and Wozniak formed Apple Computer on April 1, 1976. Wozniak left Hewlett-Packard to focus full-time on the Apple II, as Vice President of Research and Development in the new company. Jobs focused his attention on marketing, sales, and fund-raising.

Unlike the histories of UNIX and BSD, which were primarily technical achievements, the story of Apple Computer is equal parts technical wizardry and marketing savvy. It's almost impossible to tell the story of one without telling the story of the other.

Apple I to Lisa

During the early years, both the Apple I and Apple II computers utilized a tape-based version of Wozniak's Apple BASIC. A 256-byte, firmware-resident system monitor served as the operating system, providing users with a command line for running programs. Shortly after the introduction of the Apple II in 1977, Wozniak produced yet another striking hardware design in the floppy disk drive. This made it possible to move the operating system from read-only memory (ROM) to disk, and further spurred the creation and introduction of Apple Disk Operating System (DOS) to the Apple II in 1978.

In 1980, Apple Computer launched an initial public offering (IPO) of stock. That IPO is legendary in tech business circles, as it created more than 300 millionaires on its first day.

1981 brought a shocking turn of events for the small Apple family. In February, Wozniak crashed his airplane in Santa Cruz, California, causing retrograde amnesia. He didn't remember the crash and often had trouble with his short-term memory. Though his memory was restored by late in the year, Wozniak didn't return to Apple until 1983. By that time, his primary interest in the Apple line of products was in product development. Although he continued with the company until 1987, his full-time employment and influence within the company were effectively ended by the crash. The enthusiast who had almost single-handedly created a computing revolution was hardly more than another employee in a quickly growing corporation.

Even without Wozniak, Apple computers would undergo a near constant series of revisions through 1984. The revised machines included the Apple II+, IIe, IIe Enhanced, and III. These systems used a variety of operating systems, including Apple Pascal, Apple SOS, and Apple ProDOS.

In 1983, Apple introduced the Lisa, and another new operating system. Lisa Office System (OS) implemented a set of process-management system calls that bore some resemblance to UNIX. Among the calls were `make_process`, `kill_process`, `activate_process`, and `setpriority_process`. The initial process, `init`, was created by the operating system as the shell process when the machine was booted, serving as the parent for all other processes. Additional processes could be created only by existing processes.

Additionally, the Lisa OS filesystem bore a striking resemblance to UNIX, albeit with a few additional Apple pieces. Like UNIX, the filesystem contained files, folders, disk volumes, and printer and serial devices. The system also supported permissions on a per-file basis.

But the most striking feature of the Lisa was a full graphical user interface (GUI), as inspired by efforts at Xerox's PARC laboratory. In 1979, Jobs and a team of Apple engineers were granted full access to the PARC facilities in exchange for $1,000 of pre-IPO Apple stock. The Xerox PARC system used a method of human-machine interaction referred to as WIMP (for window, icon, menu, pointing device).

The WIMP paradigm provided nontechnical users with an easily understood visual metaphor—that of the desktop, the elements of which were most popularly accessed with a mouse—another first for personal computing. With menus, WIMP also gave users a means to access the full feature set of an application without a requirement to remember each and every element. Though the concepts of WIMP had been known in technical circles since the early 1970s, Lisa OS was the first to implement those concepts in a computing system outside a laboratory. Relying primarily on Lisa Pascal, the WIMP concept implemented by Apple would prove revolutionary.

And Finally, the Mac

The Apple Lisa was ahead of the curve in personal computing on many levels. Unfortunately for Apple, it also required hardware upgrades that pushed the cost of the Lisa to nearly $10,000—hardly a price point that would appeal to the masses.

That same year, Jobs began the search for a more seasoned chief executive officer (CEO) for Apple. The company had ambitious expansion plans in place for the years ahead and needed an executive who could oversee and implement those plans. Jobs landed on John Sculley, then CEO of PepsiCo. While Sculley had never worked in the tech sector, his reputation and resume with PepsiCo was, in Jobs's eyes, a perfect fit.

Sculley had been the youngest Vice President of Marketing in PepsiCo's history and, subsequently, the company's youngest president. He had a keen marketing eye and was unafraid to spend on advertising. He instituted the company's first consumer-research studies. He took on rival Coca-Cola head-to-head with the Pepsi Challenge, a blind taste test that served as the company's successful national marketing campaign in the mid-1970s. The campaign dramatically increased Pepsi's market share. And, at 44, Sculley was still a relatively young man—a fact of some importance to the executives at the young Apple Computer company.

Among the ambitious plans Sculley was tasked to implement was the introduction of yet another computer line, scheduled for early 1984. That computer, the Macintosh, would leverage and advance the GUI concepts first made publicly available in the Lisa. The single 400KB operating system floppy disk was known as Mac System Software.

Aside from the low-level operating code, the Macintosh ROM load contained the Toolbox and the Finder. The Toolbox was a collection of shared libraries used in the applications and made available to developers for use in future Macintosh application development. The Finder was a system browser, allowing users to view the contents of the filesystem and to launch applications. However, use of the Finder required users to shut down other running applications, as the Macintosh was a single-tasking computer. The Macintosh also contained a 7.86 MHz Motorola MC68000 processor; 64KB ROM; 128KB random-access memory (RAM); and an 8-bit, four-voice sound generator, capable of converting text to speech. An all-in-one unit, the Macintosh weighed just over 16 pounds.

To kick off the launch of the Macintosh, Apple hired director Ridley Scott to produce a television ad intended to air only once: during the broadcast of Super Bowl XVIII on January 22, 1984. At a cost of more than a million dollars, the ad portrayed computer users as conformists in dark-gray suits of sackcloth, herded by helmeted police into a large and dark arena beneath a huge video monitor. From the screen, Big Brother lauded the age of information purity and scorned "contradictory thoughts." From the back of the arena, a heroine raced down the center aisle, flinging a heavy sledgehammer through the video screen, leaving the users stunned. The closing caption and voice-over read like this: "On January 24th, Apple Computer will introduce the Macintosh. And you'll see why 1984 won't be like '1984.'"

Two days later, Jobs introduced the Macintosh at the annual Apple shareholders' meeting. He gave a brief prepared speech and a demonstration of the Macintosh's graphics capabilities, and then said, "Now, we've done a lot of talking about Macintosh, lately. But, today, for the first time ever, I'd like to let Macintosh speak for itself."

To a thunderous round of applause, the Macintosh began.

Hello, I'm Macintosh. It sure is great to get out of that bag.

Unaccustomed as I am to public speaking, I'd like to share with you a maxim I thought of the first time I met an IBM mainframe: never trust a computer you can't lift.

Obviously, I can talk, but right now I'd like to sit back and listen. So, it is with considerable pride that I introduce a man who has been like a father to me . . . Steve Jobs.

The applause in the Cupertino theater continued unabated for more than five minutes. Although the Macintosh was by all accounts a huge success, Apple had difficulty competing with an increasing number of IBM-clone personal computers. CEO John Sculley, intent on driving the company to profit, instituted tighter engineering procedures and reviews, predevelopment marketability studies, and engineering staff reductions. With control of the company he had started now all but ceded to Sculley, Jobs found himself in almost constant conflict with the CEO. By 1985, both Sculley and the board of directors had had enough. Jobs was stripped of his duties as head of Apple's Macintosh division. Nine years after the company's formation, his time and influence had ended.

The Convergence: Mac OS X

Financially buoyed by his time at Apple, Jobs purchased Pixar, a visual effects studio, for $10 million in 1986, and then founded a new company, NeXT, Inc. NeXT would produce the NeXTStep operating system, a UNIX-like system, and the hardware on which it would run.

NeXTStep would eventually serve as one basis of the rebirth of Apple and the Macintosh. However, the convergence of the Macintosh and UNIX actually began in the early 1990s, with a version of AT&T UNIX known as Apple UNIX. Apple UNIX was the operating system used on the Apple Macintosh Quadra machines. The Quadra 700 and Quadra 900 were introduced in 1991 and were built around the Motorola 68040 CPU. With the known reliability of UNIX and powerful 25 MHz CPUs, the Quadras were marketed as high-end professional machines, geared to replace the Macintosh II.

NeXTStep

NeXTStep was a direct descendent of 4.3BSD. Its distinction from BSD rested in its use of the Mach microkernel, originally designed as a drop-in UNIX kernel replacement. Developed at Carnegie Mellon University in 1985, the Mach microkernel provides operating system and application services by calls to user-mode servers. This is in contrast to the monolithic kernel design of BSD, wherein applications obtain services (such as operating system services) by making system calls directly to the service. These services don't exist in the kernel space of the Mach kernel—they exist in user space. The kernel merely routes the interprocess communication (IPC) call to the appropriate server, which then handles the request to the application. The result is that the Mach kernel is a much lighter structure, with a lot of the "heavy-lifting" done in user space. In almost all other respects, NeXTStep was a standard BSD operating system.

Initially, the Mach microkernel was, in fact, slower than the monolithic BSD kernel. When the Mach 3 kernel moved the processes of permissioning and security to the applications, it performed its tasks in only one-quarter the time required by a system with a monolithic kernel. Mach was also designed from the ground up with multitasking and multiple-processor support built in. NeXTStep was quickly accepted by many in the computing community as the next-generation operating system.

NeXTStep was also renowned at the time for its use of the Objective-C language. Objective-C is an extension to the C language that adds object-oriented programming. Unlike other C extensions (C++, for example), Objective-C uses a small-footprint runtime. As a result, Objective-C programs, while powerful, are generally relatively small. Additionally, these programs can be compiled with the GNU Compiler Collection (GCC) compiler, included in all implementations of BSD.

The NeXT computer hardware was equally advanced. The initial machines, released in 1989, were composed of the 25 MHz Motorola 68030 processor, up to 64MB RAM, a 10-Base 2 Ethernet port, a 40MB to 660MB hard drive, and an 1120×832, 17-inch grayscale display. The "cube" form factor was also unique, carrying a feel of the forward-thinking design principles required by Jobs at Apple. The machines were widely accepted among the computing cognoscenti. Among their users was Tim Berners-Lee, who used the NeXT computer to create the first web browser and web server in 1991.

While the NeXT computer was accepted as an advanced computing workhorse, its high hardware manufacturing costs, like those of Apple's Lisa, would eventually determine its fate. By 1993, it was clear that profitability was nowhere on the horizon. NeXT returned to its original software-only business plan, changing the name to NeXT Software, Inc., and laying off more than half its employees. A partnership with Sun Microsystems, funded by $10 million cash from the Santa Clara, California, company, kept the software business moving forward, though slowly. The partners created OpenStep, a version of NeXTStep minus the Mach kernel, with a commitment to use the software in future Sun SPARC machines. By 1996, still heavily loaded with debt, NeXT Software was ripe for an acquisition.

Back at Apple

Following Jobs's departure from Apple, the company went through a period in which it seemed, at once, overambitious and underachieving. The company took on some daunting development tasks, beginning with a port of the Mac OS to the new PowerPC platform. The development came at a huge financial cost and bore little practical result. To great fanfare, Apple announced the Copland project, a complete update to the operating system. The rewrite was highly anticipated by Mac users, but was never completed. And the product line was fragmented into increasingly smaller chunks, creating a growing impression of Macintosh computers as simply niche machines.

Interest in UNIX and Linux operating systems did continue during this period. At the annual Apple Worldwide Developers Conference in 1996, Apple announced MkLinux, a microkernel-based Linux system intended to bring Linux to the PowerPC platform on the Mac.

By 1996, Apple faced a severe shortage of cash. CEO Gil Amelio cut the workforce, dropped the Copland project, and went looking for a suitable operating system for the Mac. When negotiations with Be Inc., headed by former Apple employee Jean-Louis Gassée and the creator of BeOS failed, Amelio went to NeXT, a company with a strong product and reputation, but little cash of its own. In 1997, Apple acquired NeXT for a staggering $429 million. The deal also included 1.5 million shares of Apple stock, all of which were awarded to Steve Jobs.

Jobs returned to the company as a consultant, and by late 1997, had replaced the newly ousted Amelio as interim CEO.

Apple had returned to its roots, bringing back its founder to head the company. In 2001, Jobs would remove the "interim" from his CEO title. The company had also found the operating system that would take it into the next century in NeXTStep. Over the next four years, NeXTStep would be ported to the PowerPC platform, while maintaining synchronous Intel builds. Critical pieces—such as Cocoa, the Dock, the Services menu, and the Finder's browser view—were all ported directly from NeXTStep and utilized in the new operating system. Jobs introduced Mac OS X, with its internal BSD and Mach kernel, at the January 2000 Macworld conference in San Francisco, California. Apple had created a twenty-first century operating system by returning to technologies born in the 1970s.

Why BSD in Mac OS X?

Following the acquisition of NeXT and the return of Steve Jobs to the company, NeXTStep began a deliberate metamorphosis to Darwin, the system that would become the core of Mac OS X. While retaining its BSD underpinnings, object-oriented libraries, strong graphics orientation, and development tools, the Darwin kernel was hybridized. The XNU kernel took shape with elements of Mach, FreeBSD, and code created in-house by the Apple team.

The decision to develop NeXTStep around the BSD base and the "plug-in" Mach kernel had already proven to be a wise choice for NeXT, Inc. and NeXT Software. For many reasons, the decision to port that system to the PowerPC platform with its BSD base intact made great sense for Apple, as well. These reasons included BSD's history, portability, open source base, economics, and extensibility.

History

UNIX and its various derivatives had been well known and highly regarded since the late 1970s. It was the operating system of choice for business, academia, and, since the early 1980s, government research programs. The large, active code base made it possible to customize a full operating system for almost any need. The huge code archive also made it possible to modernize and implement some tools that were too esoteric for the existing user base, but that might serve a consumer operating system well.

BSD also had a large and dedicated user base. Bugs in the system were fixed quickly. The code was under constant review and revision by the community. That community, in fact, made sure that each new tool added to BSD underwent thorough testing under the UNIX philosophy that it should "work well with other tools." That established process and history would potentially reduce the development time for the Apple team.

Release timing was important to Apple, as well. A large element of its decline in the early 1990s was due to the company's inability to stick to a regular operating system update schedule. The historical view of BSD clearly proved that this critical release cycle could be established and followed at Apple.

And history had proven the reliability of the BSD system. BSD-installed machines amassed months, sometimes years, of uptime without a reboot. This was often accomplished despite long periods of intense processing. Apple's primary operating system competition in the consumer computing space, Microsoft Windows, was already scorned in many circles for its tendency to crash at critical moments. While stability was certainly important in commerce, academia, and governmental use, the engineers and marketing groups at Apple saw it as no less important at the consumer level. Stability was a competitive advantage, even with low-intensity users. The BSD base of NeXTStep, and later Mac OS X, was known first and foremost for its long track record of power and stability.

Portability

Portability was another important piece of the decision to retain the BSD underpinnings of NeXTStep in Mac OS X. BSD had proven its portability almost from the beginning, In fact, the FreeBSD group members took no small measure of pride in the fact that their Intel version was the only Intel UNIX that could run reliably as a server. The inclusion of FreeBSD had also helped to make NeXTStep and OpenStep fully operable on a number of platforms, including x86, SPARC, and HPPA.

The NeXTStep engineers, many of whom came to Apple with the acquisition, had begun their foray into the hardware world by porting the system to the Motorola 68030-based architecture. Versions of NeXTStep also existed for the reduced instruction set computing (RISC) and Intel architectures, the latter having been maintained in parallel with the Motorola development. In fact, given the concurrent PowerPC and Intel builds maintained by Apple, and the hiring of a number of FreeBSD core developers from Wind River Systems, it has been speculated that Apple's 2005 PowerPC-to-Intel transition was long planned. In any event, it was a transition made much easier by the BSD foundation of NeXTStep and Darwin.

Open Source Base

The open source basis of Mac OS X was actually misrepresented in Steve Jobs's hyperbolic announcement of the operating system at the 2000 Macworld conference in San Francisco. Two pieces of that announcement in particular made more of those origins than was supported by reality:

- Calling Mac OS X "very Linux-like," Jobs noted that it uses "FreeBSD UNIX, which is the same as Linux." While there are similarities, there are also many differences between the two operating systems.

- Jobs also noted that Mac OS X was "completely open source." Again, that's not exactly true. While the Darwin code is, in fact, open source, many elements of Mac OS X are not.

While the FreeBSD basis of Mac OS X moved the Macintosh into the modern age, it is not the completely free and open source operating system painted by Jobs's Macworld announcement. But the timing was right, even for an open source–based operating system with many proprietary elements. By the time that introduction was made, hard-core computer users and developers had already begun a slow but steady migration to open source.

The concept of free and open source software (FOSS) was increasingly popular, growing from its origins in the Free Software Foundation of Richard Stallman in the 1980s.

In the early 1990s, Linux had become the most well known of an increasing number of FOSS applications. Interestingly, Linux creator Linus Torvalds later noted that it was because of the legal action surrounding BSD in those years that he wrote another operating system. He might have chosen BSD had it been widely available.

The philosophy of open source was further advanced in 1997 by Eric Raymond's publication of "The Cathedral and the Bazaar." In that work, Raymond quotes Torvalds as saying, "Given enough eyeballs, all bugs are shallow." This was one of the fundamental philosophical frameworks around which computer users rallied: the concept that software built, shared, and maintained by a large community of users was, by its nature, better. While not unique to open source, the concept found its strongest example in FOSS.

By 2000, open source software had begun to find its way into both server rooms and technical publications around the world. The continued use of open source tools in Mac OS X allowed Apple to stake a claim to some of that growing buzz. While some greeted the announcement with skepticism, many open source developers were surprised by what appeared to be a significant philosophical shift for the once secretive company.

The easy availability of the Darwin code from Apple's web site also ensured that curious developers would tinker with and improve on the product. The decision to continue using open source tools in Mac OS X created, to paraphrase Torvalds, "enough eyeballs to keep the bugs shallow." It allowed Apple to call upon a large pool of user-created tools. It helped to ensure that the in-house developers would always have the latest improvements in critical development tools. And it did so at little financial risk for Apple. Given the financial state of the company at the time of the NeXT acquisition, it's plausible to believe that open source both saved and renewed Apple.

Economics

As noted, the financial health of Apple at the time of the NeXT acquisition in 1997 was poor, and worsening. The first quarter of 1997 would bring 12-year stock price lows and mark the largest financial losses in Apple history, totaling some $700 million. Of predecessor Gil Amelio's business strategy, Jobs famously quipped, "Apple is like a ship with a hole in the bottom, and my job is to point the ship in the right direction."

Simply put, the financial health of the company allowed no room for immediate bold development initiatives. NeXTStep already existed, and it was in a state in which the only initial cost was that of porting it to the PowerPC platform.

Additionally, the Apple engineering staff had been nearly wiped out under the direction of a changing stream of CEOs. Much of the engineering staff after the NeXT acquisition was brought from NeXT itself. The engineers and developers were, in effect, already up to speed on the state of the operating system. The transition required few resources for retraining, research, and development. By basing Mac OS X on NeXTStep, They could hit the ground running, while realizing a significant cost savings.

Extensibility

Based on BSD, NeXTStep was highly extensible. The basis of NeXTStep was BSD's native C. The power of C had already been proven and could be extended easily as the operating system grew to meet new demands. With additional Objective-C frameworks, the extensibility of BSD and the NeXT tools brought efficiency in both process and economics.

How Is BSD Implemented in Mac OS X?

The full set of UNIX user-space tools available in FreeBSD is available in Mac OS X natively. While there are some core differences between UNIX and Linux, there are enough similarities between BSD and Linux that many common tasks in Mac OS X will seem familiar to Linux users.

If your preference is to use the command line as often as possible, for example, you can do so in Mac OS X. With the bash shell in place, it's possible to port administrative and other scripts from a Linux system to Mac OS X. As the minimal UNIX filesystem structure is intact in Mac OS X, moving and implementing these scripts can be nearly seamless, though some modification may be required to adjust the path of some system binaries called by the script.

As already noted, the core of Mac OS X is based on FreeBSD and is a true UNIX. Mac OS X 10.5, in fact, has been certified by the Open Group as UNIX 03–compliant.

In the Mac OS X implementation, FreeBSD is paired with the XNU kernel—a hybrid Mach microkernel containing additional Apple modifications. The kernel fully supports the following:

- Preemptive multitasking
- Protected memory
- Interrupt management
- Kernel debugging support
- Console input/output (I/O)
- Real-time support

Mac OS X also implements a suite of core services, which include system services such as the following:

- CFNetwork, a user-level networking API
- OSServices, a collection of system APIs
- WebServicesCore, APIs for using web services with SOAP and XML-RPC
- SearchKit, a framework for multilingual searches and indexing

Additionally, Mac OS X implements application services and application environments. The application services include graphics and windowing services, printing services, launch services, event services, and so on. The application environments include execution environments, such as those for BSD, Cocoa (the object-oriented application development API), and Java.

Why Switch from Linux to Mac?

Finally, we get to a question central to the rest of this book: why bother to switch from a Linux-based system to Mac OS X? There are three main reasons: hardware control, common code, and release stability.

Hardware Control

Apple, unlike its primary competitors, is in the business of both software and hardware. While the hardware for Apple's machines is chosen in part for profitability, it's also chosen for reliability and stability.

Hardware components are selected only after rigorous testing using the latest iteration of Mac OS X. While that sounds almost intuitive, the result of controlling the hardware running Mac OS X is that Apple's developers have a known hardware platform for which to develop. By itself, that practice eliminates a large number of the issues seen in other systems, including incompatibility between off-the-shelf components and operating system code. It allows Apple's developers to create device drivers that can be thoroughly tested prior to the release of a new Mac OS X version or a new hardware platform. It allows them to compile in hardware-specific optimization features within the operating system itself.

It's hard to overstate the importance and value of this controlled hardware environment. We've all experienced the frustration of incompatible drivers and other code in competing operating systems. Aside from the frustration, the practice of allowing a multitude of hardware components to utilize the operating system code means that we can never be sure that the code created by hardware vendors will interact optimally with the code created for the operating system. In the open source community, much of this code is, in fact, reverse-engineered. By first controlling the hardware, then developing to that hardware, Apple ensures that its operating system and hardware will work together seamlessly.

Common Code

The APIs, development frameworks, and integrated development environments (IDEs) for Mac OS X are included on the installation disc. Mac owners literally have access to most of the same tools used by the Apple developers to create Mac OS X. That means that applications created specifically for the Mac will have a consistent feel and operation.

A broad range of purely open source development tools is also available to install on the Mac with minimal effort. The Mac development tools can be used in tandem with these open source development tools. From within the same environment, developers can create cross-platform open source applications or applications specifically for the Mac.

Release Stability

Because Apple's operating system and application developers are working with known hardware, using common code for development, Apple's operating system releases are extremely stable. That commonality allows Apple's quality assurance testers to create test cases that will encompass the full range of possible issues in the code.

Summary

UNIX, BSD, and Mac OS X have clearly followed a long path to the convergence represented by the current Macintosh operating system. They're marked by many similarities and many significant differences. UNIX and BSD users will find the underlying Mac OS X environment very familiar, while Linux users will find enough commonality with their own operating system to provide a lot of comfort. Add to that the hardware control, common code, release stability, and beautiful look and feel of Mac OS X, and a move from Linux to Mac becomes much more attractive.

In the next chapter, we'll take a deeper look at the differences and similarities between Mac OS X and Linux to lay a solid foundation for your personal migration.

■ ■ ■

## CHAPTER 2

The Comparison: Linux vs. Mac OS X

BSD, Linux, and Mac OS X are clearly branches straight from a single tap root: the UNIX operating system. As you learned in Chapter 1, UNIX rose to meet many new computing challenges in the 1970s, and matured at a dizzying pace in the 1980s. BSD was the result of the work of computer science students at UCB. Linux was the creation of a Finnish computer science student in Sweden. Mac OS X took critical elements of BSD—FreeBSD in particular—and rolled them into yet another powerful and groundbreaking operating system. In their own way, all three moved computing into new and previously unknown realms.

Now that you have an understanding of both the philosophical and historical similarities between BSD and Mac OS X, let's look closely at how those similarities, as well as the differences, take shape in today's Mac operating system.

Mac OS X and Linux Filesystems

In many ways, the filesystems of Mac OS X and most commonly used Linux distributions are very similar. However, there are some specific implementation differences between the filesystems. To best explore those differences, we'll cover the following topics:

- The Apple filesystem, focusing on the evolution from MFS to HFS+

- The filesystem layouts of Linux, FreeBSD, and Mac OS X

- The Linux ext2 filesystem, with its modern ext3 journaling layer

- A comparison of some critical features of HFS+ and ext2/ext3

The Apple Filesystem

In 1985, computers were moving toward a new model for data storage. Hard drive manufacturing costs, while still very high by today's standards, were beginning to fall. Designers and manufacturers were packing more data onto smaller drives and gaining quicker access to that data from the other computer systems. Hard drive technology promised considerably more data storage capacity. These new technologies also provided a much more stable and reliable means for storage than the sometimes fragile floppy disks and mini disks of the day. However, the increasing size of hard drives brought its own set of problems.

By 1984, Apple had rolled the Macintosh File System (MFS) into its newest computers. MFS was designed to overcome some of the inefficiencies inherent in the floppy and mini disk storage of the day. To speed access times, all the filesystem metadata—the data about the data—was stored in a single file. This helped to speed access times on these external disks, but did little to protect that data from corruption. With virtually no redundancy, data stored on these disks was at a high risk of loss. If the single metadata file were corrupted, it would be nearly impossible to retrieve any data from the disk.

With those primary issues in mind, the Hierarchical File System (HFS) was introduced by Apple in 1985 to replace MFS. HFS serves as the basis of the Mac OS X filesystem today, but with many changes and improvements.

HFS

Compared with MFS, HFS takes a markedly different approach to the metadata that describes the files on the system. Apple created a filesystem based on *B*-tree* structure. The B*-tree structure is, as the name implies, a tree-like structure based on data *trunks*, *branches*, and *leaves*. This structure stores the system file metadata in a *catalog file*, which can be searched more quickly. The catalog file also provides a higher level of redundancy for these files, moving much of the critical data into nearly independent files and away from the flat-file structure of MFS. B*-tree data structures have the advantage of faster access on a hard drive than is available with most filesystems.

Note While the term *B-tree* is commonly used to describe the trunk-and-leaf structure of the HFS filesystem, the B*-tree structure differs from a true B-tree. In the B*-trees implemented in HFS, branch and leaf nodes must be two-thirds full prior to the creation of new nodes, rather than the half required by B-trees. This also requires that adjacent nodes share a common key identifier. When the two nodes are full, they're split into three. B*-trees are also distinct from *B+ trees*, which chain all leaf nodes together in a *linked list*. Despite these important differences, the term B-tree has been used generically to describe all these tree-like data structures.

The HFS catalog file contains a record of all files and directories stored on the system, tracked by unique identifiers. These identifiers are similar to the node IDs used by UNIX filesystems. In practice, each file and directory is recorded twice in the catalog file. The first is the *thread record*. In the case of files, the thread record contains the file name and the ID of its parent file. Directories follow the same structure, with the catalog file recording the directory name and the ID of its parent directory. These thread records are identified by a combination of the parent ID and the file or directory name. Metadata for the files and directories is stored in the *file record* or the *directory record*.

Aside from the structure of the metadata, HFS also uses a system of forks to address data. Each file is split into two distinct forks:

- *Data fork*: For the most part, the data fork contains the user-created data in the file.

- *Resource fork*: The resource fork contains a resource header, the actual file resources, and a map of those resources. The resources may include icons, windows, controls, dialog boxes, machine code, and so on—anything that will be required to present the data. The resource forks are identified by a standardized set of keys known as *resource identifiers*.

HFS was first utilized in the Macintosh Plus and was hard-coded into the 128KB ROM. The system was implemented in 512-byte *logical blocks*, which were then bundled into *allocation blocks*, as illustrated in Figure 2-1. In this scheme, logical blocks 0 and 1 are the boot blocks, containing all the data necessary to boot the system. Logical block 2 is the Master Directory Block (MDB), containing volume data such as timestamps and a mapping of the other volume structures. Logical block 3 contains a volume bitmap that tracks the use of all allocation blocks. In that bitmap, bits represent allocation blocks in a 1:1 ratio—one bit for each allocation block. The bit determines the current status of the block: in use or not in use.

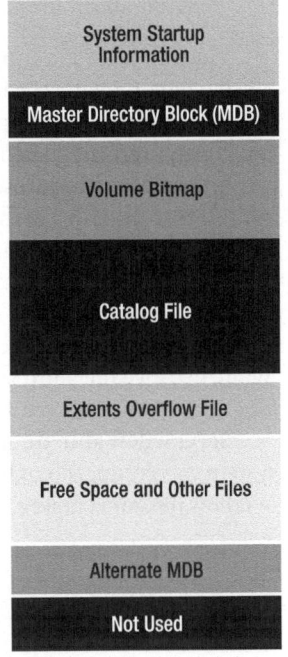

Figure 2-1. *Logical block structure of the HFS filesystem*

The 1:1 bit-to-allocation block ratio was a very limiting factor in the original HFS filesystem. The system allocated a single file to each allocation block, limiting the number of allocation blocks available on a single volume to 65,535. Because files and allocation blocks were paired in this 1:1 ratio, the resulting number of files on a single volume was also constrained to 65,535.

Furthermore, as disks increased in size, so did the allocation block size, while the number of allocation blocks remained the same. The result was a terrible inefficiency in the use of larger hard drives. Since each file was assigned one allocation block, systems with a large number of small files used a disproportionate amount of storage. A 5KB file, for example, was handled in the same way as a 25KB file: they were both assigned a single allocation block. In other words, smaller files were allocated the same amount of space on a drive as larger files.

Users of early HFS-based Macintosh systems resorted to many schemes to use disk space more efficiently. Perhaps the most popular was one that later carried into other consumer operating systems: the practice of creating multiple partitions on a single hard drive. With smaller partitions, HFS created smaller allocation blocks, thus reducing the sometimes ludicrously large storage allocation for smaller files. The practice also allowed for a larger number of files on the drive. Each partition was viewed as a volume by the system, containing the same 65,535 allocation blocks.

The limited number of allocation blocks and files was but one issue with early versions of HFS. The filesystem had performance issues, namely that only a single application at a time could write to files in this structure. That led to long queue times and applications that seemed to overpower the system. As hard drives continued to grow and application demands increased, a revision to the original HFS filesystem was in order.

HFS+

HFS+ was first incorporated into the Mac with the introduction of Mac OS 8.1, in January 1998. It contained significant changes from the original scheme of HFS, including the following:

- Support for 255-character Unicode file names

- 32-bit block addressing

- 32-bit allocation mapping table

The new Unicode support represented a more significant change to Mac OS than first blush might indicate. Until the point of the change, Mac OS assumed that the character set used MacRoman encoding. File names were compared and sorted with that assumption, causing unpredictable behavior with names using another character encoding.

The new block addressing allowed HFS+ to handle much larger file sizes. These block addresses were 16-bit in the original HFS.

The 32-bit allocation mapping table, also extended from 16 bits, gave the system access to more than 4.3 billion allocation blocks, for a 65,000-fold increase. An increase in the number of allocation blocks based on the new 32-bit mapping table made the allocation blocks smaller and, therefore, much more numerous in a drive of equal size with a 16-bit mapping table. Again, because the address space for each file in HFS+ was handled by a single allocation block, this revision extended the file storage capabilities from 65,535 files to 4.3 billion.

Several new structural features were added to the HFS filesystem. Where the HFS filesystem was composed of five principal elements (boot block, MDB, volume bitmap, extent overflow file, and catalog file), the HFS+ filesystem contained seven:

- The boot blocks, as in HFS, are contained in logical blocks 0 and 1.

- The MDB is contained in logical block 2. This is much the same as the HFS implementation.

- Logical block 3 contains the volume bitmap. This is, again, relatively unchanged from HFS.

- The startup file is used to boot operating systems without HFS or HFS+ support.

- The alternate volume header is a copy of the volume header, located in the next-to-last logical block. This provides redundant storage of filesystem critical data. This was also part of HFS.

- The final logical block is reserved for Apple's use during the manufacturing process.

HFS+ Evolution

HFS+ would continue to evolve from the Mac OS 8.1 version of 1998 to the Mac OS X version of 2001. By the time of the release of Mac OS X 10.0 (Cheetah) on March 24, 2001, Apple had officially moved the core operating system to Darwin, the first release version of Mac OS based on FreeBSD. Darwin made use of the XNU kernel—an Apple modification of the Mach kernel—and large chunks of FreeBSD. In fact, Mac OS X also used pieces from projects such as MkLinux, NetBSD, and OpenBSD.

Significantly, Apple added optional support for *journaling* in Mac OS X 10.2.2. With the following full-point release, Mac OS X 10.3 (Panther), Mac volumes supported journaling by default.

Like journaling on other systems, the new system in Mac OS X 10.3 ensured that all changes to the filesystem were recorded. The scheme in Mac OS X follows a simple rule: either all changes are made or none will be made. The journal stores a record of all pending data changes to the system. Each set of changes is referred to as a *transaction*. When the journal file is written to disk, the transactions are made following the all-or-nothing rule. When all the changes have been made and the transaction has been removed from the journal, the changes have been *committed*.

A special block exists in the root directory of the volume, exclusively for the use of the journal: .journal_info_block. This block contains the journal header and buffer file, .journal, which is hidden from all users except the system user. The journal buffer contains all of the transactions that have yet to be written to media as a circular linked list, which means that transactions may "wrap-around" to the beginning of the buffer. The journal header describes which part of the journal buffer is currently in use. If the journal is not empty—that is, not all transactions have been completed—the journal must be *replayed* to complete the transactions, in accordance with the all-or-nothing rule.

In Mac OS X 10.3, a variant of HFS+, HFSX, was introduced. This version added support for case-sensitivity for file and folder names.

Mac OS X 10.3 also added *adaptive hot file clustering*. Volume metadata items (allocation bitmap, extents overflow file, catalog file, and journal file) are located together at the beginning of the disk. Since these may change with every file action, they're high-access items. Placing them in a static location on the drive shortens the access time to make necessary changes. The location of this set of files is known as the *metadata zone*.

With adaptive hot file clustering, other small high-access files are defragmented (reduced to a single extent) and placed in the metadata zone, as well. Hot files are determined by measuring the number of bytes read from a file during the recording period, divided by the file's size in bytes. Again, this placement in the metadata zone shortens the time necessary to access these files and to write changes to the system metadata.

Finally, Mac OS X 10.3 also opened up extended file attributes, a feature of Mac OS X that had previously been reserved for future use. These attributes permitted features such as POSIX access control lists and extended metadata. *Access control lists* allow much finer granularity of UNIX file permissions on the system. *Extended metadata* is intended to further sharpen the accuracy of the Mac OS X Finder, a system-wide search tool.

Note Access control lists are an attempt to move from file-based permissions to role-based permissions. Users assume a role in the system, with permissions addressing those roles. Each entry in an access control list specifies a subject and an operation, such as "tony, write" on the file testfile.txt. This allows for much tighter control of file and filesystem operations.

Mac OS X 10.4 (Tiger) added *inline attribute data records* to the seven existing structural elements of the operating system. Inline attributes are yet another B*-tree structure, which contain the following:

- *Inline attribute data records*: Small data attributes that can fit within the file itself. This field in HFS+ is currently reserved for future use.

- *Fork data attribute records*: References to a maximum of eight extents that can hold a collection of attributes larger than those contained in the inline data attribute records.

- *Extension attribute records*: Extension to a fork data attribute when its eight extents are already in use.

Mac OS X 10.5 (Leopard) added more than 300 changes and improvements, many of which were feature additions and bug fixes for user applications. Leopard also introduced a number of new developer technologies, several of which will be covered in Chapter 8. Five additional security improvements were rolled in:

- *Application layer firewall*: Mac OS X already ships with the BSD ipfw firewall (a topic covered in some depth in Chapter 7). The application layer firewall is exposed to the user and operates at the socket level, bound to processes rather than packets.

- *Secure guest account*: This feature allows for the temporary creation of a secure guest account. This account is destroyed when the guest user logs out of the system.

- *Library randomization*: This feature is intended to address vulnerabilities that corrupt program memory based on known memory addresses. Randomizing the memory location of libraries can prevent these types of system attacks.

- *Role-based access control (RBAC)*: RBAC creates a system by which permissions can be granted based on operations rather than or in addition to the traditional user- or file-based permissions.

- *Read-only support for the ZFS filesystem*: ZFS was designed by Sun Microsystems for the Solaris operating system. ZFS supports large storage capacities, continuous integrity checking, automatic repair, and snapshots.

Filesystem Layouts

Although there are many similarities between the filesystems of Mac OS X and most UNIX-based systems, the filesystem layout can be a bit baffling to new Mac OS X users. In short, Mac OS X hides much of the filesystem from users, displaying only those filesystem elements that can be written to and read from by the currently logged-in user. Here, we'll take a look at the Linux, FreeBSD, and Mac OS X filesystem layouts.

Linux Filesystems

Table 2-1 describes the standard Linux filesystem hierarchy, as described by the Linux Standard Base (LSB).

Table 2-1. *Linux Filesystem Layout As Defined by the Linux Standard Base*

Directory	Contents
/	Top-level, root directory of the filesystem hierarchy
/bin/	Command binaries for all users
/boot/	Boot loader files (can be installed on a different partition)
/dev/	System devices
/etc/	Host system configuration files
/etc/opt/	Configuration files for the /opt directory
/etc/X11/	Configuration files for the X11 windowing system
/etc/sgml/	SGML configuration files
/etc/xml/	XML configuration files
/home/	User home directories
/lib/	Libraries for /bin/ and /sbin/ binaries
/media/	Mount points for removable media
/mnt/	Mount point for temporarily mounted filesystems
/opt/	Optional software packages
/proc/	Virtual filesystem tracking processes and kernel activities
/root/	Home directory for the root user
/sbin/	System binaries
/srv/	Site-specific data served by the system
/tmp/	Temporary files
/usr/	Top-level directory for the user data
/usr/bin/	User command binaries
/usr/include/	Include files
/usr/lib/	Libraries for binaries in /usr/bin/ and /usr/sbin/
/usr/sbin/	User binaries
/usr/share/	Data independent from the system architecture
/usr/src/	Source code
/usr/X11R6/	X Window System
/usr/local/	Host-specific local data
/var/	Variable files: logs, spools, etc.
/var/lib/	System state information
/var/lock/	Lock files
/var/log/	System log files

Continued

Table 2-1. *Continued*

Directory	Contents
/var/mail/	User mailboxes
/var/run/	System information since last boot
/var/spool/	Spoolable tasks awaiting processing
/var/spool/mail/	Deprecated user mailbox location
/var/tmp/	Temporary files to be preserved between system boots

FreeBSD Filesystem Layout

The layout of a FreeBSD filesystem is similar to Linux, although you'll find some small differences. Table 2-2 describes the FreeBSD filesystem hierarchy.

Table 2-2. *FreeBSD Filesystem Layout*

Directory	Contents
/	Root directory of the filesystem
/bin/	User utilities fundamental to both single-user and multiuser environments
/boot/	Programs and configuration files used during operating system bootstrap
/boot/defaults/	Default bootstrapping configuration files; see loader.conf(5)
/dev/	Device nodes; see intro(4)
/etc/	System configuration files and scripts
/etc/defaults/	Default system configuration files; see rc(8)
/etc/mail/	Configuration files for mail transport agents such as sendmail(8)
/etc/namedb/	Named configuration files; see named(8)
/etc/periodic/	Scripts that are run daily, weekly, and monthly, via cron(8); see periodic(8)
/etc/ppp/	PPP configuration files; see ppp(8)
/mnt/	Empty directory commonly used by system administrators as a temporary mount point
/proc/	Process filesystem; see procfs(5), mount_procfs(8)
/rescue/	Statically linked programs for emergency recovery; see rescue(8)
/root/	Home directory for the root account
/sbin/	System programs and administration utilities fundamental to both single-user and multiuser environments
/tmp/	Temporary files[a]
/usr/	The majority of user utilities and applications
/usr/bin/	Common utilities, programming tools, and applications
/usr/include/	Standard C include files

Directory	Contents
/usr/lib/	Archive libraries
/usr/libdata/	Miscellaneous utility data files
/usr/libexec/	System daemons and system utilities (executed by other programs)
/usr/local/	Local executables, libraries, etc., and also used as the default destination for the FreeBSD ports framework[b]
/usr/obj/	Architecture-specific target tree produced by building the /usr/src tree
/usr/ports	The FreeBSD ports collection (optional)
./usr/sbin/	System daemons and system utilities (executed by users)
/usr/share/	Architecture-independent files
/usr/src/	BSD and/or local source files
/usr/X11R6/	X11R6 distribution executables, libraries, etc. (optional)
/var/	Multipurpose log, temporary, transient, and spool files[c]
/var/log/	Miscellaneous system log files
/var/mail/	User mailbox files
/var/spool/	Miscellaneous printer and mail system spooling directories
/var/tmp/	Temporary files[d]
/var/yp	Network Information Service (NIS) maps

[a] *The contents of /tmp are usually not preserved across a system reboot. A memory-based filesystem is often mounted at /tmp. This can be automated using the tmpmfs-related variables of rc.conf(5) (or with an entry in /etc/fstab; see mdmfs(8)).*

[b] *Within /usr/local, the general layout sketched out by hier(7) for /usr should be used. Exceptions are the man directory, which is directly under /usr/local rather than under /usr/local/share, and the ports documentation is in share/doc/port.*

[c] *A memory-based filesystem is sometimes mounted at /var. This can be automated using the varmfs-related variables of rc.conf(5) (or with an entry in /etc/fstab; see mdmfs(8)).*

[d] *The /var/tmp/ files are usually preserved across a system reboot, unless /var is a memory-based filesystem.*

Mac OS X Filesystem Layout

Mac OS X approaches the filesystem layout from the perspective of multiple privileged and unprivileged users. The system is divided into four filesystem *domains*:

User: This is the domain in which a logged-in user has complete control of resources. The User domain is determined by the user's home directory, and can reside either on the boot volume (/Users) or on a networked volume. Table 2-3 describes the basic system setup for the User domain (it may contain additional directories). Figure 2-2 shows the typical contents of a user home directory in Mac OS X.

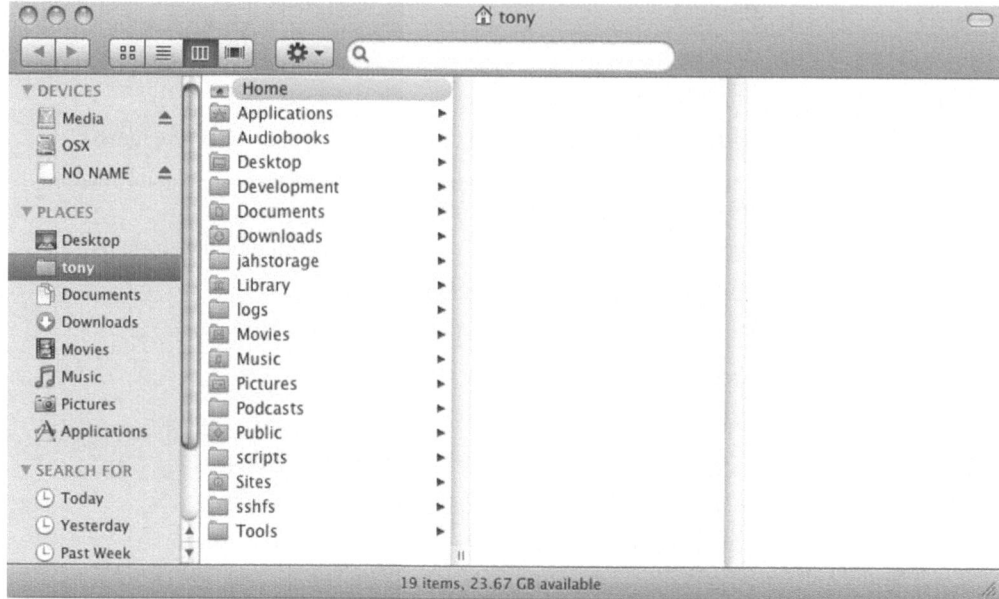

Figure 2-2. *The typical contents of a user home directory in Mac OS X*

Local: The Local domain contains resources that are available to all local users on the system. These are noncritical applications, utilities, startup items, and global application settings. Apple-installed applications and utilities are located in the Local domain /Applications and /Applications/Utilities directories. These resources are available to the current user on the local system, but are unavailable to users on networked computers.

Network: The Network domain contains resources shared by all system users on a local area network (LAN). These items are typically located on a network share and placed under the control of a network administrator. Table 2-4 describes the filesystem contents of the Network domain on a Mac OS X system.

System: The System domain contains Apple-installed system-critical software. This domain contains a single directory: /Library, which holds the core services, applications, and frameworks that make up Mac OS X. This directory is inaccessible to individual users.

Table 2-3. *Contents of the User Domain on a Mac OS X System*

Directory	Description
~	Denotes the top level of the user's home directory
~/Library/Fonts	Font storage in the user's home directory
~tony	Top level of user tony's home directory
Applications	Applications available only to the current user
Desktop	Items displayed by the Finder on the current user's desktop

Directory	Description
Documents	Current user's personal documents
Library	Application settings, preferences, and system resources applicable to the current user
Movies	Digital movies in all formats
Music	Digital music in all formats
Pictures	Image files in all formats
Public	Items shared by the current user with other system users
Sites	Web pages for the current user's personal web site[a]

[a] *These web pages are accessible to other users only when Web Sharing has been enabled by the owner/user.*

Table 2-4. *Contents of the Network Domain on Mac OS X Systems*

Directory	Description
/Network/Applications	Applications accessible to all users on a LAN system
/Network/Library	All resources, including settings, preferences, and system resources available to users on a networked system
/Network/Servers	Mount points for any NFS shares on the system
/Network/Users	Home directories for all LAN users[a]

[a] *These home directories may also be stored on the users' local servers or on other LAN-accessible servers.*

The commonality of directory names within the domains is by design. These common directory names store common file types. The system searches the domains sequentially—User, Local, Network, and System—until it finds the necessary resource.

Exposing the Filesystem

To get a better look at the components of the filesystem, you can use the commands listed in Table 2-5.

Table 2-5. *Commands for Viewing the Filesystem Components*

Command	Purpose
ls	List directory contents
cd	Change directory
df	Display disk free space
dirs	Display list of remembered directories
fdisk	Partition table manipulator
fsaclctl	Enable/disable access control list support

Continued

Table 2-5. *Continued*

Command	Purpose
fs_usage	Filesystem usage (process/pathname)
GetFileInfo	Get attributes of HFS+ files
quota	Display disk usage and limits

The ext2/ext3 Filesystem in Linux

The majority of Linux distributions have moved to ext3 as the default filesystem. If you're using Fedora, Ubuntu, SuSE, Mandriva, Debian, or any of the other popular Linux distributions, you're already familiar with ext3. Based on ext2, the core of ext3 is an extremely stable and time-tested filesystem, with few open issues.

ext2, introduced in 1993 and based on the Berkeley Fast File System (BFFS), was created with full and easy extensibility in mind. ext2 has proven stable and extremely reliable in both consumer and commercial Linux applications.

ext3 adds a journaling layer to ext2. Announced by its author, Stephen Tweedie, in a 1999 kernel group mailing, ext3 allows on-the-fly upgrades from ext2. This upgrade is primarily the implementation of the journaling layer. At the time of its inclusion in the 2.4.15 Linux kernel in 2001, ext3 was hailed as the next great iteration in a system already recognized as a modern robust filesystem. Aside from journaling, ext3 is, in fact, ext2.

Like the HFS+ filesystem, transactions in ext3 are recorded, replayed, and committed. This helps prevent and/or correct filesystem corruption by completing transactions that may have been buffered or left otherwise incomplete during an event such as a kernel panic or dirty system shutdown. Without the journaling layer, ext2 required a full system scan with tools like e2fsprogs, including fsck. These tools are still available in ext3 as an element of the ext2 underpinnings. And, while these tools provide a full range of options to correct filesystem errors, they can take quite a long time to run—time that may be best used on other tasks in a critical production environment. The journaling layer in ext3 is a means to bring a corrupted system back to a known state in a comparatively short time and efficient fashion.

ext2 implements a system of *blocks* organized in *block groups*. Metadata for these blocks is stored in a *superblock*, a *block group bitmap*, and an *inode bitmap*. These items occupy the space just before the block group on the drive. The superblock contains a *group descriptor table*, populated with *group descriptors* that store the value of the block bitmap, the inode bitmap, and the start of the inode table for every block group. The superblock is critical to the overall operation of the ext2 filesystem. As a result, a duplicate copy of the superblock is stored in every block group of every block on the system. This structure is the reason most often cited when noting that Linux systems don't require routine defragmentation, as is required by Windows systems. In effect, each block and superblock is distinct from all others, reducing the possibility of external fragmentation when writing new data to a disk.

Note In both ext2 and ext3 Linux systems, it's possible to repair a corrupted filesystem using a duplicate superblock. To do so, it's necessary to find the next superblock with the `newfs` command, then run `fsck` using the first alternate superblock. This is important because `fsck` may not run at all when asked to check a corrupted superblock.

The maximum number of subdirectories supported by ext2 is 32,768. However, a directory containing more than 10,000 subdirectories may prompt a user warning that operations may take an abnormally long time.

Comparison of HFS+ and ext2/ext3

Tables 2-6 through 2-9 provide a quick overview and comparison of some critical features of HFS+ and ext2/ext3.

Table 2-6. *HFS+ and ext2/ext3 File Constraints*

Feature	HFS+	ext2/ext3
Maximum file name length	255 UTF-16 characters	255 bytes of any data type
Maximum file size	8EB	2TB
Maximum volume size	8EB	32TB

Table 2-7. *HFS+ and ext2/ext3 Block Features*

Feature	HFS+	ext2/ext3
Block suballocation	Not supported	Not supported
Extents	Supported	Not supported
Variable block size	Not supported	Not supported

Table 2-8. *Primary Features of HFS+ and ext2/ext3*

Feature	HFS+	ext2/ext3
Hard links	Not supported	Supported
Sym links	Supported	Supported
Block journal	Not supported	Not supported
Metadata journal	Supported	Supported
Case sensitivity	Supported	Supported
Case preservation	Supported	Supported

Table 2-9. *Metadata Capabilities of HFS+ and ext2/ext3*

Feature	HFS+	ext2/ext3
File owner	Supported	Supported
POSIX permissions	Supported	Supported
Creation timestamp	Supported	Not supported
Last access timestamp	Supported	Supported
Last modified timestamp	Not supported	Supported
Copy create timestamp	Not supported	Not supported

As these tables show, in many critical measures, HFS+ stacks up well against ext2/ext3—even exceeding some of the Linux filesystem's capabilities. In particular, HFS+ allows file and volume sizes that are considerably greater than those of ext2/ext3. By default, both implement metadata journaling, reducing the number of writes necessary to capture transactions. HFS+ also provides support for full data journaling (although full redundancy results in a substantial performance hit).

Permissions in Mac OS X

Mac OS X, as you've seen, is at its core a BSD system. Accordingly, Mac OS X implements the BSD permissions structure.

File Permissions

The permissions on individual files will look familiar to most Linux users. Figure 2-3 shows that the output of ls-l in Mac OS X is the same as the output in Linux. For example, using the ls -l command, the /net directory on my Mac OS X system returns the following:

```
dr-xr-xr-x  2 root  wheel  1 Jul 20 17:36 cortex
```

As on a purely BSD system, the listing denotes that cortex is a directory, and that it allows read and execute access to the owner, group, and world. Similarly, the ls -la command reveals the following:

```
dr-xr-xr-x   2 root  wheel     1 Jul 20 10:47 .
drwxrwxr-t  41 root  admin  1462 Jul  2 16:36 ..
dr-xr-xr-x   2 root  wheel     1 Jul 20 17:41 broadcasthost
dr-xr-xr-x   2 root  wheel     1 Jul 20 17:41 cortex
dr-xr-xr-x   2 root  wheel     1 Jul 20 17:41 localhost
```

The -la option returns a long directory listing containing all the hidden files. In this case, that includes the dot files necessary for moving within directories.

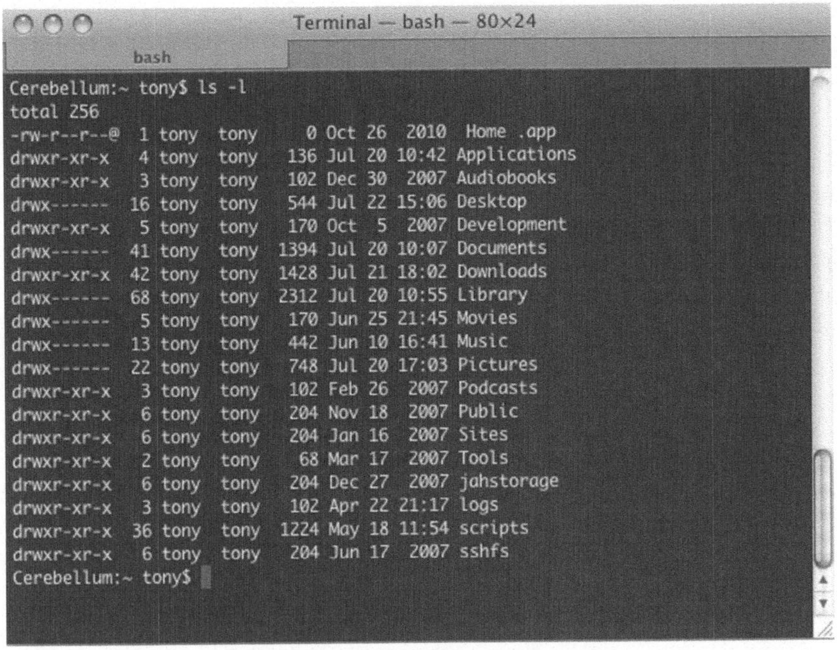

```
○ ○ ○                    Terminal — bash — 80×24
         bash
Cerebellum:~ tony$ ls -l
total 256
-rw-r--r--@  1 tony  tony     0 Oct 26  2010  Home .app
drwxr-xr-x   4 tony  tony   136 Jul 20 10:42 Applications
drwxr-xr-x   3 tony  tony   102 Dec 30  2007 Audiobooks
drwx------  16 tony  tony   544 Jul 22 15:06 Desktop
drwxr-xr-x   5 tony  tony   170 Oct  5  2007 Development
drwx------  41 tony  tony  1394 Jul 20 10:07 Documents
drwxr-xr-x  42 tony  tony  1428 Jul 21 18:02 Downloads
drwx------  68 tony  tony  2312 Jul 20 10:55 Library
drwx------   5 tony  tony   170 Jun 25 21:45 Movies
drwx------  13 tony  tony   442 Jun 10 16:41 Music
drwx------  22 tony  tony   748 Jul 20 17:03 Pictures
drwxr-xr-x   3 tony  tony   102 Feb 26  2007 Podcasts
drwxr-xr-x   6 tony  tony   204 Nov 18  2007 Public
drwxr-xr-x   6 tony  tony   204 Jan 16  2007 Sites
drwxr-xr-x   2 tony  tony    68 Mar 17  2007 Tools
drwxr-xr-x   6 tony  tony   204 Dec 27  2007 jahstorage
drwxr-xr-x   3 tony  tony   102 Apr 22 21:17 logs
drwxr-xr-x  36 tony  tony  1224 May 18 11:54 scripts
drwxr-xr-x   6 tony  tony   204 Jun 17  2007 sshfs
Cerebellum:~ tony$
```

Figure 2-3. *Permissions in the Mac OS X terminal window*

Permissions can be changed by the owner of any file using the same methods available in BSD. These include the notation method (chmod +x *file*) or the octal method (chmod 644 *file*). Ownership and group membership can be changed using the BSD methods, as well, including with the Directory Service command-line tool dscl.

Root and Administrative Access

UNIX-based systems divide user privileges into user and root access. The permissions based on these groups can be subdivided in many ways by the further use of grouping. Both individual users and groups can be granted permissions to read, write, and execute files. These permissions are created by the root user—the all-seeing, all-powerful user on a UNIX system.

Mac OS X disables the root account by default. Instead, administrative access is granted to the user installing the system. This is accomplished by adding the user to the admin group. The admin group has limited administrative access to the system. When administrative access is required to complete a task, the user is prompted for the local user password. If the request is made during the use of a GUI-based application, Mac OS X requests the user password in a pop-up window.

Mac OS X also makes use of sudo access when working in the terminal. As the root user is unavailable by default, this sudo access follows the permissions structure of the wheel group.

To enable the root user in Mac OS X versions prior to 10.5 (Leopard), the netinfo application was required. This application has since been removed from Mac OS X. To enable the root user in Leopard and later, double-click the Applications folder in the Dock, double-click the Utilities folder in the Applications window, and double-click the Directory Utility application in the Utilities window. Select Edit from the menu, and click Enable Root User. You'll be prompted to enter a password for the root user. This will allow any user with the root password to gain full access to the system.

■**Note** Many modern Linux systems, such as Ubuntu and Fedora, disable root access by default. This is intended as a measure of strong security on these systems. The use of the wheel group allows the creation of administrative privileges that lie somewhere between user and root access. On both Fedora and Ubuntu, root access can be enabled, much like in Mac OS X. In both systems, a persistent root login is created by use of the `sudo -i` command. As with the warnings provided by Apple, Ubuntu and Fedora highly discourage full root access. All three provide a means to disable the root account when the activity requiring persistent root access is completed.

Terminal Access in Mac OS X

You'll find a full complement of BSD and Linux tools in the Mac OS X environment. As you might expect from a UNIX-based system, Mac OS X includes a Terminal application, allowing quick access to the command-line power of BSD.

Starting Bash

The default user shell on Mac OS X 10.3 and later is bash (previously it was tcsh). The Terminal application is available from the `Applications/Utilities` folder.

Since Mac OS X 10.5, the Terminal application offers a tabbed terminal, allowing a user to segment task types into different terminal tabs under a unified window, as shown in Figure 2-4. It's also fully customizable in look, feel, and behavior via the Terminal Preferences option in the menu.

Mac OS X also includes the full BSD man page system, allowing quick access to application or command usage instructions from the terminal window.

As the Mac OS X system is subdivided into domains, opening a terminal window lands the user in the home directory. For example, opening the terminal on my system when logged in as tony places me in the `/Users/tony` directory. The command-line prompt, in that case, displays the following:

```
Cerebellum:~ tony $
```

This line indicates that I'm awaiting an action on the machine named Cerebellum, in the home directory of user tony.

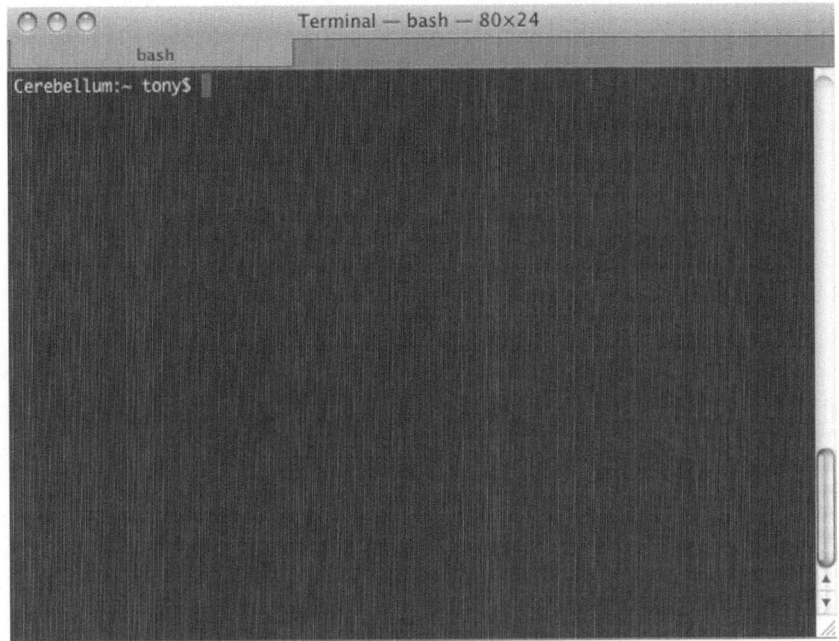

Figure 2-4. *The terminal window in Mac OS X*

Setting Linux System Variables in Mac OS X

As Mac OS X is based on BSD, you'll find quite a bit of commonality with the shell in Linux. Many of the same principles apply. Your shell environment is fully customizable from ~/.bash_profile, including aliases, environment variables, and shell variables.

Table 2-10 lists common environment variables on a Mac OS X system. For a full list of current system variables, use the env command in a terminal window.

Table 2-10. *Common Mac OS X System Variables*

Variable	Description
HOME	Full path of the user's home directory
USER	Login name of current user
LOGNAME	$USER
PWD	Full path of current working directory
PATH	List of directories containing commands
SHELL	Full path to user's shell

As noted, one way to set the system variables is to modify the ~.bash_profile file. For example, if you need another entry in the PATH variable, you can add it to the end of the current variable, separated by a colon. In Mac OS X 10.5 and later, the system administrator can add to

PATH by adding a file to /etc/paths.d describing the path addition, or by adding a new line to /etc/paths.

Environment variables can also be set by editing the ~/.MacOSX/environment.plist file.

```
<?xml version ="1.0" encoding="UTF-8">
<!DOCTYPE plist SYSTEM file://localhost/System/Library/DTDs/PropertyList.dtd>
<plist version="0.9">
<dict>
        <key>EnvironmentVariable</key>
        <string>/new/path</string>
    </dict>
</plist>
```

This edit adds the /new/path value to the EnvironmentVariable key, creating a system-wide addition to the environment variable.

The PATH variable can be set temporarily, as well, with a life of only a single terminal session. The following command will append the current PATH variable with /usr/local/bin:

```
export PATH=$PATH:/usr/local/bin
```

Again, this reflects the BSD underpinnings of Mac OS X. Modifying system variables in Mac OS X is identical to the process in BSD and Linux systems. All system variables can be set in Mac OS X using either method.

Interfaces in Mac OS X

Ethernet interfaces follow the BSD naming scheme. Ethernet interfaces in Mac OS X are named using the convention en*x*, where *x* is the number of the Ethernet interface.

The interfaces can be configured through the command line or through an easy-to-access GUI tool in the Mac OS X System Preferences pane.

Configuring Ethernet Interfaces from the Command Line

The current interface configuration can be read using the ifconfig command from the terminal:

```
$ ifconfig en0
en0: flags=8863<UP,BROADCAST,SMART,RUNNING,SIMPLEX,MULTICAST> mtu 1500
    inet 192.168.1.110 netmask 0xffffff00 broadcast 192.168.1.255
    ether 00:16:cb:a7:74:a4
    media: autoselect (100baseTX <full-duplex,flow-control>) status: active
    supported media: autoselect 10baseT/UTP <half-duplex> 10baseT/UTP <full-duplex>
10baseT/UTP <full-duplex,hw-loopback> 10baseT/UTP <full-duplex,flow-control>
100baseTX <half-duplex> 100baseTX <full-duplex> 100baseTX <full-duplex,hw-loopback>
100baseTX <full-duplex,flow-control> 1000baseT <full-duplex>
1000baseT <full-duplex,hw-loopback> 1000baseT <full-duplex,flow-control> none
```

You can also configure the interfaces using the same ifconfig command:

```
$ ifconfig en0 192.168.1.100 netmask 255.255.255.0 up
```

This command returns the following – a configuration, very similar to that seen in the preceding bare `ifconfig` command:

```
en0: flags=8863<UP,BROADCAST,SMART,RUNNING,SIMPLEX,MULTICAST> mtu 1500
     inet 192.168.1.100 netmask 0xffffff00 broadcast 192.168.1.255
     ether 00:16:cb:a7:74:a4
     media: autoselect (100baseTX <full-duplex,flow-control>) status: active
     supported media: autoselect 10baseT/UTP <half-duplex> 10baseT/UTP <full-duplex>
10baseT/UTP <full-duplex,hw-loopback> 10baseT/UTP <full-duplex,flow-control>
100baseTX <half-duplex> 100baseTX <full-duplex>
100baseTX <full-duplex,hw-loopback> 100baseTX <full-duplex,flow-control>
1000baseT <full-duplex> 1000baseT <full-duplex,hw-loopback>
1000baseT <full-duplex,flow-control> none
```

Using the GUI to Configure Ethernet Interfaces

The Ethernet interfaces can also be configured via the GUI, in the Network options of System Preferences, as shown in Figure 2-5.

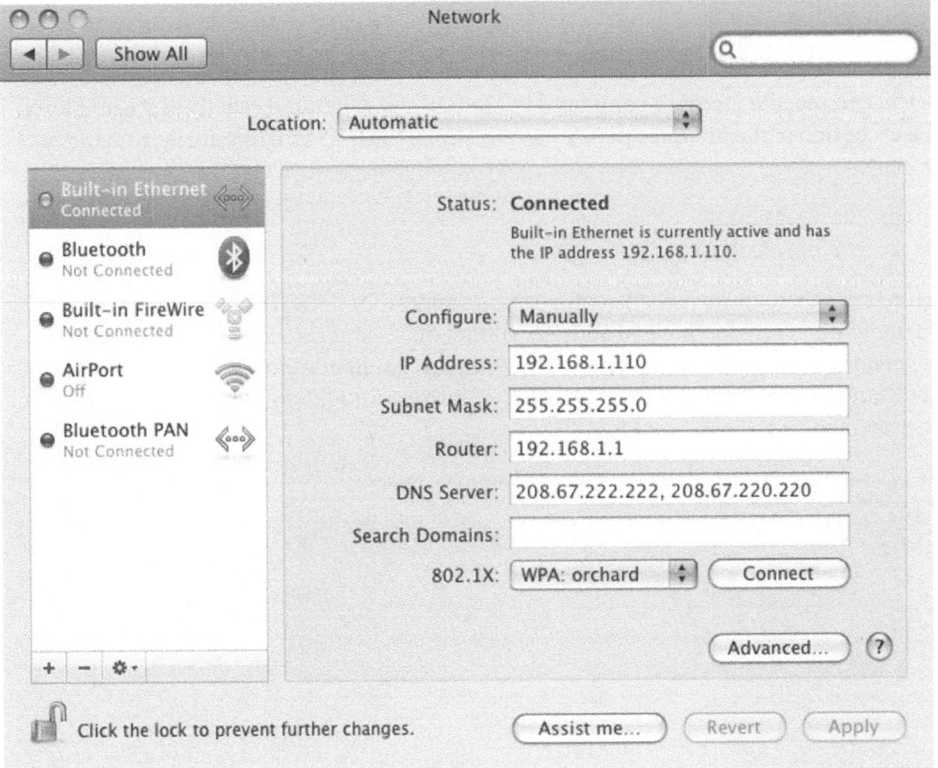

Figure 2-5. *Manually configuring the network interfaces with the GUI tool in Mac OS X*

You can set the following options:

- *Configure*: Determines whether the IP address will be set manually or via the Dynamic Host Configuration Protocol (DHCP).

- *IP Address*: This field is accessible only if the Configure field is set to Manually. Otherwise, the IP address is set by DHCP.

- *Subnet Mask*: Defines the subnetwork on which the computer resides.

- *Router*: The address of a router or gateway device.

- *DNS Server*: Comma-delimited list of Domain Name System (DNS) servers used to perform DNS lookups.

- *Search Domains*: Allows the user to enter comma-delimited domains that are accessed frequently. For example, if you frequently access apple.com, that domain can be entered in the Search Domains text box. This will allow you to enter only developer in your browser's address bar to access developer.apple.com.

- *802.1x*: Selects a default wireless network.

The command-line equivalent to the configuration shown in Figure 2-5 would be as follows:

```
$ ifconfig en0 192.168.1.110 netmask 255.255.255.0 up
```

As you can see, the ifconfig command in Mac OS X is structured exactly as it is in Linux, with the exception of the interface name. As with Linux, the DNS lookups are written to /etc/resolv.conf.

```
nameserver 208.67.222.222
nameserver 208.67.220.220
```

Figure 2-6 shows the advanced configuration window for networking. This provides the tools to manually configure the IPv4 address, subnet mask, and gateway, and to configure IPv6, if needed. Additional tabs in the window establish configuration for DNS, Windows Internet Name Service (WINS), AppleTalk, 802.1x, Proxies, and Ethernet. Figure 2-7 shows the Ethernet tab.

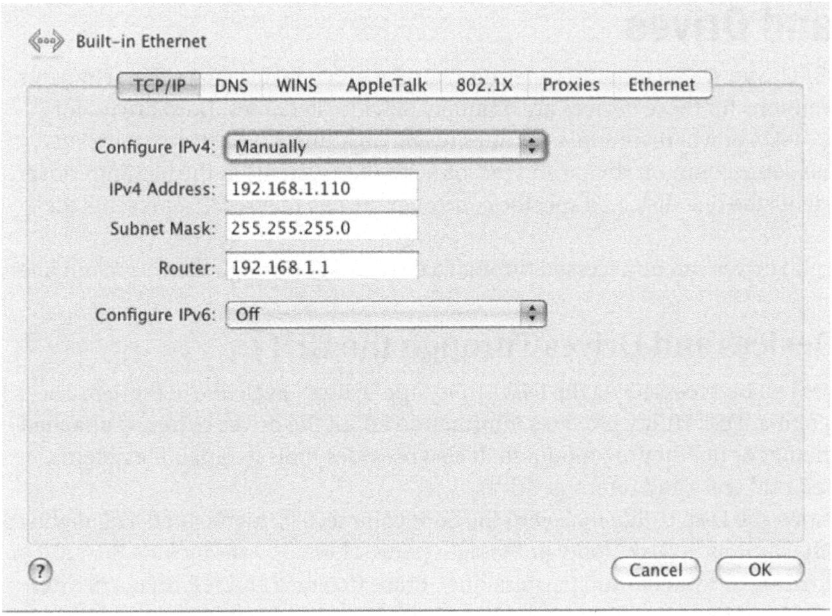

Figure 2-6. *Advanced network configuration in the GUI tool in Mac OS X*

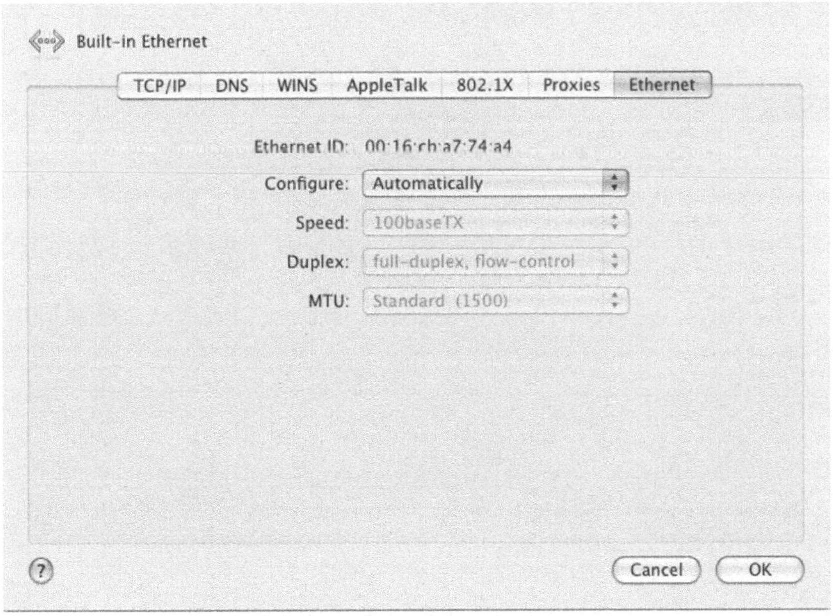

Figure 2-7. *Additional Ethernet configuration with the GUI tool in Mac OS X*

Devices and Drives

Consistent with BSD, Mac OS X contains a /dev directory to abstract devices to files. However, the naming conventions for these devices are uniquely Macintosh names. Hard drives, for example, may be disk0, or where multiple volumes reside on a single disk, disk0s1, disk0s2, and so on. There is some common rhyme and reason with BSD systems in the naming convention. disk0 represents the first disk on a specific controller, just as /dev/hdd0 represents the first hard drive.

The devices and drives can be accessed through a GUI tool or through the command line.

Accessing Devices and Drives Through the GUI

Devices and drives can be accessed via the Disk Utility application, available in the Applications/Utilities folder. Disk Utility provides information about the drives currently attached to the system, whether or not they are mounted. It also provides tools to repair filesystems, repair permissions, and erase and reformat drives.

Figure 2-8 shows the Disk Utility tool, with the boot volume, OSX, highlighted. Highlighting a volume opens the options in Disk Utility in the right pane. These options include First Aid (verifying and repairing filesystems and permissions), Erase (to erase and reformat a drive), RAID (for RAID configuration), and Restore (to restore a full image to a drive).

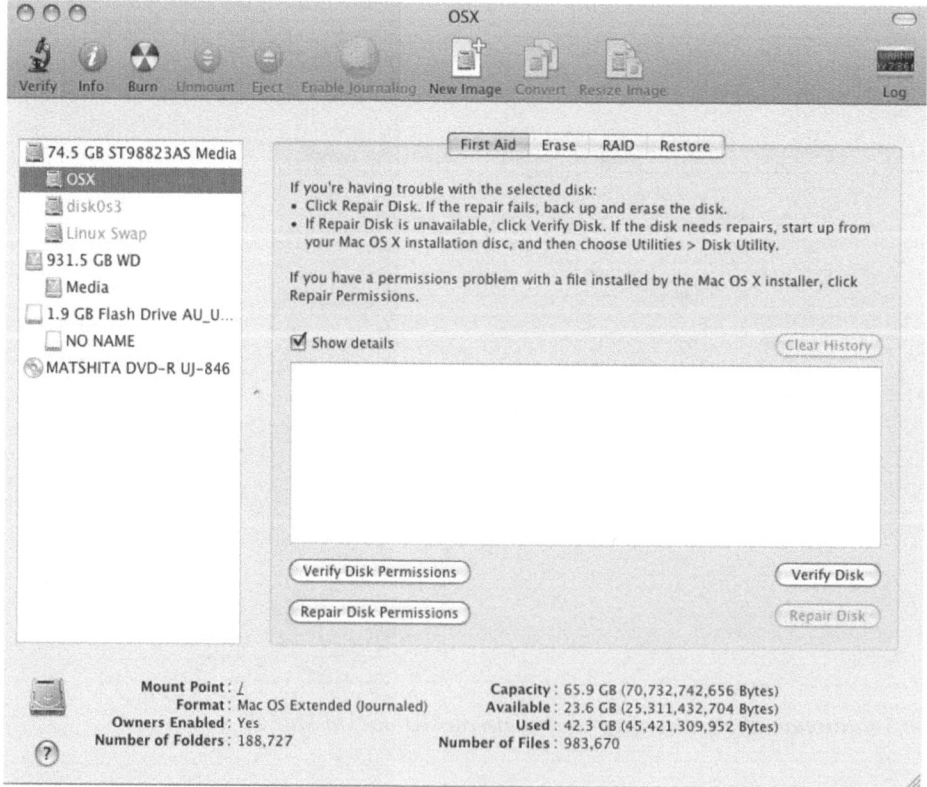

Figure 2-8. *Disk Utility in Mac OS X*

Read-only GUI access to the Mac OS X devices and drives can be found in System Profiler, available in the `Applications/Utilities` folder. This is an informational tool only.

An equivalent tool exists in Linux. Figure 2-9 shows the network configuration tool in the GNOME desktop environment, in Ubuntu.

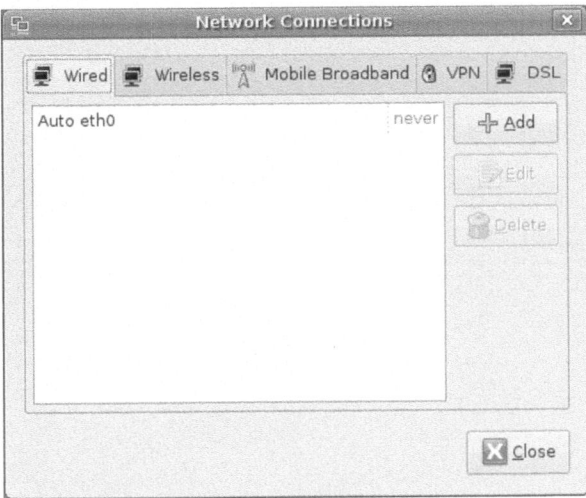

Figure 2-9. *The Network Connections window in Ubuntu*

Accessing Devices and Drives from the Command Line

Mac OS X also offers command-line access to the `diskutil` tool. This allows the user command-line access to all the options offered in the Disk Utility tool, described in the previous section. These options include mounting/umounting drives, verifying disks and permissions, repairing disks and permissions, erasing and reformatting disks, and configuring RAID.

Summary

This chapter reviewed the similarities and differences between Mac OS X and UNIX, and BSD. You saw that the Mac OS X filesystem (HFS+) and ext2/ext3 filesystem (common on many Linux distributions) are similar, although there are some differences. We then covered Mac OS X permissions, terminal access, interface configuration, and device and drive access. In the next chapter, we'll move on to a way to ease the transition from Linux to Mac OS X: via dual-booting or running virtual Linux.

■ ■ ■

## CHAPTER 3

Dual-Booting and Virtualization

Sometimes it's easiest to make the transition from Linux to the Mac in a dual-boot configuration. Or maybe you would prefer to start with a virtual machine, running Linux within Mac OS X. Either is possible and reasonably easy to configure on the Mac.

Creating a dual-boot configuration is the job of Boot Camp (although it's intended for dual-booting with Windows), a built-in component of Mac OS X. For virtual Linux installations, VMware or its free counterpart VirtualBox make short work of creating a virtual machine and installing Linux within it. Your preferences will certainly be personal and based on your own use of the machine. This chapter details the process for each of these options, leaving the choice of which is best up to you.

Dual-Booting Linux and Mac OS X

Dual-booting Linux on the Mac has some distinct advantages, including the following:

- Speed
- Full use of the hardware capabilities without an additional abstraction layer between the hardware and the software
- Full read and write capabilities

If you're not bothered by rebooting the machine to get to your Linux installation, the speed and storage made possible by dual-booting make it an attractive option.

Note Interestingly, Apple Mac OS X 10.5 (Leopard) was released in late 2007 with dual-booting in mind. Boot Camp, a Mac OS X partitioning tool, was included in the release. Boot Camp had been in beta use since 2006, and included on nearly all Intel-based Macs since their introduction, allowing new Mac users to also install Windows on their new machines. While the Mac is complete with software suitable for substitution for nearly any Windows application, it's still difficult to pull some users away from the tools they understand best. Looking at the recent market-share numbers, Boot Camp may have helped achieve the goal of moving Windows users to the Mac.

Critical to the process of installing a new partition on the Mac is the concept of nonde-structive partitioning. In a sense, that's the most important piece of Boot Camp: the ability to resize existing partitions without destroying the existing data. In Windows, this has long been possible with Partition Magic. In Linux, GParted has recently risen to prominence for its nondestructive partitioning features. These applications are, for the most part, easy to use and very robust. That's what you'll find with Boot Camp, as well.

In order to load Linux on the Mac, however, you'll probably want to download and install a copy of rEFIt on the Mac, so we'll look at how to do that first.

Loading Linux with rEFIt

Macs make use of the Extensible Firmware Interface (EFI). This is a replacement for the older and less efficient Basic Input/Output System (BIOS) of Intel-based computers. EFI, developed by Intel in the mid-1990s, has some distinct advantages over the older BIOS system:

- EFI contains both architecture-specific and processor-independent device drivers for use in booting the system. The processor-independent environment is referred to as the EFI Byte Code (EBC). Because the EFI contains an interpreter for EBC images that reside in the environment, the EFI boot loader is almost completely hardware-independent. EFI can also make use of its own graphics capabilities prior to loading the architecture-specific graphics drivers.

- The EFI boot loader is an application that's part and parcel of EFI. This means that there's no longer a need for a dedicated boot-loading mechanism.

- EFI also supports both the BIOS standard master boot record (MBR) and the GUID partition table (GPT) used by the Mac. In fact, this support of both standards is the pri-mary reason you'll need to install rEFIt on the Mac in order to dual-boot Linux. rEFIt will read and take advantage of the MBR records created by Linux.

- EFI provides a shell environment, much like the Grub boot loader in Linux. Like Grub, the EFI shell can be used to further tailor and customize the EFI boot process.

rEFIt handles all these options, helping to translate from the GPT boot scheme to the MBR boot scheme of Linux.

Note that rEFIt isn't necessary to boot Linux from the Mac. The Mac volume chooser (activated by holding the Option key at bootup) will recognize all "blessed" bootable drives. However, if the installation was created with Boot Camp, the Linux option may be listed as Windows. rEFIt refines the existing tool and makes the multiple-boot experience more accu-rate and much better.

■**Note** The Myths and Facts page of the rEFIt site (http://refit.sourceforge.net/myths/) notes that Boot Camp isn't actually necessary in order to install Windows or Linux. The rEFIt developers make a com-pelling case, noting changes to OS X in the release of 10.4.6. However, having made the strong case against Boot Camp, they conclude that though Boot Camp isn't necessary, it is helpful. The rEFIt developers make much the same case about Linux BIOS compatibility mode: it's not necessary, as elilo will boot Intel Macs. Again, though, they conclude that BIOS compatibility requires less effort.

Downloading and Installing rEFIt

rEFIt is available as a free download at `http://refit.sourceforge.net/`. Two versions of the application exist: an automatic installation package and a manual installation version.

To install the automatic version, follow these steps:

1. Download and mount the rEFIt image by double-clicking the icon.

2. Double-click the `rEFIt.mpkg` file in the mounted rEFIt image.

3. Follow the instructions to select the Mac OS X volume in which rEFIt will be installed.

4. Reboot the system when the installation is complete. The rEFIt menu will appear at bootup.

Here's the procedure for manually installing rEFIt:

1. Download the Mac disk image version of the application.

2. Double-click the icon of the downloaded application.

3. Copy the `efi` directory from the downloaded image to the root level of the Mac.

4. Open a terminal window and enter the following commands:

```
cd /efi/refit
./enable.sh
```

5. Reboot the system when complete. The rEFIt menu will appear at bootup.

The rEFIt menu allows you to choose which system you'll boot into, much like Grub (or the even older LILO). It also provides the rEFIt shell and the ability to shut down or restart the system from the rEFIt menu.

Should you choose to uninstall rEFIt, that's also easily done. While booted into the Mac system, remove the `efi` directory from `/Volumes/[boot volume name]`. Also be sure to remove the `rEFItBlesser` folder from within the `Library/StartupItems` directory.

Configuring and Customizing rEFIt

rEFIt is customizable in many ways. To make machine-specific changes to rEFIt's operation and behavior, you'll need to edit the `refit.conf` file. This is located in the `efi` directory in the boot volume at `/Volumes/[boot volume name]/efi/refit/refit.conf`.

As with many similar configuration files, options for rEFIt's operation can be turned on or off by commenting or uncommenting application directives in the configuration file. The following is a representative example from the actual `refit.conf` file.

```
#
# refit.conf
# Configuration file for the rEFIt boot menu
#

# Timeout in seconds for the main menu screen. Setting the timeout to 0
# disables automatic booting (i.e., no timeout).
#
timeout 20
```

```
# Disable menu options for increased security. These are intended for a lab
# environment where the administrator doesn't want users to mess with the
# operating system. List the names for the options you want to hide from
# the boot menu. Currently supported:
#  shell        - remove the EFI shell
#  tools        - remove all EFI tools (shell and gptsync)
# Use text mode only. When enabled, this option forces rEFIt into text mode.
#
#textonly

# List legacy options first. When enabled, legacy BIOS based boot options
# (e.g. Windows, Linux via LILO or GRUB) will be listed first. This is
# intended as a quick fix to change the default boot choice until full
# configurability arrives.
#
#legacyfirst

# EOF
```

rEFIt will find any bootable operating system on any drive attached to the system. As you would expect, the first drive listed in the menu is the default. For example, I use a 320GB FireWire drive attached to the Mac mini for regular backups. One partition contains Time Machine backups (covered in more detail in Chapter 7), and another partition on the same drive is reserved for cloned and fully bootable backups of the hard drive. The latter partition is labeled Rollbacks on the FireWire drive. The rEFIt boot menu displays Rollbacks, OSX (hard drive), and Linux as the boot options. No further configuration was necessary to make this possible.

However, if I wanted to have the Linux installation on the Mac as the default boot installation, I would just need to make a simple change to the refit.conf file: remove the comment hash from the legacyfirst directive in the file. As is noted in the file, this command lists the Windows or Linux installations first in the boot menu (both use the "legacy" or MBR boot method).

The default option will boot without further interaction at the expiration of the timeout number listed in the refit.conf file. So, if your preference is to boot immediately into Linux, set the timeout to a very small number (setting it to 0 will disable the automatic boot altogether, not prevent a user from choosing another option), and uncomment the legacyfirst directive.

Updating rEFIt

Updates to rEFIt are easily supported and installed. If you choose the automatic installer option when first installing rEFIt, the installer for subsequent versions will replace the updated files seamlessly. If you chose the manual installation option, simply replace the older files with the updated files from the newer version of rEFIt.

Creating a Bootable rEFIt CD

You can also create a bootable rEFIt CD using the downloaded .dmg image. To do so, follow these steps:

1. Right-click the rEFIt-0.11.dmg image in the Finder and select Open With ➤ Disk Utility from the context menu.

2. Select rEFIt-0.11.dmg in the list on the left side of the Disk Utility window.

3. Click the Burn button in the Disk Utility toolbar.

4. Insert a blank CD and select Burn.

This disc will provide emergency recovery with rEFIt, or it can be installed to the hard drive.

With rEFIt installed, you can now get on to the business of installing Linux on the Mac.

Installing Linux Using Boot Camp

As noted, Boot Camp is part of the default Mac OS X installation. Using Boot Camp to install Linux is clearly a bit different than its intended use. There are some additional steps necessary to install Linux using Boot Camp, which we'll walk through now.

Here are the main tasks you'll need to perform to install Linux using Boot Camp:

- Use Boot Camp to nondestructively partition the boot drive on your system.

- Reformat the FAT32 partition created by Boot Camp to a Linux-friendly filesystem.

- Install the Linux system in the newly reformatted partition.

- Synchronize the MBR and GPT tables used by rEFIt to allow either operating system to boot.

Partitioning the Boot Drive

First, you'll need to create some drive space for the installation. There are, of course, at least a couple of ways to accomplish this partitioning task. Here, I'll describe the use of Boot Camp, the nondestructive partitioner included in the Mac OS X installation. I'll explain how to use the diskutil utility in the "Partitioning from the Command Line" section later in this chapter.

To launch Boot Camp, click the Applications folder in the Dock, click Utilities, and then click Boot Camp Assistant in the Utilities window. You'll see the window shown in Figure 3-1.

Boot Camp makes a recommendation as to the size of the new partition. You can adjust the partition sizes by sliding the partition divider to the right or left.

Click Partition, and Boot Camp will create the partition, nondestructively resizing the original partition on the drive. When partitioning is complete, Boot Camp will prompt you to insert a blank CD. This will be used for Windows drivers. Because you're installing Linux, you can skip this step.

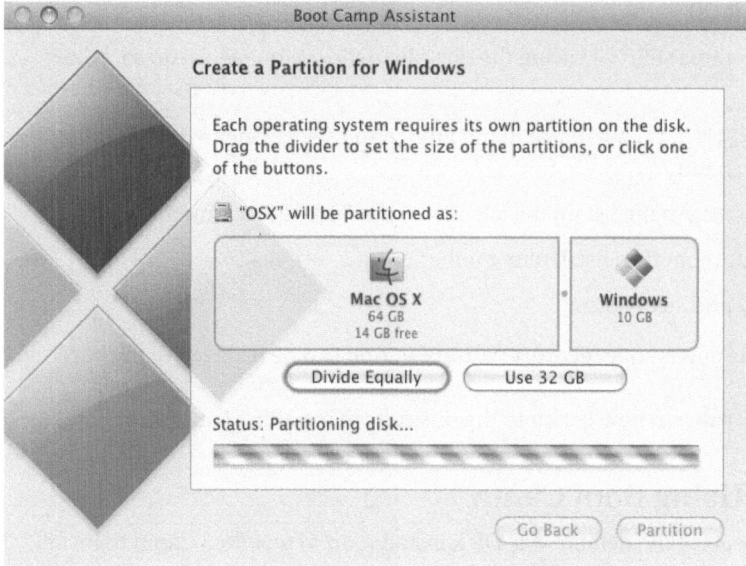

Figure 3-1. *Creating a partition with the Boot Camp Assistant*

Installing Linux

Insert the Linux installation disc in the CD drive, and reboot when the Boot Camp installation is complete. As the system reboots, hold down the C key on the keyboard. This will boot from the CD ROM drive—your Linux installation disc.

Start the installation as normal. Figure 3-2 shows the main installation screen in Ubuntu; yours will differ based on the Linux distribution you've chosen.

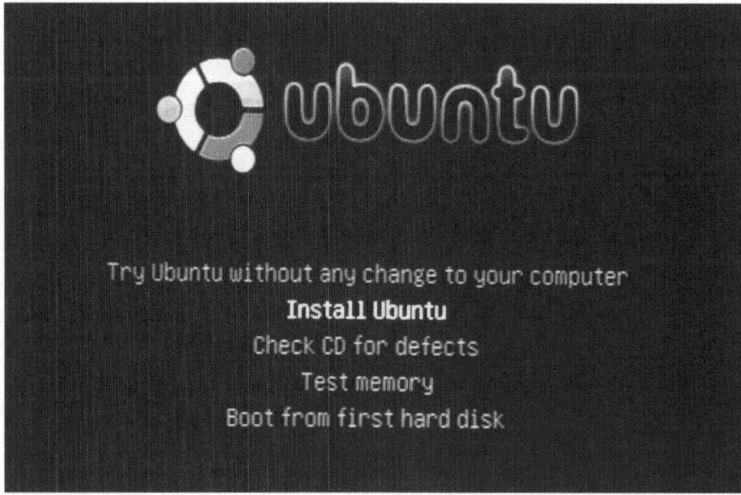

Figure 3-2. *The main Ubuntu installation screen*

Many current Linux distributions will make some recommendation for partitioning, based, in part, on any free space on the drive. Figure 3-3 shows the partitioning recommendations in Ubuntu.

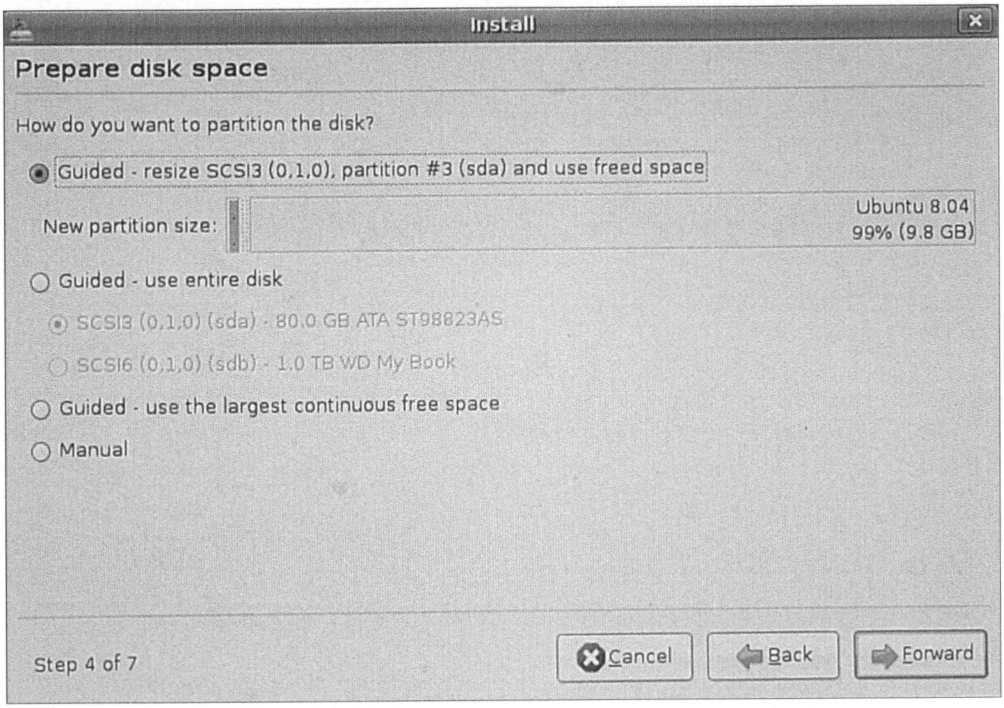

Figure 3-3. *Partitioning and formatting for Linux*

When provided the partitioning options during your Linux installation, choose the manual partitioning option offered by your chosen distribution. You'll find an MS-DOS FAT32 partition in the listed partition table. You'll need to reformat this partition to a Linux-friendly filesystem, such as ext3, ext4, ReiserFS, ZFS, or some other system. You'll also need to create the / mount point. Figure 3-4 shows the manual partition screen in Ubuntu for the free space I created with Boot Camp.

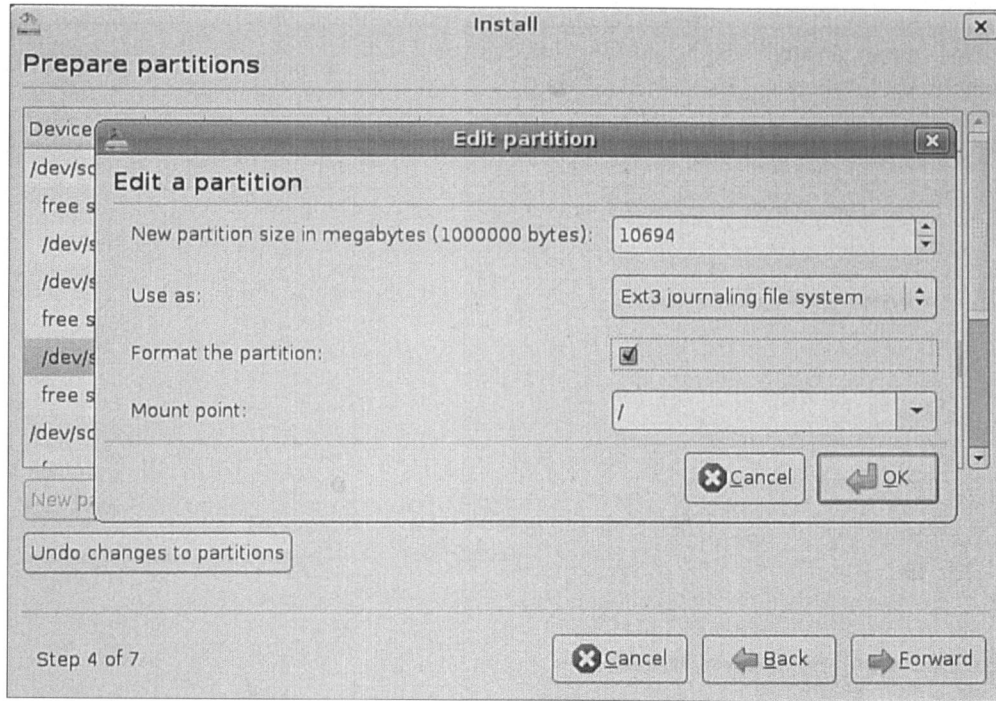

Figure 3-4. *Creating the / mount point and formatting the new partition in Ubuntu*

In most cases, all of the other default options will be acceptable in the installation. You can also customize the installation as necessary for your use.

Synchronizing the MBR and GPT Tables

After Linux is installed, reboot the system. You'll be greeted with a rEFIt menu, complete with icons and graphical representations of both the Mac OS X and Linux installations on the drive. To complete the installation, choose the Start Partitioning Tool option, by using the arrow keys, as shown in Figure 3-5. This will provide you with the option to commit the new Linux installation to the MBR.

Figure 3-5. *Altering the MBR with rEFIt*

As shown in Figure 3-6, when the partitioning is complete, the MBR and GPT tables will be in sync, allowing rEFIt to boot from either system.

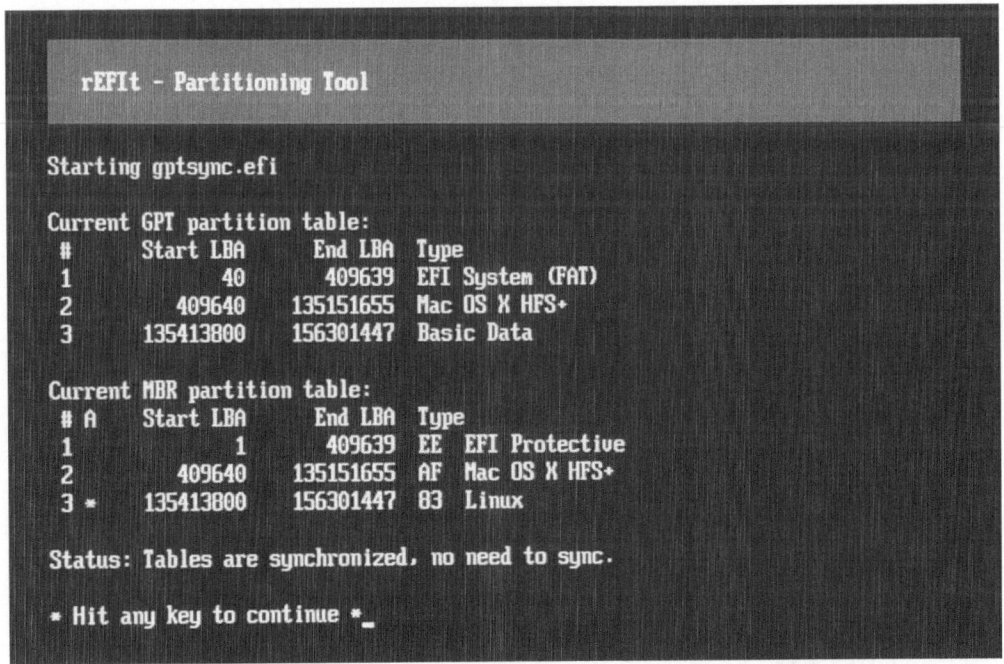

Figure 3-6. *Synchronizing MBR and GPT tables in rEFIt*

With the boot tables in sync, select the Restart option in rEFIt to reboot the system. This time, select the Linux installation from the rEFIt menu, and then press Enter.

Partitioning from the Command Line

Mac OS X includes the Disk Utility application, accessible both from the command line and from the Applications folder in the Dock, within Utilities. As any good Linux geek knows, if you can do it with a GUI tool, you can generally do it more quickly from the command line. Command-line diskutil offers more options than the GUI version and is, indeed, quicker to use.

Creating a new partition on the hard drive for your Linux installation is actually surprisingly easy using the command-line version of diskutil. Let's break out the individual pieces, then combine all the elements into a single command that will nondestructively repartition the existing boot volume and, simultaneously, create a new partition for the Linux installation.

diskutil has many options. Usage is as follows:

```
diskutil <verb> <options>
```

In other words, you're calling the diskutil application to take some defined action on the drive, and you can specify options to customize those actions. The following is a representative set of options available to diskutil (by no means is that a complete list of the options):

```
list                    (List the partitions of a disk)
info[rmation]           (Get information on a specific disk or partition)
u[n]mount               (Unmount a single volume)
unmountDisk             (Unmount an entire disk (all volumes))
eject                   (Eject a disk)
mount                   (Mount a single volume)
mountDisk               (Mount an entire disk (all mountable volumes))

repairVolume            (Repair the file system data structure of a volume)
verifyDisk              (Synonym for verifyVolume)
..resizeVolume          (Resize a volume, increasing or decreasing its size)
```

```
diskutil <verb> with no options will provide help on that verb
```

Of particular interest to the task at hand is the resizeVolume verb. This is what you'll use to shrink the current boot volume, freeing space for the new Linux partition.

diskutil clearly already knows the format of the current boot partition. So, if the only change you're making to that partition is its size, you won't need to tell diskutil how the partition should be formatted. However, you will need to let diskutil know the new size of the partition. This is the option to the command.

You also need to know how the system currently sees and labels the boot volume. To see this information, use the list verb of the diskutil command.

```
$ diskutil list
```

This returns the following output:

```
#:      TYPE NAME                    SIZE        IDENTIFIER
0:      GUID_partition_scheme       *74.5 Gi     disk0
```

```
    1:      EFI                        200.0 Mi   disk0s1
    2:      Apple_HFS OSX              74.1 Gi    disk0s2
```

This listing displays the partition number on the drive (#), as well as the partition type, name, size, and system identifier. In the case of my hard drive, the partition named OSX is the partition I would like to shrink. That's just the common name. In fact, the system sees the drive as disk0s2. This denotes the second partition on the first hard drive (where 0 is significant only in the case of the drive itself, not the partitions created on the drive).

So, you now have two of the critical pieces needed for resizing the partition on the hard drive: the verb (resizeVolume) and the name of the partition to be resized (disk0s2, in my example).

To create a new partition on the same drive, using the same command, you'll need to use several more options. The next piece is the filesystem type of the new partition. According to the help pages of the diskutil command, the following are valid:

```
Valid filesystems: "Journaled HFS+" "HFS+" "Case-sensitive HFS+"
"Case-sensitive Journaled HFS+" "HFS" "MS-DOS FAT16" "MS-DOS FAT32"
"MS-DOS FAT12" "MS-DOS" "UDF" "UFS" "ZFS"
```

The next piece of information you'll need for the new partition is an identifier. In this case, let's just call it Linux.

Finally, you'll need to make sure the system knows how big this new partition should be. diskutil provides a tool you can use to see the available size of a partition:

```
$ diskutil resizeVolume disk0s2 limits
For device disk0s2 OSX:
    Current size:       79548170240 bytes
    Minimum size:       45846577152 bytes
    Maximum size:       79682387968 bytes
```

This will give you a basis from which to resize the drive. In my case, I would like to leave 60GB on the drive as my Mac installation. With 79.6GB available, I'll make sure the newly resized boot partition is 60GB, while creating a new partition of 19.6GB. The size of a new or resized partition can be denoted in the command line with B, M, or G, for bytes, megabytes, and gigabytes, respectively.

So, with all those pieces, the following diskutil command will resize the existing partition, create a new partition of 19.6GB, create an MS-DOS FAT32 filesystem on that partition, and give it the name Linux.

```
$ diskutil resizeVolume disk0s2 60G "MS-DOS FAT32" "Linux" 19.6G
```

When this command completes, you'll be ready to install Linux on the Mac, as described in the previous section. And, with rEFIt installed, the boot-loading functions will all be handled automatically.

Removing a Linux Partition

If you were installing Windows on the Mac, Boot Camp would do yeoman-like work in removing the Boot Camp partition and resizing the old Mac OS X partition to utilize the full drive. However, Boot Camp doesn't recognize ext3 or other Linux partitions. If you create a Linux installation on the Mac, and then attempt to remove it using Boot Camp, you'll just get an error. So, it's important to understand the alternative method for deleting these Linux partitions, if necessary.

gpt is another command-line application in Mac OS X. The command name stands for GUID partition table, the standard for Macs and Mac OS X. gpt will display all the current partitions on a system and will also allow you to remove a partition that you can't remove using Boot Camp.

However, because you'll be working with gpt on the system volume—the boot drive—you'll need to exit the current Mac OS X session and restart using the installation disc. This will allow you to unmount the system volume in order to view or make the changes.

To begin removing a partition, insert the Mac OS X installation disc in the drive, reboot the system, and hold down the C key as it reboots, until you hear the disc spinning up in the disc drive.

At the installation prompt, select your language of choice. Then select Utilities and Disk Utility from the menu bar. Highlight the boot drive by clicking its icon in the left pane of Disk Utility, right-click, and select Unmount.

Now you'll be able to use gpt to remove the Linux partition and diskutil to resize the Mac OS X partition. Alternatively, open Terminal.app from the Utilities menu, and eject the volume from the command line:

```
$ disktuil eject /Volumes/[volume name]
```

To remove a partition using gpt, you'll first want to look at the names of the existing partitions:

```
$ gpt show disk0
```

This command will display all the partitions on the system. From this list, you'll cull the name of the partition you would like to remove on the boot drive. With this command, unlike the diskutil command, the partition number is displayed as the index on the drive, distinct from the drive itself.

```
start                size     index    contents
    0                   1               MBR
    1                   1               Pri GPT header
    2                  32               Pri GPT table
   34                   6
   40              409600         1     GPT part - C12A7328-F81F-11D2-BA➥
4B-00A0C93EC93B
  409640          4742016         2     GPT part - 48465300-0000-11AA-AA➥
11-00306543ECAC
135151656          262144
135413800        20887648         3     GPT part - EBD0A0A2-B9E5-4433-87➥
C0-68B6B72699C7
156301448                         7
156301455                        32     Sec GPT table
156301487                         1     Sec GPT header
```

The important elements of this return listing are the indices. As this is disk0, the specific partitions to be modified will be addressed as disk0s2 and disk0s3. In particular, disk0s3 is the Linux partition. To remove the partition, use gpt as follows:

```
$ gpt remove -i 3 disk0
```

As you might guess, this instructs gpt to remove the third partition on disk0—the partition created to install Linux in this example.

When gpt has successfully removed the partition, run the gpt show command once again to get a view of the current state of the partition table on the drive.

```
$ gpt show disk0
```

The gpt command returns a description of disk0.

```
start              size   index   contents
    0                 1           MBR
    1                 1           Pri GPT header
    2                32           Pri GPT table
   34                 6
   40            409600       1   GPT part - C12A7328-F81F-11D2-BA➡
4B-00A0C93EC93B
409640         134742016       2   GPT part - 48465300-0000-11AA-AA➡
11-00306543ECAC
135151656         262144
135413800       20887648       3   MBR Part 131
156301448                      7
156301455                     32   Sec GPT table
156301487                      1   Sec GPT header
```

disk0s3 is gone—successfully deleted by gpt.

Now, you need only to use the resizeVolume verb for diskutil to enlarge the current Mac OS X volume (disk0s2) to the maximum capacity of the drive. You'll use the verb in two different ways. First, use it with the limits option:

```
$ diskutil resizeVolume disk0s2 limits
```

This will display the maximum available space on the drive for an expanded partition:

```
For device disk0s2 OSX:
    Current size:    68987912192 bytes
    Minimum size:    47553765376 bytes
    Maximum size:    79682387968 bytes
```

Then use diskutil to actually resize the volume to its maximum size:

```
$ diskutil resizeVolume disk0s2 79682387968B
```

This command will resize the volume to the maximum size available, reclaiming all the partition space on the Mac OS X boot drive. You can reboot into the Mac OS X system.

However, this doesn't take care of rEFIt. If you're removing the Linux partition permanently, you'll probably want to remove rEFIt, as well. While booted into the Mac system, remove the efi directory from /Volumes/[boot volume name], the rEFItBlesser folder from within the Library/StartupItems directory, and the Partition Inspector from /Applications/Utilities.

Virtual Linux

Another valid option for making a gradual transition to Mac OS X is to install Linux in a virtual machine on the Mac. In this regard, you have several viable options. Virtual Linux on the Mac can be any distribution you favor. Given enough RAM on the host machine, virtual Linux runs quite well on the Mac.

Virtual machines allow a software layer, called the *hypervisor*, to access the underlying hardware resources while abstracting those resources from the user. This creates the appearance of a separate machine within the machine.

A popular "for pay" option for your virtual version of Linux is VMware. This is the option chosen by many Mac users, and the one detailed here. A free alternative is VirtualBox, which I'll cover briefly after the discussion of VMware.

Using VMware

VMware is stable and has a long history. A single user license for VMware Fusion—the VMware version written specifically for the Mac—will set you back $79.99 (at the time of publication). A fully functional 30-day trial version is also available.

Installing VMware

Most Mac applications install quite easily. You mount the provided image on your system, and then simply drag the application file from the mounted image to the Applications folder, either within the Finder or on the Dock.

In the case of VMware, an installation package is provided within the downloaded .dmg image. Double-clicking the installation package will start the installation, and will require the user's administrative (sudo) password.

The VMware installation begins by defining a virtual machine. The Virtual Machine Assistant, shown in Figure 3-7, will help you to create this virtual machine, walking you through the steps item by item. The distribution installed in this virtual machine is referred to as the guest system.

It's possible to run any Linux distribution within the virtual machine created by VMware. If you choose, you can also install Windows in a separate virtual machine. VMware provides a drop-down list with a full range of guest system options, as shown in Figure 3-8.

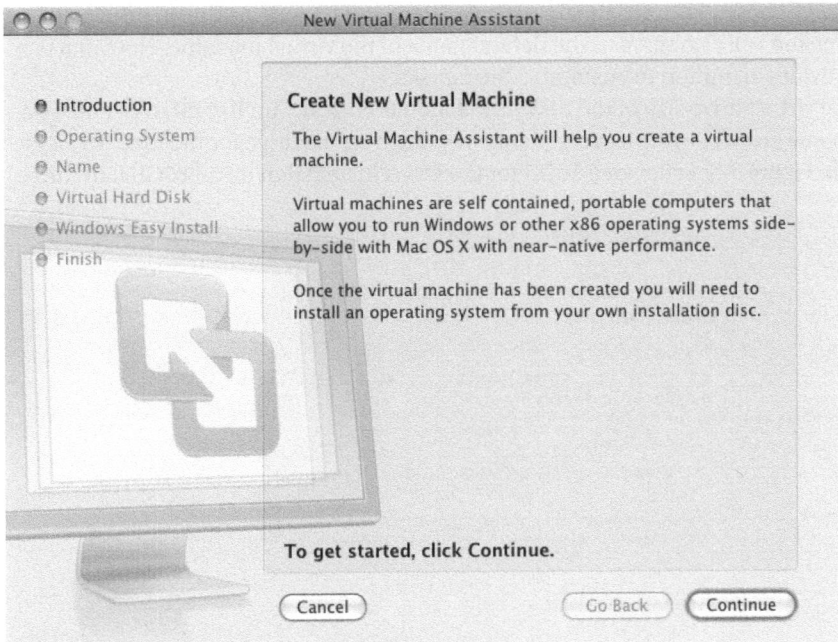

Figure 3-7. *The VMware Virtual Machine Assistant*

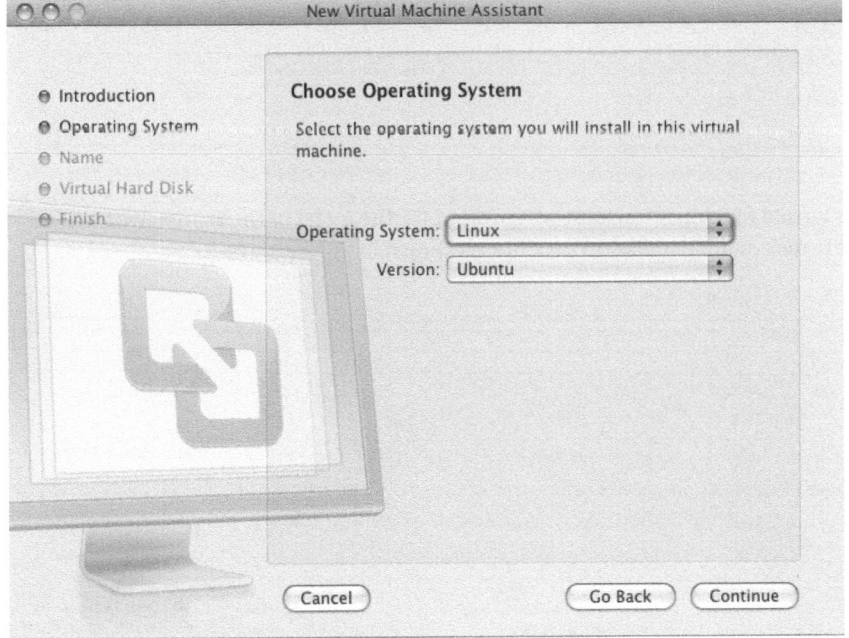

Figure 3-8. *Creating the new virtual machine with VMware*

In my case, I've chosen Linux as the operating system and Ubuntu as the distribution (version). The version will also serve as the default name of the virtual machine. Note that VMware also provides an option to customize the name.

Defining the virtual drive size of the new installation is critical. You'll want to define a size that allows for some growth, while leaving plenty of storage on the drive for the Mac OS X system. As shown in Figure 3-9, I allocated 10GB for the Linux installation on an 80GB hard drive.

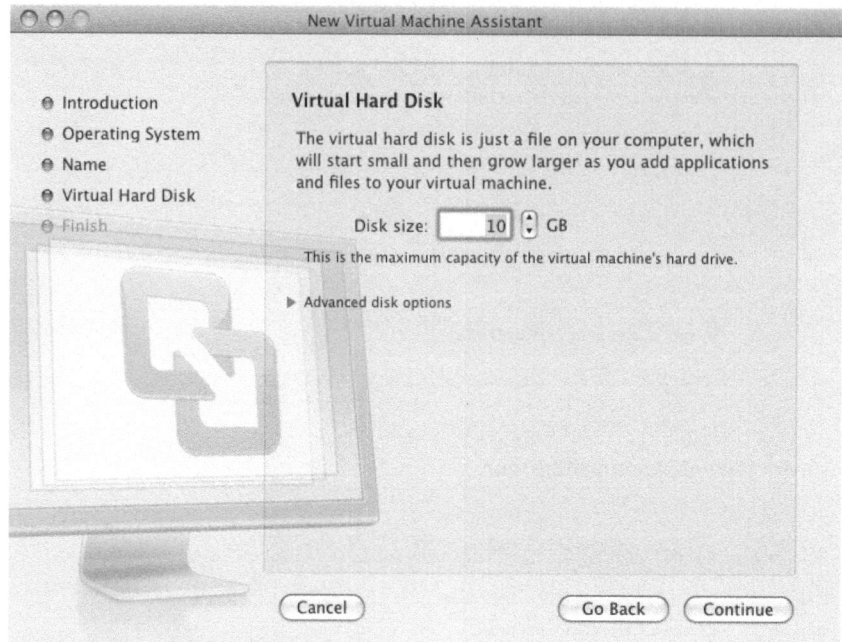

Figure 3-9. *Sizing the virtual machine*

Finally, the Virtual Machine Assistant will prompt for the installation source, which is an actual installation disk or an installation disk file, as shown in Figure 3-10.

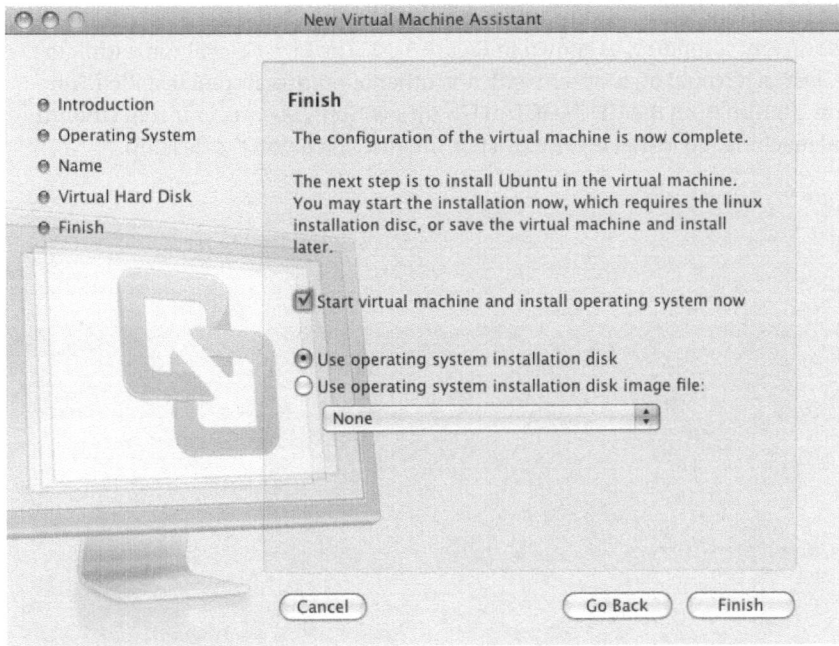

Figure 3-10. *Selecting the installation source for the virtual Linux installation*

After completing the virtual machine installation, VMware displays a library of virtual machines, as shown in Figure 3-11, and starts the virtual machine in which your Linux distribution will be installed.

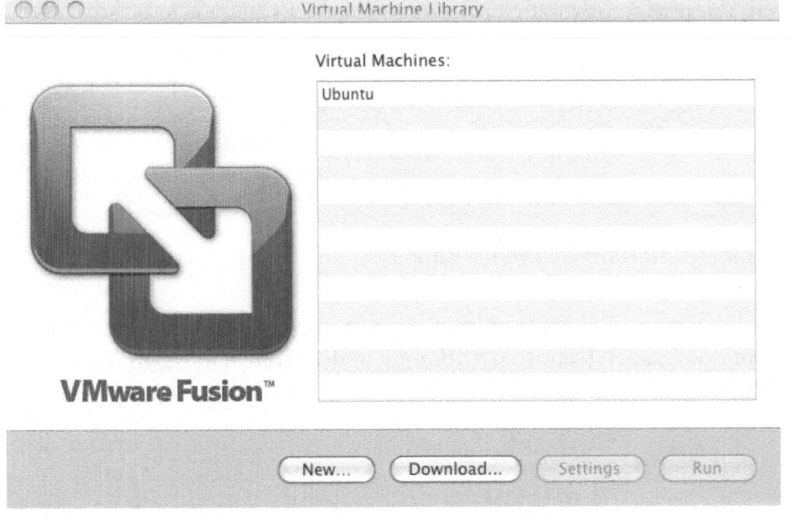

Figure 3-11. *The library of installed virtual machines*

The installation of Ubuntu in VMware looks and performs much the same as a standalone installation on any computer, as shown in Figure 3-12. The Live CD will run within the virtual machine, just as it would on a system with any other operating system installed. You can choose to run Ubuntu from the CD itself, run Ubuntu within VMware, or install Ubuntu within the virtual machine. To install it, double-click the Install icon on the desktop.

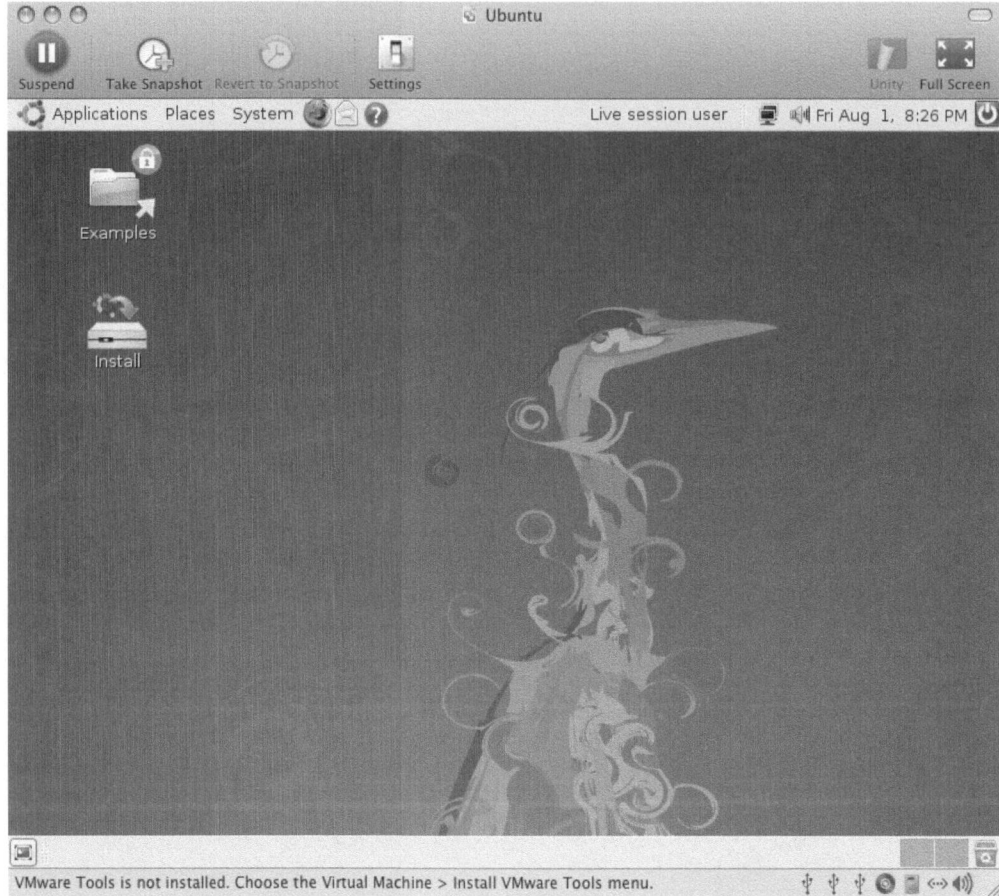

Figure 3-12. *The Ubuntu Live CD running within VMware*

The partitioning tool in Ubuntu will see the virtual drive created by VMware as a normal drive. It's acceptable to use the guided Ubuntu partitioning tool, as shown in Figure 3-13, creating a large ext3 partition and a small swap partition on the VMware virtual drive.

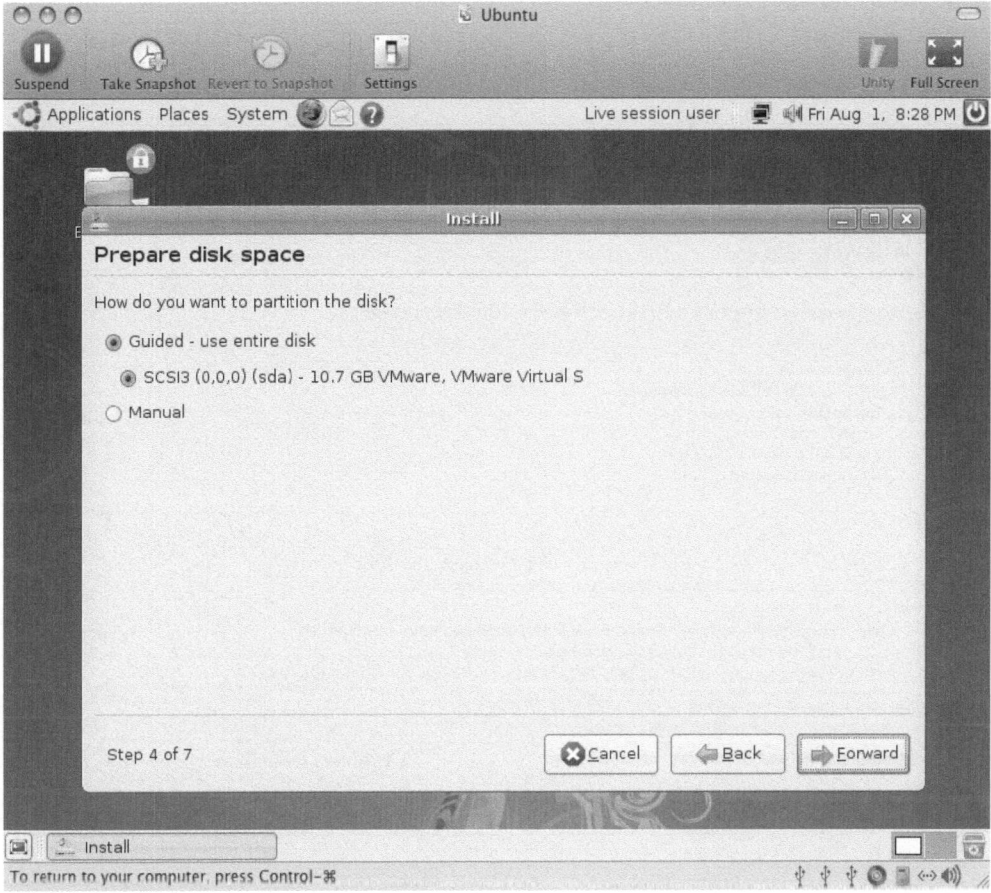

Figure 3-13. *The Ubuntu partitioning tool*

After creating a user on the system who will have administrative privileges, the installation begins, as shown in Figure 3-14.

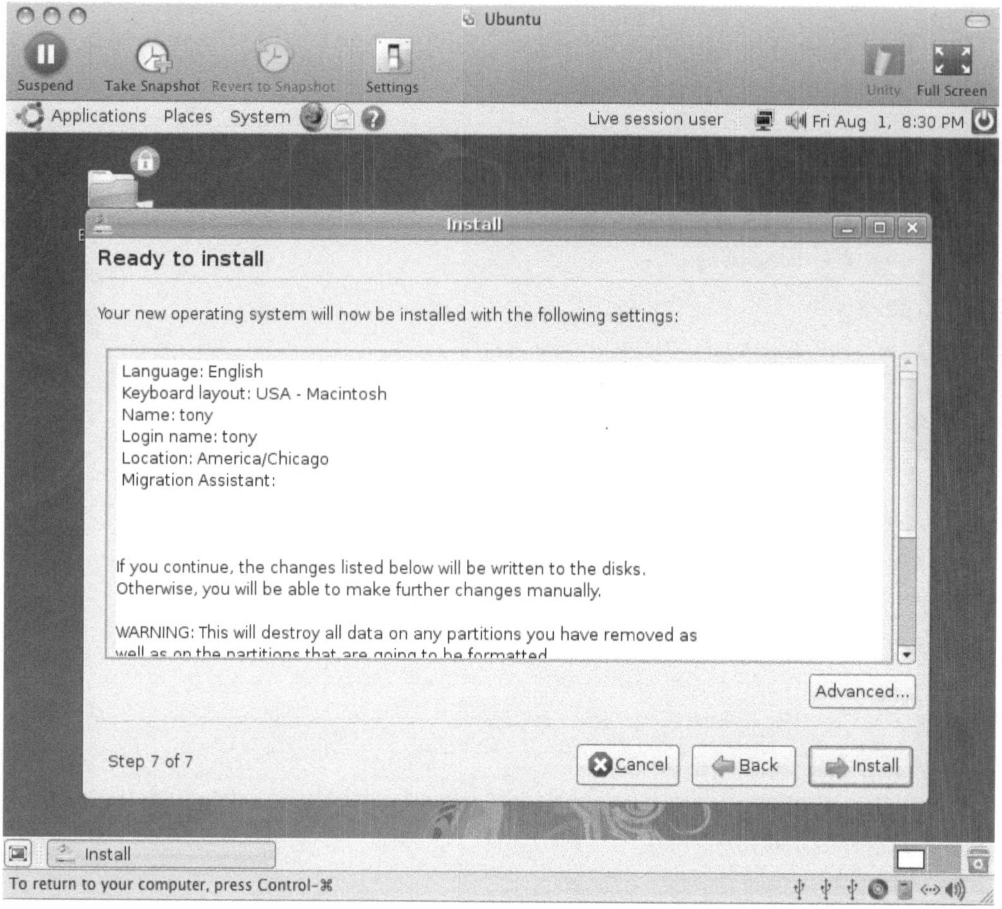

Figure 3-14 shows a screenshot of an Ubuntu installation running within a virtual machine. The window title bar shows "Ubuntu" with buttons labeled Suspend, Take Snapshot, Revert to Snapshot, Settings, Unity, and Full Screen. The menu bar reads: Applications Places System, Live session user, Fri Aug 1, 8:30 PM. The Install dialog displays:

Ready to install

Your new operating system will now be installed with the following settings:

Language: English
Keyboard layout: USA - Macintosh
Name: tony
Login name: tony
Location: America/Chicago
Migration Assistant:

If you continue, the changes listed below will be written to the disks.
Otherwise, you will be able to make further changes manually.

WARNING: This will destroy all data on any partitions you have removed as
well as on the partitions that are going to be formatted.

Advanced...

Step 7 of 7   Cancel   Back   Install

Install

To return to your computer, press Control-⌘

Figure 3-14. *Beginning the Linux installation within the virtual machine*

I also recommend that you install the VMware Tools package on the system when the Linux installation completes. As shown in Figure 3-15, the tools will allow you to more efficiently manage memory and to take advantage of improved graphics in the virtual machine. In order to install these tools, the guest system must be fully booted and operational.

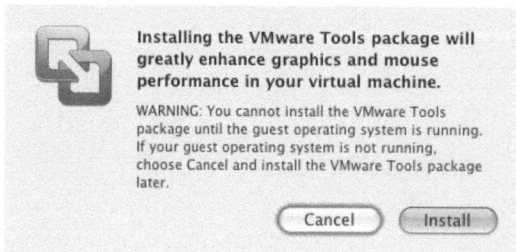

Figure 3-15. *The VMware Tools Package installation prompt*

To install the VMware Tools package, select Virtual Machine from the Mac OS X menu bar, and choose Install VMware Tools. This will open the archive manager in Ubuntu, with both an .rpm and a .tar.gz version of the VMware Tools package, as shown in Figure 3-16. Extract the .tar.gz package to the desktop, and then close the archive manager. You'll find the install script, vmware-install.pl, in the vmware-tools-distrib directory on the desktop.

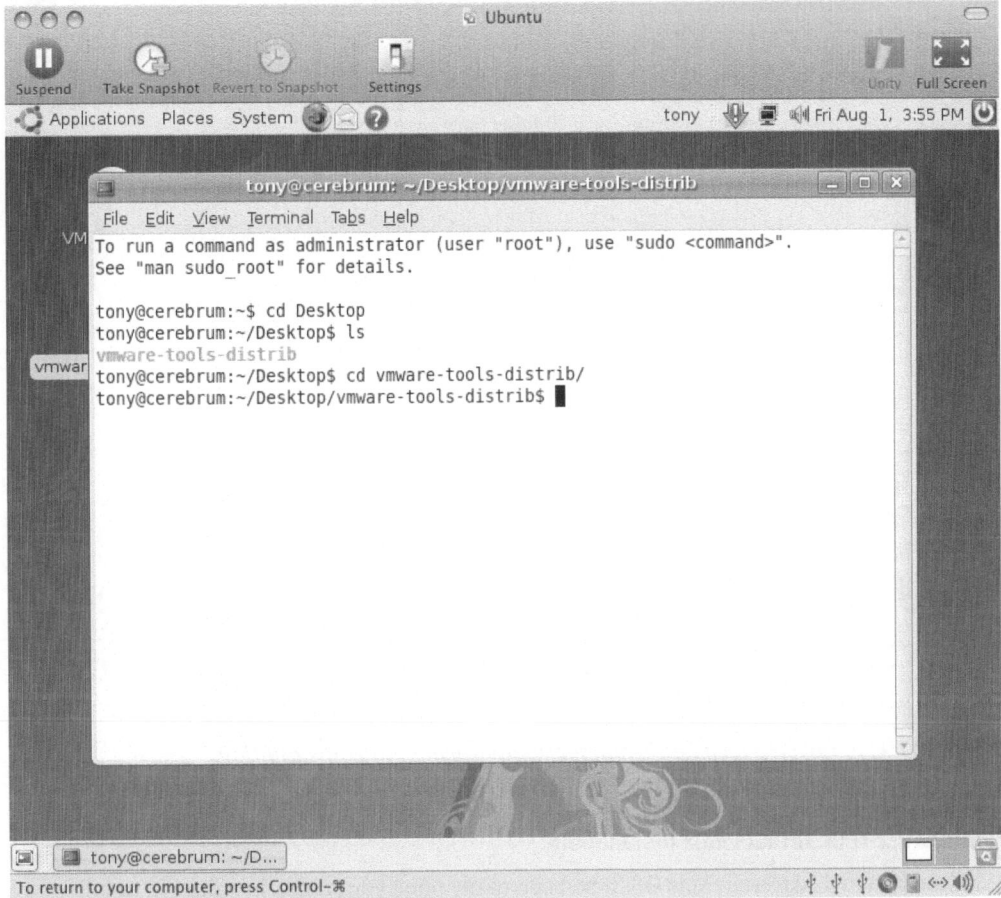

Figure 3-16. *Installing the VMware tools*

At the end of the installation process, you'll choose a screen resolution in which your VMware Linux installation will start, as shown in Figure 3-17. After a quick reboot of the system, your Linux installation in VMware Fusion will be complete.

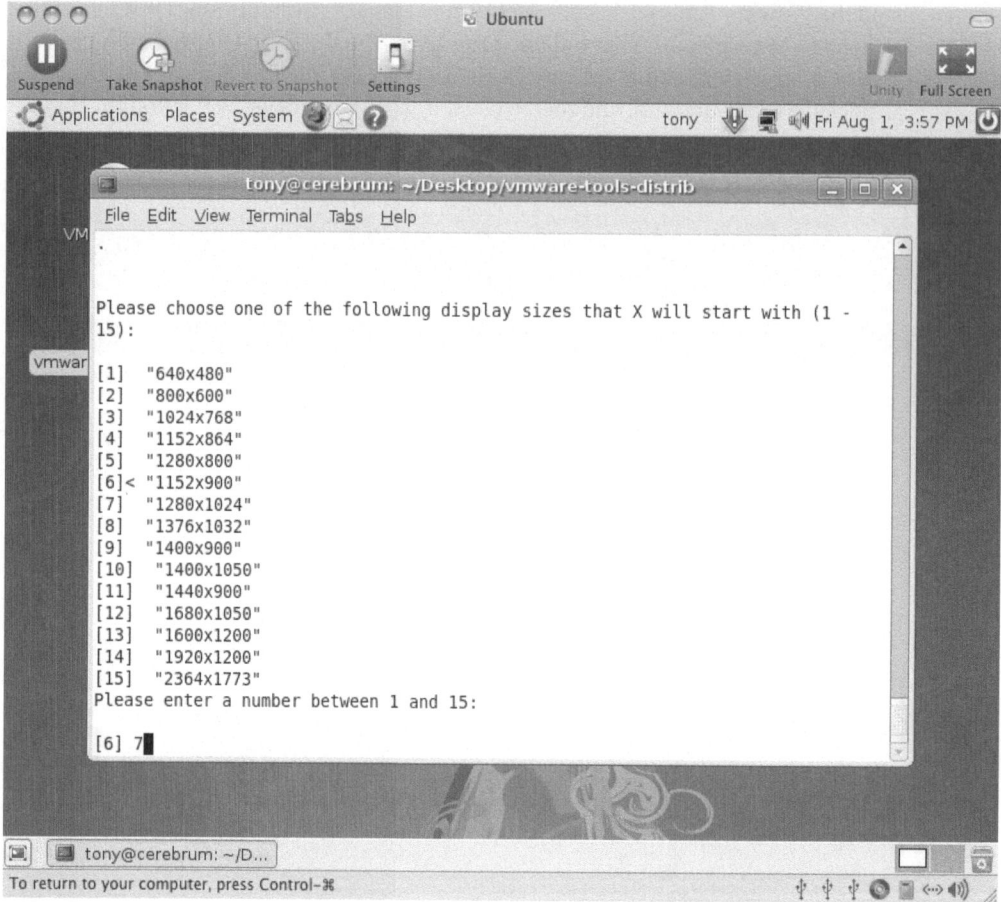

Figure 3-17. *Choosing a screen resolution for your VMware Linux installation*

Configuring Your Virtual Linux Installation

With the virtual desktops in Mac OS X, you can easily open your Linux installation to full-screen size from the VMware interface and cycle between desktops on the Mac. Configured in this way, the Linux installation appears as it does on any computer, with full functionality.

To return control of the window to Mac OS X, use the Apple+Control key combination. This will reduce the Linux installation screen to the size chosen during installation of the VMware Tools package. You can also use the Apple+Tab key combination to cycle between open applications, choosing VMware. This will move you to the virtual desktop running your Linux installation.

By default, the networking tools in VMware will create a virtual network interface, using Network Address Translation (NAT) for the actual Ethernet interface on the Mac. You'll need to provide Domain Name System (DNS) information in the network configuration tools of the Linux distribution. You may also need to reboot the Linux installation within VMware in order to bring up the new network settings.

All the Linux developer tools are available, as well—this is a full Linux installation, after all. And, all the peripheral hardware is available to the virtual machine, too. You can set up printer access from Linux on the Mac, just as you would an actual stand-alone Linux machine.

Uninstalling VMware

Uninstalling VMware is easy. The VMware installation image contains an uninstallation package. Running this package will remove VMware from the system, but will leave the virtual machines intact.

If you prefer to uninstall the virtual machines as well, you will need to remove the folder in which they are stored. By default, the virtual machines are installed in `~/Documents/Virtual Machines`. By uninstalling VMware with the uninstallation package, and then dragging the virtual machines folder to the trash, you can completely uninstall the virtual Linux machines.

Using VirtualBox

While VMware is the most widely recognized virtualization tool, it's not the only one. Of particular note is VirtualBox, an open source tool that is, in every operational respect, nearly identical to VMware. Because of those similarities, I won't go into any detail here on the installation or operation of VirtualBox. The primary factor separating the two virtual machine tools is, quite simply, the price.

Although it is released under the GNU Public License (GPL) 2, the licensing of VirtualBox isn't quite as precise as that might indicate. Originally released as a fully open source tool, VirtualBox was purchased by Sun Microsystems in 2008 and forked into two separate products, including the GPL-licensed VirtualBox Open Source Edition (OSE). However, Sun requests that developers interested in redistributing the OSE version do so only after contacting Sun. So, even the open source version of VirtualBox now contains some use and redistribution restrictions.

The choice of a closed source license with known terms in VMware or an open source license with changing terms in VirtualBox will be yours to make.

Summary

This chapter covered your options for smoothing the transition from Linux to the Mac: dual-booting or running a Linux virtual machine within Mac OS X.

Creating a dual-boot configuration with Boot Camp, a built-in component of Mac OS X, is relatively easy. Using this approach, you can simply choose which operating system you want to run at bootup.

Creating a Linux virtual machine with VMware is not difficult either. Overall, the experience with VMware is pretty positive, provided your Mac has ample RAM. The screen responsiveness is good, even in full-screen mode. Moving from the virtual machine to the real Mac OS X environment is a simple matter of using the Apple+Control key combination, even in full-screen mode.

Now that you have an idea of how these two approaches work, you can choose the one that suits your own preferences.

In the next chapter, we'll look at building out the Linux environment on Mac OS X with development tools and third-party software installation tools.

CHAPTER 4

■ ■ ■

Building Out the Linux Environment

Up to this point in the book, I've spent a fair amount of time laying the foundation: the UNIX and BSD origins of Mac OS X; the similarities between Mac OS X, BSD, and Linux; and the best ways to install Linux on your Mac without blowing away the Mac OS X installation. But none of that really gets to the heart of Mac OS X for Linux geeks.

The real beauty of Mac OS X is how easily most Linux and UNIX users can make the change from their original operating systems to Mac OS X. It's not a perfect match, but it's close enough to be surprisingly painless overall. In other words, there are more than enough similarities between the operating systems to make the differences far less painful than you might expect. If you have a good Linux foundation, you'll find the differences to be pretty easy to overcome. In fact, after years of using Linux exclusively, I made the change almost overnight. I didn't miss the power of Linux in the least once I committed to the change.

However, that change does require some preparation. Many of the development tools for Mac OS X are made available on the installation disc, but they're not installed by default. Those tools provide a full IDE and the foundation for a complete suite of open source tools, as well.

In this chapter, we'll start down the path of building out the development and BSD environment. We'll walk through the process of installing Apple's Xcode tools package, as well as your choice of utilities for obtaining open source tools for Mac OS X, similar to the BSD ports system. These are the real heart of the development and system administration power of Mac OS X. They're necessary for harnessing the full power of your Mac OS X system.

Xcode Tools

The first piece of the Linux pie in Mac OS X is Xcode, Apple's suite of free tools for Mac OS X developers. Xcode is available on the installation disc, but it's not installed by default on a new system.

The Xcode tools package includes an IDE, a tool for GUI development (Interface Builder), the GNU Compiler Collection (GCC), and support for many popular and powerful programming languages (such as C, C++, Objective-C, Java, Python, and Ruby). The package also includes make tools for both GNU and BSD, `autoconf`, `automake`, and other tools necessary for compiling and installing open source applications. Additionally, the Xcode package contains the complete set of reference documentation necessary to learn and use the tools. These tools will create the base environment on which the Linux environment will be built within Mac OS X.

■**Note** Prior to Xcode, Apple provided the Project Builder IDE with its operating systems. Project Builder was another legacy tool of the NeXT operating system that, in many ways, served as the foundation for Mac OS X. It contained earlier versions of many of the same tools as Xcode. Xcode is an update to Project Builder and has been further extended by third parties to include support for Pascal, Ada, Perl, and other programming languages and environments.

The open source analog for Xcode is Eclipse. These two tools take very similar approaches to providing a rich IDE. Both provide support for many of the same development models and languages, and they create similar development work flows.

Xcode Installation

As noted, the Xcode tools are available on the installation disc provided with your Mac. They're also available at the Apple Developer Connection web site. In general, the Xcode packages available online will be the most up-to-date versions. We'll walk through the installation of both the provided and online versions of Xcode.

Installing Xcode from the Apple Developer Connection

Downloading and installing Xcode from the Apple Developer Connection site will guarantee that you're working with the most current version of the Xcode tools. You'll need a good network connection and ample time, though. Xcode version 3.1 (current at the time of this writing), weighs in at a hefty 1GB.

To download the latest version of Xcode, visit the Apple Developer Connection site at `http://connect.apple.com/`. If you're not already a member, you'll be asked to fill out a short registration form, followed by a brief survey on your development needs. You'll then gain access to the Apple Developer Connection Member site, where you'll find the Xcode download at Downloads/Developer Tools.

■**Note** In the past few years, Apple's iPhone has become one of the hottest smart phones on the market. It has also become a leading development target, with thousands of iPhone applications available through the iTunes Store. That's due, in part, to the easy availability of the iPhone SDK. If you're one of those developers who intends to develop primarily for the iPhone, the SDK is also available from the Apple Developer Connection site. As it includes Xcode, downloading and installing the iPhone SDK alone will provide you with all the tools you'll need.

To begin the installation, from the Xcode Tools screen, shown in Figure 4-1, double-click the XcodeTools.mpkg file. You'll be greeted with a welcome screen, followed by a license agreement screen. Once you've accepted the license agreement, you'll have the option of choosing a destination for these files. Finally, you'll be presented with a list of packages for installation, as shown in Figure 4-2. Select the packages you will need, which will most likely include the Mac OS X package. You'll also want to select the WebObjects package if you plan to develop web applications.

Figure 4-1. *Starting the Xcode installation from the Apple Developer Connection site*

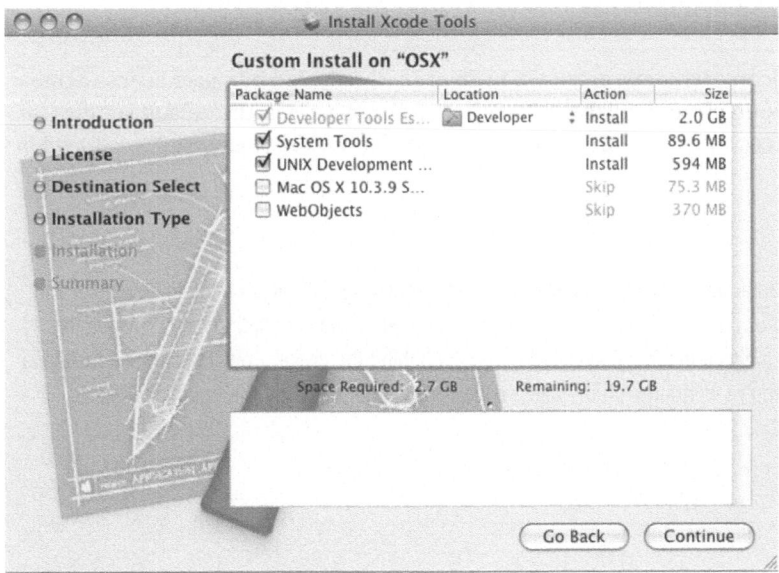

Figure 4-2. *Choosing Xcode packages to install*

Installing Xcode from the Mac OS X Installation Disc

To install Xcode from the Mac OS X disc, insert the Mac OS X installation DVD into the Mac DVD drive. You'll see the window shown in Figure 4-3. Double-click the Optional Installs folder, and then click the Xcode Tools folder. In the next window, double-click the XcodeTools. mpkg file to start the installation program.

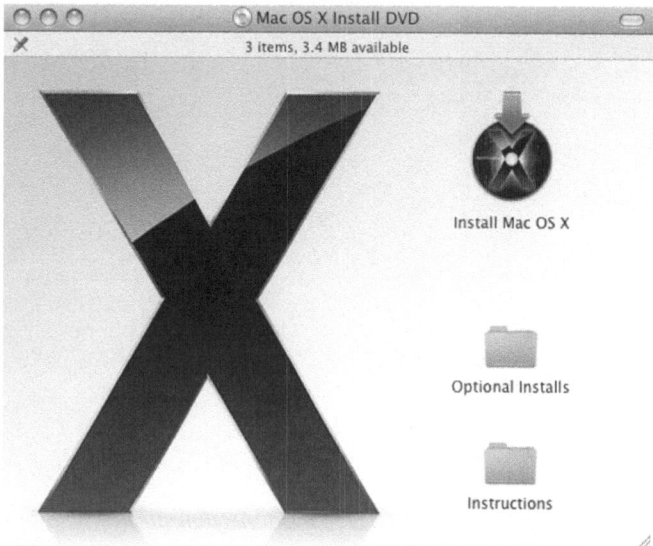

Figure 4-3. *Starting the Xcode installation from the Mac OS X installation DVD*

You'll see the welcome window, as shown in Figure 4-4, followed by a user license agreement and the opportunity to customize the installation. In most cases, the default settings for the installation are acceptable. To start the standard installation, just click Install, as shown in Figure 4-5.

■**Note** If you intend to later install and use open source tools requiring X11, you'll need to download and install the X11 tools from http://xquartz.macosforge.org/. While the installation DVD provides the option to install X11, the tools on the installation DVD are a bit behind the curve. Downloading and installing X11 will guarantee that you're working with the latest code written and tested by the Apple engineers.

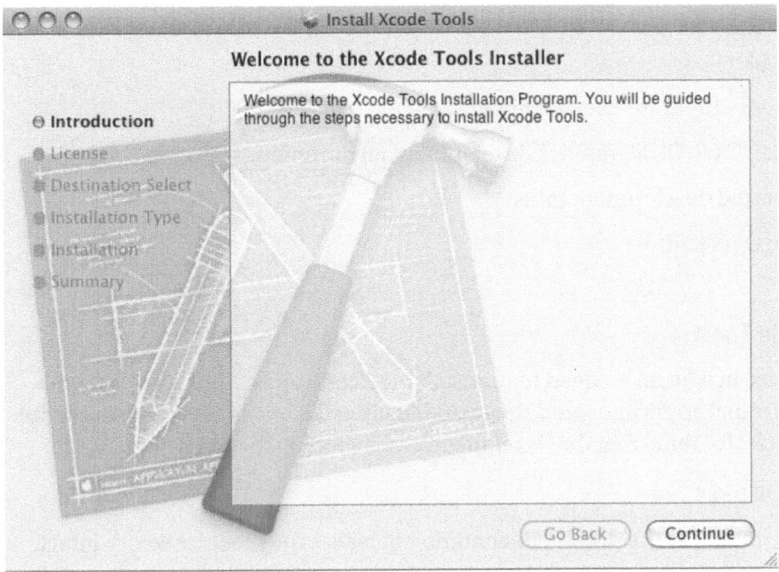

Figure 4-4. *The Mac OS X installation DVD's welcome window*

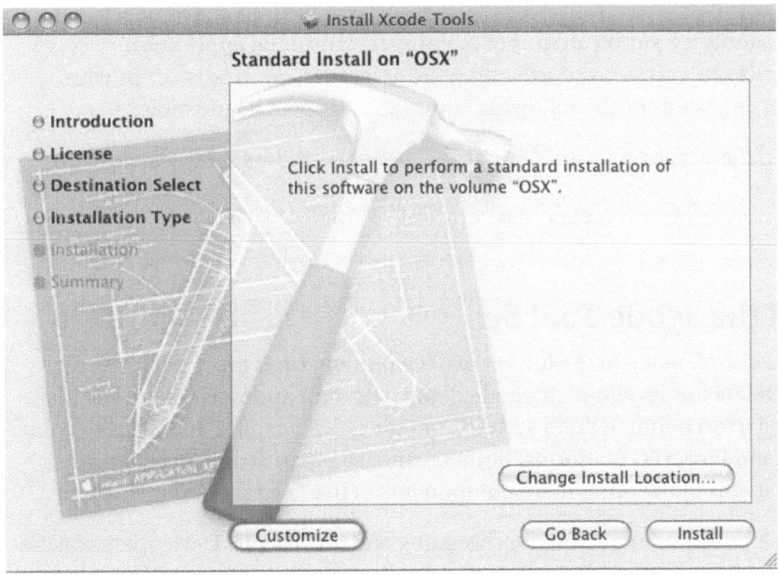

Figure 4-5. *Performing a standard Xcode installation from the Mac OS X installation DVD*

When the installation completes, you'll find the Xcode tools on the boot drive, in the `Developer/Applications` subdirectories, as follows:

- `Audio` (audio and multimedia interface creation tools)
- `Dashcode` (tools for creating Mac OS X Dashboard widgets)

- Graphics Tools

- Interface Builder

- Performance Tools (tools for code profiling)

- Quartz Composer (Mac OS X graphics development environment)

- Utilities (assorted development tools)

- Xcode (the Mac OS X IDE)

Uninstalling the Xcode Tools

In the rare circumstance in which you need to uninstall the Xcode tools, Apple recommends doing so using the Terminal application and the included uninstall script. The uninstall script recognizes several *modes* for removing the developer tools, including the following:

- all: Removes all tools.

- systemsupport: Removes the developer content, but leaves the Xcode directory intact.

- unixdev: Removes all UNIX development support, leaving the Xcode directory and supporting files intact.

- codedir: Removes only the Xcode directory.

Uninstalling these tools is a simple matter of opening the Terminal application (/Applications/Utilities/Terminal), and executing the uninstall-devltools script with the appropriate mode. For example, the following command removes all the tools:

```
$ sudo /[boot volume]/Developer/Library/uninstall-devtools mode=all
```

You'll be prompted for your administrative password, and then the Xcode tools will be uninstalled.

An Overview of the Xcode Tool Set

Xcode is, in fact, a generic reference to the full set of development tools provided by Apple. That set includes a rich IDE for development, code debugging, and optimization on the Mac. The IDE is built around a text editor, a build system, and the GCC compiler, modified to compile for both the Intel and PowerPC platforms, both 32- and 64-bit, with one invocation.

Here's a quick overview of the other main components of the Xcode tool set:

Interface Builder: A powerful Apple tool for designing and testing UIs. Developers can create interfaces for both Carbon- and Cocoa-based applications. Most Apple GUI elements are available from the Interface Builder tool, so your applications can have a look and feel common to other Apple applications.

WebObjects: A development framework for creating scalable, object-oriented web applications. Based in Java, these applications can be easily deployed on nearly any platform. The WebObjects package is installed by default when you install Xcode from the Mac OS X installation DVD. You'll need to explicitly select the WebObjects package when installing Xcode from the Apple Developer Connection site.

Instruments and DTrace: Instruments is a visual code analysis tool that implements the open source analysis engine DTrace. Instruments can record and monitor network activity, CPU utilization, disk activity, and many other system behaviors.

Shark: Provides code profiling. Shark supports both 32- and 64-bit applications.

Dashcode: Provides a compact and easy-to-use IDE specifically for developing Mac OS X Dashboard widgets. Targeted at nondevelopers, Dashcode is template-based and runs within a workspace that offers quick access to a full set of customization tools.

While the tools provided in the Xcode package are powerful and very useful for Mac developers, the real need for most open source users moving to Mac OS X is the GCC compiler. For many, the GCC compiler will be the single biggest reason to install the Xcode tools. You'll need the GCC compiler—if for no other reason than to compile the truly open source tools available to Mac users.

Online Linux Tools

Let's go back one more time to the origins of Mac OS X. It began its life as NeXTStep, which was a direct descendant of OpenBSD—UNIX through and through. The real hallmarks of FreeBSD are stability, reliability, connectivity, and a robust system for finding, installing, and maintaining new applications on the system. The latter is the BSD *ports* system.

The core implementation of BSD in Mac OS X is Darwin. Many Darwin projects are released under the Apple Public Source License, which has been approved as a free software license by the Free Software Foundation, but is not recognized as compatible with the GNU General Public License (GPL). Some other projects are released under other licenses, such as launchd (Apple's init replacement), which is under the Apache License. Darwin also includes a large variety of projects from the open source community, and these are released under various licenses.

Mac OS X is compatible with the Single UNIX Specification Version 3, is certified UNIX 03–compliant, and is fully POSIX-compliant.

Apple makes much of the source code for Darwin available on the Web, from its open source site at http://www.opensource.apple.com/darwinsource/. With the GCC compiler installed with Xcode, many of these tools can be downloaded, compiled, and installed on your Mac OS X system. However, you may encounter some issues with dependencies on proprietary elements of the operating system. While most pieces will work, be aware that you may not be able to compile every piece of the Darwin system.

Two other projects exist to provide open source tools to Mac OS X users. Both of these projects more closely reflect the operation and spirit of the BSD ports system, in that they make open source tools for Mac OS X available online. Adding new tools or maintaining existing tools on your Mac system is a simple command-line operation. Both the MacPorts and Fink projects bring that online functionality to the Darwin element of Mac OS X.

MacPorts

On its home page (http://www.macports.org), MacPorts is described as follows by its developers:

> *The MacPorts Project is an open-source community initiative to design an easy-to-use system for compiling, installing, and upgrading either command-line, X11 or Aqua based open-source software on the Mac OS X operating system. To that end we provide the command-line driven MacPorts software package under a BSD License, and through it easy access to thousands of ports that greatly simplify the task of compiling and installing open-source software on your Mac.*

Installing MacPorts

You can download MacPorts from `http://www.macports.org/install.php`. Installation packages are available in several forms, including a Mac `.dmg` disk image, source code in both `.tar.bz2` and `.tar.gz` forms, or Subversion (SVN) checkout. A `selfupdate` target also exists for systems that already have MacPorts installed.

In general, the easiest installation for MacPorts is with the `.dmg` package. To begin the installation, download the package and double-click the `.dmg` file. This will mount the image on the system and open a directory to expose the `.pkg` installer file, as shown in Figure 4-6. Double-click the `.pkg` file to begin the installation process, as shown in Figure 4-7.

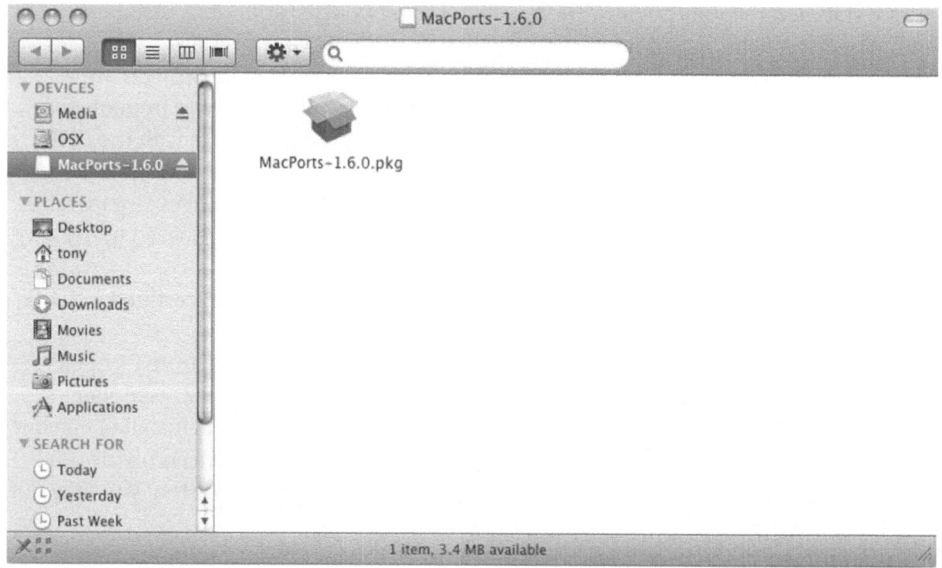

Figure 4-6. *Accessing the MacPorts installer package*

You'll be provided with some background information about MacPorts, including bug fixes in the current version. You'll also be prompted to accept the license agreement. When the installation begins, you'll be required to enter your administrative password.

By default, MacPorts installs in the `/opt/local` directory on your system, with the applications available in `/opt/local/bin`.

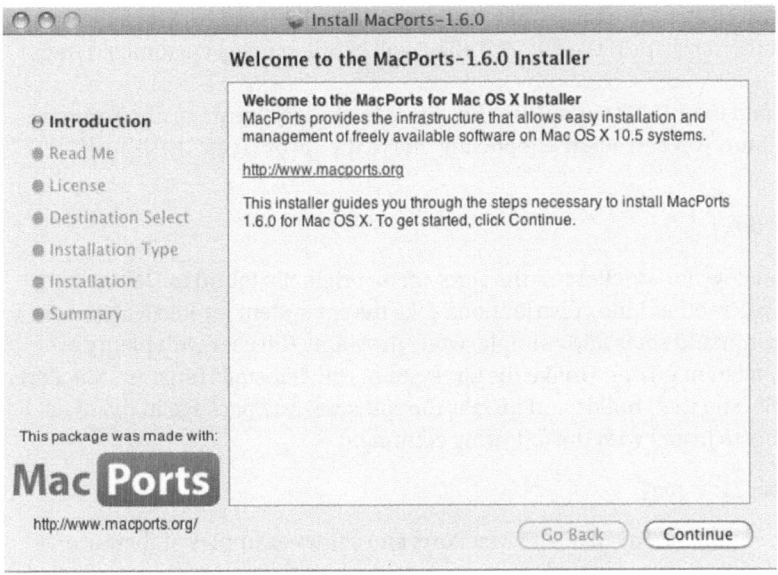

Figure 4-7. *Running the MacPorts installer*

Using MacPorts

Currently, MacPorts provides nearly 5,000 ports, or software packages, from more than 80 different software categories. These packages include all the common UNIX tools and utilities. They also include GUI applications for graphics, multimedia, security, and development, among other categories. We'll look at graphics and multimedia applications in Chapter 5, security in Chapter 7, and development in Chapter 8.

When using the MacPorts installation script, the postflight process creates a .profile file in your home directory (/Users/[*username*]). This file exports the MacPorts path (/opt/local) to the shell, adding it to the existing PATH variable. It's very similar in function to the .profile, .bash_profile, or .bashrc file in Linux. If you've already created a .bash_profile file in your Mac OS X home directory, you can simply add the contents of the .profile file to .bash_profile:

```
cd
cat ~/.profile >> ~/.bash_profile
rm ~/.profile
```

■**Note** At the time of publication, a known bug existed in the MacPorts binary installer. The 1.6.0 MacPorts package required a command-line fix for the installation to work properly. You can find all such reported problems and fixes on the MacPorts wiki at http://trac.macports.org/wiki/ProblemHotlist/.

If you have not created a .bash_profile file, you can modify the .profile file in the same way as you would edit the .bash_profile file. The effect will be the same: a customized shell environment.

It's also useful to add the EDITOR variable to the .profile or .bash_profile file. For example, if you use the vi editor, you can add the following line to the .profile or .bash_profile file:

```
export EDITOR=/usr/bin/vi
```

The loose Linux analogy for MacPorts is the apt system, originally found in Debian and since implemented in many other Linux distributions. Like the apt system (or Red Hat/Fedora's similar up2date), the command set is fairly simple, while providing the user with plenty of installation and uninstallation power. Unlike the apt system, which installs binaries, MacPorts downloads source code, and then builds and installs the software. Any package in the Mac-Ports system is available to install with the following command:

```
sudo port install [application]
```

Table 4-1 lists the commands available to MacPorts and shows examples of their use.

Table 4-1. *MacPorts Commands*

Command	Description	Use
port	The basic command for the MacPorts system.	sudo port install libmad
install	The installation command for the ports system.	sudo port install libmad
uninstall	Uninstalls a port.	sudo port uninstall libmad
selfupdate	Synchronizes the local ports tree with the global MacPorts repository. This sync includes updates to the MacPorts base system.	sudo port selfupdate
upgrade	Upgrades an installed port and its dependencies. Will also uninstall the outdated version with the -u option.	sudo port -u upgrade libmad
installed	Lists all installed ports.	port installed
outdated	Lists all outdated installed ports.	port outdated
dependents	Lists other files that are dependent on the installed port.	port dependents libmad
livecheck	Checks whether a given port has been updated at the developer's download site.	sudo port livecheck libmad
list	Provides a complete list of all available ports.	port list
search	Returns a list of all available ports matching a partial pattern.	port search libmad
info	Provides information about a specific port, including the port description and maintainer.	port info libmad
contents	Displays files that have been installed by a port.	port contents libmad
sync	Synchronizes the local ports tree with the global MacPorts repository, without checking for upgrades to the MacPorts base system.	sudo port sync

Command	Description	Use
clean	"Cleans" all files created by ports during installation. Includes the options all, dist, archive, and work.	sudo port clean –all libmad
deps	Lists port dependencies.	port deps libmad
variants	Lists all variants for a given port.	port variants libmad

As you can see, MacPorts provides a robust system for installing, uninstalling, and maintaining the Darwin-based open source tools on your Mac system. But it's not the only tool available for these tasks.

Fink

Another option for using open source tools in tandem with Darwin is Fink. Like MacPorts, Fink is designed to allow users to install and update software from online code repositories. Unlike MacPorts, Fink is based on the Debian model of dselect and apt. Because of that, Fink has a much more Linux-like feel. Additionally, the Fink project lists more than 9,000 packages available in 24 categories.

Installing Fink

To install Fink, first, download the package from http://finkproject.org/. You can choose either the binary distribution or the source file.

The binary distribution will mount and open an installation image, as shown in Figure 4-8. Double-click the Fink Installer package to start the installation program, as shown in Figure 4-9. Next, you'll be prompted with an information window, as shown in Figure 4-10, followed by a license agreement.

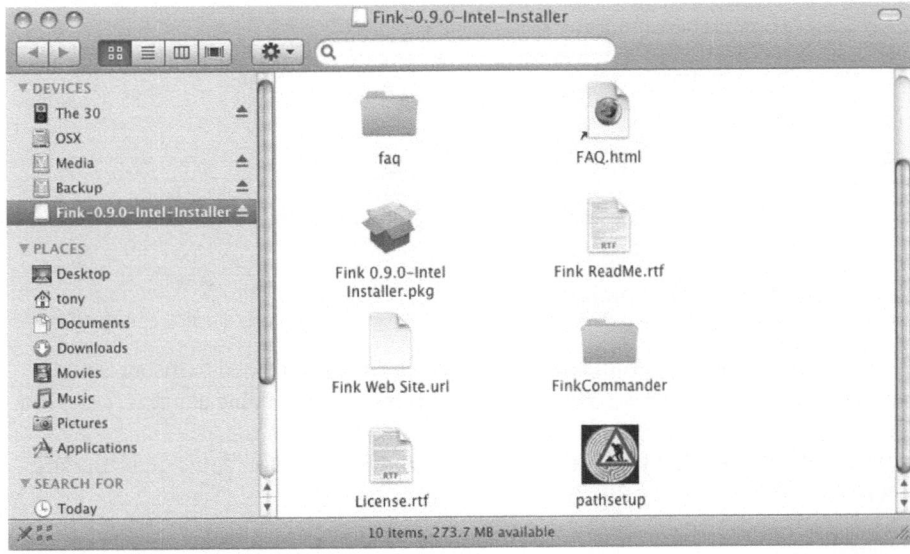

Figure 4-8. *Accessing the Fink installer package*

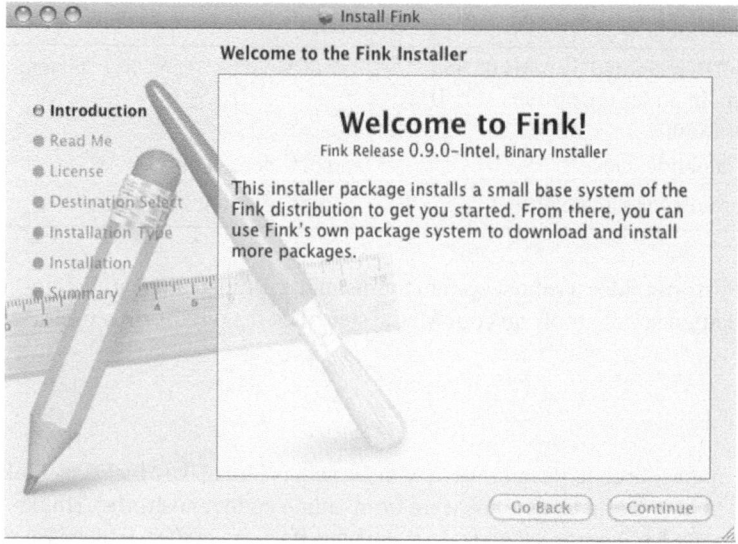

Figure 4-9. *Starting the Fink installation*

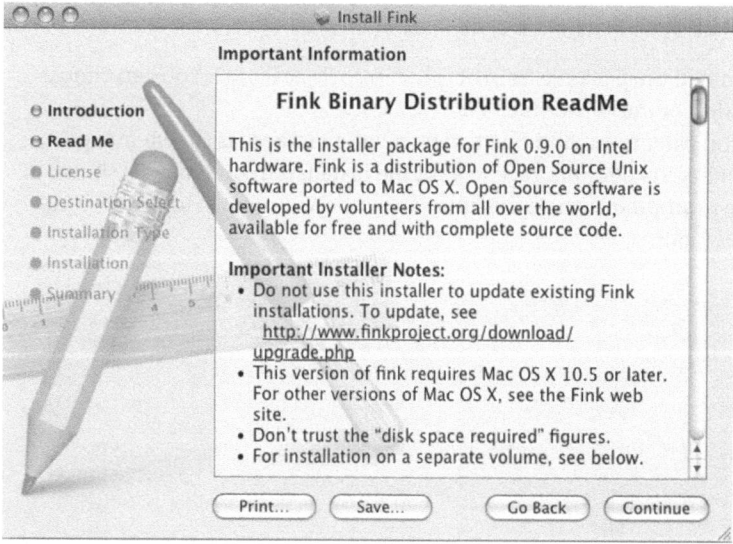

Figure 4-10. *Fink installation information*

If you intend to use packages from Fink that require a GUI, you'll need to install the X11 package as well. An updated version of the Darwin X11 package is available at `http://xquartz.macosforge.org/`.

Next, it's recommended that you open a terminal window and make some quick updates to Fink, as follows:

```
$ fink scanpackages
$ fink index
```

These steps will completely update your Fink installation.

Using Fink

Fink has several methods for updates and for self updates. You can choose your preference from the command line when you perform an update. That choice will become the default. For example, should you prefer to self update via HTTP or FTP, use the following command:

```
$ fink selfupdate
```

If your preference is to update using rsync, use the following command:

```
$ fink selfupdate-rsync
```

In general, the rsync mirrors are only an hour or so behind the CVS servers.

If you're behind a firewall that blocks rsync, you may be able to update via CVS, using the following command:

```
$ sudo fink selfupdate-cvs
```

This option also assures that you're using the most recent Fink code.

Fink is easy to configure for package access. From a terminal window, enter the following command:

```
$ sudo fink configure
```

This will allow you to select code repositories for the apt system in Fink, and your chosen methods of code downloads. This is very similar in look and function to the apt configuration in Debian-based Linux distributions. In that regard, Fink becomes more like MacPorts, as well.

If you've been using a Debian-based Linux distribution, the other Fink tools will look familiar. Fink allows you to use dselect, should you choose, as shown in Figure 4-11.

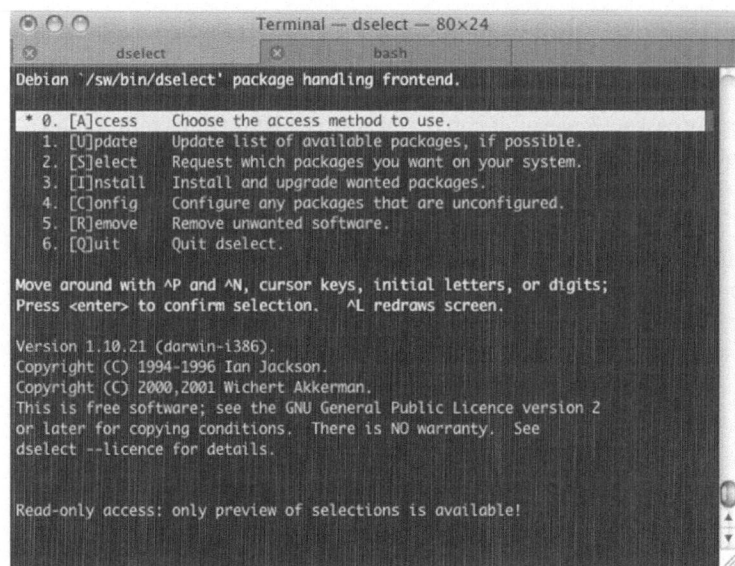

Figure 4-11. *Using Fink dselect*

GUI package management is also available with Fink, in a fashion similar to the Synaptic Package Manager application of many Debian-based Linux distributions, as shown in Figure 4-12.

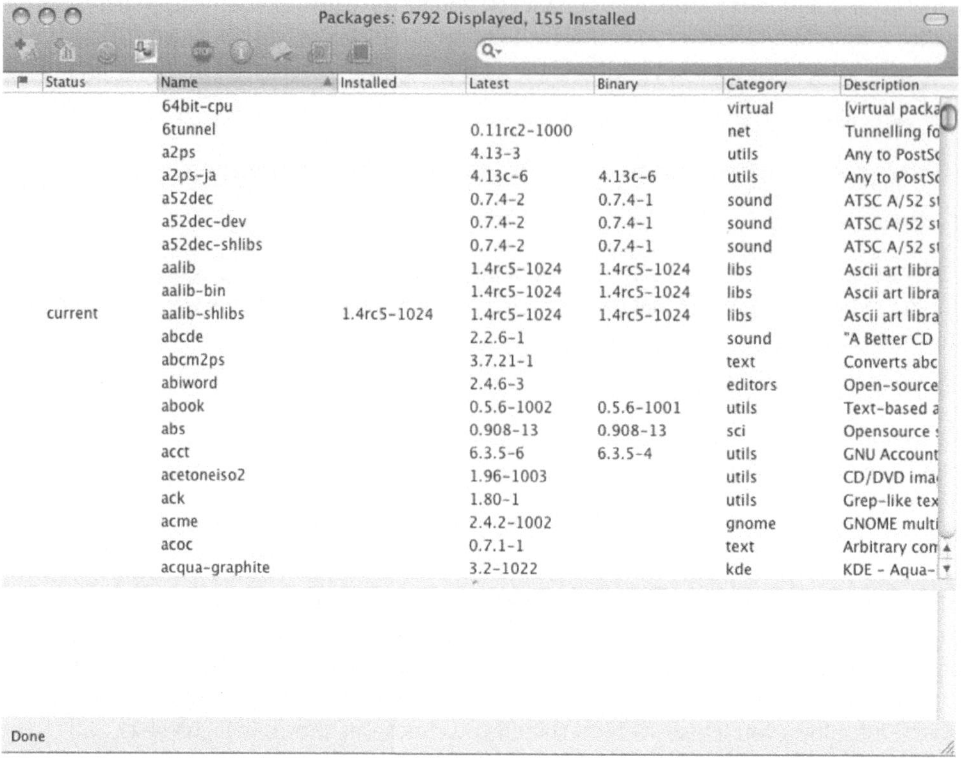

Figure 4-12. *Available packages displayed in Fink*

The `apt` system in Fink attempts to download and install binary packages for Darwin. In fact, that's possible in many cases. However, if you prefer source installations rather than binary installations, Fink provides this capability, as well.

```
$ fink install normalize
```

In this case, Fink will find the source, and then compile and install the `normalize` package.

Fink has a small but powerful command set. The commands are constructed and used in a fashion similar to what you've already seen with MacPorts. Table 4-2 lists the commands and shows examples of their use. Several of the commands are aliases to similar commands in the Debian package management system (`dpkg`).

Table 4-2. *Fink Commands*

Command	Description	Example
install	Used to install packages. Downloads, configures, builds, and installs applications.	`fink install libmad`
remove	Removes packages, using dpkg --remove.	`fink remove libmad`
update-all	Updates all packages to the latest version.	`fink update-all`
list	Provides a list of all available packages, including installation status and latest version.	`fink list`
describe	Provides a description of a named package.	`fink describe libmad`
fetch	Downloads a package without installing it.	`find fetch libmad`
fetch-all	Downloads all package source files without installing them.	`fink fetch-all`
fetch-missing	Downloads all package source files not currently installed on the system.	`fink fetch-missing`
build	Builds a package without installing it.	`fink build libmad`
rebuild	Builds a package, overwriting an existing .deb file.	`fink rebuild libmad`
reinstall	Reinstalls a package via dpkg, even when that package is already installed.	`fink reinstall libmad`
configure	Starts the Fink configuration process.	`fink configure`
selfupdate	Initiates the process of upgrading Fink to a new release.	`fink selfupdate`

Though the fink command is the preferred option, users can also use common apt commands (all of which are implemented in the Fink system), as listed in Table 4-3.

Table 4-3. *apt Commands for Fink*

Command	Description	Example
install	Installs the specified software package	`apt-get install libmad`
update	Updates the list of packages from the repositories listed in sources.list	`apt-get update`
upgrade	Updates out-of-date software packages	`apt-get upgrade`
dist-upgrade	Updates out-of-date software packages and may install additional dependent packages	`apt-get dist-upgrade`
setup	Provides an interface to modify the list of repositories	`apt-get setup`
search	Searches for a specific package	`apt-cache search libmad`
remove	Uninstalls software packages	`apt-get remove libmad`

Summary

With this chapter, you started the process of building out the development and BSD environment in Mac OS X. We focused on installing Xcode, Apple's suite of tools for OS X developers, and two tools that parallel the BSD ports system: MacPorts and Fink.

The next chapter covers using graphics, multimedia, and office productivity tools in Mac OS X.

CHAPTER 5

■ ■ ■

Using the Many Apple and Linux Tools

Over the years, Apple has earned a reputation for several core strengths. It's well known for its ability to process graphics, video, and audio. Mac is the standard in several industries, including audio editing and production, publishing, and graphic design. Apple computers running Mac OS X are finding an increasingly larger role in movie production, as well.

Many of these core strengths can be attributed to software written for the platform. This includes suites by Adobe, such as Photoshop, Flash, After Effects, and Illustrator. Apple has a history of working closely with software designers within these core competencies.

Apple also provides the software infrastructure to continue to uphold these strengths. Remember that Mac OS X started life as NeXTStep, an operating system that was highly regarded for its graphics and multimedia capabilities. The underpinnings of Mac OS X are strong in these areas, providing a set of graphics and multimedia tools that stands head and shoulders above those offered by most other operating systems.

Aside from its strengths in multimedia, Mac also performs well in the area of productivity and office tasks. Microsoft maintains a Mac OS X build of Office, including Word, Excel, and PowerPoint. Additionally, Apple has created iWork, a Mac OS X-native office suite that includes Pages (word processing), Numbers (spreadsheet), and Keynote (presentations).

If you're making the change from Linux to Mac, you'll want to know about the Mac multimedia and office productivity tools, and the corresponding open source tools. In this chapter, we'll explore those tools. But first, it's useful to understand a bit about the underlying graphics and multimedia technologies in Mac OS X.

A Brief Overview of Graphics and Multimedia on the Mac

While specific applications will utilize the core Mac OS X graphics and multimedia technologies in their own ways, the basics are the same. Mac OS X can also take advantage of X11 and X.Org, the open source X windowing systems.

The reputation of the Macintosh as an outstanding graphics platform extends back almost to its beginnings. And, while Apple has consistently improved the graphics performance of the Macintosh, few improvements were as striking or as strong as those made with the introduction of Mac OS X. With roots in the NeXT-developed Display PostScript, Mac OS X now makes full use of a powerful set of PostScript-style display tools. These include Portable Document Format (PDF) primitives to cache window graphics as bitmaps. These primitives are easily leveraged by the application frameworks and provide the foundation for the strong graphics performance of Mac OS X.

But graphics in Mac OS X don't end with PostScript and PDF primitives. The system adds an even more complex and powerful set of graphics tools for maximum performance. All represent the state of the art in graphics creation and manipulation. These tools include OpenGL and QuickTime.

OpenGL provides an industry-standard tool set for 3D image creation and manipulation. The OpenGL standard also defines required hardware features and support. This guarantees consistent performance on all platforms that implement the OpenGL standard.

QuickTime provides a tool set for creating and playing audio, video, and images. Supported formats include MPEG-4 and H.264 for video, Advanced Audio Coding (AAC) for audio, and literally hundreds of graphics formats, including Portable Network Graphics (PNG), Joint Photographic Experts Group (JPEG), Graphics Interchange Format (GIF), and Tagged Image File Format (TIFF).

Mac OS X contains a set of frameworks that handle all multimedia tasks. At the top level, these frameworks consist of Core Audio and Core Graphics. The Core Graphics framework in Mac OS X is composed of additional frameworks (or subframeworks, if you will), such as Core Image and Core Video. As a suite, Core Graphics provides all the essential graphics manipulation elements for a broad range of tasks, from rendering to compositing. The Core Image framework in Mac OS X exposes and leverages a system-wide Mac OS X API for powerful graphics creation and manipulation. Core Image also makes it possible to share image-processing capabilities between both built-in and third-party graphics applications. Core Audio and Core Graphics work together to provide all the necessary elements for image, video, and audio processing, and help push Mac OS X to the forefront in multimedia production and editing.

Core Graphics

Also known as Quartz, the Core Graphics framework is an imaging and windowing technology that relies heavily on the PDF drawing model. Quartz provides advanced windowing capabilities—including translucency, drop shadowing, and window buffering—and lies at the heart of all image functions in Mac OS X. The key components of Quartz include the following:

- Quartz 2D is the vector drawing-based API—the native Mac OS X drawing API.
- Quartz Compositor composites application drawings into a single image.
- Window Server manages all system windows.

Quartz 2D is the Mac OS X drawing engine—the core of graphics on the Mac. It's the basis for both the beautiful interface and any applications written for Mac that require graphic creation and manipulation. As part of the Core Graphics framework, Quartz 2D can interact with all other Core pieces in Mac OS X, including Core Image, Core Video, and QuickTime.

While the underpinnings of graphics in Mac OS X are so complex as to fall well outside the scope of this chapter, it's important to have at least a rudimentary understanding of how Mac OS X graphics are created. The following are some important Quartz 2D concepts:

Page: Quartz 2D takes advantage of image layering. An object drawn on the canvas, or *page*, cannot be modified except by the addition of a new layer. Drawing order is extremely important in this scheme, as subsequent solid layers (layers that are near or at the top of the stack on the page) may completely obscure previous layers. This provides the environment for extremely detailed and flexible graphics creation. Apple refers to this method of drawing as the *painter's model*, based on the analogy of adding paint to a canvas.

Context: The output of these drawing operations can take any number of forms, such as a page of paper passed through a printer, a PDF-based virtual page, or a file. This is referred to as the *context* of the drawing. Mac OS X recognizes five contexts: window, PDF, bitmap, layer, and printer. Any of these five contexts can serve as the destination for a drawing in Mac OS X.

Paths: In Quartz 2D, *paths* are defined as the shapes created by a graphics application. These can be simple lines and curves or more complex shapes incorporating many simple shapes.

Color spaces: These provide a reference for the interpretation of color information in Mac OS X. Wikipedia describes a color space as "an abstract mathematical model describing the way colors can be represented as tuples of numbers, typically as three or four values or color components" (http://en.wikipedia.org/wiki/Color_space). Several color spaces can be used, including Blue, Green, Red (BGR); Red, Green, Blue (RGB); Cyan, Magenta, Yellow, Black (CMYK); and Hue, Saturation, Brightness (HSB). In practice, these color schemes create a 3D representation of colors along x, y, and z axes. When a 3D color model is created using these schemes, any point in any of the three axes will be assigned a unique color value. As the starting points—the color models—vary, a value in the RGB model may differ greatly from the same value in the HSB model. In short, it's important to understand and define the color space when creating or manipulating graphics in Mac OS X.

Alpha values: Graphics created in the Quartz 2D model also contain an *alpha* value. Quartz uses the alpha value to determine how a new color will be composited to a page. The alpha value is, in practice, a measure of a color's opacity—how transparent will the new color be on the page? A color with an alpha value of 0 is completely transparent; an alpha value of 1 sets the color as completely opaque. Full opacity will completely cover and obscure images in the lower layers.

Transforms: Quartz 2D also provides a full range of image *transforms*. These transforms allow image scaling, translation, and rotation.

Patterns: Another important tool in the Quartz 2D kit is *patterns*. According to the *Quartz 2D Programming Guide*, "A pattern is a sequence of drawing operations that is repeatedly painted to a graphics context" (http://developer.apple.com/documentation/GraphicsImaging/Conceptual/drawingwithquartz2d/dq_patterns/chapter_7_section_1.html#//apple_ref/doc/uid/TP30001066-CH206-TPXREF101). Mac OS X includes a number of built-in patterns and full capabilities for unique pattern creation.

Shadows: These are simply images at least one layer below the top image, offset so as to depict the effect of a light source on the top object. The Aqua interface itself—the collection of Mac OS X windows and buttons—is heavily dependent on shadows. Nearly all windows in Mac OS X are drawn with shadows of one depth or another. This helps to provide Aqua with a 3D look and feel. As shadowing relies on an additional image below the primary layer, these images can be blurred or sharp-edged, depending on the desired shadowing effect.

Transparency layers: Objects can be stacked on a page and offset with shadowing using transparency layers. A *transparency layer* is the result of combining two or more objects into a single composite object.

Gradients: These are blends of colors, either circular (radial) or straight (axial).

Bitmaps: A *bitmap* is a sampled image in which each pixel represents a single point in the image. Bitmap types include TIFF, PNG, and JPEG.

Aside from graphics creation and manipulation, Quartz 2D also provides the input to the PDF engine on which Mac OS X relies to store those graphics, text, and images. Virtually all applications on the system turn to Quartz 2D to create these digital paper documents. These documents can then be further optimized, based on the context in which they will be viewed. These contexts can include web or print. Graphics and PDF files can be viewed in Mac OS X in the native Preview application, which also provides some rudimentary manipulation tools.

These critical elements of Quartz 2D provide Mac OS X with industrial-strength graphics creation and manipulation capabilities. They also provide the foundation on which the clean Mac OS X user interface, Aqua, is built.

Quartz interacts with the open source graphics tools we'll discuss later in this chapter. It works quite well with the Darwin X server that's necessary for many of the GUI-based open source tools.

Core Video

As mentioned earlier, Core Video is a part of the Core Graphics framework. Graphics and video follow a similar rendering path in Mac OS X, as illustrated in Figure 5-1.

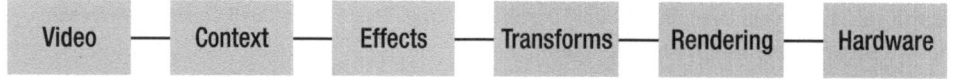

Figure 5-1. *The video rendering path in Mac OS X*

Note In its role as the Mac OS X window manager, Quartz Compositor follows a similar work flow for rendering the working environment —windows on the desktop, for example—in Mac OS X. Quartz Compositor receives a bitmap of window contents, mixes new elements into the scene, and then displays the new image. Unlike UNIX-based window managers, Quartz Compositor does not allow any other process access to the graphics frame buffer. This means that, ultimately, even a running X-based window server will be subservient to the Quartz Compositor, although that will generally be transparent to users.

A critical piece of the multimedia display puzzle is the refresh rate of the display. While we see refresh rates as static numbers, those numbers are, in reality, theoretical. They can be affected by any number of factors. Core Video synchronizes the media refresh rate with the display refresh rate using a *display link*. Based on display type and latencies, this special timer makes intelligent choices about when a frame should be output. This largely solves older video synchronization and rendering issues.

Core Video Buffers

Core Video also implements several buffer types. These buffers store video images on the system for display or compression. The buffer types provided by Core Video include the following:

- Pixel buffers for storing images in main memory
- Image buffers that store video frames
- Core Video OpenGL buffers that provide a wrapper around a standard OpenGL buffer
- Core Video OpenGL textures that provide a wrapper around a standard OpenGL texture

These buffers provide quick memory access for an application. Core Video creates a buffer pool that allocates the number of usable buffers. Buffers are used as needed, and then released back to the pool, rather than allocating and deallocating memory on each request. And these pools can exist in either main memory or video memory.

Core Video Frames

Core Video *frames* are the single images that compose a video. Video frames in Core Video can contain additional information that's useful for rendering. These additional properties are referred to as *attachments* and include the following:

Clean aperture and preferred clean aperture: To avoid artifacts at the edge of the image caused by processing, video frames are generally larger than the target image. The preferred clean aperture is the suggested cropping size for a single frame. The clean aperture is the actual size of the frame after cropping.

Color space: As with static images created with Core Image and Quartz 2D, Core Video frames will reference a color space. Again, this reference ensures that the correct x, y, z axes are used in creating the colors within the frame.

Square pixels/rectangular pixels: The choice of square versus rectangular pixels in a frame is most relevant to video created for television broadcast, as opposed to streaming or stored playback on a computer. Television pixels are rectangular; computer pixels are square.

Gamma: This value is used to balance the display output with its input. This produces output more closely aligned with what the human eye expects to see.

Timestamps: A timestamp notes when a frame appears in a movie. This takes the form of *HH*:*MM*:*SS*:*FF*, where *FF* is equal to a fraction, based on the *timebase* of the move. A timebase is a fixed period of time against which other events or time periods are gauged. So, the fraction in the video frame timestamp is expressed as a fraction of the timebase used in the video.

Note The concept of timebases extends back nearly to the beginning of the electronics age. In the case of video, timebases were a critical subsystem in the video cassette recorders (VCRs) of the 1980s and 1990s. Unlike audio, a video signal is information-dense, including picture, sync, and subcarrier information. The signal on video tape is written in a diagonal pattern to maximize use of the full tape width. This tape is pulled across a drum for reading. If the speed and alignment of the drum were perfectly in sync with that of the record head used to create the video, and if it were possible to keep that perfect speed constant, there would be no need for timebases. In VCRs, the timebases served to adjust the servos of the mechanical parts, allowing either perfect sync between the medium and the read head or video signal correction when that sync could not be achieved. In digital tools, such as QuickTime, the timebase defines when temporal events will occur; a time is reached, a frame rate is reached, and so on.

Quartz Composer

As is typical with Mac OS X, a Quartz development tool exists, and it is included with the installation medium. Quartz Composer is built on OpenGL, Core Image, and Core Video. It provides an easily implemented API and a GUI-based tool for development.

Applications created with Quartz Composer can be played in QuickTime, embedded in a Cocoa application, run as a system screen saver, or run from within the Composer itself.

Built-in Mac OS X Multimedia Tools

Recognizing the niche its hardware holds in the multimedia space, Apple has created a well-regarded suite of multimedia software tools that are included with new Mac computers. The iLife suite includes iPhoto, iMovie, iDVD, iWeb, and GarageBand. These tools provide consumer-level functionality for managing and editing multimedia—whether that's audio, video, or graphics.

iPhoto

iPhoto is a rudimentary photo editor with strong photo-organizing tools. Users can rotate, crop, resize, transform, and adjust images. iPhoto's primary strength is its tagging and management features. Figure 5-2 shows iPhoto's main interface, and Figure 5-3 shows an image open for editing.

Figure 5-2. *The main iPhoto interface*

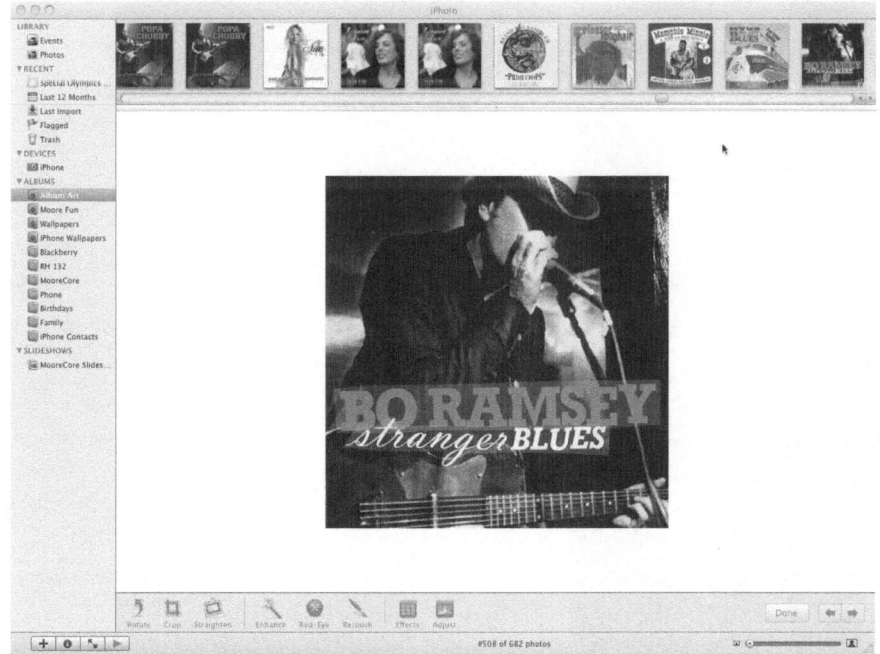

Figure 5-3. *Viewing and editing images in iPhoto*

The editing interface in iPhoto is easy to use and includes a basic set of editing tools within the main interface. iPhoto also provides tools to adjust most elements of a photo, including exposure, saturation, and contrast, as shown in Figure 5-4. In addition to the other tools, iPhoto includes some preset stock photographic effects, including sepia tones, color boosting, color fading, and matte, as shown in Figure 5-5.

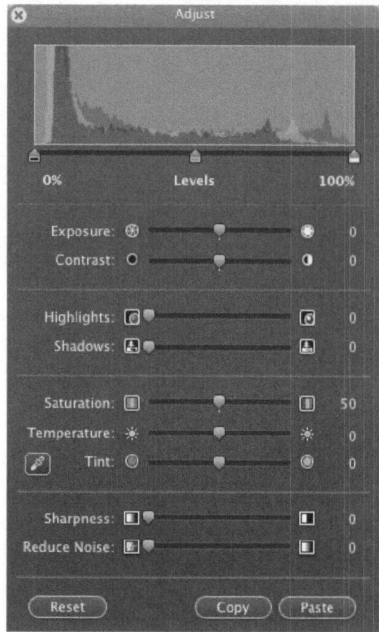

Figure 5-4. *Image adjustments in iPhoto*

Figure 5-5. *Image effects in iPhoto*

Note The editing features in iPhoto are perfect examples of Core Image *image units,* which are graphics packages that contain the architecture for accessing effects and image filters. These image units are available to all Mac OS X developers.

iMovie and iDVD

iMovie, shown in Figure 5-6, is the video-editing application included in the Mac iLife suite. Videos can be imported from a camera or a file, and edited nonlinearly. Assets can be included from the other Mac OS X tools, including iTunes and iPhoto. Built-in tools include those for adding titles and captions. When editing is complete, final videos can be sent directly to iDVD for DVD mastering, or exported to a number of formats suitable for a range of purposes, from the iPhone to YouTube.

Figure 5-6. *Editing video in iMovie*

iDVD is the native Mac OS X DVD creation and mastering tool. Figure 5-7 shows its opening window.

Figure 5-7. *Creating a new DVD project in iDVD*

iDVD includes several tools for quickly creating and burning DVDs. As shown in Figure 5-8, Magic iDVD allows a user to drag an existing Apple-format movie into a window, select a theme, import any additional graphics from the other iLife tools, and burn a DVD with a single mouse click. iDVD also includes OneStep DVD, which is even easier to use than Magic iDVD. A user can attach a video camera via FireWire, insert a blank DVD, and burn the movie to disk simply by clicking one button in the window.

Note Unlike iMovie, which recognizes USB, iDVD requires a FireWire connection.

Figure 5-8. *Editing video in iDVD*

iDVD features a strong consumer-grade tool set for DVD editing and mastering. These tools include prebuilt interface elements, including themes and buttons, as shown in Figure 5-9.

Figure 5-9. *Applying a menu theme in iDVD*

As with its counterparts in the iLife suite, iDVD is tightly integrated with the other iLife tools. This means that it has a similar look and feel, and allows quick imports of media from iTunes, iPhoto, and iMovie.

iWeb

iWeb is the "what you see is what you get" (WYSIWYG) web site development tool for Mac OS X. It's tightly integrated with Apple's online offering, MobileMe. Sites created in iWeb can be directly uploaded to a MobileMe account, using iWeb's built-in FTP tool, and current MobileMe sites can be added to iWeb, for easy editing.

Note MobileMe is an Apple offering, providing subscribers with online space for web sites, backup, mail, and storage. Many of the Mac OS X tools are MobileMe-aware, so they can be easily configured to connect to a user's MobileMe account. In recent years, MobileMe has evolved to include synchronization services between Mac OS X-based desktop computers and the iPhone. Finally, it also provides a conduit for Apple's Back to My Mac service, a secure remote desktop application. MobileMe is subscription-based, requiring an annual fee.

---

iWeb includes a full selection of theme templates, as shown in Figure 5-10. With the chosen template in place, all elements of the page are editable from the iWeb WYSIWYG interface, as shown in Figure 5-11.

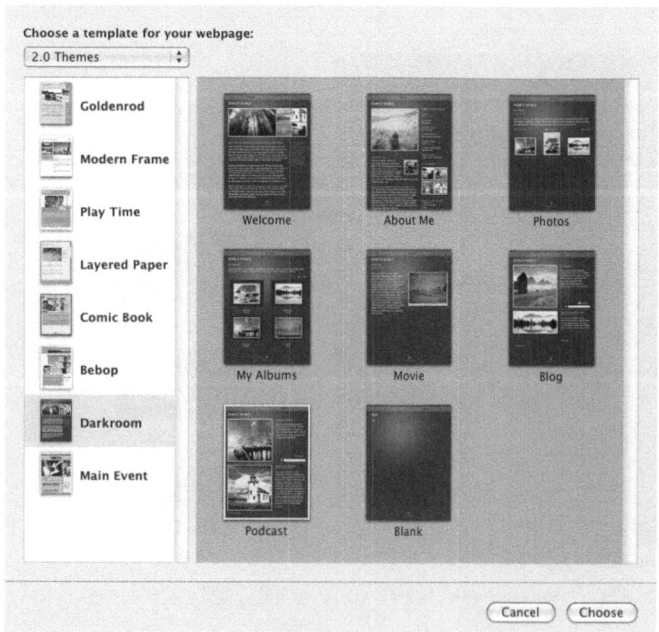

Figure 5-10. *Choosing a template from iWeb*

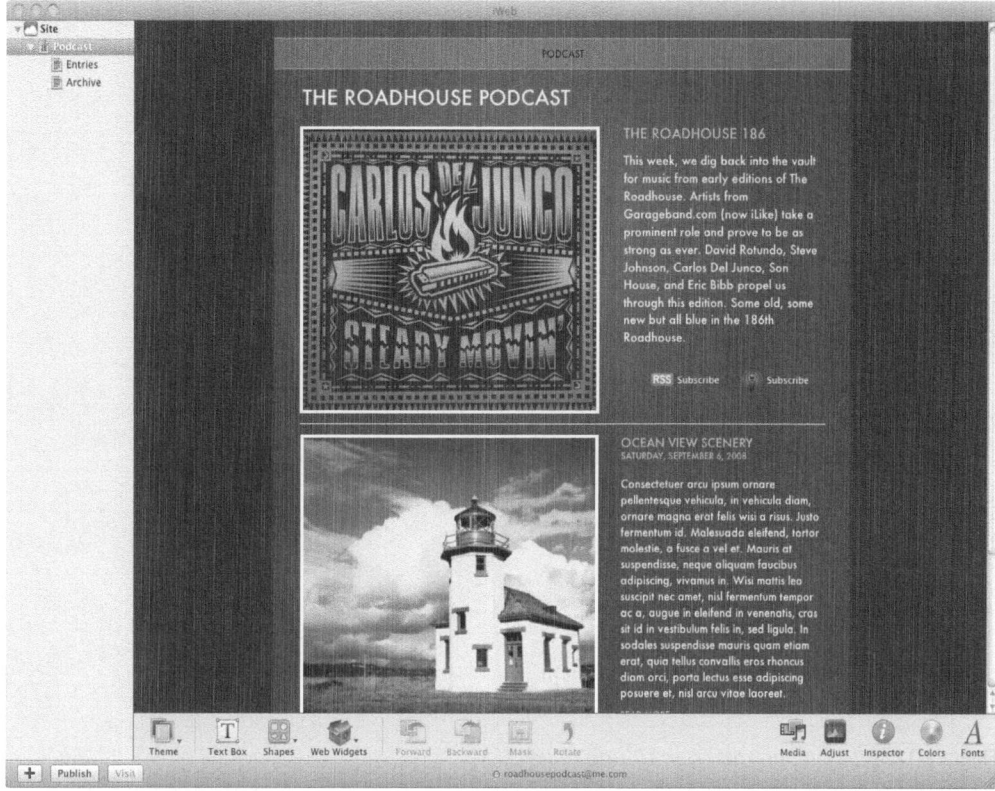

Figure 5-11. *Using the WYSIWYG iWeb editor*

As with the other iLife tools, iWeb has full access to media from iPhoto, iTunes, and iMovie. Media from these other tools can be easily imported into iWeb. Figure 5-12 shows an example of accessing iPhoto images from iWeb.

Figure 5-12. *Selecting photos from iPhoto in iWeb*

GarageBand

GarageBand is the audio creation and editing application in the iLife suite. It is, perhaps, the most advanced piece of the iLife package, with many features targeted at professional musicians.

GarageBand provides the tools to edit existing projects, create new projects (both music and podcasts), or, like iDVD, to use built-in audio to create a Magic GarageBand project with minimal effort. Figure 5-13 shows GarageBand's opening window, which offers access to these features. Figure 5-14 shows the main GarageBand editing window.

Figure 5-13. *Creating a new audio project with GarageBand*

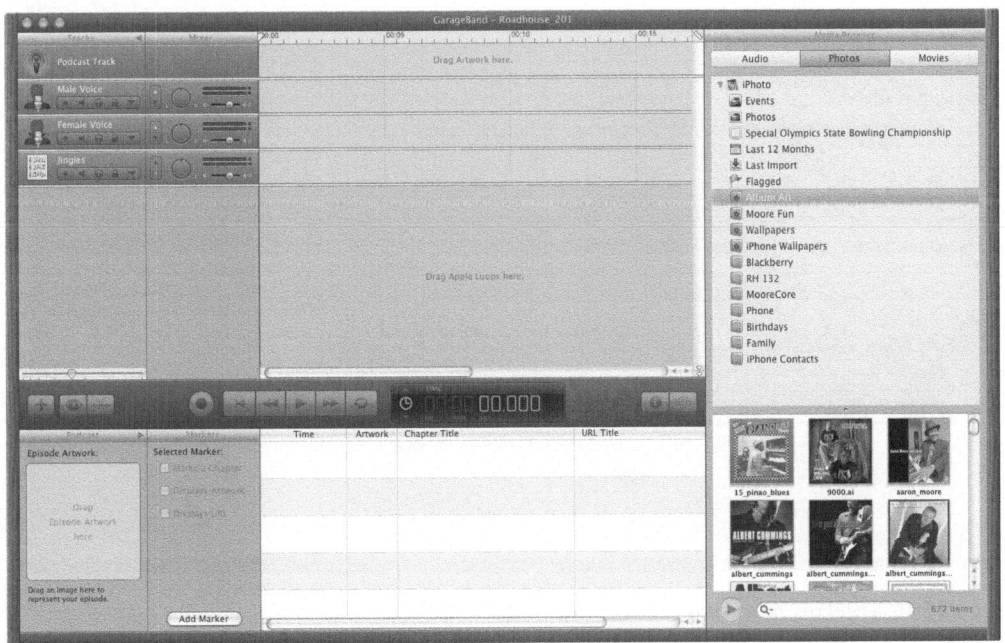

Figure 5-14. *The main GarageBand editing window*

GarageBand provides access to additional assets, including music from iTunes and graphics from iPhoto. You can add existing audio or record new audio live, as shown in Figure 5-15.

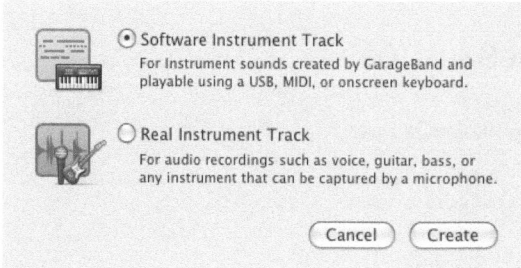

Figure 5-15. *Adding a new track to a GarageBand project*

GarageBand also provides a rich set of sound effects and sample sounds. The library includes loops that can be used to construct songs in GarageBand, as well as radio-type sound effects for use in podcasts, as shown in Figure 5-16. These audio effects can be applied to instruments, voices, or externally imported tracks.

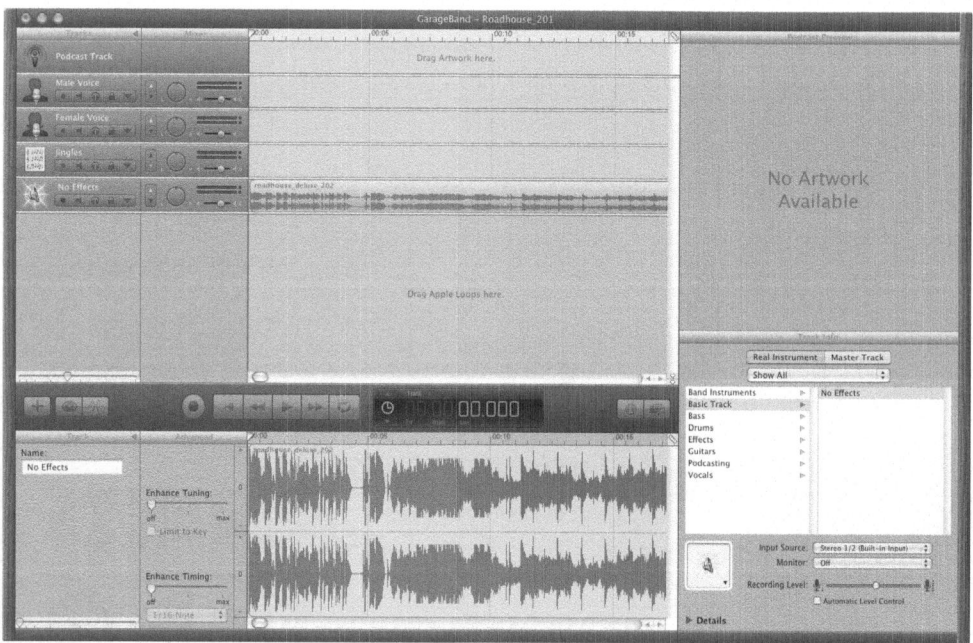

Figure 5-16. *Tracking a waveform in GarageBand*

GarageBand uses MIDI to interface with external musical instruments. You can select the instrument for which audio is being composed; for instance, if the external MIDI instrument is a simple keyboard, the instrument being composed can be a grand piano. Via the MIDI interface, GarageBand can capture and notate music as it's played on the external instrument, as shown in Figure 5-17.

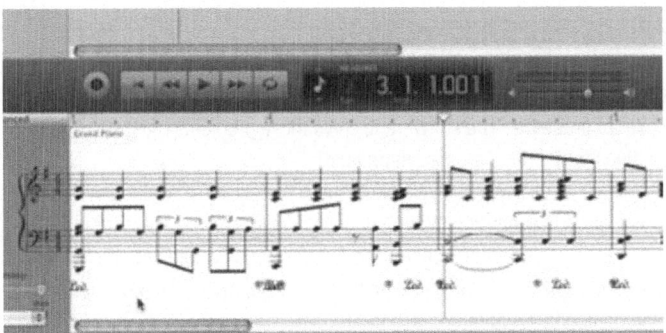

Figure 5-17. *Musical notation created by GarageBand*

When projects in GarageBand are complete, they can be sent to iTunes, sent to iWeb, sent to iDVD, saved to disk, or burned directly to a CD or DVD. Figure 5-18 shows an example of exporting a project from GarageBand.

Send your song to your iTunes library.

iTunes Playlist:	Anthony Steidler–Dennison's Playlist
Artist Name:	Tony Steidler–Dennison
Composer Name:	Tony Steidler–Dennison
Album Name:	The Roadhouse Podcast

☑ Compress

Compress Using:	AAC Encoder
Audio Settings:	Custom...

192 kbps, Highest Quality, Stereo, optimized for MMX/SSE2. Estimated size: 84.5MB.

Cancel   Share

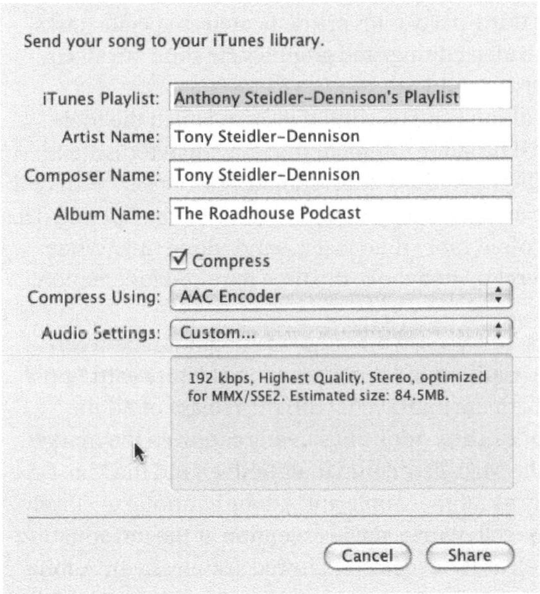

Figure 5-18. *Exporting a finished project from GarageBand*

APPLE'S PROFESSIONAL TOOLS

The iLife suite, for all its strengths, is a consumer-grade package. Professional video, audio, and image editing present a much more complex set of problems. The software to solve those problems must provide granular control and a wide range of options for the final processed product.

Apple's Final Cut Studio meets the needs of professional video and audio editing. It's in wide use in television, film, and video production, as well as live sporting event broadcasts. Aperture is Apple's professional-grade image management tool. It also provides some light editing functions. Compared with the Adobe tools discussed in this chapter, these tools are relatively new to the market. They are, however, gaining a strong foothold in a market previously dominated by Adobe.

Third-Party Multimedia Tools

With its strong APIs, Apple has created a platform on which any dedicated company can build multimedia capture and editing tools. Many third-party tools are dedicated to specific tasks within the multimedia realm. Audio editing, video editing, and graphics creation are all covered to one degree or another by smaller tools.

The difficulty lies in creating a full suite of multimedia editing tools in which the tools are closely integrated, as they are in the Mac iLife suite. Although the individual tools stand well on their own, the model created by Apple is that these tools should work closely with one another, creating a tool set that's stronger as a whole than the sum of its individual pieces. This approach recognizes that handling media is often more than just a stand-alone task. When software makes it easy to move between several related tools, the time required for creation and editing is reduced.

Adobe Systems has, in the past few years, recognized the value of integration between its set of multimedia tools. Based in San Jose, California, Adobe has a long history with Apple and Mac. It's a relationship that extends back to the mid-1980s with the release of Adobe Illustrator. As a partial result of that long relationship, Adobe has nearly captured the market for third-party multimedia applications on the Mac. Few companies understand the Mac OS X graphics and multimedia APIs as intimately as Adobe. Apple and Adobe continue to closely coordinate efforts across product releases, as well. With a single exception at the introduction of the Intel-based Mac OS X, Apple version releases have been followed seamlessly by Adobe version releases. The Adobe suite of tools remains the premiere multimedia editing suite for the Mac and Mac OS X, and those are the tools we'll look at here.

Note While rumors seem to constantly suggest that Apple is on the verge of buying Adobe, or that Apple has its own Adobe-killer applications under in-house development, these rumors have yet to play out as true. In general, the relationship between the companies seems nearly as cordial and symbiotic as it has always been.

The Adobe Multimedia Tools

The set of Adobe applications for multimedia is stunning in its depth. Every element of these tasks is covered in one software application or another. These tools were originally created and released as stand-alone applications, with little attention to how each interacted with the other. Following the release of Mac OS X and the iLife suite, Adobe took note of the tight integration among the iLife tools. The Adobe developers began to pay more attention to how closely their own tools worked together, with the result being a tight fit between video, audio, and graphics. This includes the ability to export from one application directly to another, much as is possible with the iLife suite.

The Adobe library of multimedia tools covers nearly all tasks in the typical work flow. The individual software packages developed and sold by Adobe are all top-of-the-class tools, as recognized by professionals and amateurs alike. While Adobe's strategy has moved toward a model of bundling these tools in recent years, they are still available as individual packages, dedicated to specific tasks. Table 5-1 lists the principal Adobe tools and their uses.

Table 5-1. *Adobe Multimedia Tools*

Tool	Use
Photoshop	Graphics editing and manipulation
Illustrator	Vector graphics editing and manipulation
InDesign	Desktop publishing
Acrobat Professional	PDF display and creation
Flash	Animation
Dreamweaver	WYSIWYG web design
Fireworks	Web graphics design and manipulation
After Effects	Motion graphics and video effects
Soundbooth	Audio editing and production
Premiere	Video editing and production
Encore	DVD authoring
OnLocation	Video production
Contribute	WYSIWYG web design

The Flash, Dreamweaver, and Fireworks tools were originally created by Macromedia, a strong rival to Adobe. In 2005, Adobe purchased Macromedia and rolled these tools into the Creative Suite lines. The addition of these tools brought Adobe to a point of near monopoly, particularly in the web space. The addition of Flash to its lineup brought the fastest rising web graphics technology into the Adobe tent. Furthermore, the strong reputations of both Dream- weaver and Fireworks burnished a new focus for Adobe on the Web. The company that was founded around the go-to desktop publishing application has made a strong transition to the technologies of the Web. That flexibility is another reason Adobe has survived so well over the years.

As mentioned, Adobe has recently begun to capitalize on the tight integration approach, and is now marketing packages of tools designed for specific types of tasks. At the top level, these packages are the Design and Web packages. These are further divided into Premium and

Standard packages. At the top of the Adobe food chain are the Production Premium and Master Collection bundles. The Production Premium package provides all the necessary pieces for high-end video production and postproduction. The Master Collection package contains all the Adobe tools in a single bundle. These bundles are clearly targeted at folks who make a living in multimedia. Ranging from $999 US to $2,500 US, the pricing of these packages is well beyond the means of the average user. Table 5-2 lists the various Creative Suite packages available from Adobe and the applications included in each.

Table 5-2. *Adobe Creative Suite Packages*

Bundle	Tools	Approximate Cost (USD)
Design Premium	Photoshop, Illustrator, InDesign, Acrobat Professional, Flash, Dreamweaver, Fireworks	$1,800
Design Standard	Photoshop, Illustrator, InDesign, Acrobat Professional	$1,200
Web Premium	Photoshop, Illustrator, Acrobat Professional, Flash, Dreamweaver, Fireworks	$1,600
Web Standard	Flash, Dreamweaver, Contribute, Fireworks	$1,000
Production Premium	Photoshop, Illustrator, Flash, After Effects, Premiere, Soundbooth, Encore	$1,700
Master Collection	Photoshop, Illustrator, InDesign, Acrobat, Flash, Dreamweaver, Fireworks, Contribute, After Effects, Premiere, Soundbooth, Encore	$2,500

Let's look at some of the critical features of the three primary pieces of the Adobe package: graphics manipulation in Photoshop, video editing in Premiere, and audio editing in Soundbooth.

Adobe Photoshop

The ins and outs of Photoshop have made many a book author a buck or two. Photoshop is so dense with features, tweaks, and tricks that even an entire book could hardly hope to cover them all. Photoshop is, in short, the standard by which all other graphics creation and manipulation applications are judged. But it comes at a price. At the time of publication of this book, a single-user license for Photoshop listed at $649 US. If you're making a living as a graphic artist, that's just the price of admission, and probably a tax write-off, as well.

Even though you may not be inclined to drop more than six bills for Photoshop, there are some features that are relevant to our discussion, because they are widely considered as critical to the success of Photoshop. You may want to look for similar features in the open source graphics applications available for Mac OS X. These features include the following:

Nondestructive editing: This type of editing leaves the original image data intact, allowing the user to revert to previous edits of an image at any time. Nondestructive editing is made possible through adjustment layers, which apply changes without permanently changing pixel values.

Painting and drawing tools: The Photoshop tool set is impressive. With a full range of brushes, pens, airbrushes, buckets, textures, and many other tools, there's very little a user can't accomplish. The primary tool set is contained in a single toolbar, located along the left side by default. The top-level tools can be expanded to expose further options by clicking the arrow in the bottom-right corner of each tool's box.

Advanced compositing: Photoshop allows for complex stacking and combining of images. Photoshop's compositing tools utilize layering to nearly its full extent, allowing for this advanced compositing.

Raw-image processing: The raw image format has come into vogue among professional photographers in the past few years. Calling it a "format," though, may be a bit of a misnomer. A raw image contains minimal processing. It's nearly identical to what a camera sensor sees and captures, without the full data set to create an actual image. In this sense, raw images are often referred to as *digital negatives*—they contain all the image data but cannot be viewed by themselves as images.

Image formats: Photoshop supports a very broad range of image formats. In short, if you've seen an image format, Photoshop or a related plug-in will probably handle and process that format.

Adobe Premiere

Premiere is Adobe's video capture and editing package. Consistent with the bundling approach, the Premiere Pro package includes Encore and OnLocation; the Standard package includes only OnLocation. Premiere is also tightly integrated with Photoshop, After Effects, and Soundbooth.

The following are some of Premiere's main features for professional video editing:

Nonlinear digital editing: Premiere advances nonlinear digital editing with a full set of tools. In video or audio, *nonlinear editing* means that an editor has access to any single frame without the need to work through other frames. Each frame is as discrete and available for editing. This is opposed to the old model of editing, in which frames of film or video were accessible only by running the video or film to the point of editing. Frames couldn't simply be plucked from the existing pool of frames without drilling down into the pool itself. In that sense, nonlinear editing is a much flatter model of editing, designed and approached as if all the frames of a video were laying in order on a table. Any frame can be removed or rearranged as easily as any other frame.

Video-editing tools: Premiere includes tools for color correction, lighting, slow-motion generation, and multiple-camera editing. The editing tools can output video to High Definition (HD) and support High Definition Video (HDV), a format that uses compression to squeeze HD content onto the same storage medium as is used for standard definition recording. The editing tools will also output video to the Sony-created Digital Video (DV) format. Like HDV, DV uses MPEG-2 compression to fit high-definition video onto smaller form-factor media.

Disc output: Premiere will output edited video directly to DVD or Blu-ray discs. This is important to many multimedia professionals as, due to the shorter wavelength of its laser, Blu-ray is capable of storing up to ten times more video information than standard single-layer DVD discs. This means that discs can be used not only for finished video products but, in some cases, also as one-off storage of raw media. For finished products, Blu-ray also supports the full 1080p video format—the highest quality video format currently available. Although television has yet to adopt this standard for broadcast, many movies are now in video release on Blu-ray in the 1080p format. All reputable HD television sets support the 1080p format, as well. The ability to output a completed video file directly from Premiere to disc promises producers and editors significant time savings when mastering their final product.

Output formats: Premiere can export finished video to a wide range of formats. Video edited in Premiere can be exported to Flash, and to formats supported by mobile phones and other mobile devices. These formats include MPEG-4 (m4v), H.261, H.264, and FLV. This flexibility in formats provides authors with a full range of options for distributing their work.

Camera setup and calibration: Premiere, using the OnLocation package, provides tools for camera calibration, for monitoring the input and output signal levels, and for adjusting those levels where necessary. The monitoring tools include a waveform monitor for monitoring the video-voltage level with respect to time, an audio spectrum analyzer used to monitor the spectral composition of the audio waveform, and a vectorscope displaying the x-y relationship of two video signals. These tools are all available in real time, as video is being captured, and allow for quick, on-the-fly adjustments when shooting on location.

Video effects: Premiere includes a full set of video effects that can be implemented either in postproduction or in real time while shooting. These effects include brightness and contrast adjustments, color balancing, cropping, directional blurring, fast and Gaussian blurring, lens flare, replication, posterization, and many more. The flexibility provided by the ability to apply these effects either on the fly or in postproduction can shorten production time considerably.

Soundbooth

Audio editing often runs hand-in-hand with video editing. In fact, you could make a strong case that stand-alone audio editing is now less common than editing audio in conjunction with accompanying video. This is especially true in an ever-more interactive multimedia world.

Given this marriage of audio and video, it's important to be able to edit audio as the integral element of the video it has become. Synchronization, for example, is critical, as are the tools to make that task more accurate and efficient. Additionally, the importance of audio definition and placement has risen in tandem with increases in video definition and advances in scaling. With high-definition, widescreen video, the placement of a sound effect in the proper temporal location within a video image is critical to telling the story. A broad audio image is necessary to support a wide video image. The breadth of that audio image now extends beyond the 180-degrees facing the viewer. It reaches a full 360 degrees behind the viewers, immersing them in sound that further supports the video storytelling. This requires the ability to intelligently and discretely assign audio to specific channels, and to do so at precisely the right time.

In short, audio editing has moved far down the road from the days of splicing magnetic tape or layering a soundtrack on film. Soundbooth offers the following features to support professional audio editing:

Soundbooth Scores: These are customizable, prerecorded soundtracks, similar to those provided by the Mac's Magic GarageBand tool. These scores can be applied to any video project, with instruments and parts dropped, added, or emphasized. Using the scores can significantly reduce the cost and time of producing video, especially for nonprofessionals on a limited budget.

Audio filters: The Soundbooth library of audio filters includes time and pitch stretching, distortion, reverb, echo, chorus, and much more. These filters provide the editor with a full range of tools for precise sound editing and customization.

Audio recording: Soundbooth isn't limited to editing existing audio files. New audio can be recorded directly into Soundbooth, either in mono or stereo.

Audio cleanup: Some types of audio problems are common from one recording to another. Rumbling, hissing, and pops can invade and significantly reduce the quality of an audio recording. Soundbooth contains tools to detect and deal with these common problems automatically.

Animation cues: Soundbooth can create markers in an audio file that will later be recognized by Flash. By using ActionScript in Flash to read these cues, sound events can trigger visual events in Flash animations. Those events can even include actions-based captioning.

Adobe Premiere integration: Audio can be sent directly from Premiere to Soundbooth, via an Edit in Soundbooth button. When edits are complete and saved, they're automatically imported back into the Premiere timeline and assets windows.

Mac OS X Third-Party Multimedia Summary

While smaller applications exist for multimedia editing and production in Mac OS X, none have the Apple history, the power, or the full capabilities of the Adobe tools. The recent Adobe move to more tightly integrate these tools into bundled packages has had mixed results. While that bundling has more closely integrated the various tasks of producing and editing sound and video, it's also impacted the pricing of the individual tools. Aside from price, it's difficult to find any multimedia tools for Mac OS X that come close to the power and flexibility of the Adobe products.

A strong case could be made that Adobe is slowly moving away from any emphasis at all on consumer-level multimedia production. In a sense, that niche is already being filled by the Apple iLife tools, included at no additional cost with new Macs and at minimal cost as a stand-alone package. While not nearly as powerful nor as flexible as the Adobe tools, the iLife suite provides all the capabilities required by the average person to edit, save, manage, and distribute multimedia files. So, while ongoing rumors that Apple is creating several Adobe killers may not be perfectly accurate, Apple has already, in an indirect but no less real sense, created similar tools to fill a niche that Adobe would probably rather be out of anyway.

Open Source Multimedia Tools

With the tight tool integration and the full resources of large software groups behind them, it's tough to make a completely fair comparison of open source multimedia tools to those of either Adobe or Apple. It's a simple statement of fact that no single suite of tools like the Adobe packages or the iLife set exists in the open source world. Then again, these large tool packages are almost antithetical to the open source philosophy of combining small tools that do one thing right. Yes, Photoshop is an image editor. It also happens to be so tightly integrated with the other Adobe applications as to be almost indistinguishable from them. For sure, Soundbooth is a strong audio editor, but its strengths lie in its use in parallel with Premiere.

All that sets aside the monetary price for each individual tool. These prices range from $99 US for Acrobat Pro to $999 US for Photoshop CS Extended. Pricing is considerably higher when reaching for the real strengths of the software—purchasing tightly integrated task-specific bundles, like those for web development, video production, or graphics creation. In short, it's tough for the average user to afford to get onboard the Adobe wagon.

While the open source community has yet to release a package of tools as tightly integrated as those produced by Apple or Adobe, the community does offer some outstanding alternatives in the form of individual tools that accomplish their tasks powerfully, cleanly, and efficiently. A full range of functionality can be found in software that addresses the tasks of audio editing and graphics creation. These tools do, in fact, meet the previously noted open source goal of tackling one task and tackling it well.

Additionally, most open source software installed on the Mac, including multimedia software, performs at least as well as when installed on other Intel-based machines. I could make the case that, for any number of reasons, it actually performs better than on some machines. I'll leave the heft of that discussion for another time. The point here is that Mac hardware is a known quantity, unlike any number of other computer brands and models on which folks run open source software. Software developed specifically for use in Mac OS X is developed for a known hardware set. That eliminates many of the problems encountered when installing and using open source software on less well-defined (or understood) hardware platforms. Open source multimedia software ported for use in Mac OS X is no exception. Simply put, that known hardware configuration is one of the most compelling reasons for moving from a generic open source hardware platform to the Mac platform.

Here, we'll look at two popular open source multimedia tools: GIMP for image editing and Audacity for audio editing.

Graphics Editing with GIMP

At the top of the heap for open source image creation and manipulation is the GNU Image Manipulation Program, known as GIMP, as shown in Figure 5-19. In effect, it's the Photoshop of open source image creation and editing. Its full feature set and ease of use make it the preferred tool for any open source user in need of a complete graphics solution.

Figure 5-19. *The GNU Image Manipulation Program: GIMP*

GIMP is similar to Photoshop in several ways, including appearance and functionality. Also, the full range of supported formats is not unlike Photoshop.

GIMP does, in fact, have some distinct advantages over Photoshop in its strong developer base and ongoing open development. There's also a pretty active community, building plug-ins and additional scripts for GIMP—something we've come to expect and recognize as one of the great strengths of the open source world.

Installing GIMP

GIMP can be installed on the Mac in a number of ways, including as a binary installation, or through either of the two open source tools for installing software we covered in the previous chapter: Fink or MacPorts.

■**Note** Recent versions of GIMP require either Mac OS X 10.5.2 or XQuartz 2.2 or greater, available from `http://xquartz.macosforge.org`. While some small font issues exist, a GIMP installation that relies on XQuartz works well.

To perform a binary installation, follow these steps:

1. Go to `http://gimp.org/downloads/` to download the binary image file (`.dmg`).

2. Double-click the image icon to mount the image.

3. Drag the application icon in the resulting window to the Applications shortcut.

4. Eject the GIMP image volume from the desktop by right-clicking and selecting Eject GIMP.

To use Fink, open a terminal window and enter the following command:

```
sudo apt-get install gimp
```

Alternatively, enter the following command to download and build the GIMP package from source:

```
fink install gimp
```

To use MacPorts, open a terminal window and enter this command:

```
sudo port install gimp
```

GIMP Editing Features

In its default configuration, the GIMP Toolbox floats on the left side of the screen. It includes many brushes, fills, pens, stamps, fonts, and other graphics editing tools.

By default, the GIMP Layers dialog box floats just to the right of the Toolbox. This dialog box provides the tools for creating and manipulating layers, channels, and paths. It also provides a visual undo history. The composition window in GIMP is layerable, and is created from any GIMP window containing the File menu option.

GIMP includes the following advanced graphics editing features:

- Layer and channel support

- Undo/redo capabilities, limited only by available disk space

- Transformation tool set

- Path tools that perform advanced selection, including polygons

- Masking support

- Subpixel sampling

- Custom brushes and patterns

- Extensibility to implement scripts, plug-ins, and other external programs

In short, GIMP provides a rich feature set for users of all skill and needs levels.

Audio Editing with Audacity

Among the open source audio tools for Mac OS X, there's little doubt which is the strongest. Audacity is a near-professional grade audio editor with a full feature set. Audacity is available for Mac, Windows, and Linux—all under the GPL at http://audacity.sourceforge.net/.

While many well-known cross-platform open source applications (including Opera, KDE, Google Earth, and Scribus) rely on the Qt framework, Audacity relies instead on wxWidgets for its cross-platform GUI, shown in Figure 5-20.

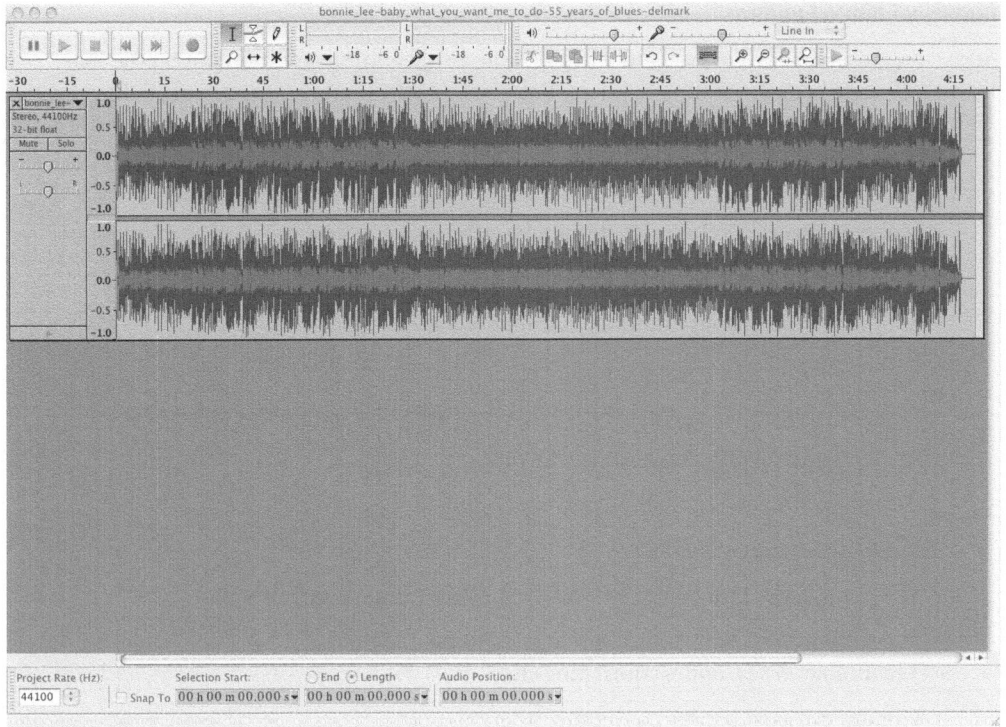

Figure 5-20. *Editing audio with Audacity*

Installing Audacity

Follow these steps to install Audacity:

1. Download the Audacity image from `http://audacity.sourceforge.net/`.

2. Mount the Audacity image by double-clicking the downloaded image icon.

3. Drag the contents of the resulting window to the `Applications` directory.

4. Eject the Audacity image by right-clicking the volume on the desktop and selecting Eject Audacity.

■**Note** The Audacity image also includes directories for Nyquist, plug-ins, and languages. Access to these tools is made a bit easier by creating an `Audacity` folder in the `Applications` directory, and then dragging the full contents of the image into the new folder. The same can be done with other applications that provide more than just a binary file.

Audacity Editing Features

Audacity creates an easy-to-use and customizable visual editing environment on the Mac, with a full range of audio editing features. The key Audacity features include the following:

- Ability to record from multiple sources

- Ability to simultaneously record and play back audio

- Ability to record 16 channels simultaneously

- Unlimited undo/redo

- Support for editing an unlimited number of tracks

- Fast editing for large files

- Ability to import WAV, AU, AIFF, MPEG, and MP3 files with proper libraries

- Ability to export MP3, WAV, and AIFF files

- Noise removal, including hiss, pop, and hum

- More than 50 built-in effects

- Ability to record and edit in 16-, 24-, and 32-bit formats up to 96 KHz

- Full support for Linux Audio Developers Simple Plugin API (LADSPA), Virtual Studio Technology (VST), and Nyquist plug-ins

- Frequency visualization via the spectrogram tool

Open Source Multimedia Summary

The open source tools for editing multimedia files pack a great punch, providing much of the same functionality as the commercial alternatives. While they're not as closely tied to each other as their commercial counterparts, they offer some additional features that may not be available in other tools. Features such as full scriptability and third-party plug-in support extend these tools to fill nearly any editing need.

The tools mentioned here are by no means the only open source multimedia packages for Mac OS X. Developers continue to create strong tools for Mac OS X, releasing them under open source licenses. Many of these packages have found their way into the Fink and MacPorts systems (introduced in Chapter 4).

Office and Productivity Tools in Mac OS X

Aside from the widely respected multimedia capabilities of Mac OS X, it also serves as a strong platform for office and productivity tools. Several office tools came to Apple Computer early in its life. Among them was VisiCalc, the first computer spreadsheet program. VisiCalc was released in 1979 for the Apple II computer. It quickly became one of the first staples of office software, pulling the Apple II squarely into its first serious use in business. Although the focus of Apple computers has changed periodically since the Apple II, and despite being overwhelmed by the PC in the business community in the early and mid-1990s, business software has remained a priority at Apple.

Microsoft Office for Mac

The primary commercial business and productivity software for Mac OS X includes the ubiquitous Microsoft Office suite of Word, Excel, and PowerPoint. Entourage provides the Outlook-equivalent e-mail and calendaring application for Mac OS X in the Office for Mac suite. Microsoft Office for Mac will set you back $150 US for the Home and Student license.

The Office applications work much the same on the Mac as they do in Microsoft Windows, with some additional look and feel tweaks for consistency with the Apple Human Interface Guidelines.

When designed based on the Apple Human Interface Guidelines, applications take on a much cleaner look than their Windows counterparts. The look includes the rounded corners, shadowing, and transparency of other Mac OS X applications.

The main menu bar in all Office applications is pared down considerably, reducing the clutter of the Windows version. Many menus have been collapsed into a single menu bar, with those menu options running one or more layers deep. Figure 5-21 shows the main Word toolbar.

Figure 5-21. *The main Word toolbar*

To give you an idea of the Office applications' interface in Mac OS X, Figure 5-22 shows creating a new Word document, and Figure 5-23 shows editing a Word document.

Figure 5-22. *Creating a new document in Word for Mac*

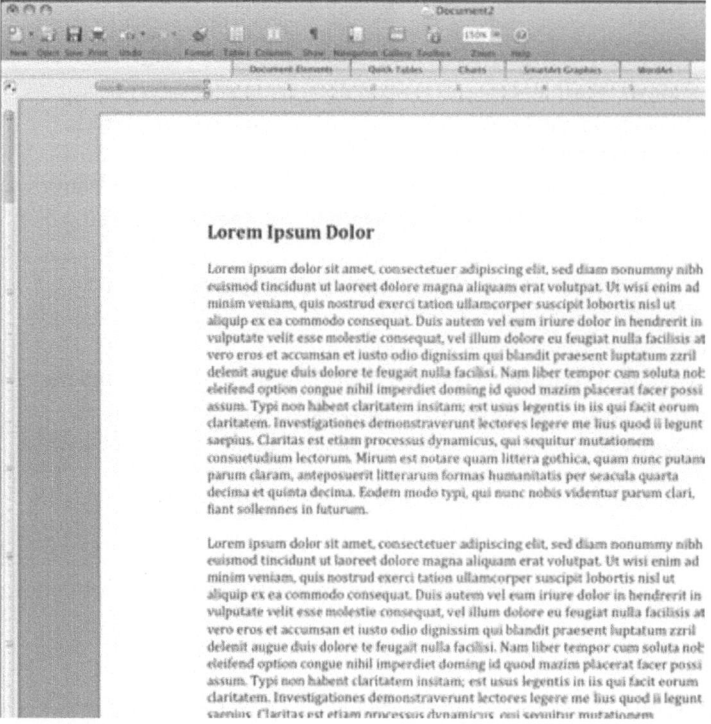

Figure 5-23. *An open document in Word for Mac*

In general, the changes to the Word, Excel, and PowerPoint applications for the Mac OS are primarily cosmetic. The known functionality across the set of tools remains nearly intact, although the user path to some of that functionality has been reduced.

Entourage is the e-mail, contacts, and calendar replacement for Outlook on Mac. The Entourage interface is a three-pane view by default, as shown in Figure 5-24. Entourage mail supports both POP3 and IMAP. It sports adequate spam filtering, message highlighting, and additional security, including image security. Entourage contacts read directly from Address Book on the Mac and render within the same interface window as Mail.

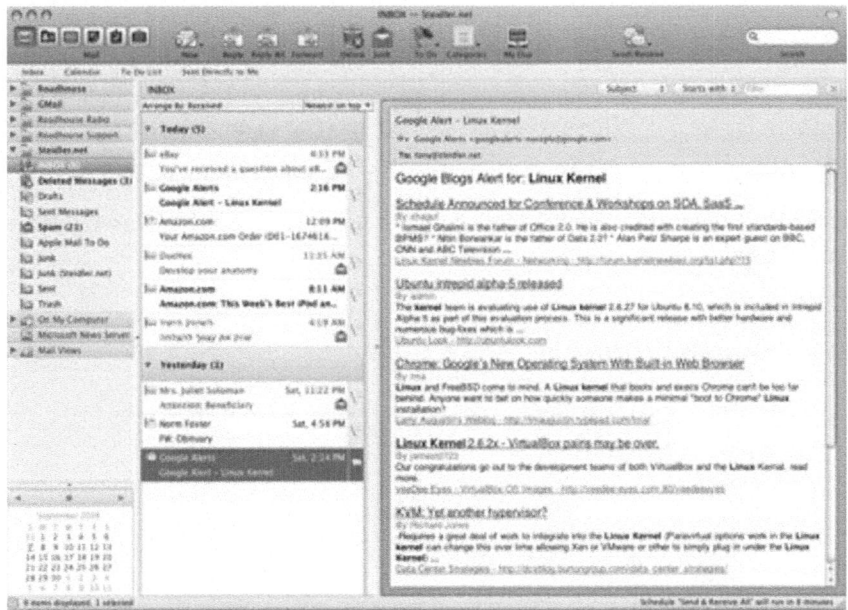

Figure 5-24. *Viewing e-mail in Entourage*

Calendaring in Entourage is far less intuitive than in iCal, Mac OS X's native calendaring application. Entourage is not integrated with iCal, by default. To see Entourage calendar items in iCal, it's necessary to create an Entourage calendar in iCal. Items created in iCal will not be seen at all in the Entourage calendar.

While the other Office applications for Mac share most of the same functionality as their Windows counterparts, Entourage feels out of place on the Mac. It's not exactly a replacement for Outlook, nor does it play well with the native Mac applications. Although it supports all modern e-mail technologies, the shortcomings of the calendar application leave it incomplete.

The Mac iWork Tools

Unless you absolutely must rely on Microsoft, there are some considerably stronger options for Mac productivity tools. One of those options is iWork, Apple's package for word processing, spreadsheets, and presentations. Unlike the iLife tools, iWork is not included with new Macs. However, iWork is surprisingly affordable at $79 US.

The iWork tools include the Pages word processor, the Numbers spreadsheet, and the Keynote presentation tool. Functions are shared across the iWork suite, simplifying overall use.

Pages

The iWork equivalent to Microsoft Word is Pages, the native Mac OS X word processing application. Pages opens with options for creating a document based on any of many included templates, as shown in Figure 5-25. These types are divided into two main categories:

- *Word Processing*: Documents such as blank pages, letters, forms, resumes, and reports.

- *Page Layout*: Documents that require more complex layouts, such as brochures, flyers, posters, and business cards.

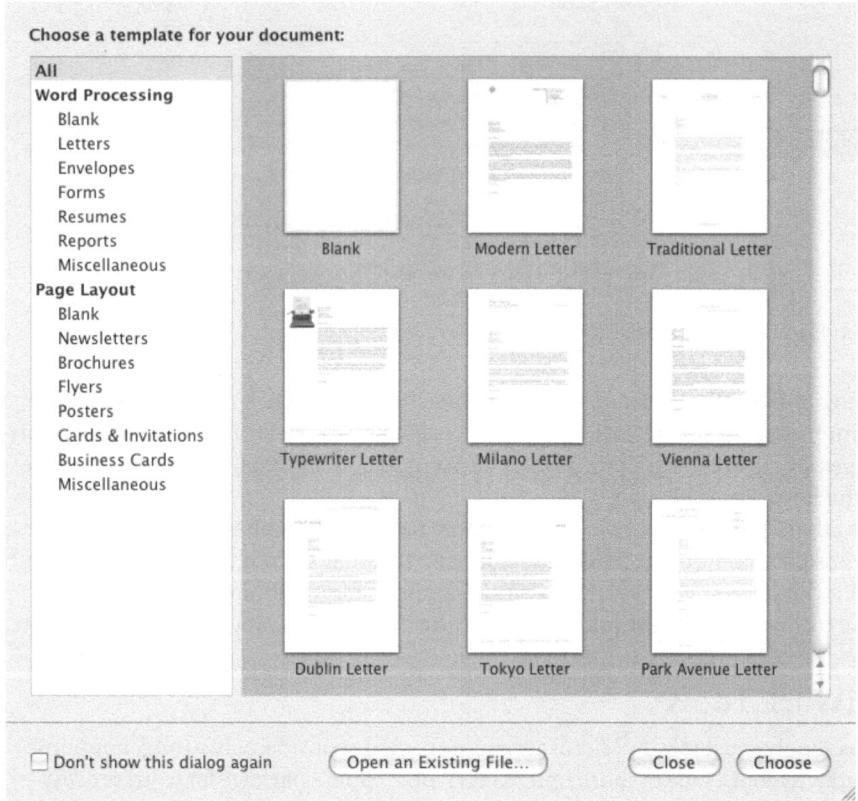

Figure 5-25. *Selecting a document template in Pages*

Templates in Pages go a step further than those in other word processing applications: they fill in the body of the template as visual support for the user. They also draw on details included in the iWork setup or information that's included in your system details. Figure 5-26 shows an example of a letter template opened in Pages.

Figure 5-26. *An open document in Pages*

Consistent with the Apple Human Interface Guidelines, the look and feel of Pages is clean, if not sparse. Menus are clearly defined, with consistent and logical submenus. Figure 5-27 shows the main Pages toolbar.

Figure 5-27. *The main Pages toolbar*

Pages will export documents to RTF or DOC format. It also supports importing and editing in those formats.

However, Pages doesn't implement some of the higher functions of other word processors, although some features can be added. For example, macros can be implemented using Apple's native scripting language, AppleScript.

In short, the feature set of Pages makes it a strong and very usable word processor, although it may not meet all the demands of hard-core business users.

Numbers

The iWork equivalent to Microsoft Excel is Numbers, the native Mac OS X spreadsheet application. Like its word processing counterpart in the iWork package, Numbers opens with a choice of spreadsheet templates, as shown in Figure 5-28. The top-level spreadsheet types include the categories Blank, Personal, Business, and Education, with several task-specific templates nested within those groups. Figure 5-29 shows an example of a spreadsheet created with a Numbers template.

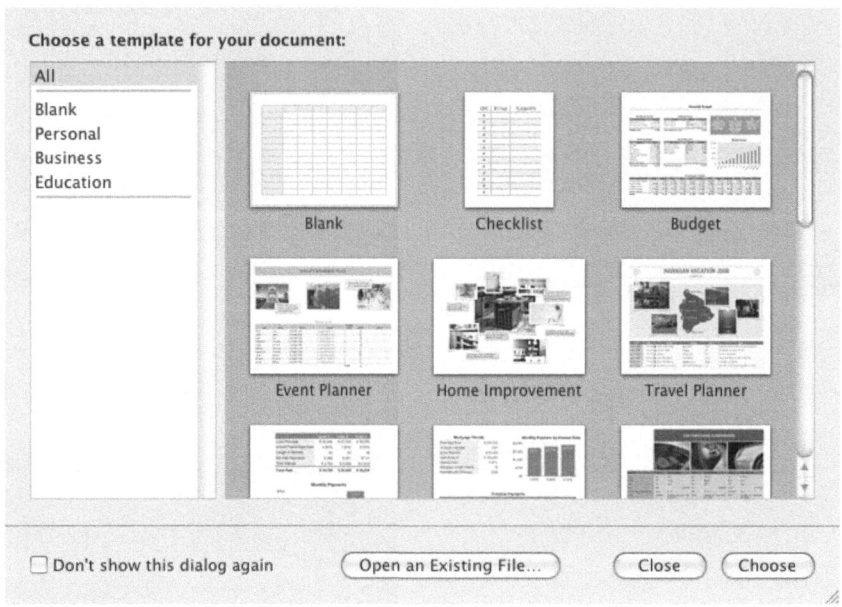

Figure 5-28. *Selecting a template for Numbers*

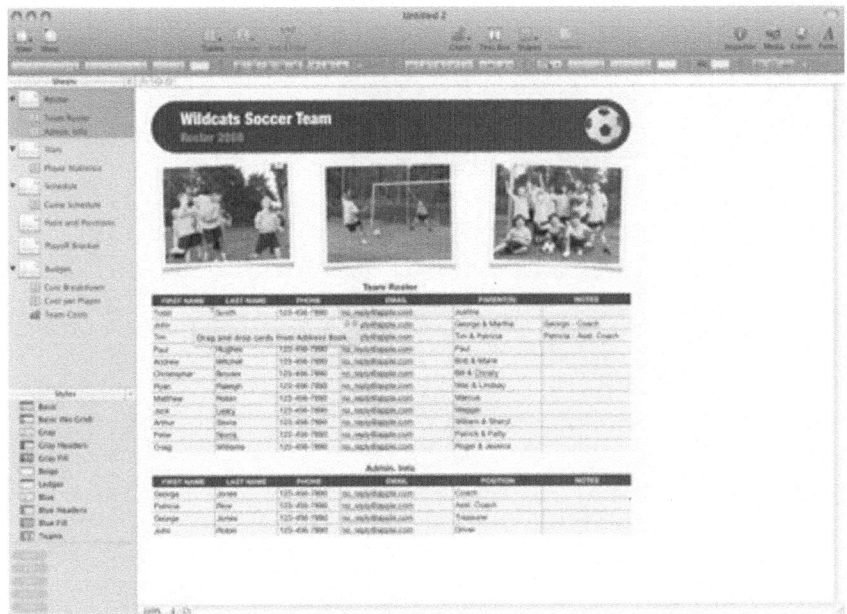

Figure 5-29. *A completed spreadsheet created with a Numbers template*

Numbers takes an interesting approach to multiple data sources within a single spreadsheet. Those data sources are placed in a sidebar within the main window, and a summary page is presented as the top page. (Note the similarity in look and feel to the iTunes application. This has been a strategy of Apple with Mac OS X native applications since 2006.)

Like Pages, Numbers is an easy-to-use application, although it's somewhat more lightweight in functionality than Excel. Again, while Numbers will meet most of the needs of a casual user, it may be lacking in features for a spreadsheet power user.

Keynote

Perhaps the most venerable application in the iWork suite is the masterful presentation package, Keynote. You may have already seen a Keynote presentation. It was the presentation tool used by Al Gore in the Academy Award–winning 2006 film *An Inconvenient Truth*. It's also the tool used in every presentation by Steve Jobs since its introduction.

Consistent with the other iWork tools, Keynote opens with template options to create a new presentation, or the capability to open an existing presentation, as shown in Figure 5-30. Figure 5-31 shows an example of editing a slide in Keynote.

Figure 5-30. *Selecting a Keynote template*

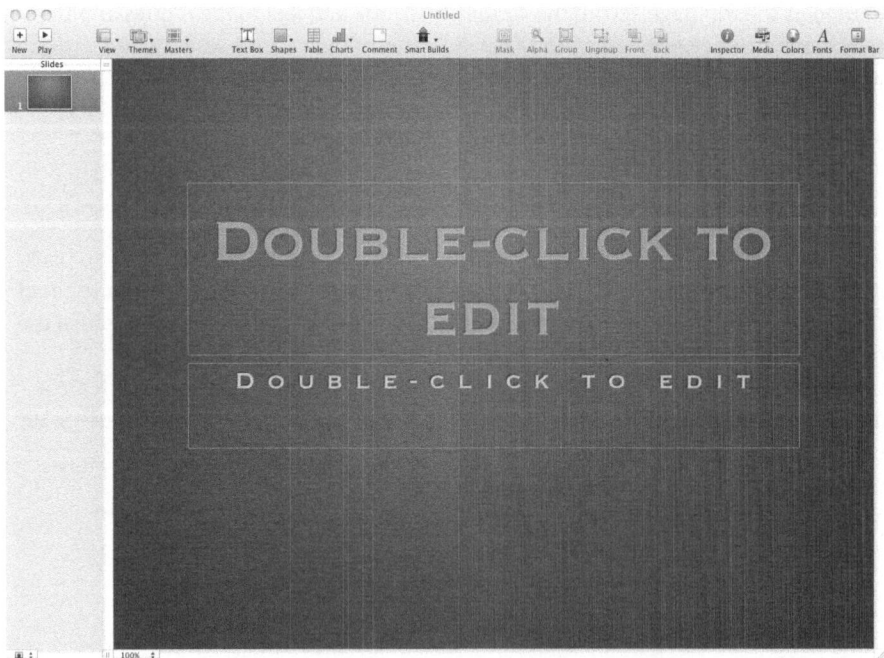

Figure 5-31. *Editing a slide in Keynote*

The many strengths of Keynote include the highly stylized templates, the huge range of available fonts, and the ease with which outside elements, such as video and other multimedia, can be included in a presentation. Keynote also provides Smart Builds, a much cleaner and more intuitive way to create transitions between slides and to build action and motion into individual slides. Additionally, Mac OS X renders the final presentation in a size that's considerably smaller than PowerPoint presentations.

Where Pages and Numbers lack a bit for word processing and spreadsheet power users, even hard-core PowerPoint users will recognize and appreciate the power and flexibility of iWork's Keynote. And Keynote includes full support for the PowerPoint PPT format.

Open Source Productivity Tools

Several open source or open source–like options exist for productivity tools on Mac. They offer a full range of functionality and, to a large extent, serve well as functional replacements for the commercial proprietary productivity software of Apple and Microsoft. In this section, we'll look at the two primary packages chosen by Mac users: OpenOffice.org and NeoOffice.

OpenOffice.org

OpenOffice.org is a productivity suite originally created as StarOffice. StarOffice was purchased by Sun Microsystems in 1999, with the first Sun build of StarOffice released in June 2000. Following that release, StarOffice was forked to a proprietary branch and an open source branch, represented by OpenOffice.org. OpenOffice.org is licensed under the Lesser GNU Public License (LGPL) and serves as the code base for StarOffice. Sun is the primary code contributor to the OpenOffice.org project.

OpenOffice.org contains the standard tools widely accepted as parts of a productivity software whole, as shown in Figure 5-32. These include the following applications:

- OpenOffice Writer is the word processing application.

- OpenOffice Calc provides the spreadsheet functionality.

- OpenOffice Impress is the presentation software.

- OpenOffice Draw is the desktop publishing application.

- OpenOffice Base is the database creation and maintenance tool.

In June 2008, OpenOffice.org released its first self-contained version for Mac OS X. The version 3 beta was the first OpenOffice.org version for the Mac that did not require a separate, running X server. Dubbed OpenOffice Aqua, the package was larger in size, but considerably quicker in use. OpenOffice Aqua is now the standard build type for OpenOffice.org on Mac.

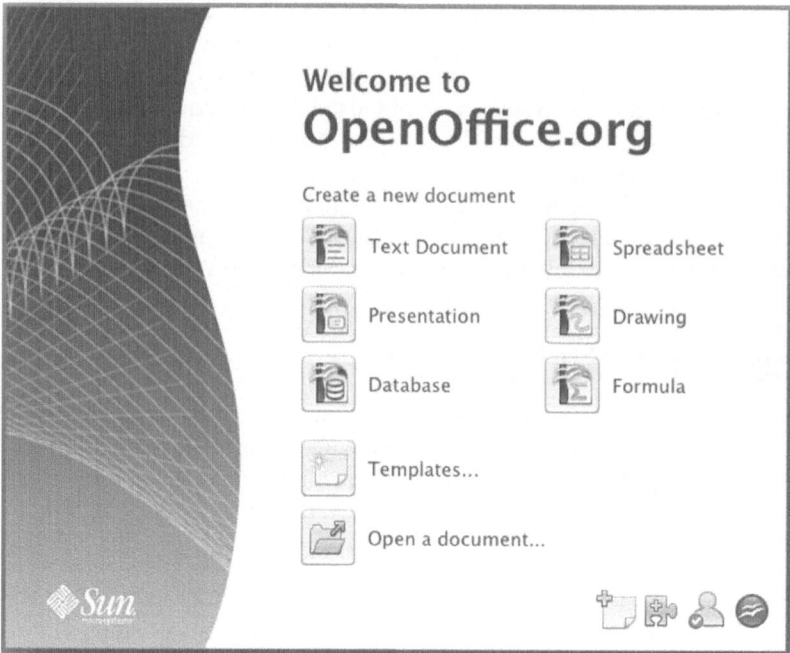

Figure 5-32. *Creating a new document in OpenOffice.org*

NeoOffice

NeoOffice is a Mac OS X productivity suite based on OpenOffice.org, but forked as a separate project. It's completely native to Mac OS X and released under the GPL. As NeoOffice is based on the OpenOffice code and model, the look, feel, and functionality of the OpenOffice.org and NeoOffice applications are nearly identical.

NeoOffice includes the following software packages:

NeoOffice Write: Write, shown in Figure 5-33, is the NeoOffice word processing application. It has a feature set that is nearly the same as Microsoft Word. Though not as clean in appearance as the recent versions of Microsoft Office for Mac, NeoOffice Write provides all the necessary functionality for both novices and power users. Documents created in NeoOffice Write are fully compatible with Microsoft Word. Word documents can also be opened and edited in Write, with the resulting documents saved seamlessly to the Microsoft DOC format.

NeoOffice Calc: Like Write, Calc is a fully functional spreadsheet application, as shown in Figure 5-34. It utilizes many routines that are similar to those in Microsoft Excel, and has a similar look and feel to older versions of the Microsoft spreadsheet program. As with Write, Calc can easily be considered feature-complete and a suitable replacement for even the most advanced Excel user.

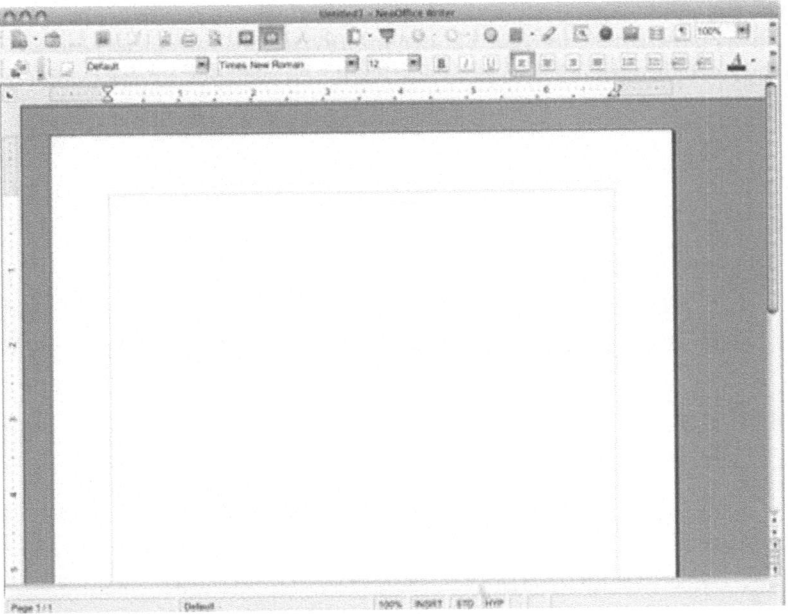

Figure 5-33. *Creating a new document in NeoOffice Write*

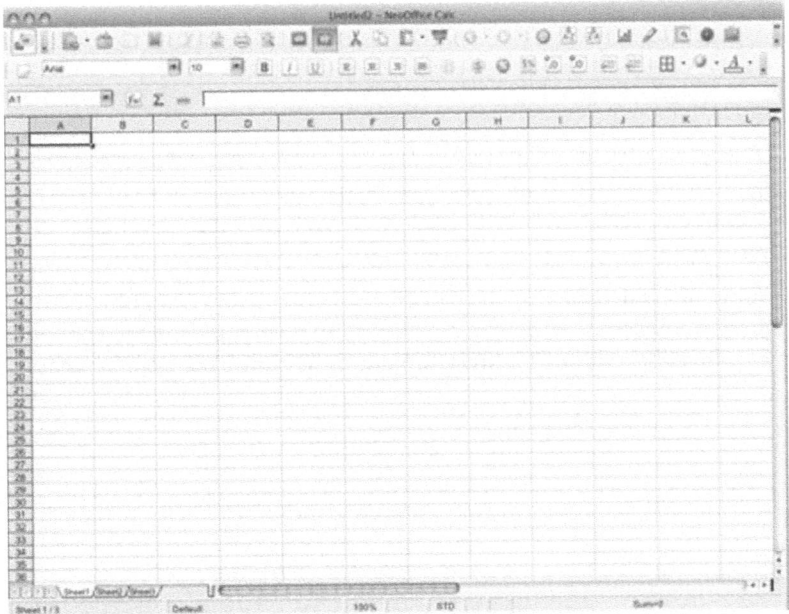

Figure 5-34. *Creating a new spreadsheet in NeoOffice Calc*

NeoOffice Impress: This application presents the familiar interface of a powerful presentation program, as shown in Figure 5-35. Though Impress is not as advanced as its counterparts in the NeoOffice suite, Microsoft PowerPoint users will find Impress suitable for their needs.

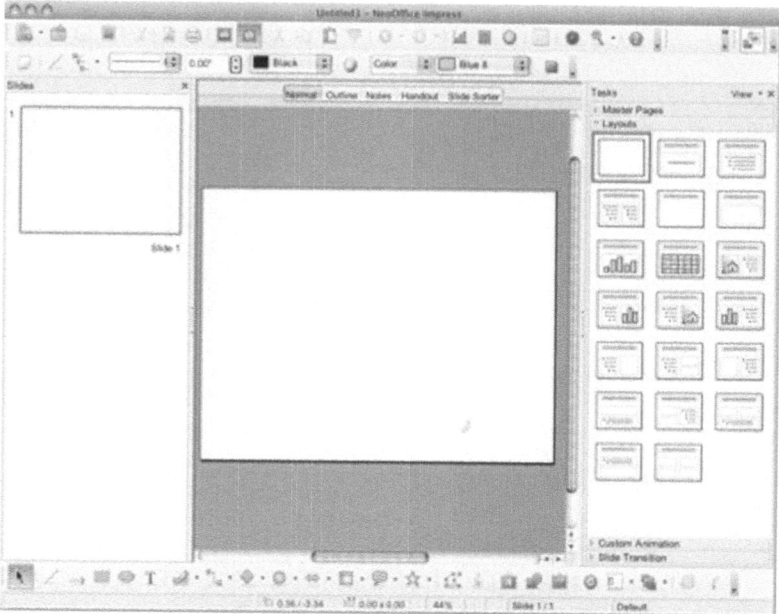

Figure 5-35. *Creating a new presentation in NeoOffice Impress*

NeoOffice Draw: While presented as a drawing application, Draw is more analogous to a desktop publishing program, geared toward page layout and design, as shown in Figure 5-36. As such, it's acceptable, though Adobe Illustrator users might hardly recognize it for its absence of powerful features.

NeoOffice Base: A stand-alone database application, Base is intended as an open source replacement for Microsoft Access. It is, however, feature-thin in comparison to Access, or to PHPMyAdmin or pure PHP scripting for MySQL. Figure 5-37 shows the New Database window in Base.

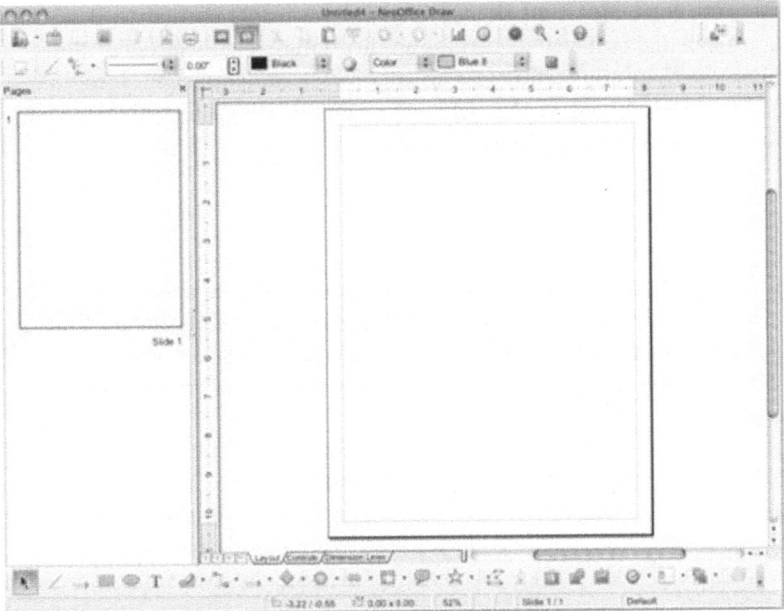

Figure 5-36. *Creating a new publication in NeoOffice Draw*

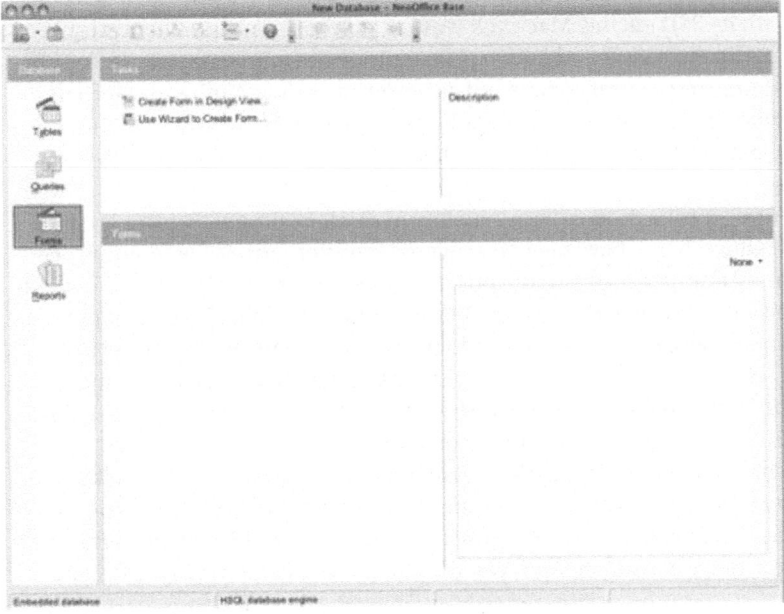

Figure 5-37. *Creating a new database with NeoOffice Base*

In most significant ways, NeoOffice is an outstanding and powerful productivity suite for Mac OS X. Its native approach makes it fast. Its various applications can edit and save files from other third-party productivity applications. As an application under the GPL, it relies strictly on donations for its development, yet NeoOffice is an outstanding alternative to commercial and proprietary productivity suites for Mac OS X.

Summary

Mac OS X has many strengths. It's a powerful and versatile platform on which to create and edit multimedia files, from graphics to video to audio. With the advanced Core Image, Core Video, and Core Audio frameworks, Mac OS X has a cutting-edge look and feel. More important, these tools make it possible to maximize the power of Mac OS X when creating and editing multimedia applications.

Those strengths are the backbone upon which Apple has built its reputation for many years. As such, Mac OS X includes a suite of tools to manage and edit personal multimedia files: the iLife package of iPhoto, iMovie, iDVD, iWeb, and GarageBand. These are powerful tools, especially when considering that they're included with the operating system.

Also available are a variety of third-party, proprietary, professionally-oriented multimedia tools, although this market is a bit dark in the shadow of Adobe Systems. Adobe's ever-growing inventory of Mac-centric multimedia tools has cornered the professional market, although the professional tools from Apple are making inroads into Adobe's dominance. Leveraging a long-standing relationship with Apple, Adobe continues to push its tools in new directions, as well as finding new income inroads through tool bundling.

And, of course, with its BSD engine, Mac OS X is also a powerful platform for open source multimedia tools. In particular, GIMP and Audacity lead the open source community for graphics and audio editing, respectively. While not as powerful as their Adobe counterparts, Photoshop and Soundbooth, these open source tools are, in fact, viable upgrades to the comparably-tasked iLife tools on the Mac. Both are developed and maintained in rich open source environments.

For many, computing means productivity. And for those users, productivity tools necessarily mean Microsoft Office. Some have never discovered the alternatives. Some simply feel they cannot use anything else, lest they lose the business edge. For them, Microsoft provides an equal to its Windows-based Office package in Microsoft Office for Mac. Feature-complete, Office for Mac is, in many ways, a good alternative to the Windows version. By complying closely with the Apple Human Interface Guidelines, Microsoft has created a cleaner, more accessible version of its hallmark Windows software for Mac. Office users will find the adjustment curve small, with no missing functionality for the power users.

Of course, Apple has created its own smaller set of productivity tools: iWork. Unlike iLife, iWork is not included in Mac OS X. Nor is it as feature-dense as the Microsoft Office for Mac package. However, like the iLife tools, the tools provided by iWork are efficient, powerful, and perfectly suited to the average consumer. And, yes, they have that distinctive Mac look and feel.

On the open source side of the productivity world, two packages stand out. In reality, they're very nearly the same. Both are based on OpenOffice.org, which was originally the German package StarOffice. The differences between NeoOffice and OpenOffice.org are primarily under the hood. The tool functions are the same. The individual tool names are the same. And the look and feel of the packages are almost identical. The single biggest difference between the two packages may be that NeoOffice was created natively for the Mac. Licensing separates the productivity tools, as well, with NeoOffice released under the GPL and OpenOffice.org released under the LGPL. However, OpenOffice.org has begun to move closer to the Mac-native model, releasing new versions that no longer require a stand-alone X server.

Now that we've covered multimedia and productivity tools, in the next chapter, we'll take a look at Mac OS X system administration.

CHAPTER 6

■ ■ ■

Routine Mac OS X System Administration

If you've administered UNIX or Linux systems in the past, or if you're making a living doing that now, you'll find many similarities between the administrative tools on those computers and those included with Mac OS X. The lineup is not a perfect match, but it's close enough in many cases. Apple has made some modifications to Mac OS X tools for its own purposes, but many of these changes will be noticeable only to the hard-core Linux and UNIX faithful.

Let's start this chapter with the similarities.

Using the Shell

The default user shell for Mac OS X is bash, the Bourne-Again SHell. Bash has been ported almost entirely intact from BSD. Prior to the introduction of bash in Mac OS X 10.3 (Panther), the default shell for Mac OS X was tcsh, the TENEX C SHell. While tcsh is a flexible and popular shell, bash has become more widely implemented. With strong similarities to the csh, the C SHell, bash offers much more flexibility in programming and scripting than its C predecessors or the tcsh shell.

A strong understanding of the shell and its scripting power is a modern prerequisite for most UNIX/BSD/Mac OS X administrators. Increasingly, the powerful shell of choice for administrators is bash.

Programming in bash isn't as complete or as powerful as full-blown programming in other languages. This programming is generally accomplished via small scripts, although bash provides the power to create very large and complex scripts. The scripting features in bash include the popular POSIX shell features: redirection, pipes, variables, conditionals, looping (including for and while loops), and functions. Bash scripts have become the backbone of many administrative tools and tasks in UNIX, BSD, and Mac OS X. Such administrative scripts can be created on the fly with any text editor, and tested line by line or command by command.

Aside from powerful programming capabilities, bash features aliasing, command prompt customization, and environment variables. These allow administrators to fully customize their daily work environment. Administrators can, in a sense, build an environment that gives them the most comfort, familiarity, and flexibility for their own uses.

Changing the Default Shell

If you're currently a system administrator and hopelessly hooked on another shell environment, it's possible to change the default shell in Mac OS X. The default Mac OS X installation includes bash, tcsh, ksh, and zsh—a lot of flexibility in shell environments. The binaries for all these shells are located in /bin.

To change the default shell, open the Terminal application and select Preferences. Choose the Settings tab and the Shell option. In the Startup text box, enter the path to your preferred shell. In Figure 6-1, this default shell has been changed to tcsh, located in /bin/tcsh. Close the Preferences window and the current terminal window. When you restart the Terminal application, the new shell you selected will be the default.

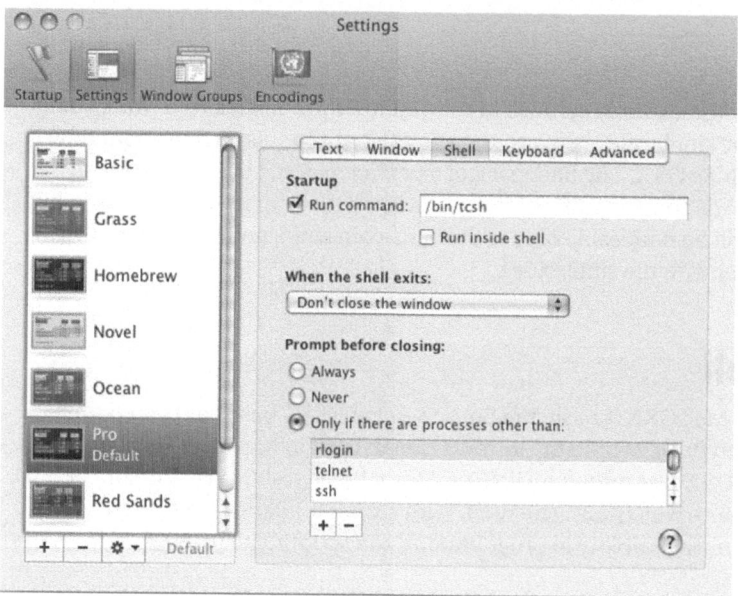

Figure 6-1. *Terminal application shell preferences in Mac OS X*

Invoking a different shell environment directly from the command line is easy, as well. Simply enter the shell environment command in a terminal window. That will execute the new shell environment. Of course, this will be a temporary invocation, replaced by the defined default shell the next time the Terminal application is opened.

Another option exists for changing the default shell in Mac OS X, although it's a bit more complicated than setting the Terminal application Preferences. From System Preferences, select your user. In the resulting window, click the lock icon in the lower-left corner and enter your password when prompted. Control-click your username in the left pane, and select Advanced Options to see the settings shown in Figure 6-2. Select the new shell from the Login Shell drop-down list. To force the change, you'll need to log out of your account and log back in.

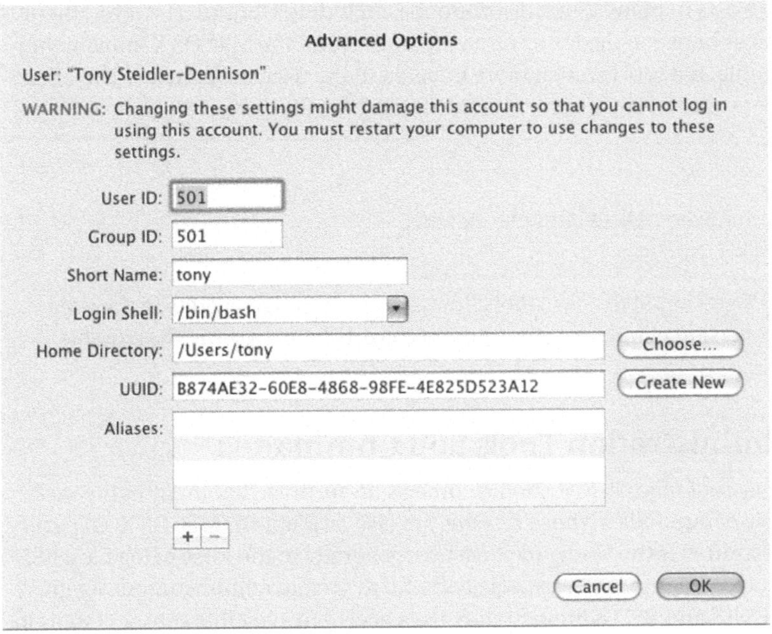

Advanced Options

User: "Tony Steidler-Dennison"

WARNING: Changing these settings might damage this account so that you cannot log in
using this account. You must restart your computer to use changes to these
settings.

User ID: 501

Group ID: 501

Short Name: tony

Login Shell: /bin/bash

Home Directory: /Users/tony   Choose...

UUID: B874AE32-60E8-4868-98FE-4E825D523A12   Create New

Aliases:

+ −

Cancel   OK

Figure 6-2. *Advanced user options in System Preferences*

To make the change from the command line, use the chsh tool in a terminal window:

```
$ sudo chsh tony
```

This command will open a window with output similar to the following:

```
# Changing user information for tony.
# Use "passwd" to change the password.
##
# Open Directory: /Local/Default
##
Login: tony
Uid [#]: 501
Gid [# or name]: 501
Generated uid: B874AE32-60E8-4868-98FE-4E825D523A12
Home directory: /Users/tony
Shell: /bin/bash
Full Name: Tony Steidler-Dennison
Office Location:
Office Phone:
Home Phone:
```

In this window, change the shell defined in the Shell line. Then save and close the file.
The default user shell will be changed to your preference.

The chsh tool also exists in many Linux distributions, including Ubuntu. However, there are significant differences between the Linux implementation and the Mac OS X implementation. In Linux, for example, the tool is much more targeted to the user shell choice. The other editing options are not available. Here's an example of using the Linux version:

```
$ sudo chsh tony
Password:
Enter the new value, or press ENTER for the default
        Login Shell [/bin/bash]:
```

While the Mac OS X version of the chsh tool allows a broader range of edits to the user information, the Linux version eliminates some possible errors by narrowing the editable information.

Using UNIX Administration Tools and Commands

Given the UNIX/BSD basis of Mac OS X, it should come as no surprise that many of the most powerful administrative commands in those systems are also available in Mac OS X. Of particular interest to administrators is the ability to parse text, generally in the form of log files. BSD is chock-full of these tools, but a subset is especially useful to system administrators. Again, the good news is that UNIX and BSD administrators have access to even this subset of tools in their native form in Mac OS X. Table 6-1 lists the tools, along with a brief description (based on the individual tool man pages), that most consider to be at the heart of system administration in UNIX, BSD, and Mac OS X.

Table 6-1. *UNIX Command-Line Administration Tools*

Command	Description
grep	Searches the named input files or standard input if no files are named, for lines containing a match to the given pattern. By default, grep prints the matching lines.
awk	Performs pattern-directed scanning and language processing. awk scans each input file for lines that match a set of patterns specified literally in prog or in one or more files specified as -f progfile. With each pattern, there can be an associated action that will be performed when a line of a file matches the pattern.
sed	Reads the specific files, or the standard input file if no files are specified, modifying the input as specified by a list of commands. The input is then written to the standard output. The sed utility is a stream editor.
sort	Sorts lines of text files. Writes sorted concatenation of all files to standard output.
uniq	Reports or filters out repeated lines in a file. The uniq utility reads the specified input file, comparing adjacent lines, and writes a copy of each unique input line to the output file.
cat	Concatenates and prints files. The cat utility reads files sequentially, writing them to the standard output. The file operands are processed in command-line order.
xargs	Constructs argument list(s) and executes the command. The xargs utility reads space, tab, newline, and end-of-file delimited strings from the standard input and executes the command with the strings as arguments.
exec	Takes a command as an argument and runs that command within the running shell's process.

Command	Description
head	Displays the first lines of a file. This filter displays the first count lines or bytes of each of the specified files, or of the standard input if no files are specified. If the count is omitted, it defaults to 10.
tail	Displays the last part of a file. The tail utility displays the contents of a file or, by default, its standard input, to the standard output.
ls	Lists directory contents. For each operand that names a file of a type other than directory, ls displays its name as well as any requested, associated information.
dd	Converts and copies a file. The dd utility copies the standard input to the standard output. Input data is read and written in 512-byte blocks.
diff	Compares files line by line.
tar	Runs the GNU version of the tar archiving utility. The man page documents the GNU version of tar, an archiving program designed to store and extract files from an archive file known as a *tarfile*. A tarfile may be made on a tape drive; however, it is also common to write a tarfile to a normal file.
cut	Selects portions of each line of a file. The cut utility selects portions of each line (as specified by list) from each file and writes them to the standard output. If no file arguments are specified, or a file argument is a single dash (-), cut reads from the standard input.

These command-line administration tools are available in their native UNIX/BSD forms to Mac OS X system administrators. As with most tools in UNIX, these utilities can be executed as stand-alone commands with the appropriate options, or called from scripts either individually or in combination. And, as noted in many of the descriptions, these tools can accept standard output as input. That means they can be strung together with output piped from one command to another. This creates a huge number of tool combinations and options for administering a Mac OS X system.

System Monitoring

Another important element of system administration is monitoring system resources and use. Mac OS X provides a full set of tools, both on the command line and through the GUI, for this system monitoring. Here, we'll look at the Activity Monitor GUI tool, and the top and ps command-line tools.

Note Several other system monitoring tools are available in Mac OS X. These include lsof, which provides a list of open files, and vm_stat, a tool to display Mach kernel virtual memory statistics.

Using Activity Monitor

The Mac OS X GUI tool for system monitoring is Activity Monitor, located in Applications/ Utilities. As shown in Figure 6-3, Activity Monitor provides a formidable level of data in an efficient format, using a combination of drop-down options, search options, and tabs.

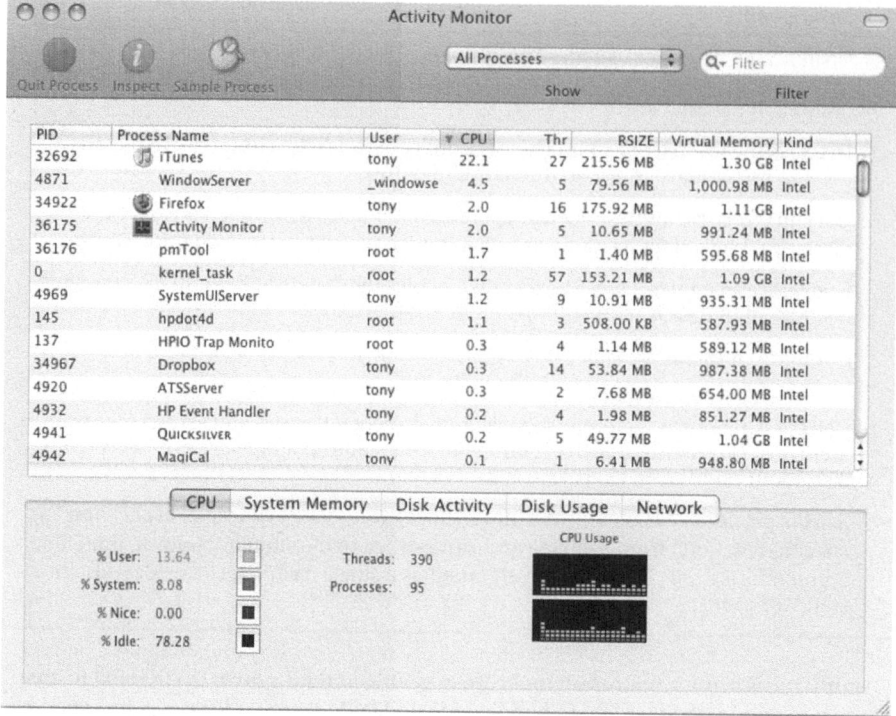

Figure 6-3. *The Mac OS X Activity Monitor main window*

As shown in Figure 6-4, Activity Monitor provides a number of ways to view the data, available through a drop-down menu in the main interface. These options include the ability to view processes by users, process type, or status.

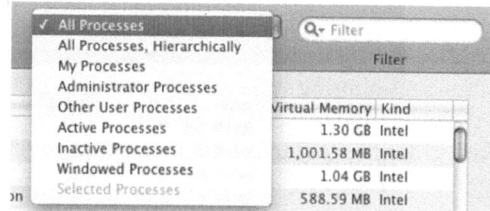

Figure 6-4. *Selecting Activity Monitor view options from the drop-down menu*

In addition to using the drop-down menu options to access views, administrators can search Activity Monitor for specific processes. As shown in Figure 6-5, the search interface is similar in look and feel to the other search tools in Mac OS X, providing full consistency across the operating system. Additionally, the text searches can be accomplished with any of the drop-down menu selections. This flexibility dramatically expands the possible administrative views of the current system.

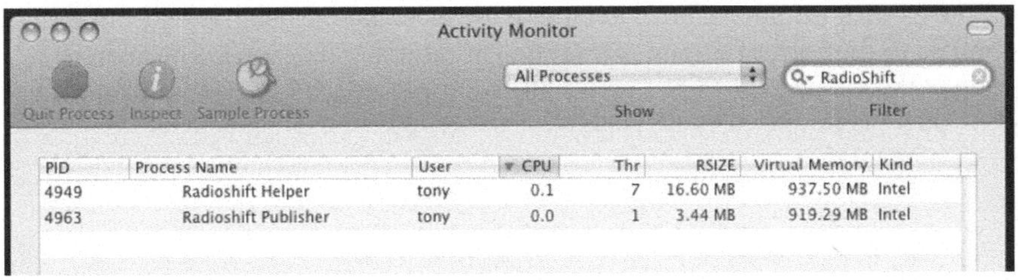

Figure 6-5. *Searching for specific processes in Activity Monitor*

The main Activity Monitor window provides a wealth of information about the current state of the system, as shown in Figure 6-6. It includes the columns of information listed in Table 6-2. You can sort all of the columns in Activity Monitor in ascending or descending order by clicking the head of the column of interest.

Table 6-2. *Activity Monitor Columns*

Column Head	Contents
PID	The process ID, a unique value assigned to each process on the running system.
Process Name	The common name assigned to each process on the running system.
User	The owner of the given process.
CPU	Current CPU use as a percentage. Percentages greater that 100 indicate use of both processors in a multiprocessor system. For example, 60% utilization of each processor in a dual-processor system would show a value of 120.
Thr	The number of threads in use by the given process.
RSIZE	The size of the resident memory allocated to the given process. This is the amount of RAM currently in actual use by the system.
Virtual Memory	The total address space allocated for the given process.
Kind	The processor type used for the noted process. This will display "Intel" for Intel-native binaries, and "PowerPC" for binaries running under the Rosetta PowerPC emulator.

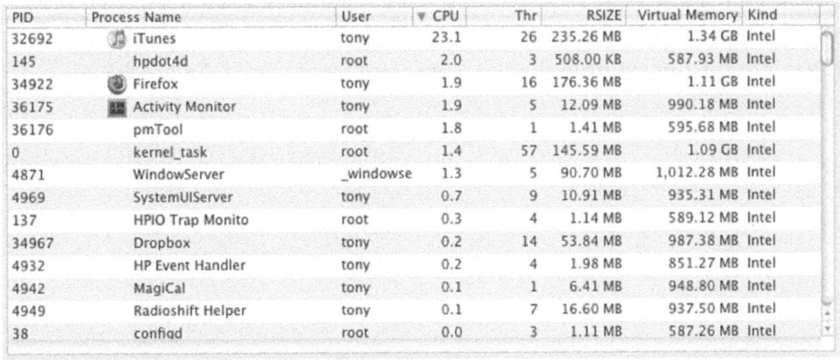

Figure 6-6. *The main Activity Monitor window, displaying pertinent information about the current system state*

Aside from the viewing options of process types and searchable strings, Activity Monitor also slices and dices the current system activity in a number of other ways. As shown in Figure 6-7, Activity Monitor provides tabs for viewing the current use of all system resources: CPU, System Memory, Disk Activity, Disk Usage, and Network.

Figure 6-7. *Additional tabbed options for viewing the current system activity*

Finally, Activity Monitor provides a graphical representation of the system use, as shown in Figure 6-8. This view includes the percentages of system resources used by both the users and the system, the percentage of nice resources (those reprioritized using the nice command), the percentage of processes currently in the idle state, the total number of running threads, and the total number of running processes. The graphical display also provides a snapshot of processor CPU usage, updated once per second.

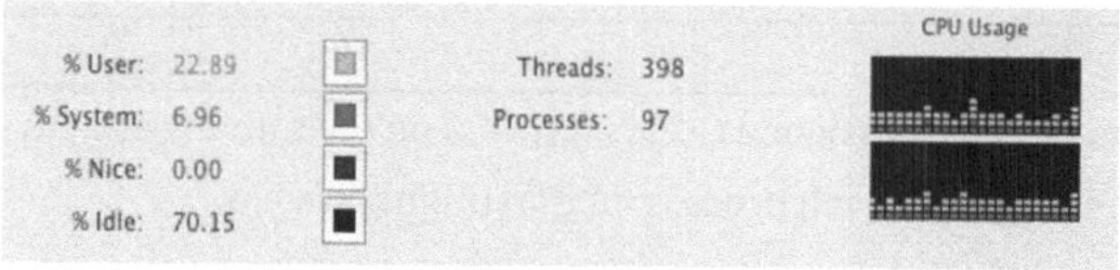

% User:	22.89		Threads:	398
% System:	6.96		Processes:	97
% Nice:	0.00			
% Idle:	70.15			

CPU Usage

Figure 6-8. *A graphical representation of current system use in the CPU tab of Activity Monitor*

Overall, Activity Monitor provides a comprehensive and flexible view of the current state of the Mac OS X system. In reality, though, it's simply a clean, graphical front end to several other UNIX command-line tools. Most prominent among them are top and ps. Using the Terminal application, system administrators can access these command-line tools to monitor system performance.

Viewing System Processes with top

The top command in Mac OS X, as in UNIX-based systems, returns a near real-time view of current system processes. This output includes a summary of process totals by type or state (running, stuck, or sleeping), a summary of the system load, the number of current shared libraries in use, memory regions in use, and both physical and virtual memory in use. This data is located at the top of the output from the top command, as shown in Figure 6-9.

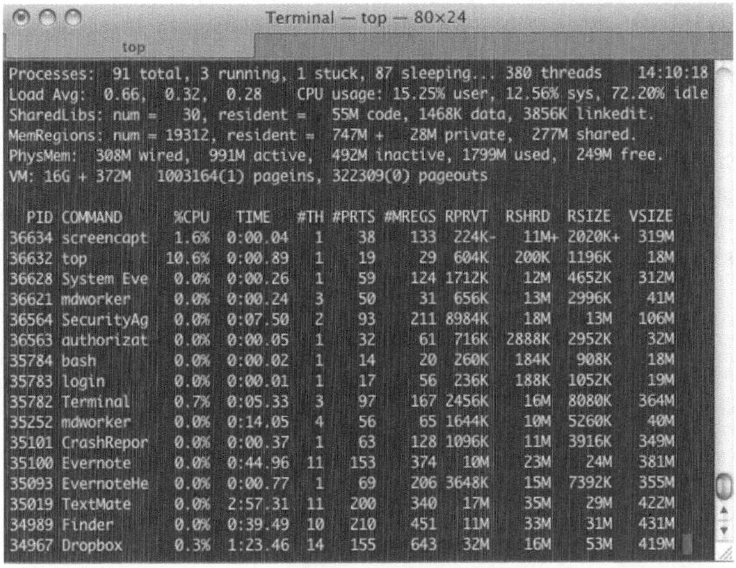

Figure 6-9. *Terminal output from the top command*

As you can see in Figure 6-9, the output breaks down system usage by individual processes. This varies a bit from the typical output of the UNIX top command. Mac OS X's top provides columns of information that differ from other top output. These columns include those shown in Table 6-3.

Table 6-3. *The top Command Output Columns*

Column Head	Contents
PID	Process ID
COMMAND	The command executed to initiate the process
TIME	The execution time of the process
#TH	The number of threads utilized by the process
#PRTS	The number of Mach kernel ports utilized by the process
#MREGS	The number of memory regions utilized by the process
RPRVT	The resident private memory size
RSHRD	The resident shared memory size
RSIZE	The total resident memory size
VSIZE	The total address space allocated to the process, including shared pages

The output shown in Figure 6-9 is the result of the bare top command. top in Mac OS X, as in its UNIX counterpart, recognizes a large pool of available options for customizing the output. These are listed in the top man page, available from the terminal window with the command man top.

Listing Processes with ps

Mac OS X also makes full use of the UNIX command that lists running processes: ps (*process status* in UNIX-ese). It lists information about all of the current processes that have controlling terminals.

Figure 6-10 displays the output from the ps command in Mac OS X, with the additional xa option. This option expands the standard output from ps to show processes that do not include a controlling terminal (x) and current processes belonging to other (or all) users (a). The output from ps breaks down as shown in Table 6-4.

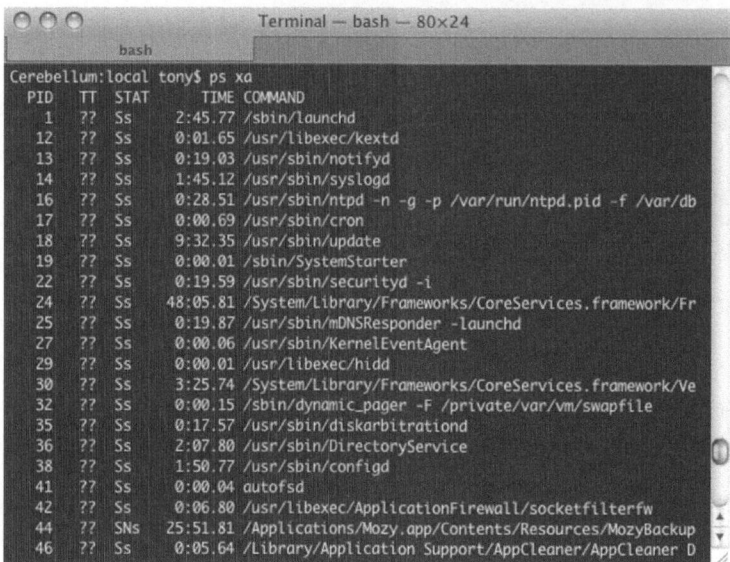

Figure 6-10. *Output from the Mac OS X ps command*

Table 6-4. *The ps Command Output Columns*

Column Head	Contents
PID	Process ID.
TT	The identification of the controlling terminal. If the noted process does not include a controlling terminal, the output of ps will include ?? in this column.
STAT	The current state of the process. These codes can include D, for uninterruptible sleep; N, for nice low priority; R, for runnable; S, for sleeping; T, for traced or stopped; and Z, for defunct (or zombie).
TIME	The total running CPU time of the process, in *MM:SS* fractions.
COMMAND	The command used to initiate the process.

User Maintenance

One of the most common jobs of system administrators is user maintenance: adding, deleting, and modifying users on the system. Administrators or individual system users may also customize the list of applications to start when logging in, or may choose to change their login password.

As with so many of the other elements of Mac OS X, most of these user maintenance tasks can be performed using either GUI tools or the command line. Let's look first at the GUI tools and how to use them for creating and deleting users in Mac OS X.

Managing User Accounts Using System Preferences

User accounts in Mac OS X are maintained in System Preferences. Figure 6-11 shows an Account window locked from modification, as indicated by the lock icon in the lower-left corner. Users with system administrator privileges can unlock the editing functions by clicking the lock, and then entering their login password.

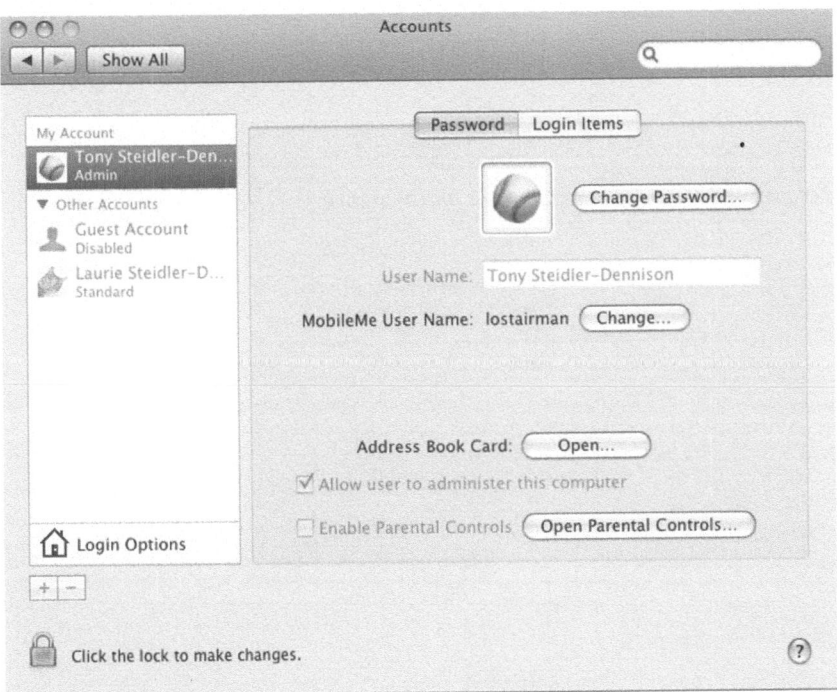

Figure 6-11. *The Accounts window of System Preferences*

When the administrative login is accepted, the grayed-out areas of the Accounts window will become editable, as shown in Figure 6-12. To add a new user to the system, click the plus sign at the bottom of the users pane. This opens a form for all the new user information, both required and optional, as shown in Figure 6-13.

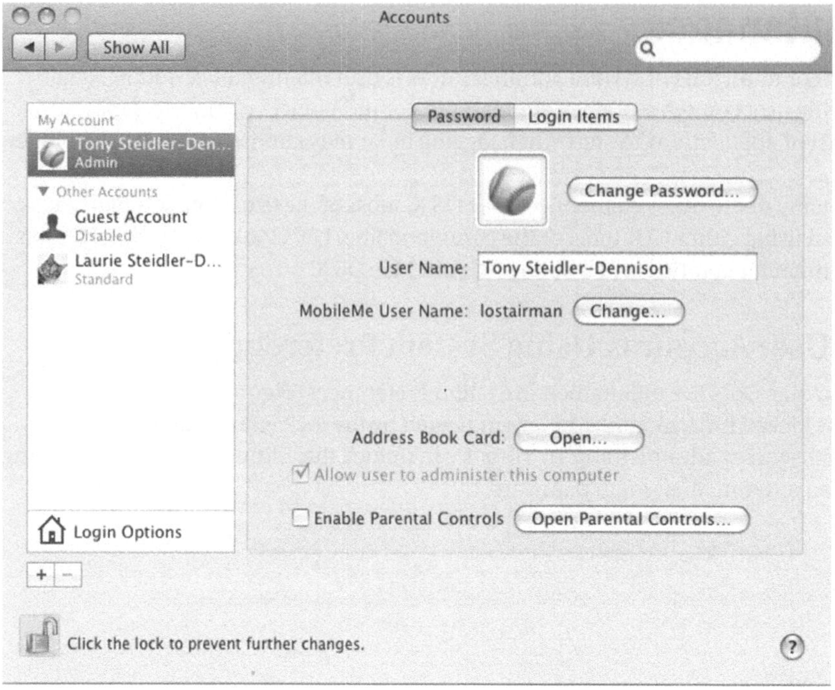

Figure 6-12. *The Accounts window unlocked for user maintenance*

Figure 6-13. *Adding a new user with the Accounts tool*

To delete a user on the system using the Accounts tool, click the minus sign at the bottom of the users pane. Figure 6-14 shows the resulting window, which provides options for the user data after deletion of the account. These options include creating a disk image for the contents of the user's home folder, leaving the home folder entirely intact, or deleting it altogether.

Checking a radio button and clicking OK will delete the account, handling the user's home folder as you specified.

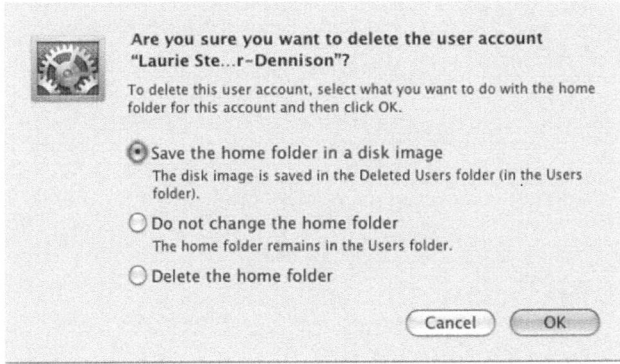

Figure 6-14. *Deleting a user with the Accounts tool*

In addition to creating or deleting users, the Accounts tool lets users set which applications on the system will start when each user logs in. To add an application to the list, click the plus sign below the applications list, and then select the application from the resulting window. Selecting the check box beside an application listed in the Login Items window, as shown in Figure 6-15, will hide the chosen application at startup.

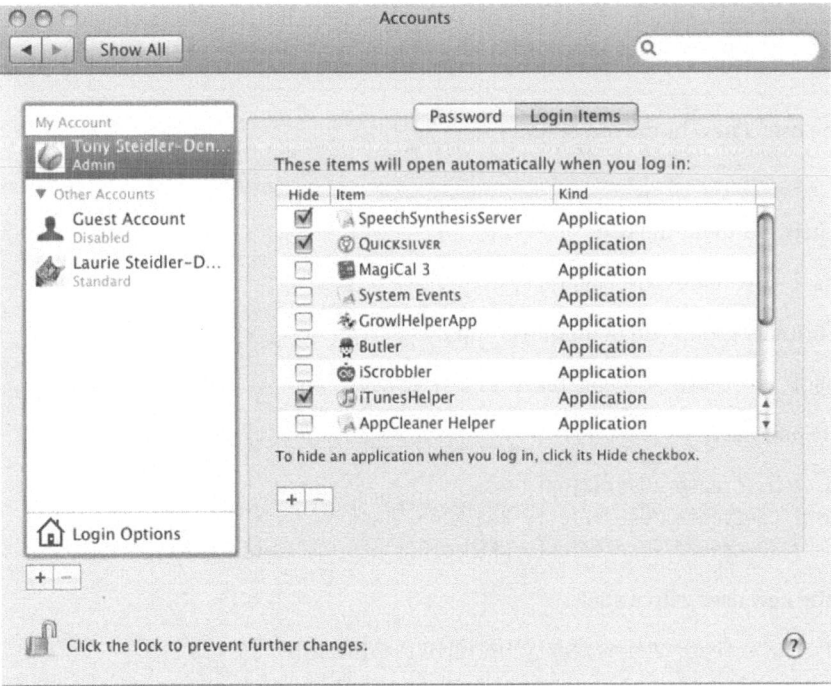

Figure 6-15. *Setting login items with the Accounts tool*

Finally, users may choose to reset an existing login password using the Accounts tool. Figure 6-16 shows the information required to reset an existing user password.

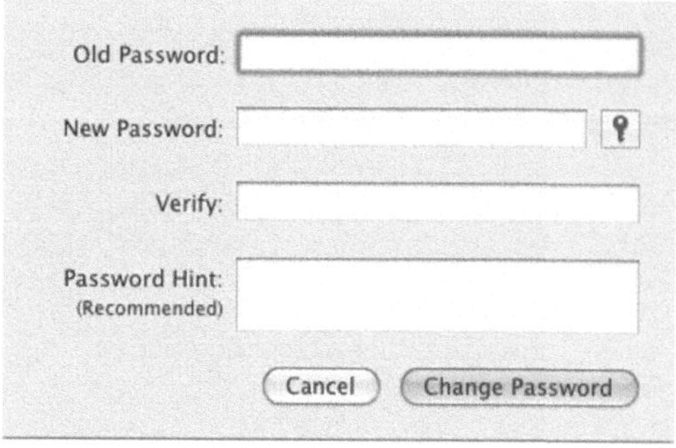

Figure 6-16. *Resetting a user password with the Accounts tool*

Managing Users Using the Command Line

Creating a new user from the command line is a bit more complicated than using the Accounts window of System Preferences. This approach doesn't employ the familiar tools from BSD, such as useradd, which includes the ability to add a home directory with the use of a single option in the command line. The tools for adding a user via the command line in Mac OS X are, instead, specific to Mac OS X.

Here are the steps necessary for creating a new user, creating the user's home directory, adding the user to a group, setting a password, and setting permissions on the user's home directory:

1. Create the user's new home directory:

   ```
   $ sudo mkdir /Users/Testy
   ```

2. Create a new group for the user:

   ```
   $ sudo dscl . -create /Groups/Testy
   ```

3. Create a primary group with a unique group ID:

   ```
   $ sudo dscl . -create /Groups/Testy PrimaryGroupID 900
   ```

4. Create the new user:

   ```
   $ sudo dscl . -create /Users/Testy
   $ sudo dscl . -create /Users/Testy RealName "Test Y. User"
   $ sudo dscl . -create /Users/Testy NFSHomeDirectory /Users/Testy
   ```

5. Provide the new user with a shell:

   ```
   $ sudo dscl . -create /Users/Testy UserShell /bin/bash
   ```

6. Create a user ID for the new user:

```
$ sudo dscl . -create /Users/Testy UniqueID 900
```

7. Add the new user to a primary group:

```
$ sudo dscl . -create /Users/Testy PrimaryGroupID 900
```

8. Create a password for the new user:

```
$ sudo passwd Testy
Changing password for Testy.
New password:
Retype new password:
```

9. Create the proper permissions for the user's home directory:

```
$ sudo chown -R Testy:Testy /Users/Testy
```

To test whether these steps properly created the new user, let's use the GUI tool to check all the users on the system. As shown in Figure 6-17, a new user, Test Y. User, has been created successfully from the command line in Mac OS X. Note that although this example was performed one line at a time, it's easy to script this command-line user-creation routine.

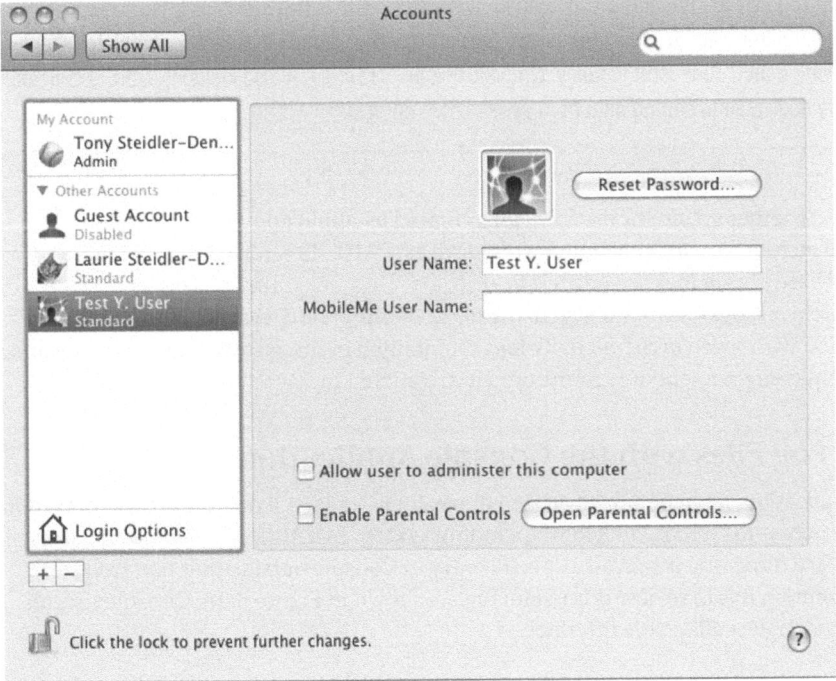

Figure 6-17. *The new system user, created using the command-line tool dscl*

Log Review and Maintenance

Another fundamental system administration task is review and maintenance of system logs. Much of the maintenance is performed automatically by launchd, the cron-like Mac OS X tool. But it's still the responsibility of the system administrator to regularly review the critical logs for security or system performance issues. It's also important to understand where those logs are located, though it you're currently an administrator on a UNIX, BSD, or Linux system, the locations won't come as much of a surprise.

Log Location and Naming Conventions

At the top of the log hierarchy in Mac OS X is the system.log file. The system log is created and maintained by the Apple System Logger, an Apple replacement for the BSD syslogd tool. The system log can be accessed quickly from a terminal window, or, like other Mac OS X tools, can be reviewed using a GUI application.

The system.log file resides in the /var/log directory. The /var/log directory also includes logs for installations, security, firewall, mail, rsync requests, connections, and the window server. Other logs exist in both the user and system Library directories.

Note The /var/log logs are not actually located in /var/log. /var is a symbolic link to /private/var. In other words, the true path to /var/log is /private/var/log, though that fact is completely transparent to a user. And, in fact, /var isn't the only symbolic link in /private. It also includes /etc, /tmp, and /cores (a directory dedicated to storing data from system core dumps).

Library logs, whether system or user, are logs created by applications on the system. Library logs also include logs for Crash Reporter, devices, RAID, directory services, Java, and sync activities. These library logs are located in /Library/Logs or ~/Library/Logs.

Mac OS X archives logs automatically, using bzip2 compression. system.log is archived daily by Mac OS X, with seven archived daily logs maintained in the system. The archiving and rotation are completed on a schedule monitored and initiated by launchd.

Reviewing Log Files with the Console Application

The Console application, launched from Applications/Utilities, is a one-step log review tool, providing quick access to all Mac OS X logs, including system.log. Although system.log lives within the /var/log directory, it's given a special entry in Console outside that hierarchy—a sign of how common it is to review this useful log. As shown in Figure 6-18, Console lists all available logs in a single, collapsible interface.

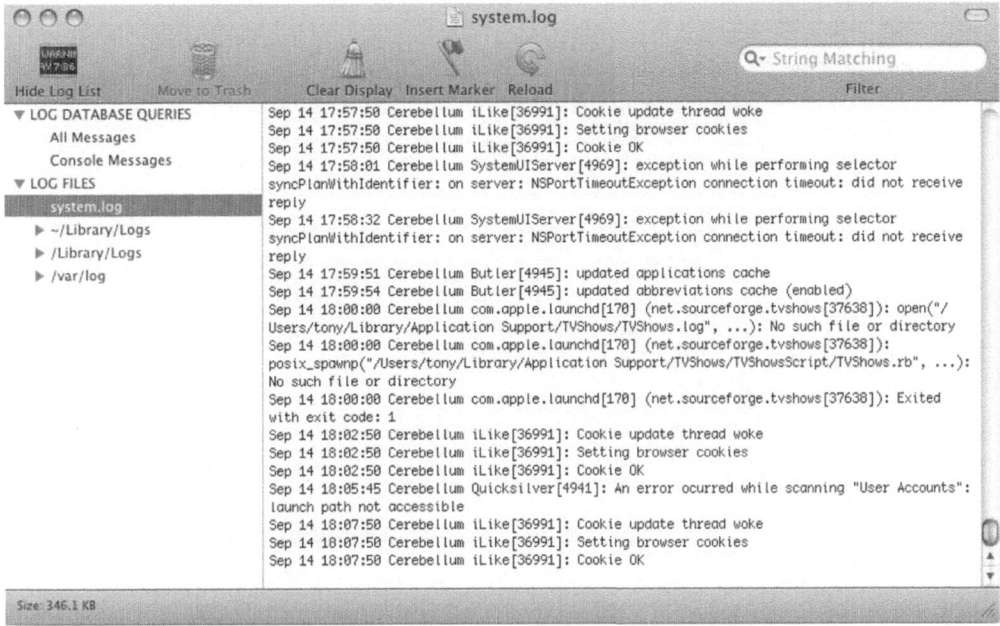

Figure 6-18. *Using the Mac OS X Console application to review the system.log file*

Like other Mac OS X applications, Console includes a search box to ease string searching while analyzing logs. Figure 6-19 shows Console's menu bar, including the search box.

Figure 6-19. *The menu bar of Mac OS X's Console application*

When reviewing or monitoring logs in real time, you can mark the start time. This is done using the Insert Marker button on the menu bar and results in a marked start time like that shown in Figure 6-20.

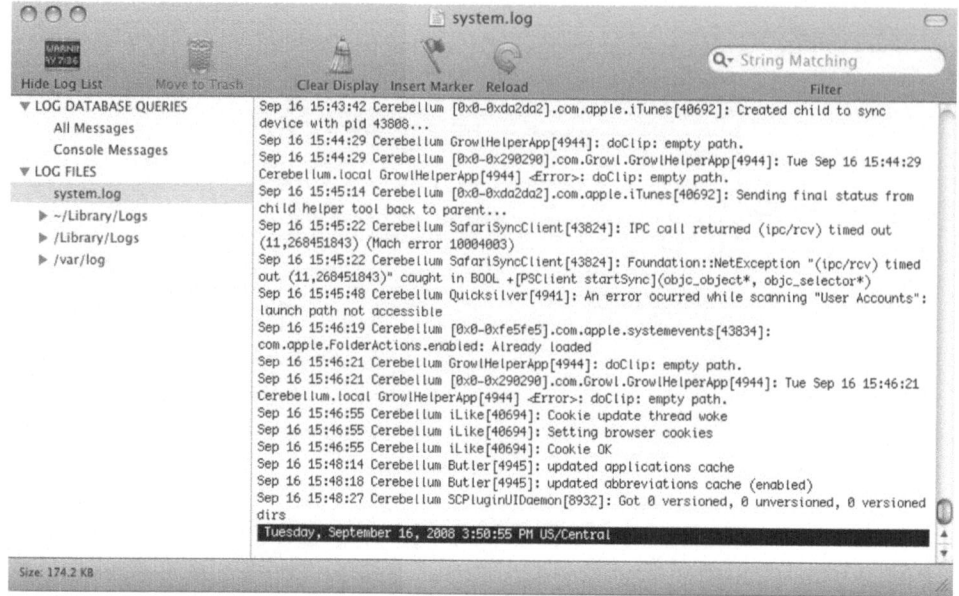

Figure 6-20. *Marking where a real-time log review begins, using the Insert Marker button*

It's also possible to hide the sidebar that lists all the logs. Clicking the Hide Log List button on the menu bar provides a full window of log messages for the current log, as shown in Figure 6-21. When clicked, the Hide Log List button changes to Show Log List, allowing the user to redisplay the list of logs at any time.

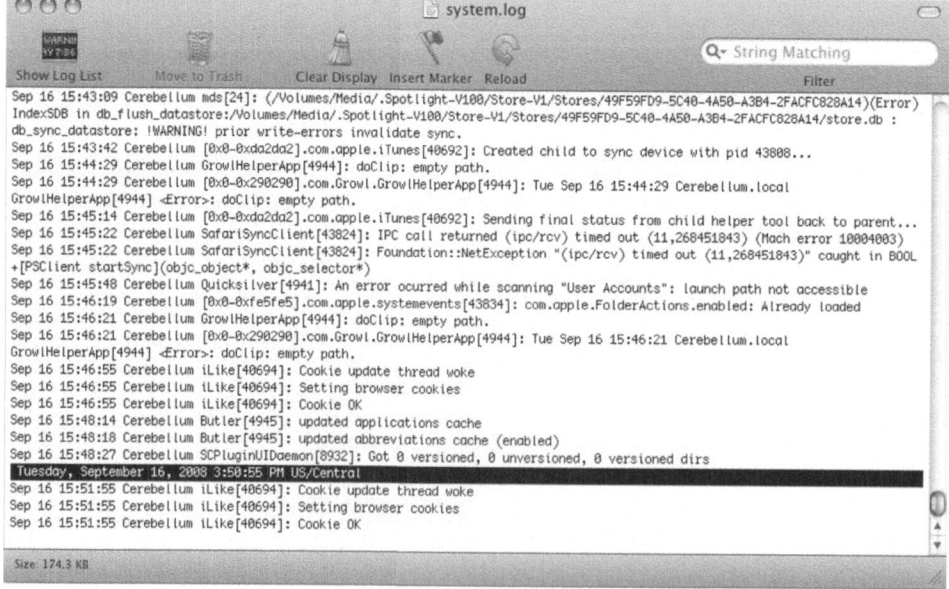

Figure 6-21. *The Mac OS X Console display with the list of logs hidden*

As mentioned, the Console application provides quick access to all Mac OS X logs. These include logs in both the user and system Library directories, and, of course, /var/log.

Any of the logs can be shown in the Finder by right-clicking the log name in Console and selecting Reveal in Finder.

Console also displays any logs that have been archived by the system, including those in /var/log/. Although the archived files are compressed, they're fully readable in Console.

Of course, all logs can also be viewed using your favorite text editor, such as vi or emacs, and UNIX tools, including less, tail, and head.

Managing Tasks with launchd

Beginning with Mac OS X 10.4 (Tiger), Mac OS X officially implemented launchd as a single replacement for both xinetd and cron. As implemented in Mac OS X 10.4, launchd completely replaces the functionality of init.

The launchd system is actually composed of two primary working pieces: launchd and launchctl. launchd runs at bootup, after the boot ROM and BootX/boot.efi complete their initial tasks. It scans through /System/Library/LaunchDaemons and /Library/LaunchDaemons, and fires up the login window.

In the /System/Library/LaunchDaemons and /Library/LaunchDaemons directories, launchd parses through <i>plist</i> ("Property List") files. These are XML-based files that provide directions for loading applications and scripts, as well as for taking periodic actions. In theory, the plist files are easier to read and create than the scripts traditionally executed by the services launchd is intended to replace.

Let's walk through the pieces of a plist file to demonstrate how they perform periodic tasks.

First, open a text editor and create a file similar to the following:

```
#!/bin/bash

cp /Users/tony/Documents/*.txt /Volumes/ThumbDrive
exit 0
```

This script will copy any files with the .txt extension in the /Users/tony/Documents directory to a USB thumb drive, mounted as /Volumes/ThumbDrive. Place this script in your /Users/[user] directory as copy_files, changing the permissions to allow execution:

```
$ chmod +x /Users/tony/copy_files
```

Next, you need to create a user plist file to provide instructions to launchctl, the other element of the launchd system. In the ~/Library/LaunchAgents directory, create a file similar to this:

```
<?xml version="1.0" encoding="UTF-8"?>
<!DOCTYPE plist PUBLIC "-//Apple Computer//DTD PLIST 1.0//EN"
 "http://www.apple.com/DTDs/PropertyList-1.0.dtd">
<plist version="1.0">
<dict>
<key>Label</key>
    <string>com.UserTony.CopyDocs</string>
    <key>OnDemand</key>
```

```
        <true/>
            <key>ProgramArguments</key>
        <array>
            <string>/Users/tony/scripts/copy_files</string>
        </array>
        <key>WatchPaths</key>
        <array>
            <string>/Users/tony/Documents</string>
        </array>
</dict>
</plist>
```

This file instructs the launchd service to execute the script you just created when a file is found in the WatchPath /User/tony/Documents. As you can see, the file provides keys and action strings. These guide the launchctl application.

You can run this new task using the launchctl application:

```
$ launchctl load ~/Library/LaunchAgents/com.UserTony.CopyDocs.plist
```

This will load the plist file into launchd. When something in the /Users/tony/Documents changes, the /Volumes/ThumbDrive/Documents directory will contain new *.txt files. All correctly coded plist files in the ~/Library/LaunchAgents, /Library/LaunchAgents, and /System/Library/LaunchAgents directories are loaded by launchd when a user logs in at the console. The plist files in /Library/LaunchDaemons and /System/Library/LaunchDaemons are loaded at system startup.

To stop the launchctl application, use the following command:

```
$ launchctl unload -w ~/Library/LaunchAgents/com.UserTony.CopyDocs.plist
```

The -w option will guarantee that the plist file isn't loaded the next time the system boots. This also sets a persistent file flag. That means that in order to load the plist file again, you'll need to launch it as follows, with the -w option:

```
$ launchctl load -w ~/Library/LaunchAgents/com.UserTony.CopyDocs.plist
```

This will remove the "ignore at boot" flag, which is a key in the plist: <key>Disabled</key><true/>.

Note As Darwin is BSD, cron still exists in Mac OS X. As in BSD, the crontab file is edited using the crontab -e command, and is available on a system or user level. If you're modifying cron at the system level, you'll need to initiate the edit command using sudo.

---

launchd utilizes the configuration file /etc/launchd.conf. All the launchd elements expose appropriate man files for a complete explanation of the functions and use. Those include launchd.plist, launchd debugd, and launchctl.

Administering Shared Resources

Another important system administration task is managing shared resources. It's already common in the workplace to share resources across a network. With multiple computers in the house and the simplicity of wireless home networks, home users are also increasingly sharing networked resources, including printers, storage, and multimedia libraries. That wireless sharing can, of course, come at a price for security—a topic we'll discuss in the next chapter. For now, let's look at the resources typically shared across a network, and how to configure and administer those resources on a Mac OS X system.

Mac OS X and Web Servers

Perhaps the best-known shared resource in modern computing is the web server. Few shared resources on any platform have had more impact on computing. Mac OS X, like its BSD and Linux brethren, is fully capable of providing the resources to serve up web pages and web applications. In fact, much of what's needed to put a Mac OS X machine on the Web is included in the initial installation.

A default Mac OS X installation includes the Apache web server, PHP, Perl, and MySQL. Those are the fundamental elements of MAMP: Mac, Apache, MySQL, and PHP (or Perl). It's possible to get this default installation up and running fairly quickly on your Mac with minimal configuration.

Configuring the Default Installation

In order to configure, test, and use the Apache server installed on your Mac, you'll need to reconfigure the sharing and security options in Mac OS X System Preferences. To allow access to the web server, select Sharing from System Preferences, and check the Web Sharing box. This will also set access to the server in the Security section of System Preferences. You can confirm the firewall settings by selecting Security from the System Preferences and clicking the Firewall tab. Web Sharing will be displayed as an allowed option in the security settings.

The MAMP tools included in Mac OS X look much the same to an administrator as the tools in a Linux or BSD system. The biggest difference between a MAMP system and the Linux and BSD tools is file location. As you've seen with other Mac OS X files, Apple follows a marginally different file structure. Some critical configuration files are located in different paths on the Mac than you've come to expect on Linux or BSD machines.

The most important of those critical configuration files is the `httpd.conf` file. In Mac OS X 10.5, this file is located at `/etc/apache2/httpd.conf`. As with other systems, this is the primary configuration file for the default Apache installation in Mac OS X. Other than the location of the file, it's identical to the one in other Apache installations. If you've configured Apache on other systems, configuring it in Mac OS X should be painless.

In general, Apache is configured by providing a series of *directives* for the server operation in the configuration file. These include the location of the root server directory, the ports on which the server will listen for requests, any task-specific modules that will be implemented in the server operation, users, and custom directory structures. The Apache project provides an outstanding configuration overview at `http://httpd.apache.org/docs/2.0/configuring.html`.

The range of options available to an Apache administrator—whether on a Linux, BSD, or Mac system—is huge and well beyond the scope of this book. With that disclaimer made, there are a few configuration options that will interest nearly any administrator.

The first thing you'll want to do for a MAMP system is to enable PHP 5. This is disabled by default in the Mac OS X installation. To enable it, open the /etc/apache2/httpd.conf file in a text editor and uncomment the line containing the following:

```
LoadModule php5_module       libexec/apache2/libphp5.so
```

Then start or restart the server with the following command:

```
$ sudo apachectl [re]start
```

It's also possible to create virtual sites with Apache in Mac OS X. This allows deep customization by web site, while maintaining a configuration file structure that's easy to follow and maintain. Several virtual sites can run from the same MAMP-installed machine with a simple configuration. Here's how to create a virtual site:

1. Create a new file named _sites.conf in the /Users/[*your user*]/Sites directory.

2. Add the following to the _sites.conf file to enable virtual hosts in your Apache installation and to create a test site for development:

   ```
   # Enable named virtual hosts
   NameVirtualHost *:80

   # Override the default httpd.conf directives.  Make sure to
   # use 'Allow from all' to prevent 403 Forbidden message.
   <Directory />
       Options ExecCGI FollowSymLinks
       AllowOverride all
       Allow from all
   </Directory>

   # A basic virtual host config
   <VirtualHost *:80>
       # Add yoursite to your /etc/hosts file so you can
       # type it directly in your browser
       ServerName yoursite

       DocumentRoot /Users/[your user]/Sites/[your site]
   </VirtualHost>
   ```

3. Add the following to the bottom of the httpd.conf file:

   ```
   Include /Users/yourusername/Sites/_sites.conf
   ```

4. Start or restart the Apache server with the following command:

   ```
   $ sudo apachectl [re]start
   ```

This virtual hosts example can serve as a model for other hosts on the system. Those hosts will be added to the _sites.conf file.

■**Caution** When configuring a virtual host that will be live on the Internet, it's not recommended that you set the `DocumentRoot` in your home directory, as shown in the example here. Instead, it's a good idea to create a directory on the system that will be accessible to the web user account (www by default in Mac OS X), and that is, in effect, segregated from the rest of the system.

This is a basic configuration for a development system. A full discussion of the configuration files and directives can be found on the Apache site at `http://httpd.apache.org/docs/1.3/configuring.html`.

As is the case with many of the software packages for Mac OS X, Apache, PHP, and MySQL are available as source packages. These can be downloaded, built, and installed with many customizations, according to your specific needs.

Installing Apache from Source

The Apache source is available from the Apache Project downloads page at `http://httpd.apache.org/download.cgi`. These are UNIX source files, provided in the `.tar.gz` format. When downloaded, the file is extracted using the following command:

```
$ tar zxvf httpd-[version number].tar.gz
```

This creates an `httpd` directory containing the source files. To configure, build, and install these files, use the following commands:

```
$ cd httpd-[version number]
$ ./configure -prefix=PREFIX
$ make
$ sudo make install
```

`PREFIX` provides the server installation path, if you would prefer installation at a location other than the default of `/usr/local/apache2`. If, for example, you set the prefix to `/usr/local/`, the install script will create the appropriate subdirectories within that path. The `httpd.conf` configuration file, in that case, would be located at `/usr/local/conf/httpd.conf`.

You can test the new Apache installation with the following command:

```
$ PREFIX/bin/apachectl -k start
```

This will start the server with a web page accessible at `http://localhost/`.

Installing PHP from Source

The latest PHP source code is available from the PHP site at `http://www.php.net/downloads.php`. The code is available in both `.tar bz2` and `.tar.gz` formats. To unpack the `.bz2` format files, use the following command:

```
$ tar vxjpf php-[version number].tar.bz2
```

Unpack the `.tar.gz` files with the following command:

```
$ tar zxvf php-[version number].tar.gz
```

As with Apache, the PHP code is built and installed with the following commands:

```
$ ./configure
$ make
$ sudo make install
```

Installing MySQL from Source

MySQL source code is available from the MySQL downloads page at http://dev.mysql.com/downloads/mysql/5.1.html#downloads. Unlike Apache and PHP, MySQL is available for download as both a .dmg image file and as a source file. In either case, you may need to register in order to download the files.

The .dmg file contains an installer file. With the image mounted, double-click the installer and follow the directions for installation.

As with the Apache and PHP source, the source files can be unpacked, built, and installed with the following commands:

```
$ tar zxvf  mysql-[version number].tar.gz
$ cd mysql-[version number]
$ ./configure -prefix=PREFIX
$ make
$ sudo make install
```

Configuring the Apache, MySQL, and PHP setup on the Mac is, in most other ways, identical to the process in Linux. For a more detailed view of building, configuring, and administering your server, please refer to *Beginning PHP and MySQL: From Novice to Professional, Third Edition*, by W. Jason Gilmore (Apress, 2008).

Using the MAMP Application

Another option exists for building and installing a web server on your Mac OS X machine. Developed by Living-e, the MAMP application is a single binary file containing Apache, PHP, and MySQL for the Mac. It also contains the PHPMyAdmin application for creating and maintaining MySQL databases.

The download from Living-e is dual-purpose, providing both the basic MAMP application and the MAMP PRO application. According to the Living-e web site, the PRO version is the "commercial, professional grade version" of MAMP.

To install MAMP, download the MAMP application from http://mamp.info/en/download.html, double-click the .dmg file, and drag the MAMP application to your Applications folder.

Printer Sharing

You can configure network printer sharing in Mac OS X in a number of ways. Sharing with fellow Mac users is configured most easily and quickly using the Print & Fax GUI tools in System Preferences. Sharing with Windows users on the network is also easiest to set up using the GUI, although the sharing tool in the background will be Server Message Block (SMB). Sharing with Linux, UNIX, or other Mac users can be easily accomplished with Common UNIX Printing System (CUPS) or Line Printer Daemon/Line Printer Remote (LPD/LPR). Let's walk through the graphical options for sharing the printer.

Sharing a Mac-Connected Printer

Sharing a printer connected to a Mac OS X system using the GUI is very easy. The GUI tool will make the printer available on the network and visible to Mac, Windows, and Linux users alike. In the System Preferences window, select Print & Fax. If you currently have a printer attached to the Mac, you'll see it listed in the left pane of the Print & Fax window, as shown in Figure 6-22.

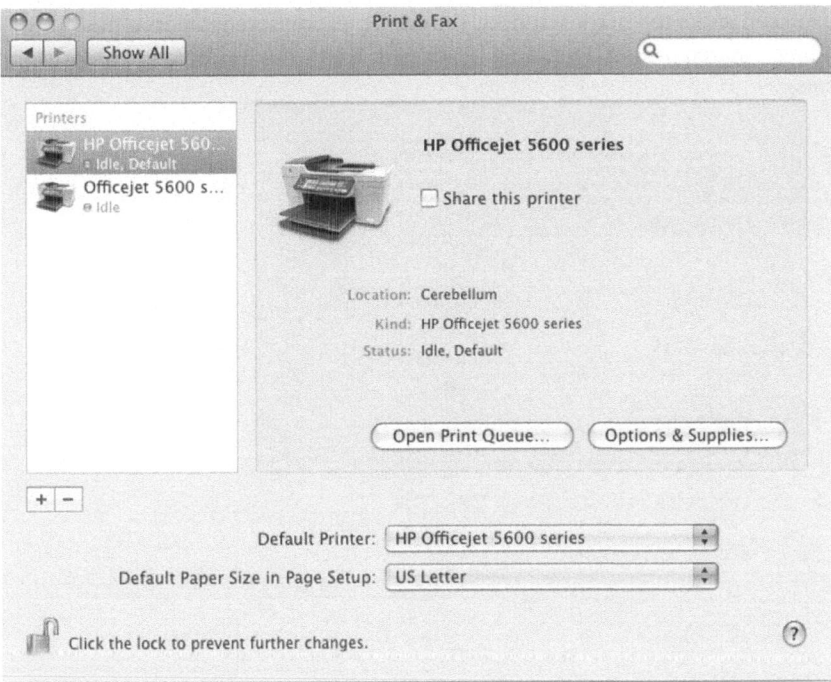

Figure 6-22. *The Print & Fax window in System Preferences. A combination printer/fax machine is displayed in the left pane as two separate devices.*

If you have not added a printer to the system, the left pane will be empty. You can add a printer by clicking the plus sign at the bottom of the printer pane and following the directions that appear.

The example in Figure 6-22 shows that I'm using an HP printer/fax combo—an HP Office-Jet 5610. This particular printer is a printer/fax/scanner combination. The printer and fax machine show up as separate items in the pane, to facilitate providing separate configurations for these two devices. However, the printer itself is the default, as noted in the caption under the printer in the printer pane, reading, "Idle, Default." Both are currently connected and operational, as indicated by the green light to the left of the status message for both the printer and the fax.

As you can see from Figure 6-22, sharing a printer with other Mac or Linux computers on the network is very easy. Select the Share this printer check box in the main printer window to make it available on the network. This will make the printer available to all other Mac and Linux computers on the network.

Connecting a Mac Client to a Shared Printer

To use a shared printer on another Mac on the network, you'll just need to open System Preferences, select Print & Fax, and add the printer (by clicking the plus sign in the printer pane). The Mac will connect to the printer. Set it as the default printer by right-clicking the printer icon in the printer pane and selecting Set default printer. The client Mac will now use the shared network printer as the default.

Figure 6-23 shows an example of adding a shared printer to another computer on the network using LPD. As seen at the top of the window, the configuration screen offers a multitude of options for adding a shared printer, including IP address, Bluetooth, AppleTalk, and other common protocols.

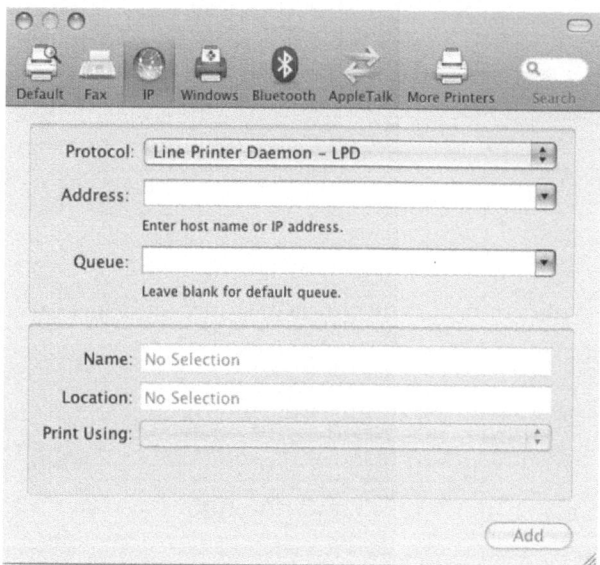

Figure 6-23. *Adding a networked printer to a Mac client machine via the System Preferences/Print & Fax tool*

Connecting a Windows Client to a Shared Printer

To use a newly shared printer with a Windows machine on the network, you'll need some additional configuration to share the printer attached to the Mac via SMB. Here are the steps:

1. Open the Mac System Preferences window and select Sharing.

2. Check the File Sharing and Printer Sharing options in the left pane.

3. Highlight the Printer Sharing option and select the printer to be shared by checking the check box.

4. Highlight the File Sharing option and click Options.

5. Select the user who will be allowed to connect to the printer by checking the appropriate check box.

6. Enter the user's password in the pop-up window.

7. Check the "Share files and folders using SMB" option.

8. Close the Sharing window.

9. Set up the Windows printing client from the Windows machine.

SMB File Sharing

Setting up SMB file sharing on the Mac is as simple as setting up printer sharing. In fact, if you've set up printer sharing from a Windows machine, you've already accomplished much of the process. Here are the steps:

1. Open the Mac System Preferences window and select Sharing.

2. Check the File Sharing option in the left pane.

3. Highlight the File Sharing option and click Options.

4. Select the "Share files and folders using SMB" option.

5. Select the user account that will be used to access the shared files and folders, and then click Done.

6. Check the list of shared folders in the small Shared Folders subwindow.

7. Optionally, remove a folder you would prefer not to share by highlighting the folder and clicking the minus button at the bottom of the Shared Folders window.

8. To add a shared folder, click the plus button, select the folder to which you would like to provide shared access, and then click Add.

9. If you would like to require the administrative password in order to make future changes, click the lock icon in the lower-left corner of the Sharing window.

These shared folders can be mapped as drives to a client Windows machine or added to shared directories on a Linux machine, without further modification on the Mac. This process shares the folders and files via SMB.

NFS File Sharing

Setting up Network File System (NFS) file sharing on the Mac is nearly as simple as setting up SMB sharing. It's best done from the command line, using the following instructions:

1. Open a terminal window.

2. Edit the /etc/exports file, adding the following line, using values specific to your network:

```
$ /Users/[shared directory] -network 192.168.1.0 -mask 255.255.255.0
```

3. Ensure that the nfsd daemon is enabled with the following command:

```
$ sudo nfsd enable
```

This example will require customization of the directory you would like to share, and assumes that your local network is a 192.168.10.x network. Adjust your entries accordingly.

You can test whether the NFS mount is actually enabled with the following command:

```
$ showmount -e
```

If the configuration is successful, the output from the showmount command will display the shared directory and the network on which it's shared. And, with that simple configuration, other machines on the network can now connect to the shared directory on the Mac using NFS.

Summary

In this chapter, we've covered the fundamentals of system administration on the Mac. In general, you'll find that Mac OS X provides the common UNIX/BSD/Linux command-line tools for system administration. Beyond those tools, Mac OS X also offers a robust set of GUI-based system administration tools.

Mac OS X provides a full range of shells, including bash, tcsh, csh, ksh, and zsh. Although bash is the default shell for Mac OS X, you can easily configure the system to make any of the other provided shells the default.

A number of commands are available in Mac OS X that are commonly used for system administration. These commands are common to most UNIX/BSD systems, and provide a near seamless administrative experience for those most familiar with UNIX, BSD, and Linux. These and other system tools can be fully explored using the installed man page system.

As with so many of the other tasks, Mac OS X offers both graphical and command-line options to monitor the system. The Mac OS X Activity Monitor tool provides a wealth of information about the current state of the system within a single window. This includes information about the running processes, processor use, and memory use. As a BSD-based system, Mac OS X also provides the common system monitoring tools top and ps to monitor the system from the command line.

Mac OS X can also function as a "headless" system, bypassing the Aqua interface altogether. In this command-line-only mode, Mac OS X can provide a variety of network server functions.

Mac OS X provides several means to add and maintain system users. The GUI Accounts tool in System Preferences allows a system administrator to add and remove users with a few mouse clicks. Users can also select applications to run at login with this tool. While a bit more complex, user maintenance can also be performed from the command line, primarily using the dscl tool.

That BSD base provides other familiar functionality for Linux system administrators. Log files are located in the standard location: /var/log. An administrator can use BSD tools to review the logs, or can choose to use the Mac Console application, a log review tool that brings all system logs into a single interface. Console also allows an administrator to monitor logs in real time, and to mark the starting point at which the real time review began.

Apple's launchd application is currently a drop-in replacement for the init and cron services of BSD. Using an XML-based system, launchd reads through both system and user plist files to execute and schedule tasks on the system. The inclusion of launchd beginning with Mac OS X 10.4 (Tiger) is the first step in the consolidation of several BSD tools into a single utility.

Finally, Mac OS X is a complete system for printer and file sharing. SMB and NFS comprise the primary means to share printers and files, with Mac OS X again providing both GUI and command-line tools for configuration.

In the next chapter, we'll continue with the important system administration tasks of handling backups and security.

CHAPTER 7

■ ■ ■

Backup, Security, and Automation

Among all the tasks performed by system administrators, few are more important or more mundane than those pertaining to backup, security, and automation. Protecting data, both from catastrophic crashes and from unfriendly intruders, is more critical than ever. As storage capacities have increased, more data is stored on single drives, vulnerable to hardware failure. As more computer users maintain full-time network connections, more computers are vulnerable to attack. Implementing measures to prevent or mitigate the damage from these events is the task of every system administrator, whether administering a small home network or a massive corporate network.

Backup tasks can be created, thoroughly tested, and scheduled, requiring only minimal additional human intervention. Security measures can be implemented and monitored with little further effort. In other words, the ability to automate both backup and security tasks greatly improves the probability that these critical tasks will be successful.

In this chapter, we'll take an in-depth look at the range of tools available to accomplish backup and security tasks, both in GUI form and from the Darwin-based command line. We'll also explore the options for testing and automating backup tasks, for recovering data, and for providing the highest practical level of security on your Mac OS X-based system.

Backup and Recovery Overview

As a computer user of any stripe, it's an admonition you've heard regularly: back up your data. If you've never lost data on your system, either you're not a real power user or you're extremely lucky. Most users like us—those who are prone to dig deeply into a system in search of the perfect tweak—have lost important, irreplaceable data at some point in our computing lives. Unfortunately, that critical data loss is usually what it takes to make the case for the importance of regular data backups.

So, assuming that you understand and believe in the importance of these regular backups, you're certainly wondering what tools exist in Mac OS X to achieve those backups with minimal muss and fuss. How can you configure regular backups? What are the best options for creating and administering those backups? How can these backups be automated and scheduled for routine background operation? Which backup type makes the most sense for specific data types? In the event of a disaster, what's the best way to recover these backups? What are the best Mac OS X tools? What are the best command-line tools? These are all critical questions and, of course, questions that are best answered before a catastrophic crash rather than after.

Fortunately, Mac OS X provides a wide range of backup and recovery options, in both GUI form and as UNIX-based command-line Darwin tools. All the various options can be scheduled to perform backups regularly without further intervention, using launchd or cron. And, with straightforward recovery options, you can feel comfortable that your critical data won't be lost on your Mac OS X system.

The Mac Approach to Backup and Recovery

As you might guess, many of the best native Mac OS X backup options are GUI-based. Mac OS X itself includes an outstanding and easy-to-use backup tool, and many third-party tools provide similar or more powerful backup and recovery features. Let's start with the built-in Mac OS X tool for backup and recovery.

Time Machine Backups

With the launch of Mac OS X 10.5 (Leopard), Apple released a native backup tool that is both robust and easy to configure. Time Machine, the Mac OS X native backup tool, was one of the most highly anticipated and widely praised elements of the Leopard release. By automatically scheduling hourly backups to an external drive or to another Mac using the Personal File Sharing service, Time Machine made the tedious task of backup creation infinitely easier for all users. By doing so, Apple all but guaranteed that users of its operating system would no longer lose critical data, either as a result of human error or a system crash.

The process of creating Time Machine backups is, in fact, invisible to the user. It requires only an easy, one-time setup. Unless an accidental deletion or system crash occurs, Time Machine requires no further attention. It creates and maintains incremental backups, accounting for the amount of storage remaining on the external drive. These backups can be full-drive backups or may exclude specific user-configured files. Furthermore, these backups can be stored on an external drive that's hard-wired to the machine—USB or FireWire—or sent to a network storage device, either wired or wireless. In fact, a network of Mac computers within a home can back up to the same dedicated network backup device, with backup profiles for each individual machine.

Mac OS X provides tools to restore any piece or all of each Time Machine backup. Individual files can be recovered easily using the Time Machine GUI. Entire systems can be restored using the Mac OS X Utilities menu. Overall, Time Machine provides seamless backups and easy restoration of lost system files.

Time Machine is accessible either from a menu or from the System Preferences window. Figure 7-1 shows the System Preferences window with the Time Machine option.

Figure 7-1. *The Time Machine option in the System Preferences window*

Configuring Backups

By design, the Time Machine setup window is clean and simple, as shown in Figure 7-2. As the window states, by default, Time Machine creates hourly incremental backups for the past 24 hours, daily backups for the past month, and weekly backups for anything older than a month.

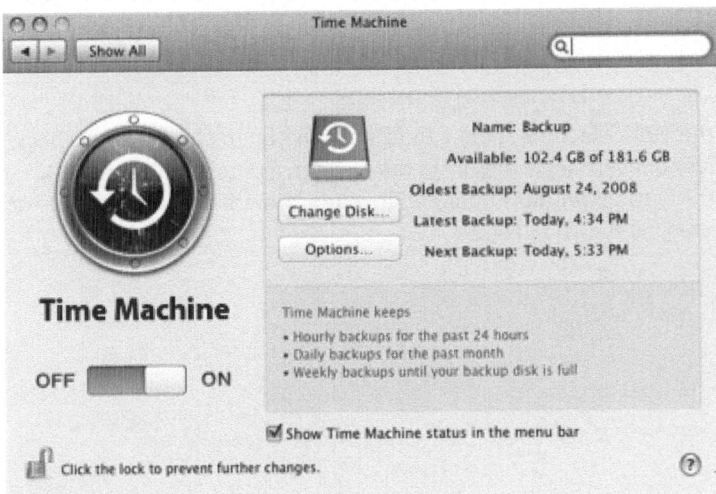

Figure 7-2. *The Time Machine setup window*

When clicked, the Change Disk button reveals all the drives the system can use to store backups, as shown in Figure 7-3. It also provides an option to set up Time Capsule. Time Capsule is Mac hardware, purchased separately and created specifically for use as a networked Time Machine backup drive.

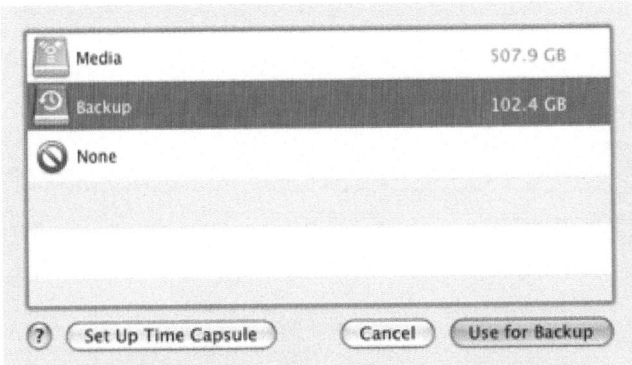

Figure 7-3. *Configuring the Time Machine backup drive*

Note Time Capsule is, in reality, Apple's entry into the Network Accessible Storage (NAS) arena. The Time Capsule hardware provides 500GB or 1TB of storage, accessible from any other machines on the network. With four Ethernet ports, it also works as an AirPort device, serving as an internal router for your home network. Additionally, it features wireless capabilities, with full 802.11 a/b/g/n support. Prices range from $300 to $500 US.

The Options button in the Time Machine setup window allows you to customize the backups, excluding complete drives or even single files from the backup, as shown in Figure 7-4. Clicking the plus button in the Options window opens a filesystem view, from which the file or drive exclusions can be selected, as shown in Figure 7-5.

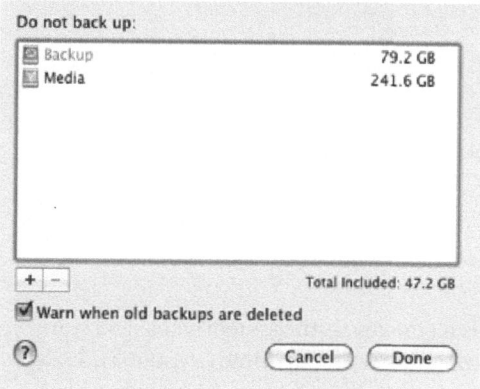

Figure 7-4. *Time Machine backup options*

Figure 7-5. *Selecting files or drives to exclude from Time Machine backups*

Time Machine can be turned on from the main window when the backups are configured properly. Or, if desired, the backups can be turned off from the same window. Figure 7-6 shows the Time Machine On/Off control.

Figure 7-6. *Turning on the Time Machine backups*

Note As with any other backups, the Time Machine backups will become quite large over time. However, these backups are intelligent, in that Time Machine is aware of the remaining space on the Time Machine drive. When backups threaten to fill the disk, Time Machine will warn the user that older backups will be deleted in order to create new ones. In any event, an external drive of less than 300GB is probably impractical if your intent is to create regular full-system backups.

Recovering Time Machine Backups

Recovering files from a Time Machine backup is as easy as the setup. The recovery interface can be launched from the `Applications` directory.

Shown in Figure 7-7, the Time Machine recovery window takes its own metaphor to the fullest possible extent. The cascade of windows in the center of the recovery window represent all the backups created by Time Machine back in time. These backups are also accessible by date, simply by rolling the mouse over the vertical timeline on the right edge of the recovery window. You can scroll through the windows using the arrows to the lower right of the cascaded windows, and select a specific window by clicking with the mouse, or you can click a specific backup along the vertical timeline. When the preferred backup is available, a file or files can be restored from that backup by selecting the file and clicking Restore in the recovery window.

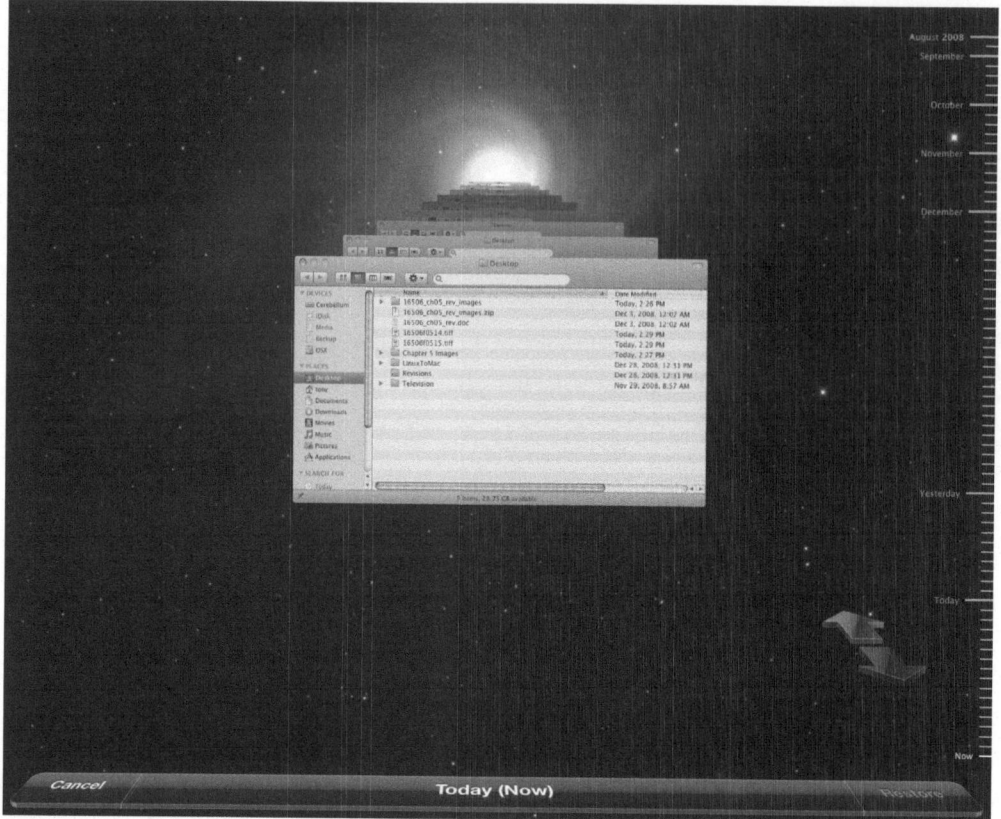

Figure 7-7. *The Time Machine recovery window*

Full, bootable system backups cannot be restored from the recovery window. In the event of a catastrophic system failure, you will need to restart the system with the installation DVD. Insert the installation DVD in the drive, and then restart the Mac. As the system starts, hold down the C button. This will start the system from the DVD, presenting the main screen. With the system booted from the installation DVD, select Utilities, and then choose Restore from Time Machine. When prompted, select a system backup to restore. These backups will be listed by the date on which they were created, and will be listed under the name of the system boot volume. Depending on the size of the system, this restoration may take well more than an hour. When the restoration is complete, you'll reboot into your restored Mac OS X system.

How Does Time Machine Do That?

As noted, Time Machine creates incremental backups, but these aren't your typical backups, as you'll see if you take a look inside the backup directories. A complete backup of the system appears to live within each instance of a backup, as shown in Figure 7-8. It doesn't seem possible that a full backup could be completed every hour, without filling up the available space on a backup drive within a matter of days. But, as noted, Time Machine isn't really doing full backups—it's doing incremental backups. And, it's doing them in a way that makes full use of UNIX file structure and permissions.

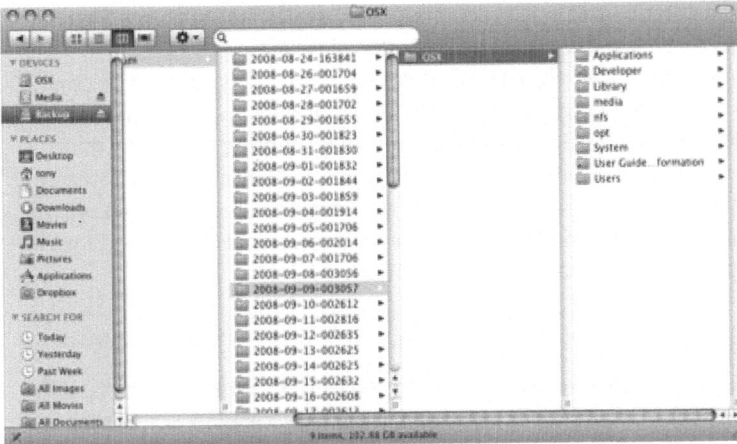

Figure 7-8. *A look inside the Time Machine backup directories*

Time Machine uses hard links in its backups. Hard links and symbolic links are integral in UNIX filesystems.

A *symbolic link*, or *symlink*, is a pointer to another file. A symlink returned in a command-line ls -l command is shown with an l in the file type slot of the file description, which is the first position. Symlinks don't contain the file data. They only point to the location of the data. At their simplest, symlinks can be thought of as shortcuts. They're files that point to the location of other files. Symlinks can be moved within a filesystem structure and will still work as shortcuts to the original file. For example, I can create a /Users/tony/scripts/test_script file that echoes a string on execution. I can then symlink that file to /Users/tony/linked_file, using this command:

```
$ ln -s /Users/tony/scripts/test_script /Users/tony/linked_file.
```

The s in the command denotes a symbolic link. The latter—the pointer file—will inherit the permissions of the former and, when executed, will actually execute the original file. If the /Users/tony/linked_file file is moved elsewhere on the system, it will still execute the original file. However, if the original file is removed, the symlink is broken, and the symlinked file will no longer work. So, in practice, you have one real file and one that's just a pointer to the other. The pointer will not work if the actual file is gone, although the actual file will still work with or without the pointer.

A *hard link*, as utilized in Time Machine, represents a second name for the same data. In other words, by creating a second name, the system sees two distinct files for the same data. The data in a single location on a disk can be accessed using either name. In other words, unlike symlinks that link to other files, hard links link to actual data. These hard links are created by issuing the ls command without any further options:

```
$ ln /Users/tony/scripts/test_script /Users/tony/linked_file
```

The return of the ls -l command on the /Users/tony/linked_file file really tells the tale. Unlike the symlink created earlier, the ls -l command returns a file, not a link. Provided executable permissions have been set, both files can be executed with the same result. Either file can go away, leaving the other completely executable. They are, in fact, separate files that execute the same data stored in the same location on the disk.

That's how Time Machine manages to create what appear to be full backups. The system creates hard links for files that haven't changed since the previous backup. Those hard links have the same names as the original file but are, in fact, new files pointing to existing data. These files require no more space on the drive than the originals, as they access the same data at the same location. Only those files that have been modified since the previous backup are actually included in the Time Machine backups. Every file on the system is accounted for, although it may not occupy additional space in the backup.

Note The concept of hard links is much more familiar to you than you might realize. A normal file in the filesystem is actually a hard link. If you create a file on the system, it's actually a link to a data location on the drive. It's also possible, using the `ls -l` command, to see how many files actually link to that data. `ls -l` returns a number in the field between the permissions strings and the file owner. This number indicates how many files link to that data on the drive.

For Time Machine backups, Apple uses a slight modification to the UNIX standard for hard links. In a normal UNIX system, hard links can be created only on files. Mac OS X extends this to include folders as well. That's the final piece that makes Time Machine backups possible.

In short, Time Machine is a robust and transparent way to create and restore regular system backups. Those backups can include everything on the system, from single individual files to a full, bootable operating system restoration. And by using hard links, those backups make the most use of drive space.

Many Mac OS X users, myself included, prefer to create full, bootable system backups independent of Time Machine. I tend to lean on Time Machine to restore those occasional file "gotchas," leaving the larger system backups to other stand-alone tools. Several tools from third-party developers utilize many of the best elements of the UNIX system. They're easily configurable to meet specific backup needs. Almost all incorporate the ability to schedule backups and to define those schedules from an easy-to-use interface. And, fortunately, many of these tools are free.

Backups with Carbon Copy Cloner

With the UNIX underpinnings of Mac OS X, many of the Mac OS X backup applications ultimately rely on the same tools that Linux administrators have been using for years, but do so from clean and fully functional GUI interfaces. Some administrators, in fact, find that the GUI tools actually help improve the efficiency of their administration tasks.

One such tool is Carbon Copy Cloner (CCC) from Bombich Software (http://www.bombich.com/software/ccc.html). As the name implies, CCC is intended as a tool to copy drives, or clone them. Its main interface is shown in Figure 7-9.

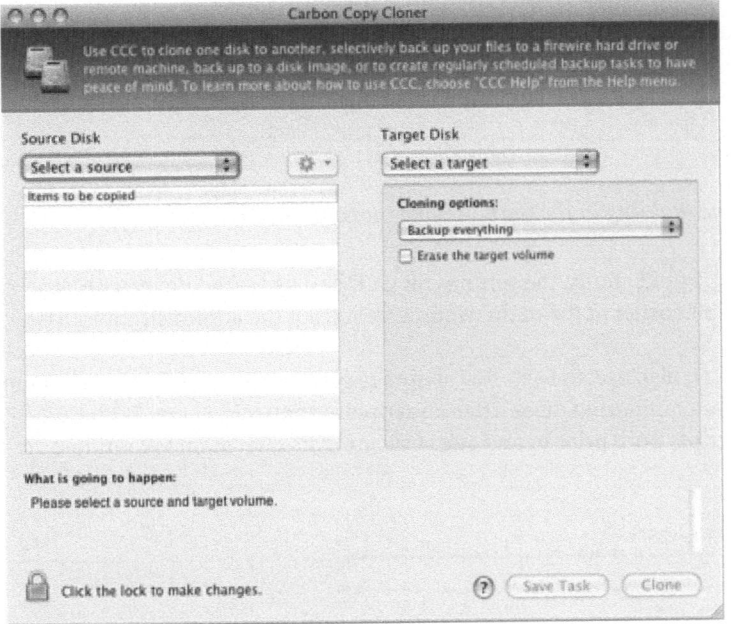

Figure 7-9. *The main interface of Bombich's Carbon Copy Cloner*

CCC is analogous to the UNIX tool dd, copying everything from a designated source to a destination, bit by bit. The end result is an exact copy—a clone—residing on the destination. These backups can be blessed by the system to be bootable. They can also be scripted within launchd or /etc/crontab to perform on a regular schedule without further intervention. You can configure the backups as either incremental or full, although the hard-linking capabilities of Time Machine are not present.

As with any other backup tool, it's necessary to select the source files and the target (the volume to which the backup will be written), as shown in Figure 7-10. In CCC, these are selected from drop-down menus in the main window. The Cloning options menu in this window provides options to create a full backup or an incremental backup of selected files. CCC also provides a look ahead at how the selected actions will direct the work flow once they are kicked off by the user, as shown in Figure 7-11.

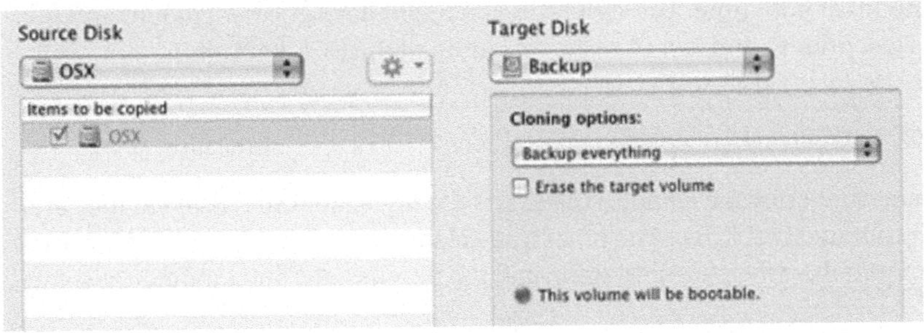

Figure 7-10. *Selecting source and target volumes in Carbon Copy Cloner*

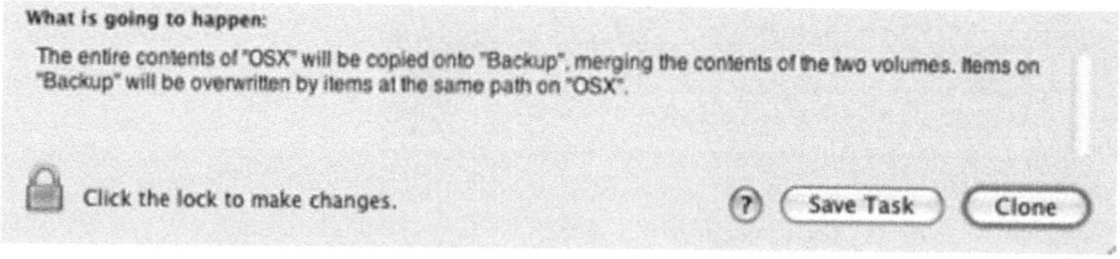

What is going to happen:

The entire contents of "OSX" will be copied onto "Backup", merging the contents of the two volumes. Items on "Backup" will be overwritten by items at the same path on "OSX".

🔒 Click the lock to make changes.   (?) (Save Task) (Clone)

Figure 7-11. *A bit of user hand-holding in the Carbon Copy Cloner main interface*

As with other Mac OS X applications, the settings for CCC can be locked down with the padlock icon in the lower-left corner of the main window, requiring the administrative password for future changes.

As noted earlier, CCC can also execute external scripts to further tailor the operation of the application. The window for configuring these external scripts is shown in Figure 7-12. CCC can execute the external scripts both prior to and after executing its own main operations.

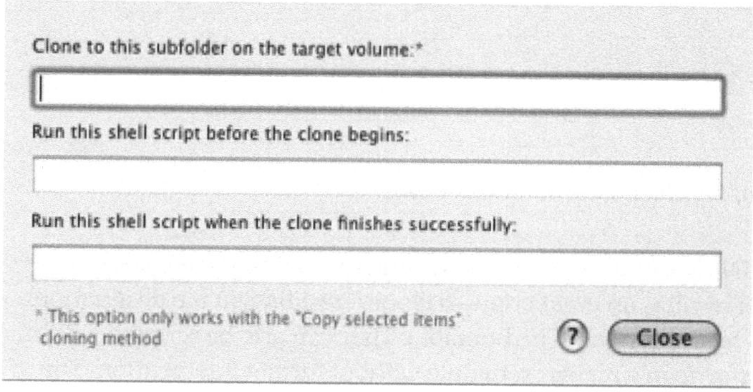

Clone to this subfolder on the target volume:*

Run this shell script before the clone begins:

Run this shell script when the clone finishes successfully:

* This option only works with the "Copy selected items" cloning method   (?) (Close)

Figure 7-12. *The Carbon Copy Cloner advanced options window*

Let's look at an example of running both preexecution and postexecution scripts with CCC. I've partitioned an external FireWire drive on my system specifically for backups, naming it (oddly enough) Backups. However, I prefer that this drive not be mounted and visible on my desktop when it's not actually in use. In other words, I want the Backups drive visible on the desktop only when it's being used as the target for a CCC backup.

To accomplish that, I've created two scripts and an entry in /etc/fstab to ensure that the drive doesn't mount at boot time. The scripts, as you might have guessed, mount and unmount the drive just prior to and just after the execution of the CCC backup.

Let's start with the /etc/fstab entry:

```
UUID=C0D690FF-6DD2-3FD3-AD45-EC1F46FDD3F1          none    hfs     rw,noauto
```

This line contains four critical elements. The first is the drive identifier, listed in the /etc/fstab by universally unique ID (UUID). The other three elements of the /etc/fstab file are the user necessary to mount the drive, the filesystem, and the permissions and automount status of the volume.

You can find the UUID of a drive by using the diskutil tool:

```
$ disktuil list
```

This lists all the available volumes on the system. On my system, Backups is listed among the other drives as disk1s3—partition 3 on the second disk (bearing in mind that zero is significant in volume names). Using diskutil again, I can get further information about that specific partition, including the UUID necessary to modify the /etc/fstab file:

```
$ diskutil info disk1s3
```

```
Device Identifier:      disk1s3
Device Node:            /dev/disk1s3
Part Of Whole:          disk1
Device / Media Name:    Untitled

Volume Name:            Backup
Mount Point:            /Volumes/Backup
File System:            Journaled HFS+
                        Journal size 16384 KB at offset 0x5af000
Owners:                 Enabled

Partition Type:         Apple_HFS
Bootable:               Is bootable
Media Type:             Generic
Protocol:               FireWire
SMART Status:           Not Supported
Volume UUID:            C0D690FF-6DD2-3FD3-AD45-EC1F46FDD3F1

Total Size:             181.6 Gi (194964635648 B) (380790304 512-byte blocks)
Free Space:             102.0 Gi (109536837632 B) (213939136 512-byte blocks)

Read Only:              No
Ejectable:              Yes
Whole:                  No
Internal:               No
```

The volume UUID, in this case, is listed as C0D690FF-6DD2-3FD3-AD45-EC1F46FDD3F1. This is used in the first field of the /etc/fstab file.

With these elements in place in the /etc/fstab file, the Backups drive on my system will not automatically mount when the system is booted.

Two other scripts are necessary to complete the process with CCC. The first mounts the drive:

```
#!/bin/sh

sudo /usr/sbin/diskutil mount disk1s3
```

The script simply uses diskutil to mount (as in Linux) disk1s3—the Backups disk that I'm prevented from mounting at bootup with the modification of /etc/fstab. This script has executable permissions and is written to /Users/tony/scripts/mount_backup.sh.

Finally, a second script will unmount the drive when CCC has completed its cloning operations.

```
#/bin/sh
```

```
sudo /usr/sbin/diskutil umount disk1s3
```

Again, I'm simply using `diskutil` to unmount the volume to which I've just written the backup. With executable permissions, this file is written to `/Users/tony/scripts/umount_backup.sh`.

Finally, I add these scripts to the advanced options window of CCC, as shown in Figure 7-13. With these pieces in place, CCC will mount the Backups drive, execute the backup, and unmount the Backups drive when the backup is complete. If further logging is required, the logging script code can be added to the `umount` script.

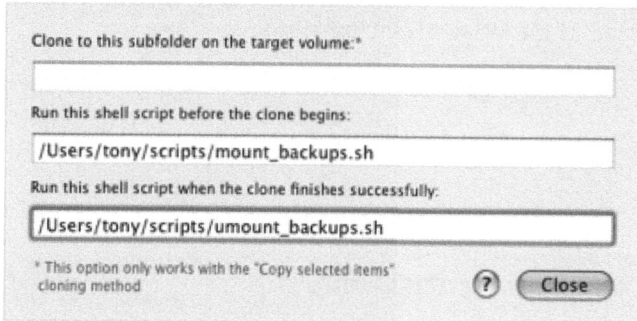

Figure 7-13. *Adding the scripts to the Carbon Copy Cloner advanced options window*

Overall, CCC is a strong backup tool with a focused mission. It's easy to configure and use for most home users.

SuperDuper for Simple Backups

Another simplified backup tool of great use to home users is SuperDuper from Shirt Pocket Software (`http://www.shirt-pocket.com/SuperDuper/SuperDuperDescription.html`). The folks at Shirt Pocket have worked to simplify the SuperDuper interface down to only the tools that are essential for creating robust backups. There's a lot to be said for the elegance of Super-Duper, even if, to some, the application may appear too simple.

SuperDuper presents most of its options in a main window. These include the selection of source and destination drives, as well as the choice of one of a number of scripted options, as shown in Figure 7-14.

SuperDuper takes a unique approach in two of its backup options, in particular. These options, known as *sandboxes*, allow you to create subsets of a normal full backup. The idea is to facilitate "system recovery without downtime" (according to a MacZealots review by Justin Williams, at `http://maczealots.com/reviews/superduper/`).

Figure 7-14. *The main SuperDuper interface*

Creation of a sandbox backup utilizes one of two scripts. One script allows both versions of the system (the sandbox and the current version) to share the current Users and Applications files. The other shares only the Users directory. In other words, you can create a full backup in a sandbox, or a backup that doesn't contain the Applications directory. That can make for a much smaller backup that allows for quicker recovery.

■**Note** While creation of the sandbox backups relies initially on one of two provided scripts, SuperDuper does provide options that allow you to copy and edit all backup scripts. So, while the sandbox scripts provide the initial basis for backups, SuperDuper scripts are, in fact, fully customizable.

The backup options provided in the "using" drop-down menu of the main window include the following:

- Sandbox – shared users (a sandbox with only the Users files)

- Backup all files (full system backup)

- Backup user files (a backup of only the user files)

- Restore – user files

- Restore – all files

- Sandbox – shared users and applications (full backup)

The options menu in SuperDuper provides additional backup customization, in two tabs: General and Advanced. Using the General tab, shown in Figure 7-15, you can repair permissions on the source drive prior to backing up. A completely clean backup can be created, erasing the original backup on the destination drive and starting from scratch. You can also create one of two incremental backup types: one in which only the newer files are copied from the source to the destination, or one in which only files that have changed since the last backup are copied from the source to the new backup.

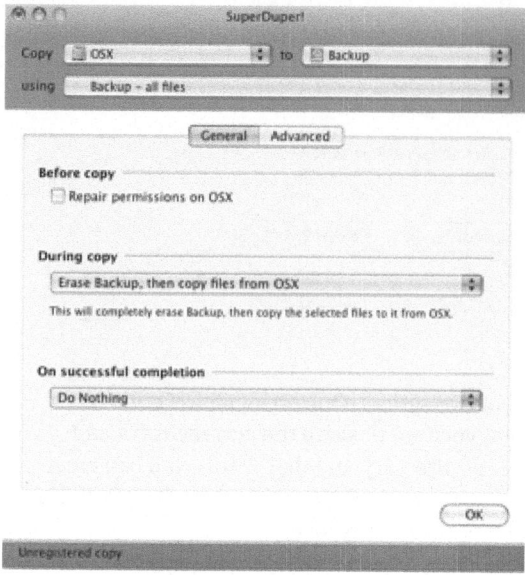

Figure 7-15. *Additional backup options in SuperDuper*

The General tab also provides several options for additional activity after completion of the backup:

- Do Nothing
- Restart from Backup
- Set Backup as Startup Disk
- Shut Down Computer
- Sleep Computer
- Quit SuperDuper!

The Advanced tab offers some powerful options. As with CCC, you can execute custom shell scripts prior to starting the actual backup. Access control lists (ACLs) can be added to the backup. A disk image of the backup can be created and written to a preferred drive or location. A new package can be installed on the backup. And, of course, a shell script can be executed on completion of the backup. In practice, you could use the same method noted in the CCC section to mount and unmount drives before and after the SuperDuper backup.

SuperDuper also includes a tool to schedule backups. Weeks of the month and days of the week are selected by clicking the appropriate button in the interface, as shown in Figure 7-16. Unless a week of the month or a day of the week is selected, the default is to perform the backup every day (all days of all weeks of the month). The backup time can be entered manually or scrolled using the arrow buttons on the right edge of the time field. The caret in the time field indicates the element of the field currently being modified. When the SuperDuper backup schedule is completed, you'll see a window that displays all the scheduled backup operations in table form, as shown in Figure 7-17.

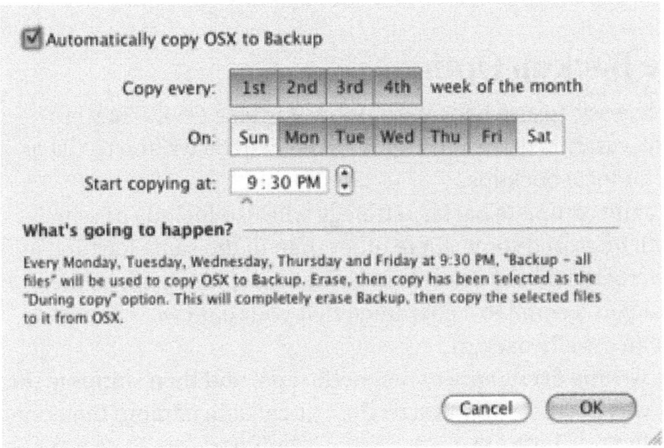

Figure 7-16. *The SuperDuper backup scheduling tool*

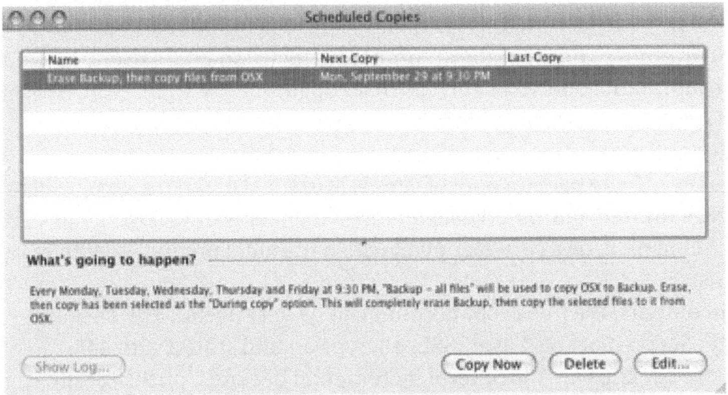

Figure 7-17. *The upcoming scheduled SuperDuper backup operations*

SuperDuper provides a simple backup tool set, while still managing to focus on the most useful options for home Mac OS X users. These options provide real flexibility in how backups are created, run, and stored. They also provide additional power in prebackup and postbackup operations, including custom scripting, backup image creation, and storage of created backups. And SuperDuper provides the tools to create sandbox backups that will considerably shorten the time necessary to recover from many system crashes.

While the tool set is much simpler than that of CCC, SuperDuper still manages to provide considerable power for the user. However, only the most basic of these features are available in the free version. In an approach that's fairly common for Mac OS X software, many of the more advanced features of SuperDuper—including sandbox creation, scheduling, and scripting—require the user to purchase a copy of the software from the Shirt Pocket site. Fortunately, as in most cases, the software pricing is reasonable for the features delivered.

Mozy and Other Off-Site Backup Options

SuperDuper and CCC provide stable, easy-to-use backup solutions for Mac OS X. They create backups that will be stored on an external drive and can, if so desired, be written to CD or DVD. In other words, they're great for local backups.

It's pretty widely accepted that any complete backup strategy will also include off-site backups. These are backups that will be stored somewhere other than in the same location as the machine from which they were created. In the event of a real catastrophe—such as fire, earthquake, or tornado—the closest you'll come to a guarantee that your data will be recoverable and intact is the restoration of an off-site backup.

Off-site backups used to mean writing everything to magnetic tape, and then shipping the tapes off to storage. Even though it was necessary and saved the critical data of more than one company, it was a tedious process that was hated by most system administrators.

However, as the number of broadband connections and the speed of broadband itself have increased, sending off-site backups over the network has become an increasingly popular method of guaranteeing the safety of your critical data. Over the past several years, many companies have sprung up to provide just such services. And, because broadband has moved so quickly into the home environment, many of these companies focus on home users, using easy interfaces and built-in automation. Services such as IBackup (`http://www.ibackup.com`), Mac Backup (`http://www.macbackups.com`), and CrashPlan (`http://crashplan.com`) make the off-site backup process quick and easy.

Another recent entry to the off-site backup pool of sites is Mozy (`http://mozy.com`), which provides 2GB of online storage for free; unlimited backups are $4.95 per month. Users can sign up for a monthly plan, an annual plan, or a two-year plan, with additional pricing incentives available for the longer plans.

For critical data and documents, the free Mozy account can be very useful. The backups are transmitted using 128-bit Secure Sockets Layer (SSL) encryption and stored with 448-bit Blowfish encryption. These backups are block-level incremental backups, pushing only changed or new files to the server.

The Mac Mozy software is well designed and very easy to use. Backups are configured using the main configuration window, as shown in Figure 7-18. Mozy creates backup sets, which are groups of files and folders from your drives that will be backed up as a single unit. This is a convenient and efficient way to group together your most critical files, and to organize your backup structure.

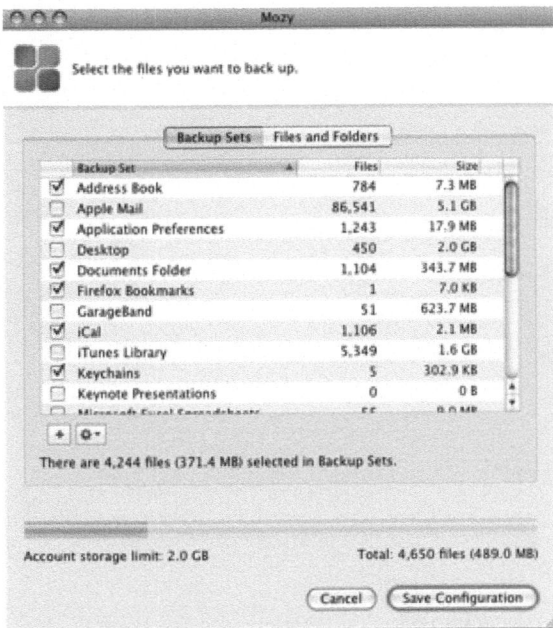

Figure 7-18. *The main Mozy configuration window*

Mozy provides some common backup directories in the initial backup set, including the Address Book, calendars, iTunes library, keychains, pictures folder, Apple mail, and others. These provide a useful starting point for critical backups. To add more backup sets to the main set, simply click the plus sign in the lower left of the main Mozy configuration window. The new group can be named in a way that makes sense to you. Add files to the set by clicking the Browse button under the search box. In Figure 7-19, I'm adding a new backup set named Radioshift Recordings, to include a directory from Radioshift (an automatic streaming audio recorder on my Mac). Figure 7-20 shows the completed new set selected for backup.

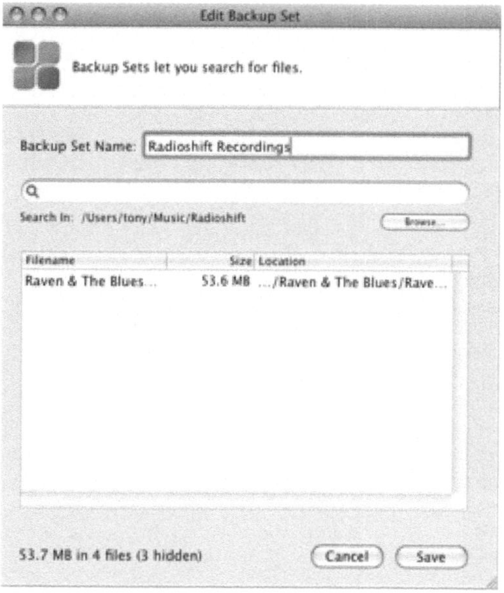

Figure 7-19. *Adding new backup types to a Mozy backup set*

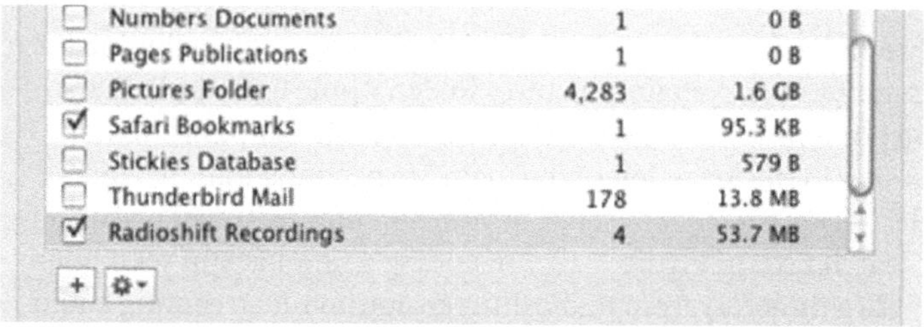

Figure 7-20. *Creating a new backup set in Mozy*

Mozy backups can be completely customized. It's not necessary to stick to the canned backup sets, or even to rely on backup sets at all. As shown in Figure 7-21, the Files and Folders tab in the main Mozy interface allows you to select specific folders and, within those folders, specific files. This sets up the potential for a very granular backup system.

Any file on the system that's accessible to the user creating the backup will be available for a Mozy backup. When you have reached the desired subdirectory or file level within a subdirectory, as shown in Figure 7-22, just check the Back up check box to add the selected file or files.

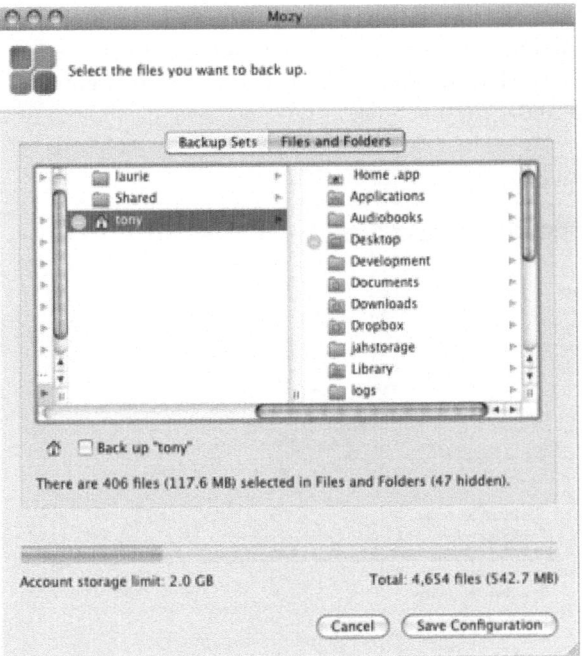

Figure 7-21. *Further customizing the Mozy backups*

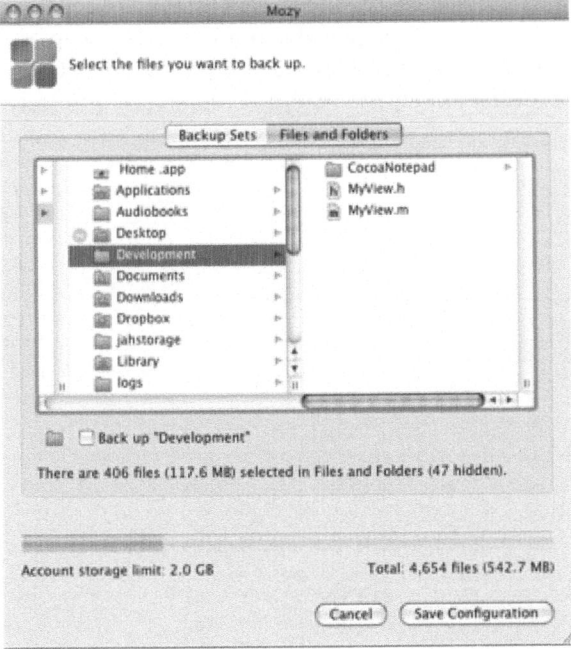

Figure 7-22. *Drilling down into the user files to add to the current Mozy backups*

Mozy also offers a view of the backup history, as shown in Figure 7-23. Full details of selected backups are provided in the lower pane of the history window, including completion status as success or failure, and reasons why a backup may have failed. These history entries also provide full details on all the files backed up at that time.

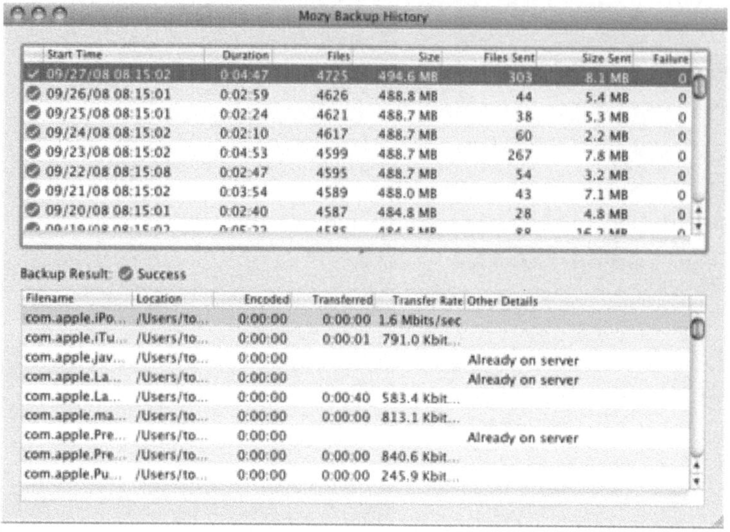

Figure 7-23. *Viewing the Mozy backup history*

If a quick summary of the backup history via the history window isn't thorough enough for you, the Mozy logs can also be viewed via the Console application (introduced in Chapter 6). Clicking the Mozy menu bar icon and selecting View Log Files will bring up the log in Console, as shown in Figure 7-24. The log file provides a complete view of all Mozy backup activity.

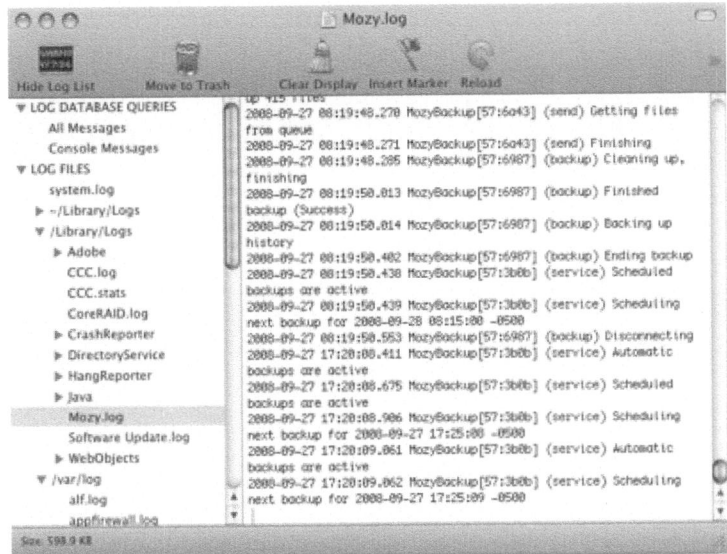

Figure 7-24. *Viewing the Mozy log in the system Console*

Restoring files from Mozy backups begins with loading all the restore information created in Mozy, as shown in Figure 7-25. When the restore options are loaded, a new window will display all the files available for restoration by Mozy. As shown in Figure 7-26. these are displayed by directory, rather than by the backup sets created earlier. Selecting a file from the window, and then clicking Restore will grab that file from your account on the Mozy servers and restore it to its original location on your local drive.

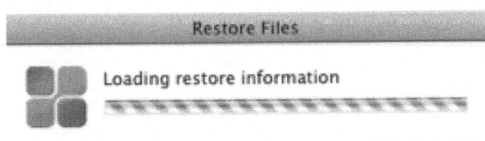

Figure 7-25. *Restoring files from a Mozy backup*

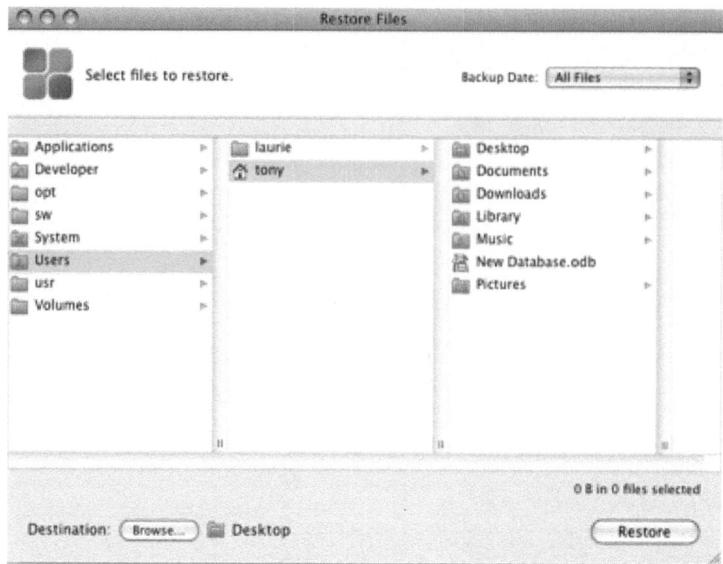

Figure 7-26. *The restore options in Mozy*

Mozy also provides a Preferences window to further customize its configuration. With the main configuration window open, select Preferences from the Mozy item in the menu bar. The resulting window provides three options:

General: As shown in Figure 7-27, the general configuration options include automatic update installation, whether to show a backup status icon in the status bar, and the option to display hidden files in the main configuration window.

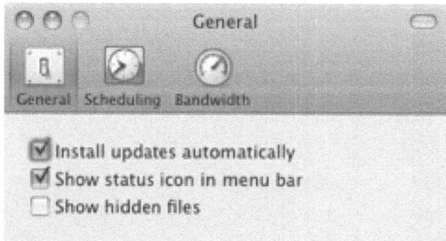

Figure 7-27. *Setting further customization options in Mozy*

Scheduling: By default, Mozy will perform a single backup each day at the time noted in the schedule window. However, that's not the real utility of Mozy. A far more useful choice for backup scheduling is to back up when the computer is idle. This is shown as the Automatic option in Figure 7-28. This option will provide backups with much more currency than the once-a-day approach. Mozy provides configuration options that account for the computer load and whether the user is actively using the system. Both load and idle time are adjustable to best meet the individual user's needs. Additionally, Mozy will alert users if backups have failed or, for any other reason, not occurred during a configurable time period. By default, this period is one week.

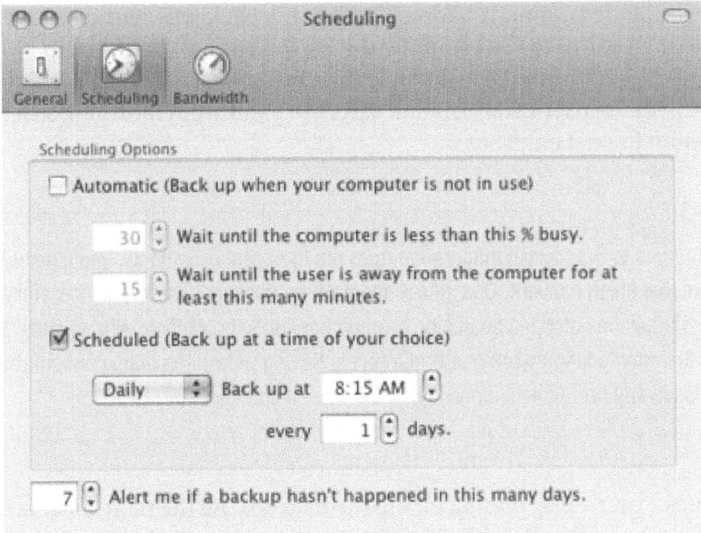

Figure 7-28. *Configuring Mozy to create scheduled backups*

Bandwidth: In effect, you're setting the bandwidth throttling options. Mozy will never use the full bandwidth of your connection, but you can determine how much it will use. Mozy also provides scheduling options to further customize the bandwidth throttling by the time of day. As shown in Figure 7-29, Mozy will use no more than 1 Mbps. If less is selected using the slider, the scheduling options will appear, allowing you to specify times of the day during which you'll throttle the Mozy backups more than the standard.

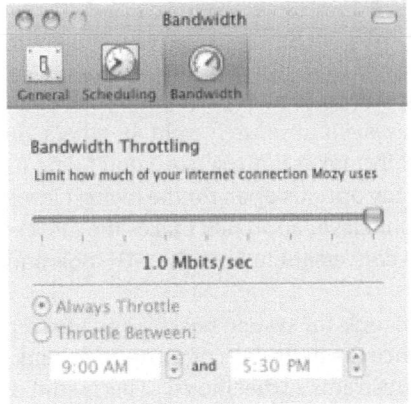

Figure 7-29. *Setting bandwidth use in Mozy*

If you've left the default scheduling times unmodified—that is, you're backing up only once per day—you probably won't need to further modify the throttling by time. Or, if a single daily Mozy backup is scheduled during a time you're normally using the computer, that time can be adjusted in the scheduling options. The ability to throttle bandwidth by time is particularly useful when using the automatic backups option. If a backup is started when the computer is idle, and the user returns to the computer during the backup, that backup will continue to completion in the background. It's possible that the bandwidth use required for that backup will interfere with the user's work. In that case, the bandwidth throttling schedule can minimize the bandwidth impact on the user.

Note In order to make changes to the Mozy configuration from the Preferences window, you'll need to let the main configuration window finish its work. Changes to the preferences can be saved successfully only when the main backup window has stopped searching through backup sets. At that point, clicking Save Configuration will save both the main configuration and preferences. Saving before the main configuration window is complete will not save any preferences options that have been changed.

Overall, Mozy provides a pretty elegant tool for off-site backups. All the right small details are covered in ways that are easily configurable. The size, time, and bandwidth usage of your backups are completely flexible. If your backup needs aren't substantial, the free 2GB Mozy accounts will more than accommodate your requirements. Even for those users who need more space, the pricing of the paid accounts is reasonable, given that one price covers unlimited backup storage and bandwidth. In the event of a catastrophe, backups are easily restored from an interface that doesn't overwhelm. And there's quite a lot to be said for the peace of mind that comes with knowing your computer could be destroyed in a disaster, but your critical data would survive to find its way onto the replacement.

The Linux Approach to Backup and Recovery

Old Linux hands might look at the GUI backup tools available for Mac OS X with some disdain. They're pretty, yes, but who needs all that overhead when the terminal will do quite well for configuring backups? Being an old Linux hand myself, I understand that view, whether or not I find it practical. In some ways and in some cases, it's absolutely right. In others, the ease with which the GUI tools allow configuration really makes more sense. I don't tend to fall completely into one camp or the other. I like to keep my options open for the highest level of convenience and efficiency. In other words, I'll use whichever approach makes the most sense for the current need. That means I need to be at least conversant in both the GUI tools and the command-line alternatives.

There's no doubt that Linux provides a rich set of tools for system backup and recovery. It is, after all, a need that has been well recognized since the early days of computing, and, accordingly, seems to be right in a good system administrator's wheelhouse. This is stuff that every admin should understand, including the tools provided with the operating system itself. In many ways, it's true that any necessary backup and recovery task can be accomplished with a few scripts and the built-in tools.

Let's take a look at a couple of those tools—tools that are also available in Mac OS X through its BSD ancestry—and some options to accomplish those backup and recovery tasks in Mac OS X. We'll start with one of the oldest tools in the UNIX toolbox: dd.

Using dd to Copy Data

The dd utility performs bit-by-bit copies of raw devices. In other words, dd sees a device as a device, rather than as the same abstraction that users see. While the dd man page states that "The dd utility copies the standard input to the standard output . . .," dd is most often used for copying data from one location to another, grabbing data, and writing it to a file, rather than to standard output. For example, in Linux, using dd to copy data from /dev/sda to /dev/sdb will copy the entire device from the source, /dev/sda, to the destination, /dev/sdb. Or using dd to copy data from /dev/sda1 to /dev/sda2 will copy the entire partition at /dev/sda1 to the /dev/sda2 partition. dd works in essentially the same fashion in Mac OS X.

The dd convention is pretty straightforward, requiring, at minimum, an input file (if) and an output file (of).

dd can also be used to make a disk image in Mac OS X. For example, to write a disk image of your main boot drive to an external drive, the following simple command will work well:

```
$ sudo dd if=/dev/disk0 of=/Volumes/Backup/OSX.dmg bs=512
```

Note that we're using the raw device designation in the input file element of the command. This command will copy the entire contents of the /dev/disk0 drive (dd if=/dev/sd0) to a new file on an external FireWire drive named OSX.dmg (of=/Volumes/Backup/OSX.dmg). dd will write this file in 512-byte blocks (bs=512). This file will be mountable on any block device, as would any other image file. Of course, the success of this command depends on the availability of storage on the destination drive. This image can be restored to the main drive as follows:

1. Insert the Mac OS X installation DVD in the DVD drive.

2. Reboot the system, holding down the C key to boot from the DVD.

3. Open the Utilities menu from the DVD.

4. Open a terminal window.

5. Use dd to copy the new image to the old drive:

   ```
   $ dd if=/Volumes/Backup/OSX.dmg /dev/disk0 bs=512 conv=sync,noerror
   ```

This command copies the new image to the boot partition on the main drive, and includes some options to account for possible errors, either on the originating or destination drive. The conv=sync,noerror option will do two things:

- Skip over any physical errors on the destination drive.

- Fill in any gaps in the data with zeros.

These two options will ensure that the new image on the original drive will work to bring up your system.

While dd is an outstanding and time-tried tool for copying data from raw devices, it's really not a good tool for copying from one directory tree to another. As dd sees devices rather than the abstractions of mount points, it also doesn't see the additional abstractions of directories. dd is perfectly capable of copying one partition to another, but not of copying one directory tree to another. So, while dd has some very strong backup functionality, it's really more analogous to a hammer where your specific backup needs require a screwdriver.

Using rsync to Synchronize Files

For all the utility of dd, dump, and restore, my favorite backup tool is still rsync. As the name indicates, rsync synchronizes files between directories. Ultimately, that's exactly what you're looking for in a backup: to leave the files that haven't changed and add the ones that have.

rsync is a powerful tool that will exclude files from a backup by reading an exclude list, and copy links, devices, owners, groups, and permissions. rsync can be executed remotely, creating backups across a network, and can also run in regular user mode. Furthermore, rsync can be used in tandem with ssh to create a secure connection for remote backups. And, of course, rsync operations can be scripted and executed automatically via cron or launchd.

A typical rsync command might look like this:

```
$ rsync -avuE --delete --exclude-from=/Users/tony/rsync_excludes \
/Users/tony/Volumes/Backup/Archive
```

This command will execute rsync as follows:

- Create an archive (-a creates a recursive copy with all attributes preserved)

- In verbose mode (v)

- Updating any existing archive of the same name (u), and preserving extended attributes and ACLs

- While deleting files (delete) on the destination that have been deleted on the source

- And excluding files (exclude-from) in /Users/tony/rsync_excludes from the backup

These options will be applied to the process of backing up the /Users/tony directory to the /Volumes/Backup/Archive directory.

The preceding command can be included in a quick bash script to execute the backup with a shorter command, or to include in cron or launchd.

To restore the backup created in this example, all that's necessary is to reverse the source and destination:

```
$ rsync -avuE --delete /Volumes/Backup/Archive /Users/tony
```

■**Note** The exclude-from option can generally be omitted from the restore command, as the files to be excluded were not included in the original backup.

If rsync is used to create a full system backup, the exclude-from option is extremely useful. Apple recommends that several files and directories, including swap files and temporary directories, be excluded from full system backups. This list of files can be rolled into a single file and, with the exclude-from rsync option, will be left out of backups.

With that information in hand, let's create a simple backup script that will perform incremental backups of a full system and make that backup bootable. Here's the backup script, saved to /Users/tony/scripts/inc_backups.sh:

```
#!/bin/sh

# mount the backup drive
disktuil mount /dev/disk1s2

# initiate the backup
# can add the -v (verbose) option to -au for test debugging
$ rsync -au --delete --exclude-from=/Users/tony/scripts/rsync_\
excludes /Volumes/Backup /

# when complete, bless the backup to make it bootable
sudo bless -folder /Volumes/Backup/System/Library/CoreServices

# umount the backup drive
diskutil umount /dev/disk1s2
```

Make sure that the preceding script is executable with this terminal command:

```
chmod +x /Users/tony/scripts/inc_backups.sh
```

Next, create a simple text file at /Users/tony/scripts/exclude-from, with the following contents:

```
tmp/*
Network/*
Volumes/*
cores/*
*/.Trash
dev/*
afs/*
automount/*
private/tmp/*
private/var/vm/*
private/var/run/*
private/var/spool/postfix/private/*
private/var/spool/postfix/public/*
private/var/imap/socket/*
```

The backup script can be manually executed or scheduled in launchd or cron. To add to launchd, create a new file contaning the following (adjusted, of course, for your system):

```
<?xml version="1.0" encoding="UTF-8"?>
<!DOCTYPE plist PUBLIC "-//Apple Computer//DTD PLIST 1.0//EN"
"http://www.apple.
com/DTDs/PropertyList-1.0.dtd">
<plist version="1.0">
<dict>
    <key>Label</key>
    <string>com.apple.backup-daily</string>
    <key>ProgramArguments</key>
```

```
      <array>
            <string>/Users/tony/scripts/inc_backup.sh</string>
            <string>daily</string>
      </array>
      <key>LowPriorityIO</key>
      <true/>
      <key>Nice</key>
      <integer>1</integer>
      <key>StartCalendarInterval</key>
      <dict>
            <key>Hour</key>
            <integer>2</integer>
            <key>Minute</key>
            <integer>25</integer>
      </dict>
</dict>
</plist>
```

When created, this file can be saved in /Users/[*you*]/Library/LaunchAgents/com.apple. DailyBackups.plist. When included in the LaunchAgents directory, this file will launch the /Users/tony/scripts/inc_backup.sh every day at 2:25 a.m.

If you're more familiar and comfortable with cron, the following entry can be added to crontab with the crontab -e command:

```
25          2          *          *          *          /Users/tony/scripts/inc_backups.sh
```

Again, the script will run at 2:25 a.m. each day, creating an incremental backup of the system and, using the bless command, making it bootable.

Security

As you can imagine, it's tough to condense the topic of security to a single section in a single chapter of a single book. The topic has filled entire libraries and served as the focus of complete careers. The increase in the number of always-on connections around the world has ramped up the necessity of talking about security, but the topic is so large that anything less than a detailed, comprehensive discussion of security will be seen as a shortcoming by some. And, of course, that detailed comprehensive discussion would take many, many volumes. Any discussion of security, in reality, creates a paradox.

Rather than allowing the sheer scale of the topic to pull us off our mission of moving you gracefully from Linux to Mac OS X, I'll cover only the basic Mac OS X-ready tools for security. As with other Mac tools, some are GUI-based, some are best implemented using the command line, some are native, and some are BSD-based.

Here, I won't discuss the deeper issues of security, or provide a plan for more esoteric security implementations. I will, instead, look at the tools, their place in the operating system, and at how they fit into the high-level security net. I'll also suggest some basic configurations and commands to point you down that long path of complete security for your system. I won't take you to the destination, but I will get you started down the road. You can find a comprehensive discussion in another recent book, *Foundations of Mac OS X Leopard Security*, by Charles Edge, Jr., William Barker, and Zack Smith (Apress, 2008). As a book devoted to the topic of security, it clearly takes the discussion I start here to another level.

By now, you're certainly familiar with the approach of the built-in Mac OS X tools, regardless of their focus: provide the high-level functionality in a clean and intuitive interface, aggregate the most important elements into a minimal number of configuration panes, and make all the options point-and-click. The native Mac OS X tools for configuring security follow that approach perfectly. By now, you're also familiar with the general layout of the Mac OS X System Preferences, where we'll begin our discussion of security.

Configuring Security Through System Preferences

As with many of the other tools we've discussed, you'll find a set of security configuration tools available from the System Preferences main window. The built-in Mac OS X security configuration is located in the Personal section of System Preferences, as shown in Figure 7-30.

Figure 7-30. *Configuring security from the System Preferences window*

As shown in Figure 7-31, the General options of the Mac OS X security configuration contain some basic but very commonsense security items. Consider the General security tab to be the highest level security options, addressing passwords, logins and logouts, and the security of remote controls. Interestingly, the window also allows you to use secure virtual memory, an option not seen or mentioned in other operating systems. This option can be important for the security of passwords or other sensitive items that may be swapped in and out of virtual memory. By securing the virtual memory, it's also possible to secure those sensitive items that have been swapped into virtual memory.

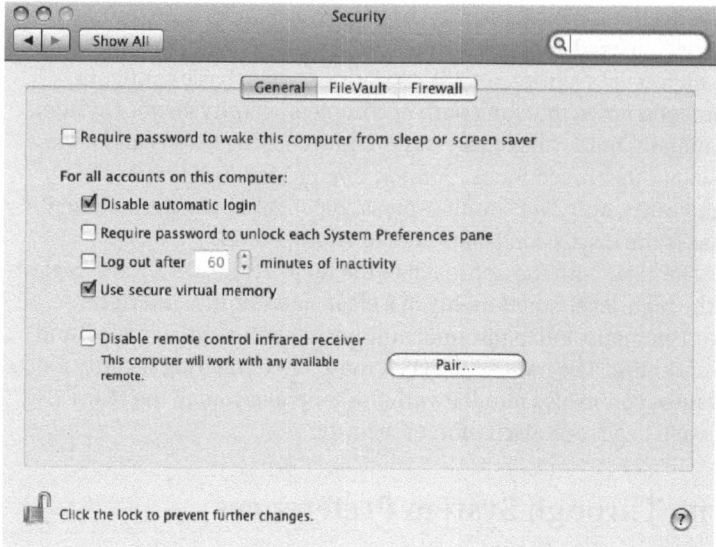

Figure 7-31. *The General options window of the Mac OS X security configuration*

Mac OS X also provides a security tool known as FileVault, configured through the window shown in Figure 7-32. FileVault encrypts the user home directories, mounting and unmounting them as users log in to the system. The directories are decrypted when mounted in the system.

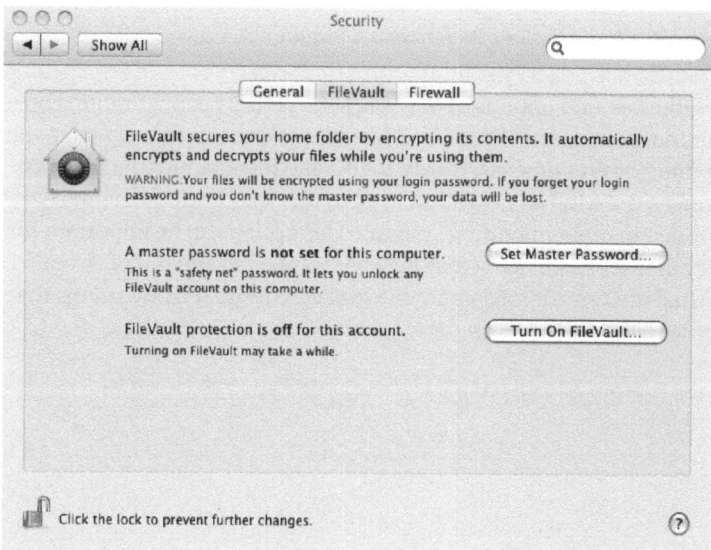

Figure 7-32. *FileVault security preferences in System Preferences*

From the FileVault tab, you can set a master password. As noted in the window, this is a "safety net" password. If the password for individual FileVault accounts is lost, the master password can be utilized to access the files locked by FileVault, and to reset the user-level password. A master password is required when choosing FileVault protection.

When it comes to setting the built-in Mac OS X firewall, basically, you can choose from three options for security levels: none, medium, or high. While that doesn't completely describe the approach, it's a good place to start your thinking. These three levels of security are represented by radio button options in the security configuration window, as shown in Figure 7-33. They work as follows:

Allow all incoming connections: This option does exactly as it notes—it doesn't lock down or otherwise prevent traffic on any system port. In reality, the system is wide open when this option is selected. This allows your system to accept requests for applications and services from other computers on the network.

Allow only essential services: This option blocks connections from other computers, as well as all requests for shared services and applications. Apple notes that in this mode, the system blocks "all connections except a limited list of services essential to the operation of your computer." Incoming connections will still be allowed for DHCP services provided by configd, mDNSResponder, and the dependent Bonjour services, as well as Internet Protocol Security (IPsec) services provided by racoon. So, this setting blocks the requests of other computers for all other services on your machine, while allowing your computer to find those critical services on other computers on the network. This is a fairly conservative mode that will likely work well for your home-connected system.

Set access for specific services and applications: The final option for Mac OS X firewall configuration is the most flexible and probably the most useful for more experienced Mac OS X users. This option allows you to choose whether to accept or deny connections on an application-by-application basis.

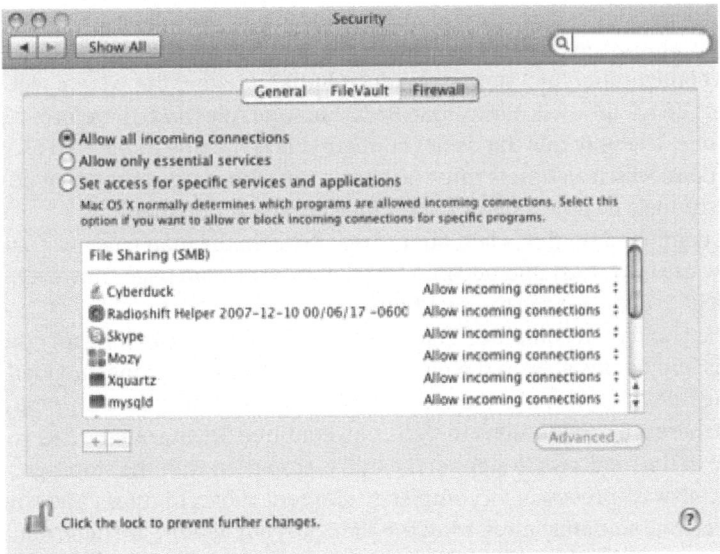

Figure 7-33. *Setting the Mac OS X application-level firewall*

When you choose the third firewall option, you can add applications by clicking the familiar plus button in the lower-left corner of the configuration window. Then you can choose to allow or block incoming connections to that application via a menu on the right side of the application pane. You can also Control-click the application name to display the location of the application in the Finder.

Applications added to this list are also digitally signed for posterity. If the application is modified at some point in the future, Mac OS X will prompt you with a choice to either accept or deny incoming connections from that application. This provides an additional level of security. The default in this mode is the same as the option to allow only essential services: only those essential services are allowed, unless and until you make the choice to allow a specific application to accept connection requests. When applications that haven't been granted explicit permissions attempt to access the network, you'll be prompted to either accept or deny the connection. That response will become the default for the application going forward. Finally, any application or script on the system can be added to this list, including command-line applications.

In general, Apple has provided an easy-to-use security configuration tool in System Preferences. This tool provides enough flexibility to meet the needs of most home users in securing their system. While it's not a complete security system—it doesn't cover all the esoteric security corner cases—it does provide strong security for the most common scenarios.

Of course, as a BSD-based system, Mac OS X does not just offer the GUI tools for security configuration. If you're willing to dig a bit deeper, you can completely customize your system security using other familiar command-line tools, such as `ipfw`.

Using ipfw As a Firewall

Mac OS X includes ipfw, a BSD firewall and traffic-shaping tool. ipfw implements *rulesets*, which are collections of rules that determine the action to be taken on packets traveling across the network interface. These rules first determine whether those packets will be allowed or denied, and then identify any further action to be taken.

The system kernel configuration determines the default rule: whether the system will allow or deny all packets. In all, ipfw will allow up to 65,535 unique rules and, therefore, unique actions on packets. The only rule that is not configurable is the rule numbered 65535. That's the default rule upon which all others must be based. Given the large number of possible rules, ipfw is an extremely flexible tool for packet filtering and traffic shaping.

ipfw utilizes a rich command set that's laid out in great detail in the man page (`man ipfw`). Your best guide for ipfw use is to study and become familiar with the man page. However, some examples are useful to demonstrate the capabilities and power of ipfw.

ipfw looks at a packet, and then compares that packet to the ruleset, searching for conditional matches. If one is found, ipfw acts on the packet based on the instructions provided by the individual matching rule. It's much like the subprocess of driving known as "stopping at a stop sign." As long as there are no stop signs in sight, you continue driving. As soon as you reach a stop sign, a rule of the road says to step on the brake, stop even with the stop sign, wait for traffic with the right-of-way (processing a completely different subset of rules), and when it's your turn to go, accelerate smoothly away from the sign. So, your actions are determined by the stop sign conditions or rules. ipfw works in this same way. When a packet that meets predefined conditions or characteristics hits the system, it's processed according to any rules matched by those conditions or characteristics.

Let's go over a blunt-force example—one that has no practical application in the real world, but serves to illustrate the potential of ipfw. My iPhone contains the Air Share application, which will connect with machines on the local network via Wi-Fi and share files across the network. The iPhone gets its IP address dynamically from my router, and, for whatever reasons, is usually assigned 192.168.1.119. I can use ipfw to deny access from the iPhone to the desktop machine with the following:

```
$ sudo ipfw enable firewall
```

This command starts ipfw with only the default rule which, on my machine, is to allow all traffic.

```
$ sudo ipfw add deny src-ip 192.168.1.119
00100 deny ip from any to any src-ip 192.168.1.119
```

This return shows me that rule 00100 has been created to deny ip **from** any **to** any src-ip 192.168.1.119. In other words, the local machine (as any) will deny any request to or from the IP address 192.168.1.119. Sure enough, when I open Air Share on the iPhone and use Go/Connect to Server from the Finder on the desktop machine, it's unable to connect to the iPhone. The attempt to connect eventually times out with an error. ipfw is denying all packets associated with the 192.168.1.119 IP address, whether they're from the iPhone or from the desktop.

■ **Note** An interesting side effect of the sample rule is that if the connection with the iPhone is made and the phone is mounted as a network drive before the rule is established, it's impossible to unmount it, even though its contents can no longer be accessed from the desktop.

To drop the "no iPhones" rule—rule 00100—I can execute the following command:

```
$ sudo ipfw delete 00100
```

As no return is issued from the system, I want to check to be sure the rule has been deleted, by asking ipfw to list all its current rules:

```
$ sudo ipfw list
65535 allow ip from any to any
```

Again, the only rule on the system is to allow all connections with all other machines—the default rule controlled by the kernel and numbered 65535.

To shut down the ipfw firewall altogether, issue the following command:

```
$ sudo ipfw disable firewall
```

■ **Note** ipfw commands that establish or delete rules require sudo access. The Mac OS X default configuration does not allow socket operations by normal users; these are accessible by only the root user.

The primary ipfw commands include those listed in Table 7-1. These commands are further modified by the use of many options to ipfw.

Table 7-1. *Common ipfw Commands*

Command	Description
add	Inserts a new rule into the ipfw ruleset
list (or show)	Displays all the current ipfw rules
flush	Removes all the user-configurable rules from the current ipfw ruleset
delete	Removes a single rule from the current ipfw ruleset
enable	Activates ipfw's firewall protections, or one of several other general options
disable	Deactivates ipfw's firewall protections, or one of several other general options
set	Disables or enables existing rule numbers; move, swap, or show existing rules

ipfw also provides *stateful* behavior; in other words, dynamic rules that match the current state of a packet can be created by existing rules. These dynamic rules exist for only as long as the state of the packet matches the original rule.

An extension to our earlier stop sign analogy can demonstrate statefulness. A new rule defines that "Any car to your right that has arrived at the intersection at the same time you've arrived will have the right-of-way and, as such, will be allowed to pull away from their stop sign first." That's a dynamic rule that applies only when another car to your right stops at a stop sign at the same time you stop. It's stateful in that its life is limited; it will apply only until the car to the right pulls away from the stop sign. Once those conditions no longer exist, the rule is no longer applicable. In IP traffic control, statefulness may, for example, temporarily open the firewall to specific traffic types. But, ipfw will do this for only as long as the matching state exists. Statefulness is a powerful tool in ipfw.

As I noted earlier, you should review the ipfw man page on your system for a full description of these commands and options. It's a powerful tool that can be used from the command line to lock down your system with nearly any degree of security you prefer.

Using WaterRoof: An ipfw Front End

Clearly, not everyone agrees that the command line is the most efficient way to administer the finer points of your system—security included. The System Preferences security options in Mac OS X are pretty powerful but, quite frankly, don't even approach the flexibility of a BSD tool like ipfw. And, of course, with security, flexibility is actually everything. The more granularly you can create your security rules, the more likely you are to defeat potential security compromises while allowing normal system operations by most users. To get there, some prefer the command line, and others prefer a GUI tool.

WaterRoof provides a clean and very detailed GUI interface to the ipfw tools. It's free and available for download from http://www.hanynet.com/waterroof/. It clearly answers the needs of those who prefer GUI configuration tools to the command line.

WaterRoof provides a clean interface to create and configure the ipfw rules. As shown in Figure 7-34, the options in the main interface include the following:

- *Static Rules*: Allows the user to create unchanging ipfw rules.

- *Dynamic Rules*: Allows the user to create dynamic ipfw rules. As noted earlier in the ipfw section, dynamic rules are used to create stateful firewalls. These rules may change depending on the state of the incoming packets.

- *Bandwidth Manager*: Allows the user to shape incoming and outgoing IPv4 traffic.

- *NAT Setup*: Allows the user to configure NAT, a process of mapping IP addresses to a different interface.

- *Net Connections*: Allows the user to block connections, switch between IPv4 and IPv6 addressing, and limit bandwidth.

- *Net Processes*: Displays current network connections, both IPv4 and IPv6.

- *Firewall Logs*: Enables, disables, and displays firewall logs.

- *Logs Statistics*: Displays a log reader, providing filtering and graphic options.

- *Ready Rule Sets*: Offers preconfigured sets of rules that can be applied for your system.

- *Configuration Wizard*: Starts a GUI to create the ipfw rules used by WaterRoof.

- *IP Reverse and Whois*: Provides a convenient way to check IP addresses.

- *Network Interfaces*: Displays a list of all network interfaces on the machine.

Figure 7-34.
The WaterRoof main interface

Unless you already have ipfw rules configured on your system, you'll use the firewall configuration wizard to create new rules for WaterRoof.

The WaterRoof Wizard provides some initial background on use of the wizard in the main screen, as shown in Figure 7-35. The first actual configuration screen in the WaterRoof Wizard provides a drop-down menu of destination types, including all the common server types, as shown in Figure 7-36. Select the service on your computer to which you'll allow others to connect. Also choose the source address type, as shown in Figure 7-37.

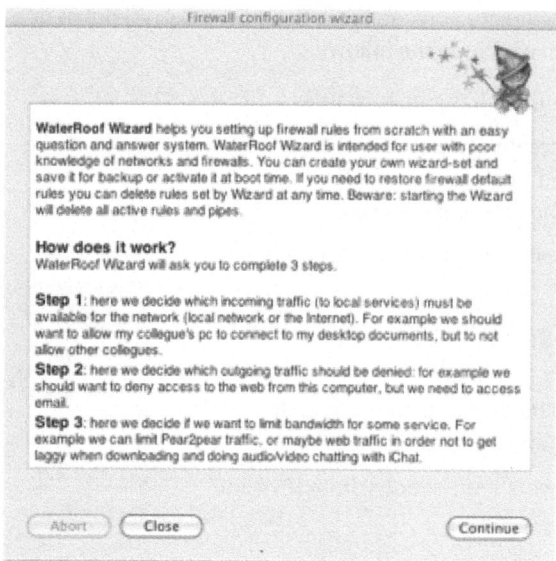

Figure 7-35. *The WaterRoof Wizard main screen*

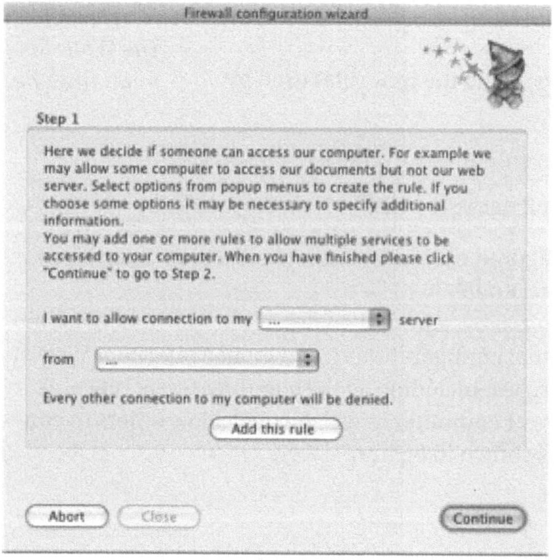

Figure 7-36. *Step 1 to configure new ipfw rules using the WaterRoof Wizard*

Figure 7-37. *Server options in WaterRoof*

Using the WaterRoof Wizard, you can configure rules to allow connections from any one of several network address types, as shown in Figure 7-38. If you choose "a computer on my network" or "my network except one host," you'll need to enter the address of that machine in a text box that appears when you make that selection.

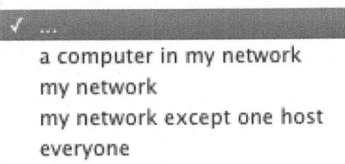

Figure 7-38. *Address options in the WaterRoof Wizard*

Step 2 in the WaterRoof Wizard allows you to define disallowed connections from your machine, as shown in Figure 7-39. As shown in Figure 7-40, several options are available for restricting the connection types available to your computer.

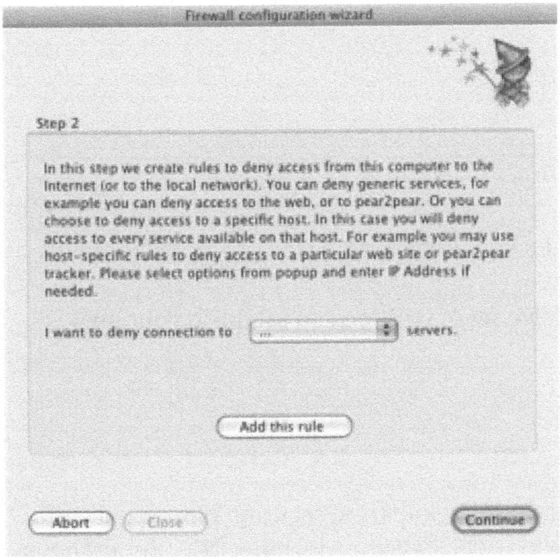

Figure 7-39. *Configuring outgoing connection rules*

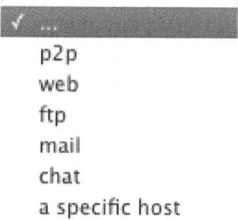

Figure 7-40. *Connection types to be disallowed from your computer*

The WaterRoof Wizard also provides tools to limit bandwidth use on your machine, as shown in Figure 7-41. It allows you limit bandwidth by connection type (web sites, mail, or P2P) and to set the allowed bandwidth for those connections.

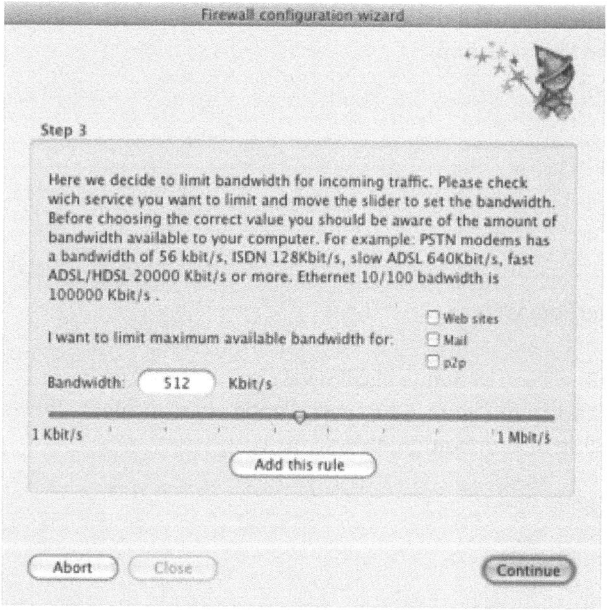

Figure 7-41. *Traffic control in the WaterRoof Wizard*

After you've created the rules using the WaterRoof Wizard, you'll be prompted for your administrative password to add the rules to ipfw.

In short, WaterRoof provides a comprehensive set of GUI tools to establish your own security and bandwidth control rules for ipfw.

Summary

This chapter covered the tools for handling Mac OS X backups and security. We started with some GUI backup and recovery tools, including Mac OS X's Time Machine, CCC, SuperDuper, and Mozy. Then we looked at two common command-line tools that are handy for backups: dd and rsync.

In the security discussion, we kept it simple and stuck to the built-in Apple firewall tools. You learned about the options available through Mac OS X preferences, the ipfw firewall, and WaterRoof, a front end for ipfw.

In the next chapter, we'll turn our attention to coding in Mac OS X.

CHAPTER 8

■■■

Mac OS X and Code

Up to this point, we've spent quite a bit of time buried in the weeds with user tools. To a large extent, we've ignored the fact that, aside from providing beautiful and functional user applications, Mac OS X is also a powerful development platform. Not only is Mac OS X loaded with the native Apple developer tools, including Xcode, but it's also very extensible using open source tools, such as Python, Perl, and PHP. A developer can create Cocoa applications native to Mac OS X, or use the Apple IDE to create tools that leverage the open source underpinnings of Mac OS X. It's also possible to add frameworks to the system that further extend the connections between these open source technologies and the native Apple development tools.

Mac OS X includes all the scripting tools you would expect in a Linux distribution. With Python, PHP, Perl, and Ruby, Mac OS X provides a powerful scripting platform, perfect for when full-blown object-oriented development is overkill. It's easy to create scripts that "do one thing and do it well." Apple also addresses this need in Mac OS X with AppleScript, a clean and easy-to-learn native scripting language.

Finally, as a developer, you understand the importance of source code and revision control. Mac OS X provides these tools as well. If you're a lone developer, it's important to understand the code control options that are available for your local machine or local network. If you work in a development house with several developers, you'll be interested in how Mac OS X can provide centralized code and revision control options, accessible on the network to all your developers. Again, the options for code control include native Mac OS X applications as well as tried-and-true open source alternatives, GUI options, and command-line tools. The flexibility you've seen in the user tools applies equally well to the developer tools in Mac OS X.

In this chapter, we'll cover development with Xcode, scripting, and code maintenance and revision control. We'll begin with a look at the Xcode IDE.

Using Xcode

As discussed in Chapter 4, Xcode is the Apple development environment provided on the Mac OS X installation DVD. Xcode has everything necessary to develop and debug applications for the Mac. Xcode is a complete IDE, including a text editor, build system, debugger, and compiler. It's the central point for development of nearly all the applications on the Mac, and the very same IDE used by developers within Apple.

Instructions for installing Xcode from the Mac OS X installation DVD are provided in Chapter 4. Once installed, the Xcode tools can be found, by default, on the boot volume. These tools are installed in the Applications subdirectory of the Developer folder on that volume.

As shown in Figure 8-1, the main Xcode window offers all the Xcode options. You can jump right into the IDE by selecting "Create your first Cocoa application." Alternatively, you can choose the other options to work with the Interface Builder, build a new database for your application data with Core Data, or use Instruments to optimize your application.

Figure 8-1. *Launching the Xcode IDE in Mac OS X*

At the top of the main Xcode window, you'll also find links to internal documentation on a range of topics. These include the iPhone Dev Center, the Mac Dev Center, the latest news on Xcode, informational mailing lists on development and Xcode-related topics, and tips for using the Xcode tools. These links point to documentation libraries built into the Xcode tool. In order to preserve storage space, many of these libraries are initially populated with minimal information locally, with the complete documentation set being available online. Additionally, some documentation sets (notably those about Java) are not available at all locally. The complete documentation libraries can be downloaded and installed locally, if needed, by clicking the Subscribe button in the left pane of the window for the documentation set you would like to install. Additionally, the documentation tool contains bookmarks, also listed in the left pane, as shown in Figure 8-2. These open the documentation in the lower pane of the main screen in the documentation library.

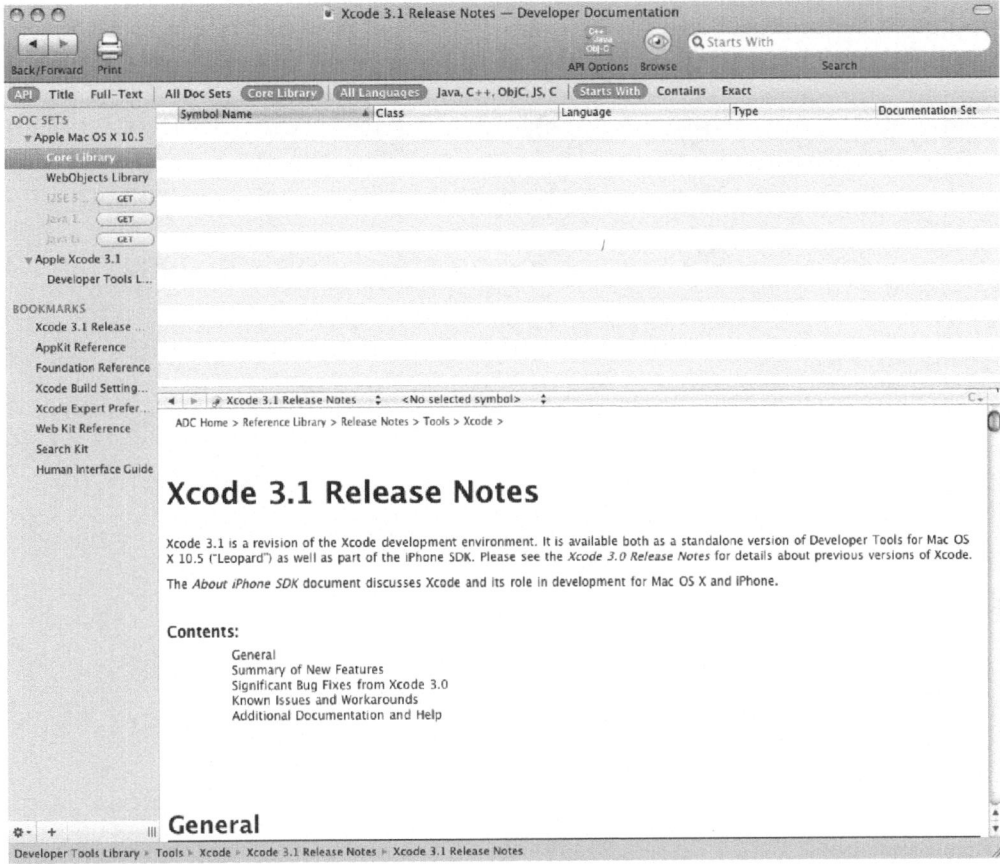

Figure 8-2. *The online documentation libraries for the Xcode tools*

Creating an Application with Xcode

When starting a new project, Xcode provides a number of templates. As shown in Figure 8-3, these are grouped into several project types, including applications, Automator actions, kernel extensions, and several others. These templates provide the basic files for your projects. Select a template category, and then select a specific template for your project. Xcode prompts you for the location where all project files will be stored, as shown in Figure 8-4.

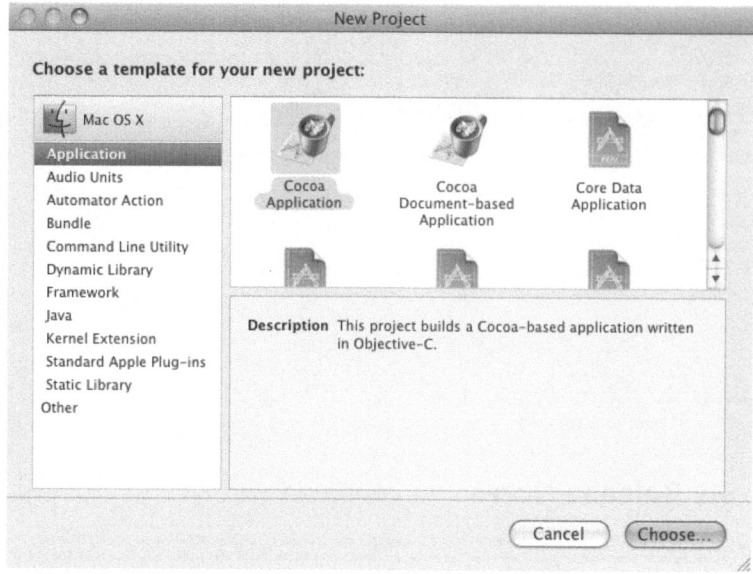

Figure 8-3. *Choosing a template for a new Xcode project*

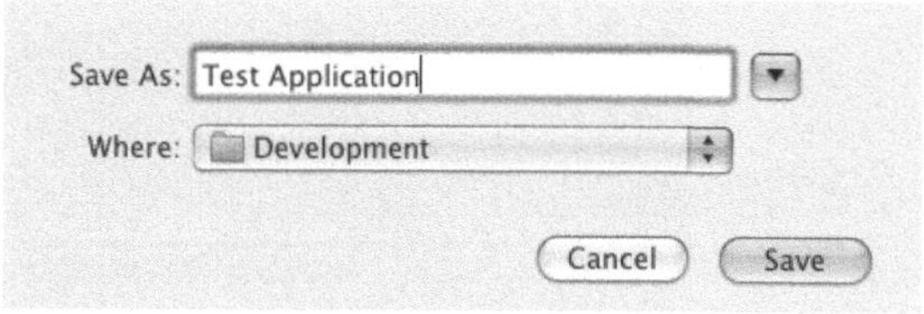

Figure 8-4. *Saving a new Xcode project*

As shown in Figure 8-5, the Xcode tool creates a basic library of files for the new application. These include header files, app files, necessary frameworks, and `plist` files, as well as several others. These are organized in the project within folders in the left pane of the Xcode window. The folders include classes, other sources, resources, frameworks, and products. Double-clicking a file name in the Xcode tool will open the file in the built-in text editor.

Xcode creates files with basic information in the header, including the code author and copyright information. This is based on information in the user's entry in the Address Book application. The files also contain the basic code necessary to create the specific file for the application, again, based on the chosen application type.

The Xcode text editor utilizes full syntax highlighting, in addition to inserting comments for the developer, specific to the project type. In the example shown in Figure 8-6, the comments provide the developer with information about the creation of a function for setting the value of input ports. This type of commenting is provided throughout all new project files.

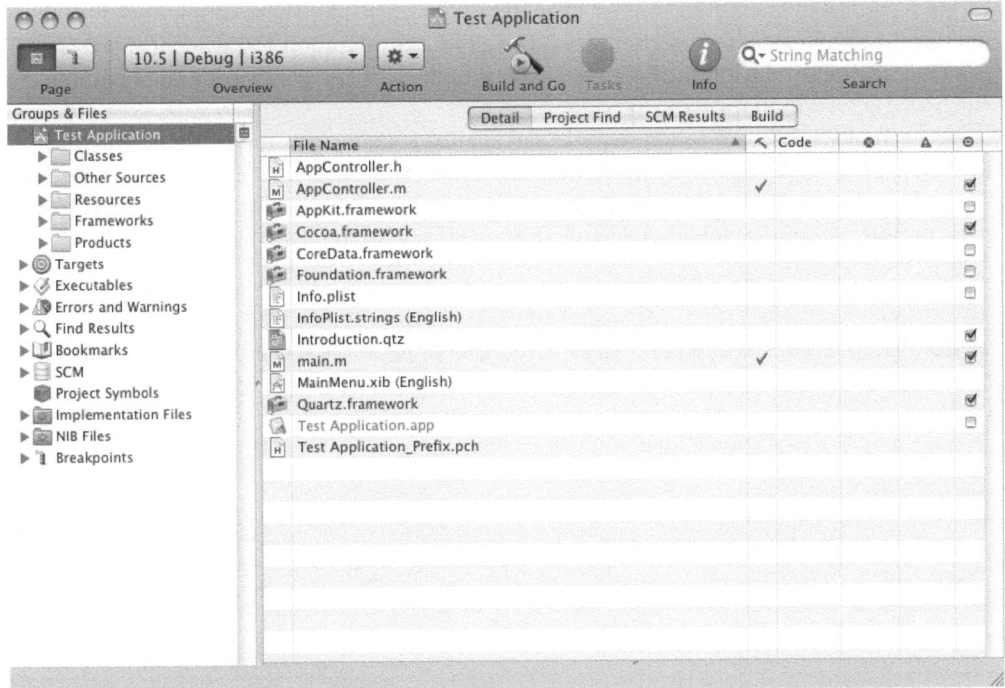

Figure 8-5. *The file library created by Xcode for a new project*

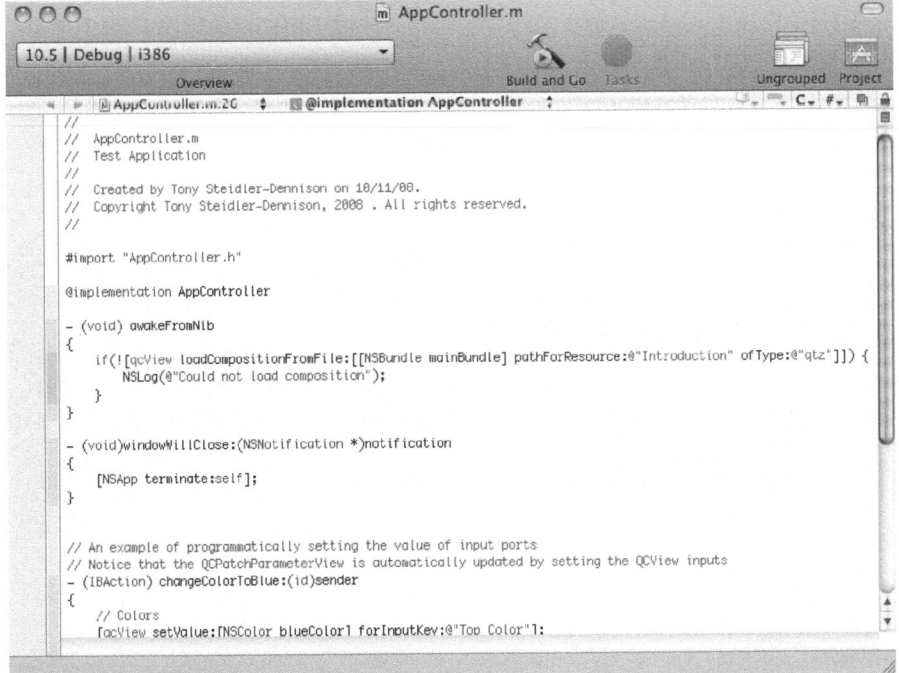

Figure 8-6. *The AppController.m file open for editing in the built-in text editor*

Applications in Mac OS X require a property list, or `plist` file. These simple XML files describe the application and user settings required for the operation of the application. The `plist` files are one of the many direct descendants of the NeXTStep operating system upon which Mac OS X is built.

As each Mac OS X application requires a `plist` file, it's only appropriate that the Xcode tool would provide the means by which to create these files. As a recent addition to Xcode, the `plist` editor is included in Xcode 3.1 and later. To launch it, double-click the `Info.plist` object in the project's `Resources` folder. A default `plist` file is shown in Figure 8-7.

Note Though Xcode includes a `plist` editor, it's not actually necessary in order to create or modify `plist` files. As XML files, the `plist` files can be created and edited with any text editor.

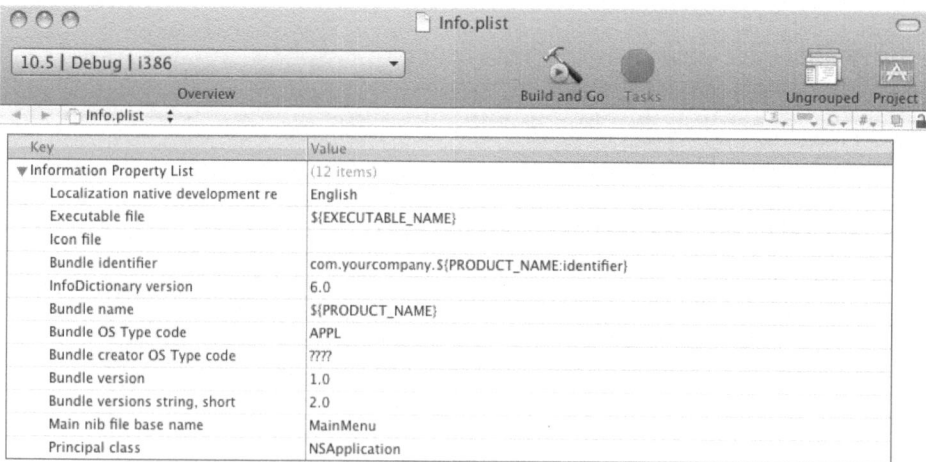

Figure 8-7. *Creating a plist file for the new application*

Working in the Main Xcode Window

Rather than launching a single file in the built-in Xcode editor by double-clicking it, you can configure the tool to provide access to all files in a single window. You can also configure external editors in the Xcode preferences. Figure 8-8 shows this configuration, opened for the `AppController.m` file. In this configuration, the editor opens in the lower pane of the main window.

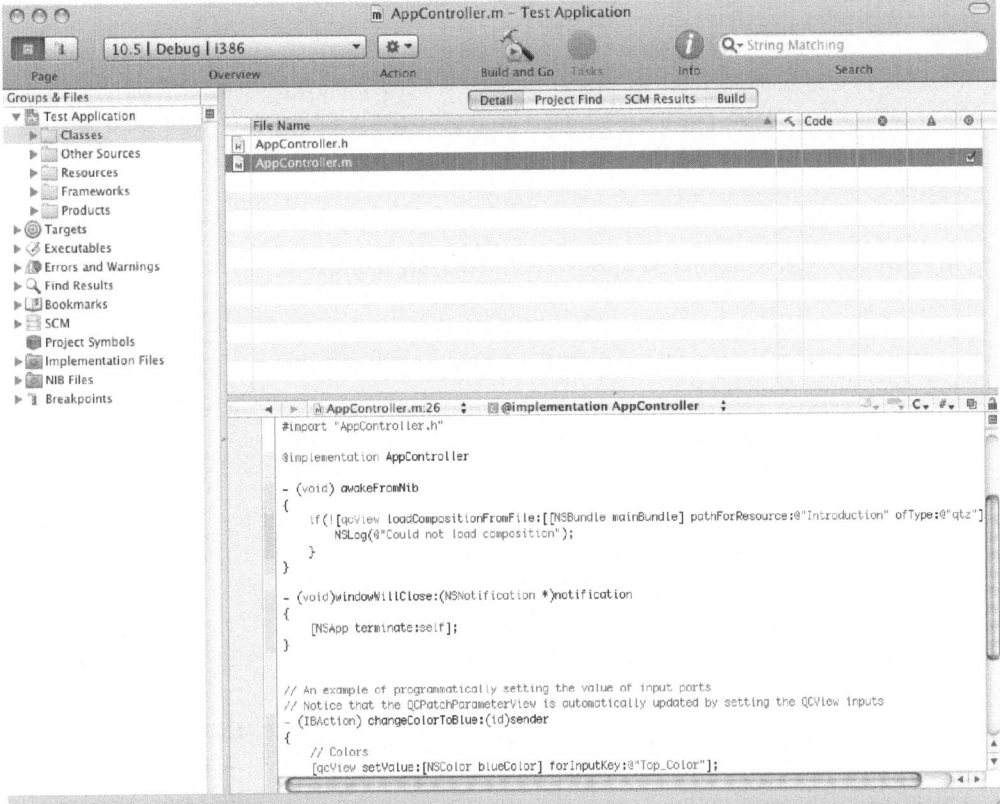

Figure 8-8. *An expanded view of the Xcode interface*

At the top left of the Xcode IDE window are options for configuring both the target environment and the window view, as shown in Figure 8-9. Your choices for window view, selected by clicking one of the two icons at the far left, are the main window or the debugging window (the bug spray icon). To designate the target environment for the application, select it from the drop-down menu in the main interface. In the example, the options for target are Mac OS X 10.4 or Mac OS X 10.5 (Target Setting).

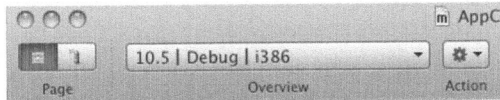

Figure 8-9. *The Xcode IDE settings*

> **Note** Xcode settings include Project settings and Target settings. Without the parenthetical indication of which settings you're modifying, such as "(Target Setting)," it's possible to confuse the settings type. Changing these settings may, in fact, give unexpected results. In other words, it's important to pay close attention to the settings type when modifying the Xcode settings.

In addition to selecting the window view and the target environment for the application, Xcode also provides several actions that are easily accessible within the main interface. Click the Action drop-down arrow to see the list shown in Figure 8-10. You can select from the following types of actions:

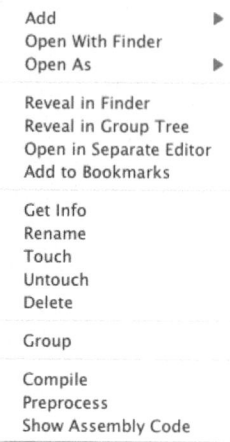

- Open and add actions, such as adding a new file, opening the current file in the Finder, or opening the current file as a new file

- Actions specific to the individual file, such as viewing the file information (as provided, in part, by the existing plist file), renaming, touching, untouching, and deleting the file

- Actions to compile, preprocess, and show the assembly code for the file

Figure 8-10.
Actions available in the Xcode interface

All in all, the most common file actions are provided from within the main Xcode window.

As shown in Figure 8-11, Xcode provides other developer options within the main window, including the ability to build an executable binary with a single button click. When the Xcode IDE is actively building a binary or is engaged in some other task that temporarily excludes user interaction, the Tasks indicator in the main window bar will become active, painting the stop sign a bright red.

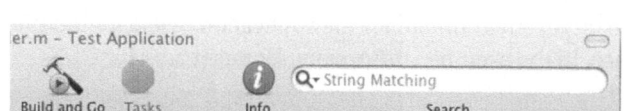

Figure 8-11. *Additional file options available within the Xcode main window*

In addition to the ability to build and compile from the main window, Xcode also provides a tool to view and edit all the available information about the current file within the main interface. The Info button at the top of the main Xcode window reveals another window with this information, as shown in Figure 8-12. This window includes several tabs of information, including general information, targets, additional compiler flags for the chosen application target, and file-specific comments.

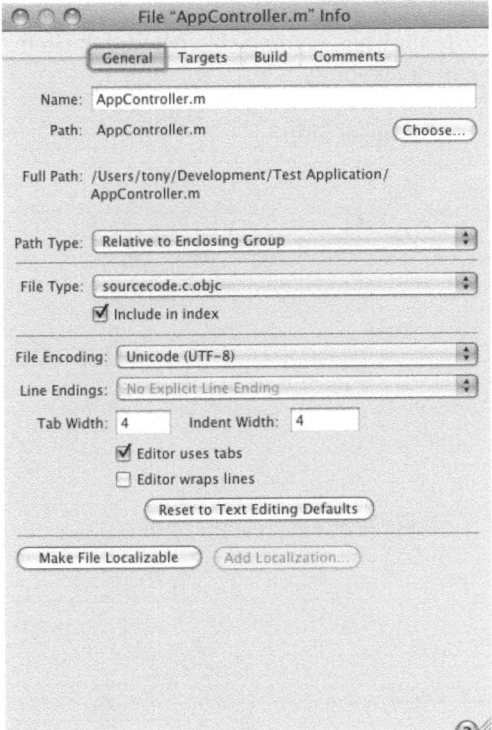

Figure 8-12. *Information about the current file available from the main Xcode interface window*

Finally, the main Xcode window includes a search interface. This provides developers with the ability to perform string searches within the selected file.

Debugging with Xcode

An essential part of creating applications is, of course, the ability to debug those programs you've created. Stepping through code execution one line at a time makes it possible to find coding errors.

In addition to the project coding and creation tools provided by Xcode, you'll also find a robust debugger. You can step through your own code line by line, or you can attach to and debug a running process that you did not initiate. And, with your own applications, you can set the debugger to attach to any process launched from Xcode only when it crashes.

Consistent with Apple's philosophy of creating tools that are flexible for developers, Xcode provides a number of ways to debug your applications. The method you choose is entirely up to you, and will undoubtedly depend on your preferred work style and environment.

Running the Debugger in the Text Editor

The Xcode debugger provides the ability to debug your code directly in the text editor. This can be a big time-saver if you're creating and debugging code on the fly. To access the debugger in the text editor, double-click the file to be debugged to open it in the text editor. Then, with the text editor in the foreground, select Run ➤ Go (Debug) from the Xcode menu.

Two pieces of the debugger in the text editor are important to you, as noted in Figure 8-13: the debugger strip and the gutter. The debugger strip, shown in Figure 8-14, includes the items listed in Table 8-1. The gutter allows you to set or edit breakpoints.

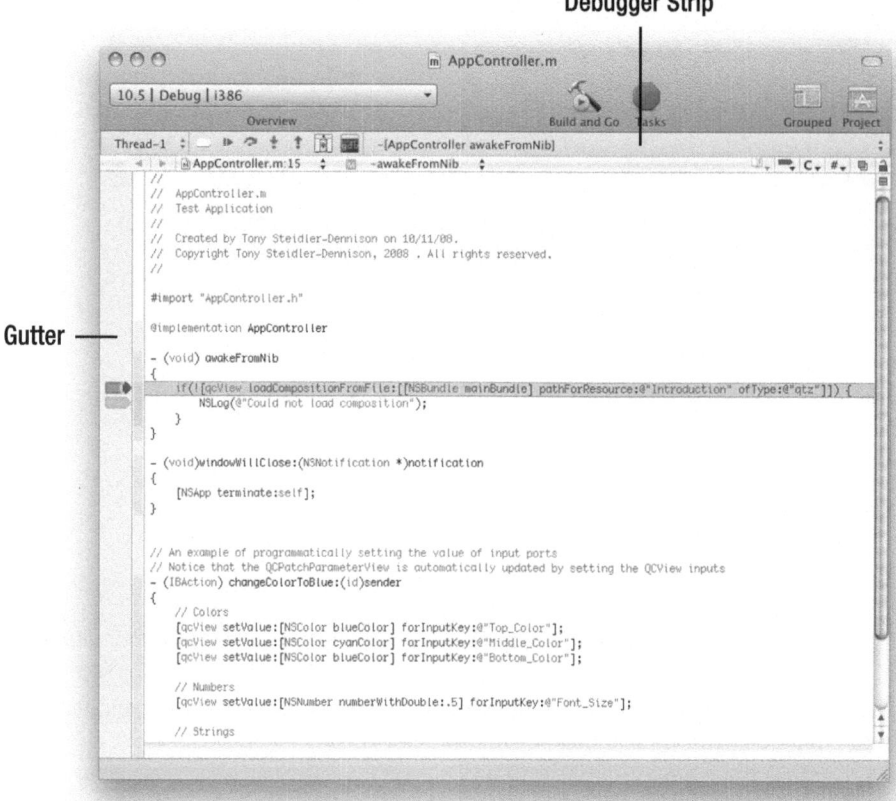

Figure 8-13. *Debugging code in the Xcode text editor*

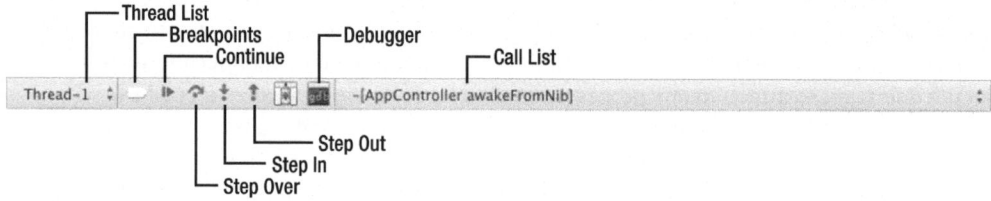

Figure 8-14. *The Xcode debugger strip*

Table 8-1. *Xcode Debugger Strip Items*

Item	Description
Thread list	Shows the thread currently under control of the debugger
Breakpoints button	Sets and deactivates the debugging breakpoints
Continue button	Continues the execution of the debugger
Step Over button	Instructs the debugger to skip, or "step over," the current line of code
Step In button	Instructs the debugger to step into a function or a specific line of code
Step Out button	Instructs the debugger to step out of a function or specific line of code
Debugger button	Opens the GDB (GNU Project Debugger) window
Call list	Shows the call stack (list of called routines)

Additionally, the debugger provides code data tips. By hovering the cursor over the code in debugging mode, you'll have access to a progressive disclosure mechanism that allows you to view and change your application's variables.

Using the Mini Debugger

The full debugging interface, while powerful, can sometimes be a bit of overkill. It's not always necessary to open a full window, nor is it desirable when what you really need is just a quick assessment of how your program is operating. For those purposes, Xcode provides a mini debugger. This small debugging interface floats above a running application, providing many of the same tools that are available in the full version.

The mini debugger, shown in Figure 8-15, includes functions to (from left to right) stop and pause the code, select the project, and activate/deactivate breakpoints within the code.

Figure 8-16 shows an example of the mini debugger in operation. In this figure, the process under control of the debugger, known as the *inferior*, is stopped.

Figure 8-15.
The Xcode mini debugger

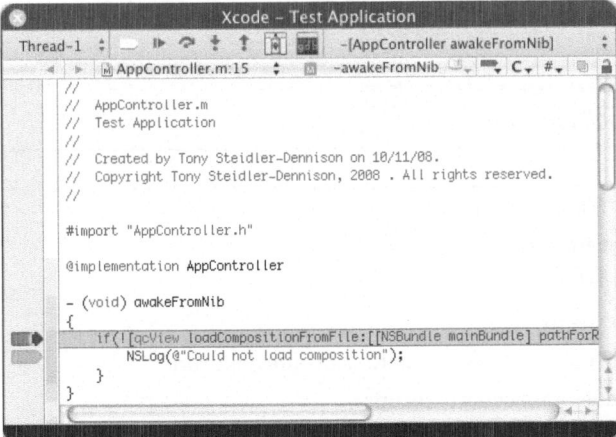

Figure 8-16. *The mini debugger in operation*

The mini debugger offers many of the same tools as the text editor debugger, including the debugger strip and the gutter. However, unlike the text editor, the mini debugger doesn't allow changes to the source files.

Using the Debugger Window

Xcode provides another interface for debugging to accompany the text editor and the mini debugger. The debugger window, shown in Figure 8-17, is the full debugging interface in Xcode.

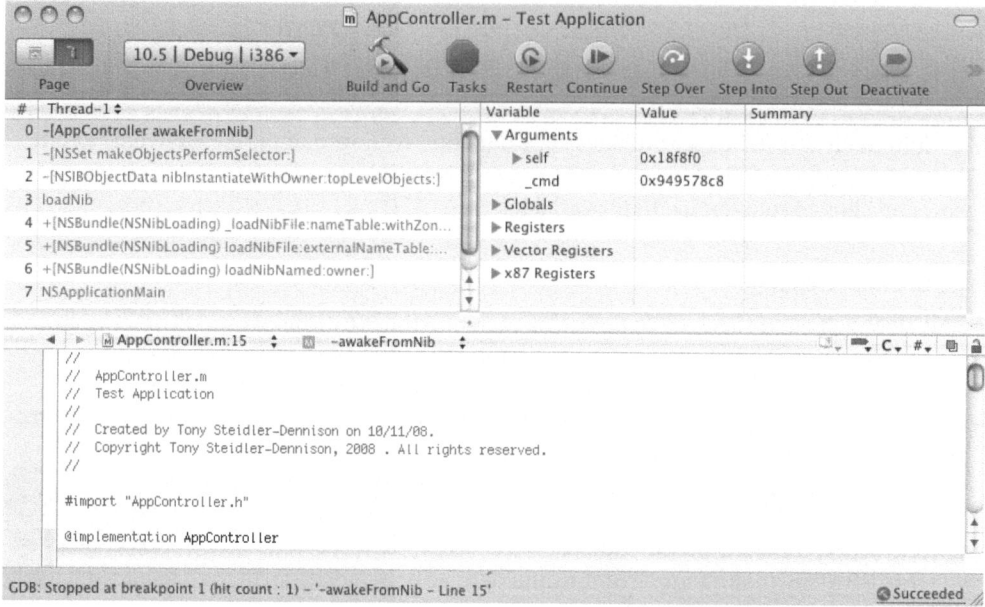

Figure 8-17. *The Xcode debugger window*

The debugger window includes the full set of debugging tools available in Xcode, as listed in Table 8-2 and shown in Figure 8-18.

Table 8-2. *Xcode Debugger Window Toolbar Options*

Button	Description
Build and Go	Builds and runs the application
Tasks (Stop)	Terminates the inferior
Activate/Deactivate	Toggles breakpoints
Fix	Builds a single file fix
Restart	Runs the application in the same state as the previous run
Pause/Continue	Pauses/continues application execution
Step Over	Steps over the current line of code
Step Into	Steps into the call to the current line
Step Out	Steps out of the current function or method

Button	Description
Breakpoints +	Adds a breakpoint
Breakpoints	Opens the breakpoint window
Console	Opens the Console window

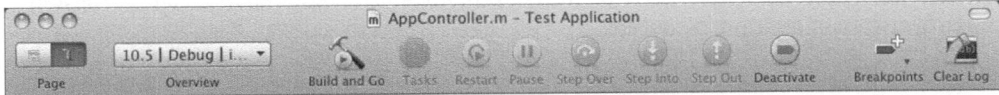

Figure 8-18. *The debugger window toolbar*

With multiple panes, the debugger window provides a wealth of other execution and debugging information. The upper-left pane contains the thread list, with the call stack of the current thread. The upper-right pane contains the variables list, displaying the variables defined in the current scope and any associated values. The lower pane contains the text editor. The status bar resides at the bottom of the window itself, just beneath the text editor. The debugger window also provides some display flexibility, with configuration options for both horizontal (as shown in Figure 8-17) and vertical display.

In short, Xcode provides a powerful set of tools for debugging your application, and maximum flexibility in how those tools are configured and used.

Xcode and Other Application Development Tools

Even though Xcode is the chosen tool for most developers creating applications specifically for Mac OS X, it's not limited to Objective-C, C++, or Java. It is, in fact, a thoroughly modern tool with the flexibility to make full use of other current programming and scripting languages. Whether you're a coder developing object-oriented applications in Python, a web guru creating database-driven sites with Ruby, or a developer who has chosen PHP as your preferred programming language, Xcode will be useful.

The benefits of using Xcode as your development tool might not be obvious until you've used Mac OS X itself for awhile. Xcode provides the native Mac OS X environment, including proper keyboard shortcuts and controls. It also "understands" Subversion, providing both development and source control within a single tool.

The following sections introduce Java, Python, Ruby, and PHP development with Xcode.

Note Xcode provides a strong set of tools for object-oriented programming and scripted solutions. *Xcode Unleashed* by Fritz Anderson (Sams, 2008) and *Beginning Xcode* by James Bucanek (Wrox, 2006) provide full, book-length views of Xcode.

Xcode and Java

Java is another development language included in Mac OS X. Java 2 Standard Edition 5 (J2SE 5) is included in the standard Mac OS X installation, with J2SE 6 available as a software update. Both 32- and 64-bit versions of Java are included in the J2SE 5 installation, while the J2SE 6 version is 64-bit and Intel only.

It's easy to create a new Java project in Xcode, as shown in Figure 8-19. As Java is a native development language in Mac OS X, no further modification is required for Xcode to see and make Java available within its tool set.

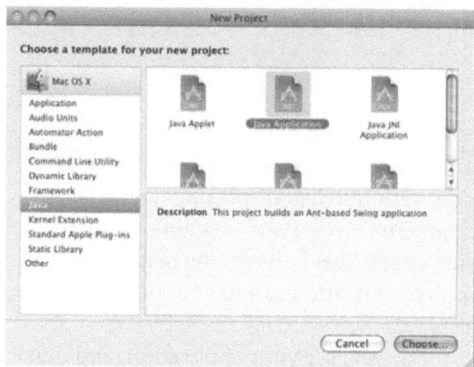

Figure 8-19. *Creating a Java application in Xcode*

Some additional tools are installed in Mac OS X specifically for use with Java. Apache Ant is the tool used by Mac OS X to compile and run Java applications. This, too, is included in the standard Mac OS X installation. The Jar Bundler allows developers to build and deploy Java JAR files as applications that can be launched in the same way as any other Mac OS X application. These JAR files won't require the use of the terminal for operation. Additionally, the Mac OS X installation includes Applet Launcher, which simplifies applet testing in Mac OS X by providing a GUI to Sun's Java plug-in. Applets can be launched from an HTML page, with applet performance and behavior settings configurable via the Java Preferences application.

Mac OS X contains some additional Java-specific development and deployment tools, including the following:

- *Java Web Start*: A tool to launch and modify settings for Java Web Start applications.

- *Java Preferences*: A tool that allows developers to specify settings for Java applications, plug-ins, and applets.

- *Input Method HotKey*: A tool that lets developers set a keyboard combination for invoking the input method dialog box in applications with multiple input methods.

- *JUnit*: A Java unit testing interface.

- *Apache Maven*: A development consolidation tool, including dependency and release management.

- *Apache Ant*: A tool to automate Java builds.

Xcode and Python

Python, the programming language creation of Guido von Rossum in 1990, has become increasingly popular in the past several years. Renowned for its clean syntax, reasonable learning curve, extensibility, and full object-orientation, Python has garnered a growing following of developers. It's often used as a scripting language to meet quick, one-off needs. Its use has also broadened to include 3D animation and rendering packages such as Maya, graphics creation and manipulation applications such as GIMP and Inkscape, and even games, including Civilization IV.

Released under a GPL-compatible license, Python has also garnered a large and robust user community. It's now a standard element in most Linux distributions. It's also included in Mac OS X, with the Python packages listed in Table 8-3 installed by default.

Table 8-3. *Python Packages Included with Mac OS X Installation*

Package	Description
altgraph	Python graph (network) package
bdist_mpkg	Tool for building Mac OS X installer packages from `distutils`
macholib	Mach-O header analysis and editing
modulegraph	Python module dependency analysis tool
NumPy	Array processing for numbers, strings, records, and objects
py2app	Tool for creating stand-alone Mac OS X applications with Python
setuptools	Utility to download, build, install, upgrade, and uninstall Python packages
xattr	Python wrapper for Darwin's extended filesystem attributes
Twisted	Event-driven networking engine
wxPython	Python bindings for the wxWidgets tool kit
Zope	Open source application server

When the `.mpkg` or source-built installation is complete, Xcode will recognize PyObjC, allowing you to create a new Python project from the menu. As shown in Figure 8-20, Xcode provides the option to create new Python Cocoa projects directly from the New Project window.

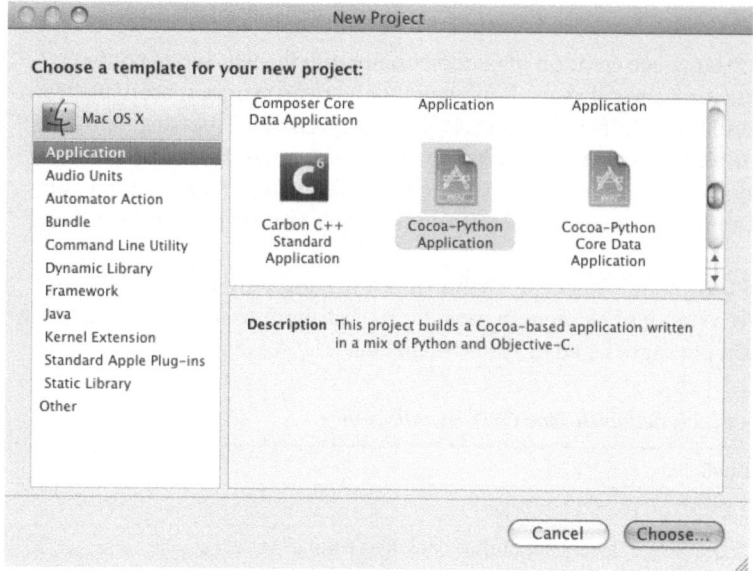

Figure 8-20. *Creating a new Python project in Xcode*

As part of the new Python Cocoa project, the Xcode tool creates the `main.py` file, as shown in Figure 8-21. The tool writes appropriate includes to the file, such as `objc` and Mac OS X classes, including `Foundation` and `AppKit`. Notice that syntax highlighting is fully functional with the PyObjC bindings in Xcode.

While all the Xcode project management tools are available for Python projects, the Xcode debugging tools do not work for Python applications. Python does, however, include the built-in `pdb` debugging module. This is a robust debugging tool, executed from the command line, as follows:

```
$ python -m pdb main.py
> /Users/tony/Development/new_python_application/main.py(10)<module>()
-> import objc
(Pdb)
```

A useful overview of the `pdb` functions is available on the Python site at `http://docs.python.org/library/pdb.html`.

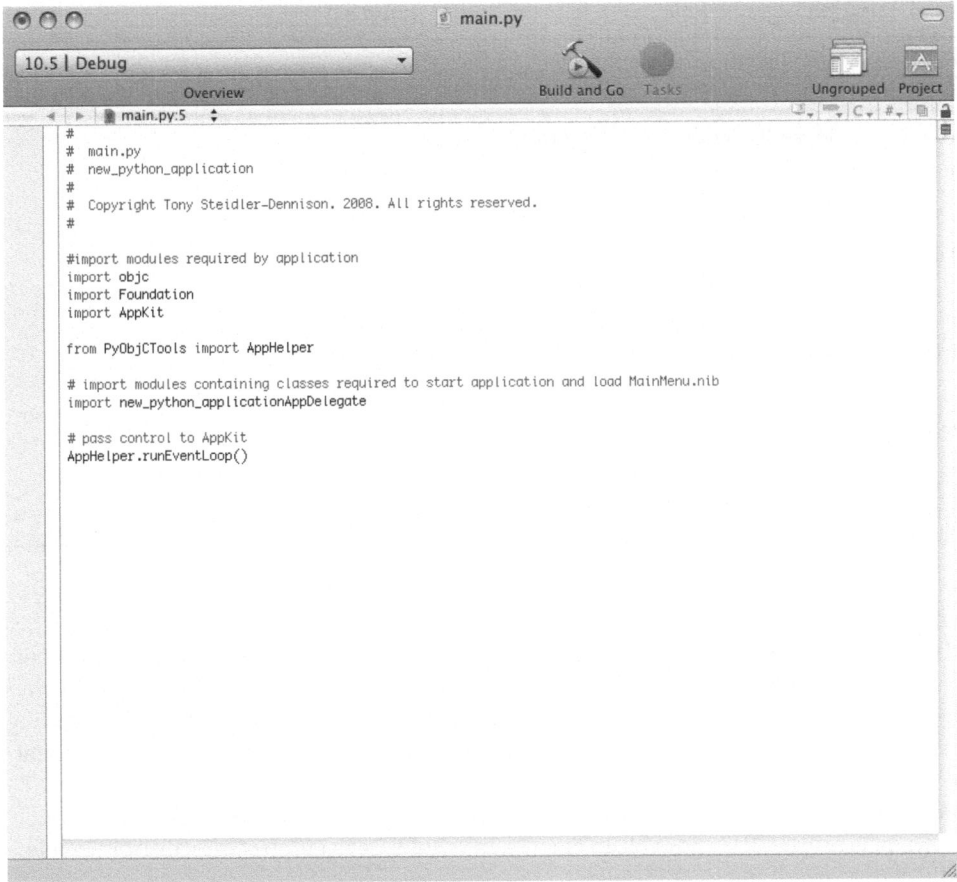

Figure 8-21. *The main.py file in the Xcode text editor*

Xcode and Ruby

Development with Ruby in Xcode is similar to Python development. Like Python, Ruby is included in the base installation of Mac OS X. This also includes Rails, the chosen framework for most current Ruby application development. A number of other Ruby utilities—Ruby gems—are included in the base installation, as well. Overall, Ruby developers will find the Mac OS X Ruby implementation to be extremely friendly and well devised. If you're already familiar with the general user interface layout of the Mac operating system, moving your Ruby development to this platform should be a painless process.

Like Python, Mac OS X provides a robust Ruby installation, including the packages listed in Table 8-4.

Table 8-4. *Ruby Packages Included with Mac OS X Installation*

Package	Description
RubyGems	Ruby package manager
rake	Make-like utility for Ruby scripts
Rails	Framework for database-backed web applications
Mongrel	HTTP library and server, used primarily to build and test Ruby applications
Capistrano	Framework and utility for executing commands in parallel on multiple remote machines, via SSH
Ferret	Search engine
OpenID	Service that provides OpenID identification to Ruby programs
sqlite3-ruby	Module that enables Ruby scripts to interact with a SQLite 3 database
libxml-ruby	Module to read and write XML documents using Ruby
dnssd	Ruby interface for DNS service discovery, implemented as Bonjour in Mac OS X
net	Pure Ruby implementations of the SSH and SFTP client protocols

Additional Ruby libraries and modules can be downloaded from `http://rubyforge.org/`. These are available in `.tgz` source code packages or as `.gem` files, available to RubyGems.

Using the RubyGems tool, a developer can add libraries and packages developed by other Ruby users. This follows the model created by Perl developers and the CPAN system. In short, these libraries represent a true implementation of modular design. With a good understanding and frequent use of the modules found on the RubyForge site, you'll clearly save development time, effort, and debugging by utilizing prewritten code.

As with PyObjC, the installation of RubyCocoa will make Ruby visible to the Xcode tool. As shown in Figure 8-22, it's possible to create a new Ruby Cocoa project directly from Xcode with the RubyCocoa framework installed.

■**Note** The RubyCocoa site (`http://rubycocoa.sourceforge.net/HomePage`) provides ample resources to get you started with Ruby development in Mac OS X., including articles on "the Ruby way," Ruby extensions, and detailed tutorials on Cocoa programming with Ruby. An even more detailed list of RubyCocoa resources can be found at the Ruby Inside site (`http://www.rubyinside.com/ the-ultimate-list-of-rubycocoa-tutorials-tips-and-tools-728.html`).

It's clear that the UNIX underpinnings of Mac OS X provide much the same flexibility for Python and Ruby development as that found in most Linux distributions. While a few extra steps may be required to configure a Mac OS X system for Cocoa development with Python or Ruby, the basic functionality of both exists in the standard installation.

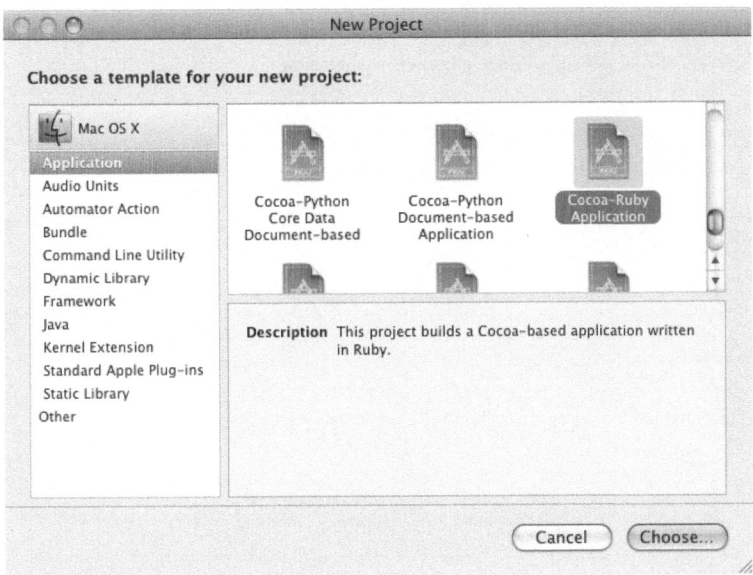

Figure 8-22. *Creating a new RubyCocoa application project with Xcode*

Xcode and PHP

Given the inclusion of Java, Python, and Ruby in the standard Mac OS X installation, it should come as no surprise that PHP is also included in Mac OS X. Mac OS X 10.5 (Leopard) installs PHP 5 by default, with built-in support for the SQLite database. The inclusion of PHP and SQLite, in combination with the default Apache installation, makes Mac OS X a strong web application development environment, requiring little additional configuration.

PHP configuration in Mac OS X starts with the setup of the built-in Apache server. To turn on the server, select Sharing from System Preferences, and check the Web Sharing check box, as shown in Figure 8-23. This enables the Apache server on your Mac OS X machine, using both a system home page and a user-specific home page, as noted in the links within the configuration window. You can check the status of the server by clicking the home page links in this window. As shown in Figure 8-24, a default home page is displayed in Mac OS X when the Apache server is properly configured. The index file is located in /Users/[user]/Sites.

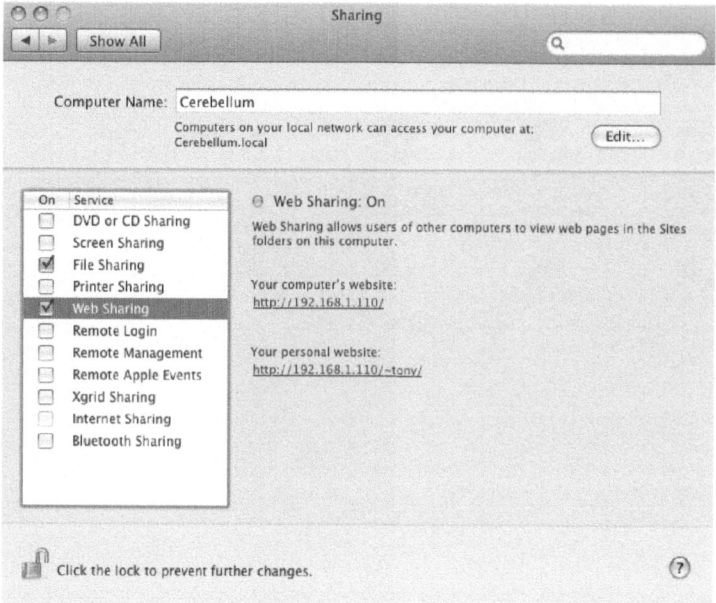

Figure 8-23. *Configuring the Apache server from System Preferences*

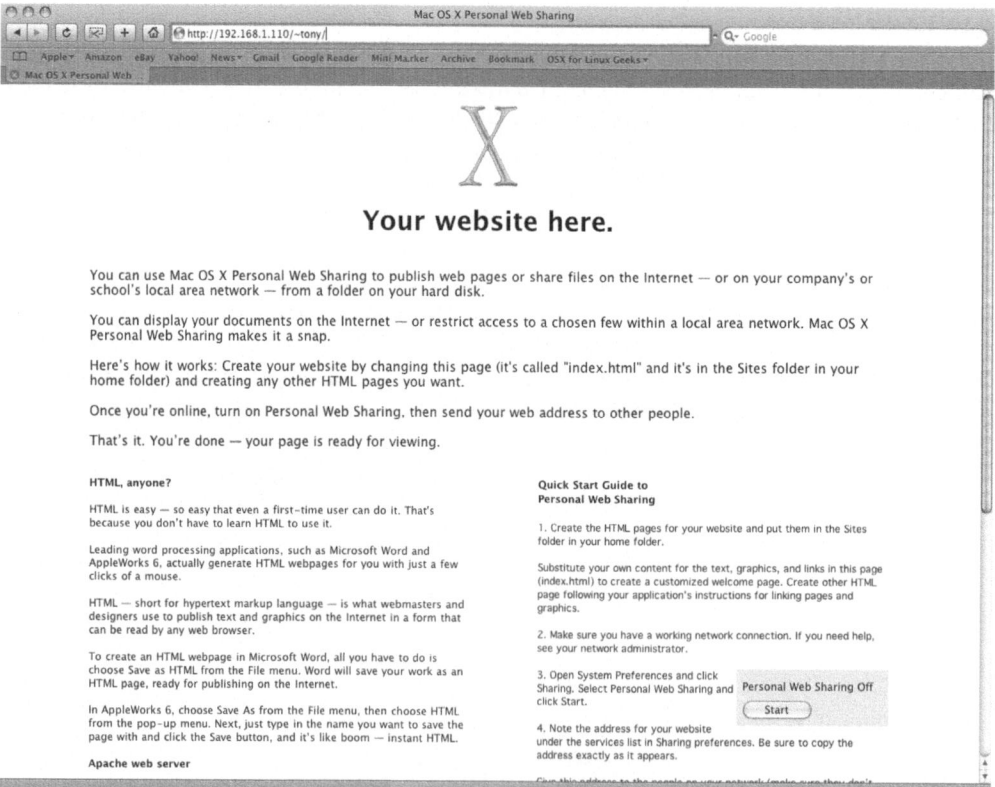

Figure 8-24. *The default user home page in Mac OS X*

While the Apache server is configured out of the box, configuring PHP requires a few additional steps. To load the PHP module in Apache at startup, uncomment the following line in /etc/apache2/httpd.conf:

```
#LoadModule php5_module         libexec/apache2/libphp5.so
```

Then restart the Apache server with the following command:

```
$ sudo /usr/sbin/apachectl restart
```

This will restart the server, loading the PHP 5 module.

You can check the PHP installation by creating a file in the server directory. Simply create a file named phpinfo.php in the document root containing the following:

```
<?php
phpinfo();
?>
```

By loading this page in your browser, as shown in Figure 8-25, you'll test the PHP configuration, as well as display all the pertinent configuration information.

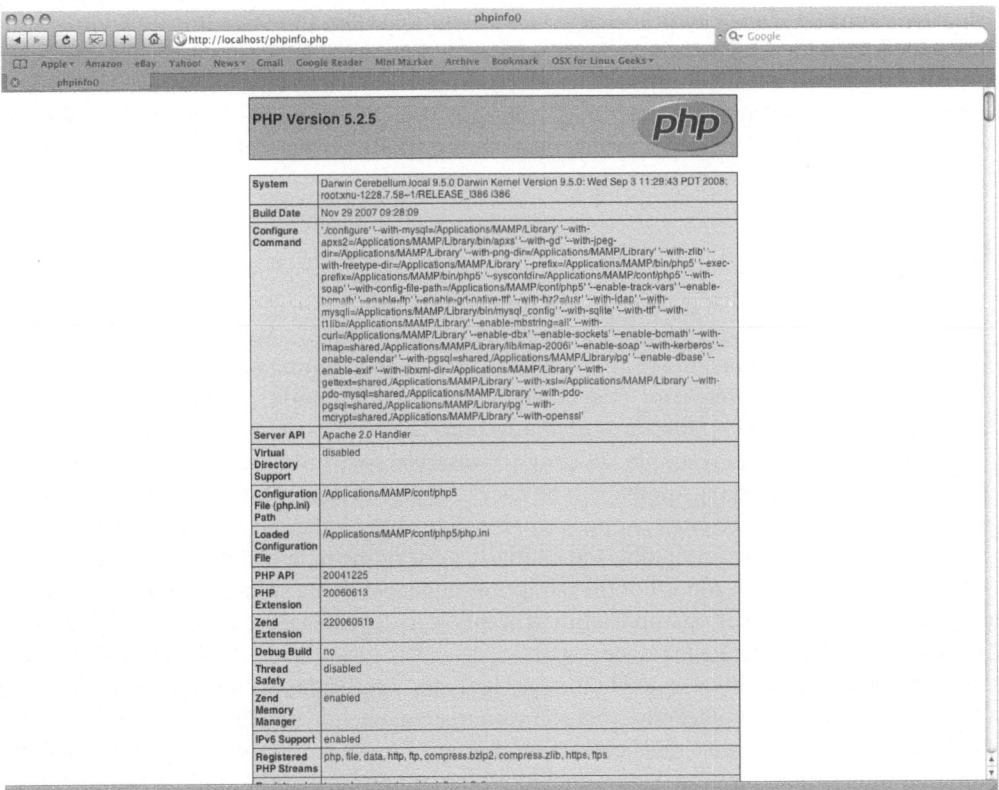

Figure 8-25. *The phpinfo.php page displayed in Safari*

Note PHP development can be greatly enhanced by the use of PEAR modules, available at `http://pear.php.net/`. Like CPAN and RubyGems, PEAR modules are prebuilt code chunks, written to accomplish a specific task. These can be easily rolled into your PHP development. Full documentation to acquire and use PEAR modules is available on the PEAR site at `http://pear.php.net/manual/`.

The inclusion of PHP in the base Mac OS X installation rounds out the remarkably complete set of development tools built into the Mac operating system. You've seen that the Mac OS X platform includes the most current programming and scripting languages, all of which are available (some with minor additional configuration) from within the Xcode interface.

Scripting

Aside from the built-in programming languages, Mac OS X supplies a great environment for scripting and scripting solutions. The UNIX basis of the operating system provides all the tools necessary for shell scripting. As with a Linux system, you can create scripts on the fly to accomplish any number of administrative tasks. Scripts can also provide some functionality in other application development.

Bash, Python, Perl, and Ruby provide strong scripting functionality, and all are available in the Mac OS X installation. In practice, scripting in Mac OS X using these languages will be virtually indistinguishable from scripting on a Linux or UNIX system. But for many, scripting in Mac OS X starts with the native scripting tool: AppleScript.

Using AppleScript

AppleScript is a scripting language that can respond to a number of events in Mac OS X by performing a set of defined operations or by providing data. An *event* in Mac OS X is an internal message containing commands or arbitrary data. The Open Scripting Architecture (OSA) is the API at the heart of AppleScript. OSA makes it possible to communicate with other scripting languages and with other applications on the system.

Lexically, AppleScript is simple, utilizing 103 reserved keywords. As with Python, the syntax is also simple, making AppleScript an easy language to learn. However, the simplicity of the language itself is deceptive. AppleScript is a rich, object-oriented scripting language, perfectly suited to creating scriptable applications, performing repetitive operations, and providing access to applications or other scripting languages in the system. Apple provides a comprehensive guide to using AppleScript at `http://developer.apple.com/referencelibrary/GettingStarted/GS_AppleScript/index.html`.

The AppleScript Utility, located in the `Applications/Applescript` directory, is used to configure the use of the AppleScript tools on your system. As shown in Figure 8-26, the configuration options include a choice between scripting editor versions, the ability to utilize GUI scripting and provide universal access (including voice control), and the ability to set up folder actions for AppleScripts. (*Folder actions* are repetitive actions taken on the contents of a folder, such as periodically checking whether the folder contents have changed, and moving any new contents to another folder.)

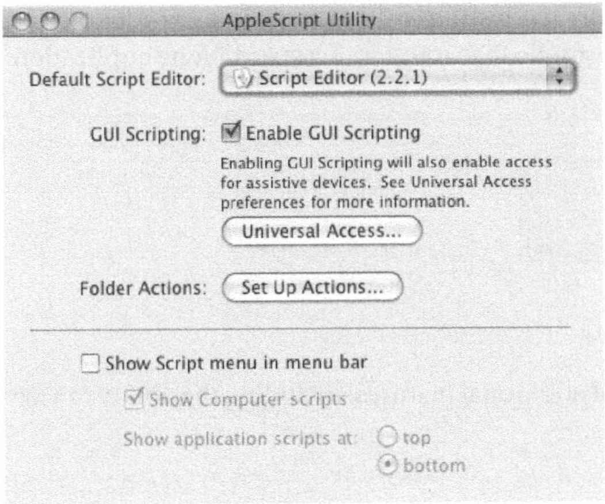

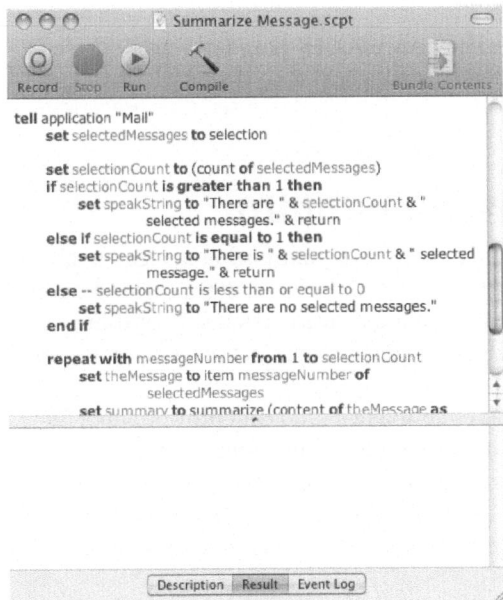

Figure 8-26. *The AppleScript Utility*

Creating Scripts with the Script Editor

Mac OS X provides the Script Editor, located in the `Applications/Applescript` directory. This is a rich editor used primarily for creating, testing and, where necessary, compiling AppleScript scripts. However, it also understands the other scripting languages on the system, including bash, Python, Perl, and Ruby.

As shown in Figure 8-27, the Script Editor utilizes a multipane window and syntax highlighting. The sample script shown in Figure 8-27 is a pure AppleScript script, with the appropriate syntax highlighting. Scripts written in other scripting languages in the Script Editor will be highlighted accordingly.

Figure 8-27. *The Script Editor*

Figure 8-28 shows the Script Editor toolbar. The buttons on this toolbar allow you to record macros, run and stop a script, and to compile that script into a stand-alone application for Mac OS X.

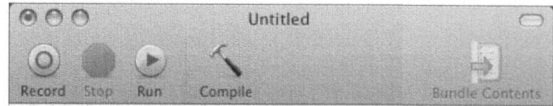

Figure 8-28. *The Script Editor toolbar*

The Script Editor provides a wide range of additional features, including the ability to view the data dictionaries of scriptable applications.

Tip Also worth noting is Automator, an Apple script-creation tool included in Mac OS X. Automator makes it possible to create scripts without actually writing any code. It's a graphical tool that provides a library of common actions in the form of graphical objects. The interface allows you to create relationships between these actions by dragging and dropping them into the proper sequence. The output is in the form of *work-flows*, which carry out the actions specified by the user. Ben Waldie's book *Automator for Mac OS X 10.5 Leopard: Visual QuickStart Guide* (Peachpit Press, 2008) provides a detailed discussion of Automator.

Using Other Scripting Languages

As noted, it's possible to use other programming languages in Mac OS X, just as you would on any other UNIX system. Bash, Perl, Python, and Ruby are all installed with Mac OS X, and are available without further configuration. Scripts in these languages can be created with any text editor or with the Script Editor. The Script Editor also provides GUI-based testing for these scripts. In practice, scripting in Mac OS X using these languages will be virtually indistinguishable from scripting on a Linux or UNIX system.

Code Maintenance and Revision Control

Mac OS X is packed with modern useful development tools: programming languages, a robust debugger, and a project organization and management tool. Combined, they provide a development environment that's very much the equivalent of most Linux systems. Everything necessary to create applications and scripts for all computing platforms is available at no additional cost and only minimal additional effort.

But even a good development environment is incomplete if it doesn't provide a tool for source and revision control. Any developer who has lost a significant chunk of irreplaceable code will vouch for the value of source control. Even lone developers have come to rely increasingly on revision control. The abilities to assess and summarize differences between files, to roll back to previous versions, and to take complete control of all source code are critical to successful software development.

From what you've seen of the built-in tools in Mac OS X, it should come as no surprise that it includes the latest and greatest source control system: Subversion. As you would find in most Linux distributions, Subversion is available both from the command line and with several well-developed front-end tools. Additionally, you can use Git with Mac OS X. Let's look at each of these revision control options, beginning with an overview of Subversion.

Introducing Subversion

Subversion has become a popular tool for version control. Developed by CollabNet in 2000 as a replacement for the Concurrent Versions System (CVS), Subversion has become the primary version control system on open source projects, including Apache, Python, Mono, GNOME, Ruby, and others. It's also moving toward prominence in the commercial world, where tools saddled with annual and per-seat licensing fees have long held sway. Both open source developers and corporate software developers have begun to appreciate the power of Subversion.

Subversion vs. CVS

Subversion offers several important improvements over the older CVS. These improvements provide users with more control over the tool, more flexibility in how versioning is accomplished, and a full set of APIs that make it extremely customizable for unique uses. These improvements are accomplished by the following:

Directory versioning: Subversion utilizes a "virtual" versioned filesystem that allows tracking of both files and directory trees. This is a significant improvement over CVS, which tracked versions only on individual files.

Versioned metadata: The metadata of all files and directories—the data describing the properties of the files and directories—can be created and modified by the user. This data is versioned with the data contained in the files themselves.

Atomic commits: Atomic commits guarantee that if an entire collection of changes cannot be committed to the repository, none are committed. This is important to the work flow of developers, as it allows them to structure their changes in a more logical fashion. It also guarantees that no problems will arise with committed code for which only a partial set of changes have been committed.

Network flexibility: Subversion can be plugged into Apache as a module. It can be used over the network as a stand-alone tool. Subversion can also be implemented within a secure Shell (SSH) tunnel across a wide network.

Binary/text parity: Both binary and text files can be committed and tracked using Subversion. The algorithm implemented to recognize and express the differences between versions is identical in both text and binary files. This results in a much more seamless work flow, in which all files are handled in the same way.

Branching and tagging: Subversion creates branches in a manner similar to hard-linking. (See the "How Does Time Machine Do That?" section of Chapter 7 for a description of hard-linking.) Both branches and tags are created and maintained using this mechanism.

True versioning: One significant drawback of CVS was its inability to distinguish files with the same name. If, for example, a file in a CVS repository was replaced with a new file of the same name, the versioning history of the predecessor file attached to the new file. Though that old versioning history may have literally no relevance to the new file, it was attached. Subversion creates a new version history with each file added to the repository, regardless of a similarity in names. Furthermore, file copies and renames are fully supported in Subversion, unlike CVS.

Open API: Subversion is implemented as a collection of shared C libraries. The APIs for these libraries are well known and well defined. As a result, Subversion can be customized, modified, and extended to more closely suit the users' needs.

Clearly, Subversion is a strong evolution from its predecessor CVS. It provides users with much more power and flexibility than its predecessors, and does so in a much more intelligent way. And, of course, it's included and ready to use in Mac OS X.

Subversion's Copy-Modify-Merge Model

Subversion implements a *copy-modify-merge* model of version control. Most older version control systems, including CVS, utilize a *lock-modify-unlock* model for version control. These models are critical for capturing all changes to a file, even when those files are under concurrent modification by different developers. The problem lies in how those changes are tracked. If the files are simply shared, without either type of version control model in place, changes made by one developer will surely be overwritten by another. That is, in the end, one of the most important reasons to use a version control system, especially in an environment where many developers will have access to a set of files.

In the lock-modify-unlock version control model utilized by CVS and other older version control systems, a file can be modified by only one user at a time. The first user to access the file in the repository "locks" the file, preventing write access by other users. Clearly, this is an inefficient model. One developer must wait for another to finish making changes to a file. Even if the second developer intends to make changes that will not conflict with changes made by the first, she will need to wait until the first user unlocks the file.

The copy-modify-merge model allows individual Subversion users to copy a file from the repository and make changes to the file locally. When complete, those changes will be merged with all other changes made to the file after the time it was checked out. At the time of the commit, Subversion notifies the "last-in" user that additional changes have been made to the file. The developer will then use the merge command to modify the local working copy of the file with changes to the file on the repository. If no conflict exists, the "last-in" file is committed seamlessly to the repository. If a conflict does exist between the changes, the user is notified of the conflicts and presented a view of both sets. One set will be selected manually and, once those changes are incorporated, the file can be committed back to the repository.

In short, the copy-modify-merge model is a much more efficient model for tracking modifications to a file. It allows multiple users to truly work on files simultaneously and handles conflicting changes to files in an intelligent fashion.

Using Subversion from the Command Line

Subversion is easy to use from the command line. The syntax is as follows:

```
svn <subcommand> [options] [args]
```

Table 8-5 lists some of the commonly used subcommands. The Subversion help (svn --help) lists the full set of subcommands.

Table 8-5. *Common Subversion (svn) Subcommands*

Subcommand	Shortcut	Description
add		Adds a new file or directory to an existing Subversion repository
checkout	co	Gets a local copy of a file or directory from a Subversion repository
commit	ci	Adds a changed local file back into an existing repository
diff	di	Provides a list of differences between two file versions
merge		Incorporates changes made after the file was checked out into the current version, or displays conflicts
update	up	Checks out the most current version of a file or directory

Options for the Subversion commands are a bit more esoteric. Subversion options are global, in that each option has the same effect, regardless of the subcommand used. Some of these option/argument pairs include those listed in Table 8-6.

Table 8-6. *Common Subversion (svn) Options*

Option	Description
--diff-cmd CMD	Uses an external tool (CMD) for diffs
--editor-cmd CMD	Uses an external tool (CMD) for editing
--file (-F) FILENAME	Uses the contents of FILENAME to execute subcommands
--force	Forces the subcommand to run
--help	Displays the svn help information
-- password PASS	Provides an authentication password on the command line
--quiet	Prints only essential information when completing an operation
--revision (-r) REV	Manually provides a revision number for the operation; can include a number, keywords, or dates
--verbose (-v)	Instructs the client to print as much information as possible while running the subcommand

Subversion also includes the svnadmin administrative tool. Like the svn command, svnadmin utilizes several subcommands, including those listed in Table 8-7.

Table 8-7. *Common Subversion Administration (svnadmin) Subcommands*

Subcommand	Description
create	Creates a new Subversion repository
dump	Dumps all changes from within a repository (most often used to move a repository from one location to another)
hotcopy	Makes a safe copy of a repository, regardless of whether other processes are using the repository
load	Loads a set of revisions into a repository, generally from a file created with the dump command
verify	Verifies the contents of a repository, including checksum comparisons of the data stored in the repository

Using Subversion GUI Front Ends

While command-line Subversion is easily the fastest possible way to utilize it, learning the subcommands and the options may not be your cup of tea. As with many great Linux command-line applications, you'll find a full range of GUI front ends for Subversion on the Mac. These tools are free or very reasonably priced, are easy to learn, and, for the most part, are very much an asset to your use of Subversion. If you're disinclined to use the command line, these tools will still maximize your efficiency and your time in using Subversion for your projects. Here, we'll look at two Subversion GUI front ends: Versions for the Mac and RapidSVN.

Versions for the Mac

Aside from providing a front end for Subversion, Versions for the Mac provides some other interesting features that you won't find in other Subversion clients.

Versions is available at http://versionsapp.com/. It is provided as a zip file containing a stand-alone application. It doesn't require any installation other than unzipping the file and dragging the binary into the Applications directory. Double-clicking will open Versions.

Figure 8-29 shows the main Versions window. On the first use, Versions provides several options for setting up a new repository or connecting to an existing one.

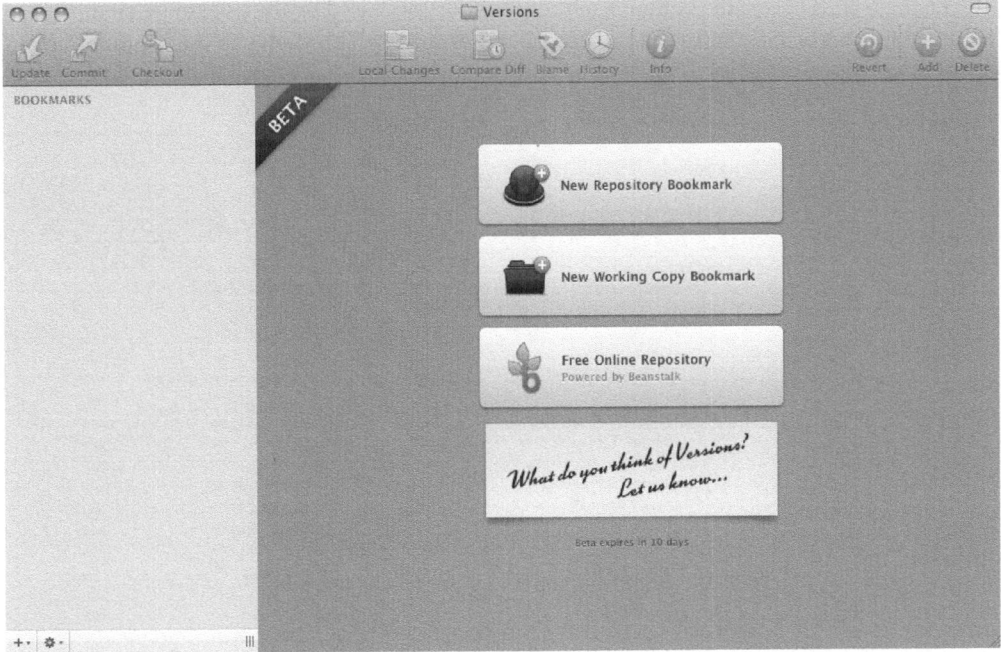

Figure 8-29. *The main Versions window*

The connections to these repositories are created in the form of bookmarks. Figure 8-30 shows an example of creating a bookmark to an existing Subversion repository (the writing repository named LinuxToMac on my system).

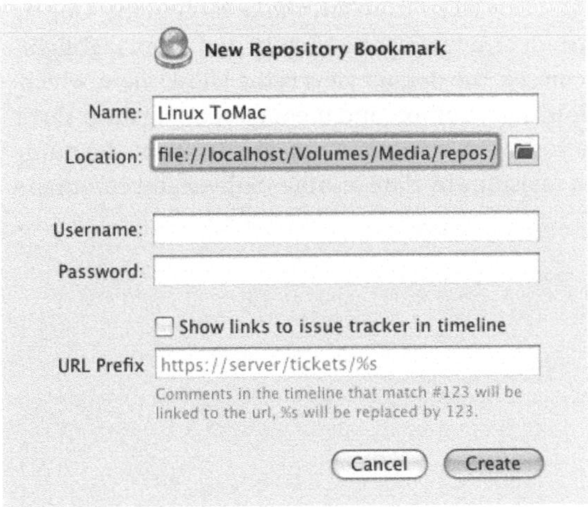

Figure 8-30. *Creating a bookmark to an existing repository in Versions*

Figure 8-31 displays the contents of the repository accessed by the bookmark created in Figure 8-30. This is the view in the Browse tab of Versions, which shows all the files and directories in the repository.

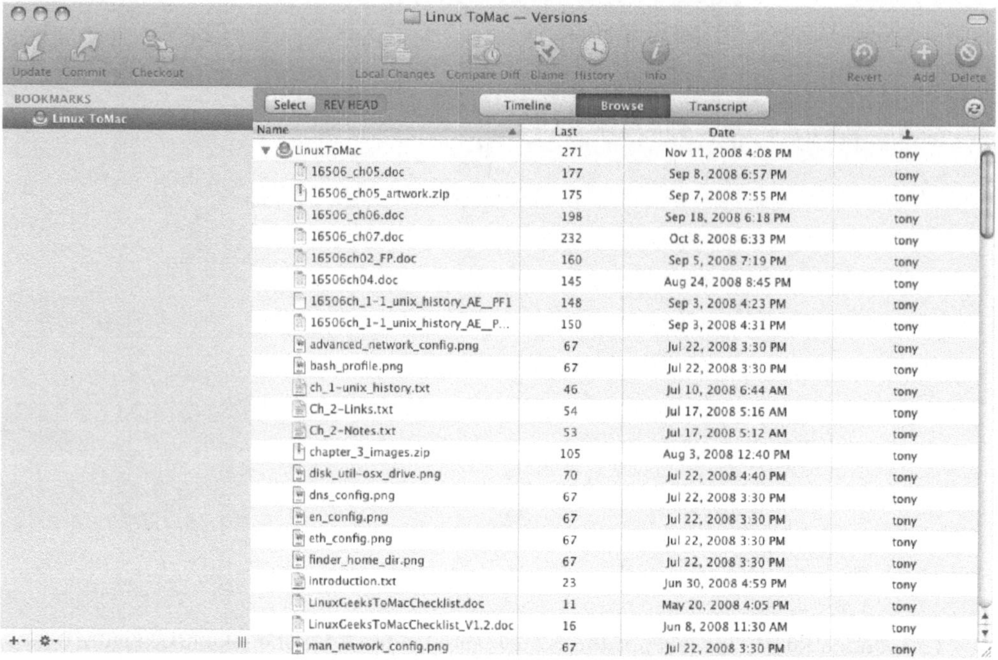

Figure 8-31. *The contents of the repository, accessed by clicking the bookmark in Versions*

By highlighting a file in the Browse tab, you can select from any of the tools in the toolbar in the main window. Figure 8-32 shows the result of selecting the History tool when highlighting the OSXLG_Chap_5_DRAFT.txt file. As you can see, the default view is the HEAD view, which reads the commit metadata, including revision, date, author, and messages. Using drop-down menus in the window, you can further refine your view by broadening or narrowing the number of viewable entries. You can also view the revisions by date or other Subversion command.

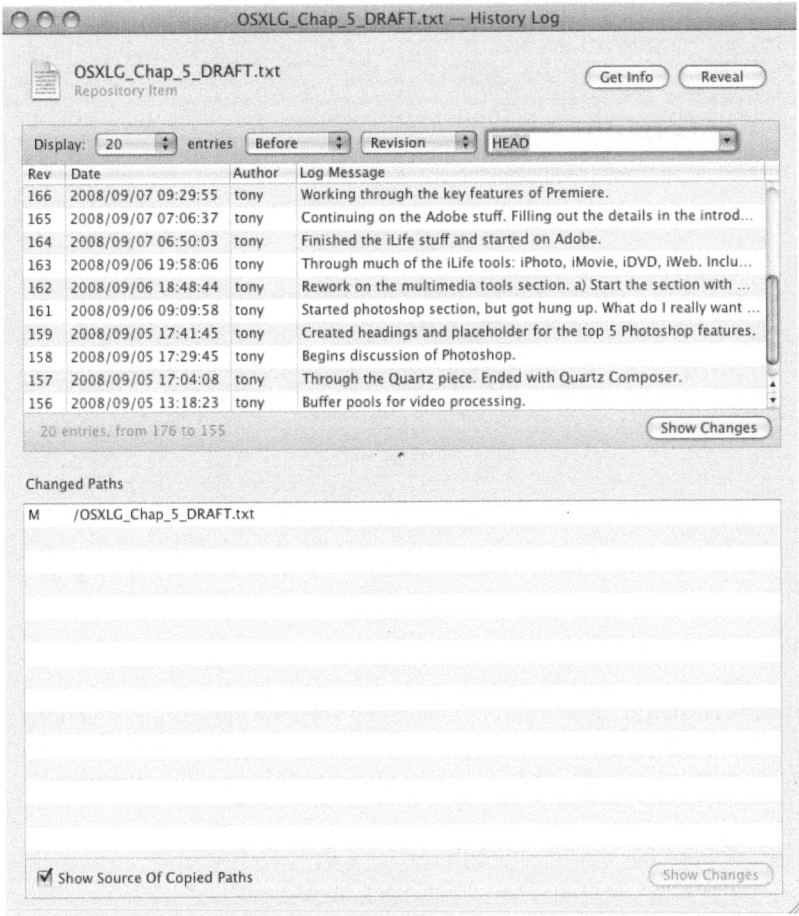

Figure 8-32. *Checking the history of a file from the Browse tab in Versions*

Figure 8-33 shows the use of the Compare Diff tool to compare two different versions of a single file. As you can see, the Versions interface puts all commits of a file side by side in the window.

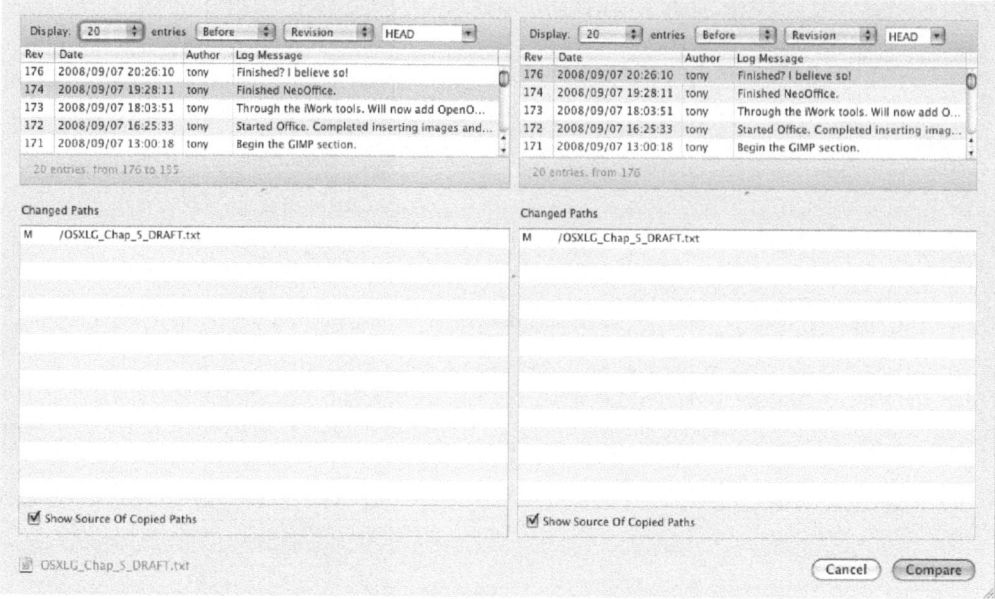

Figure 8-33. *The Compare Diff function in Versions*

Figure 8-34 shows the clean diff presentation provided by Versions. Inserts and deletions are clearly delineated in the Compare Diff window, as is a count of the number of differences. In short, Versions makes it very easy to quickly scan through changes in multiple document versions.

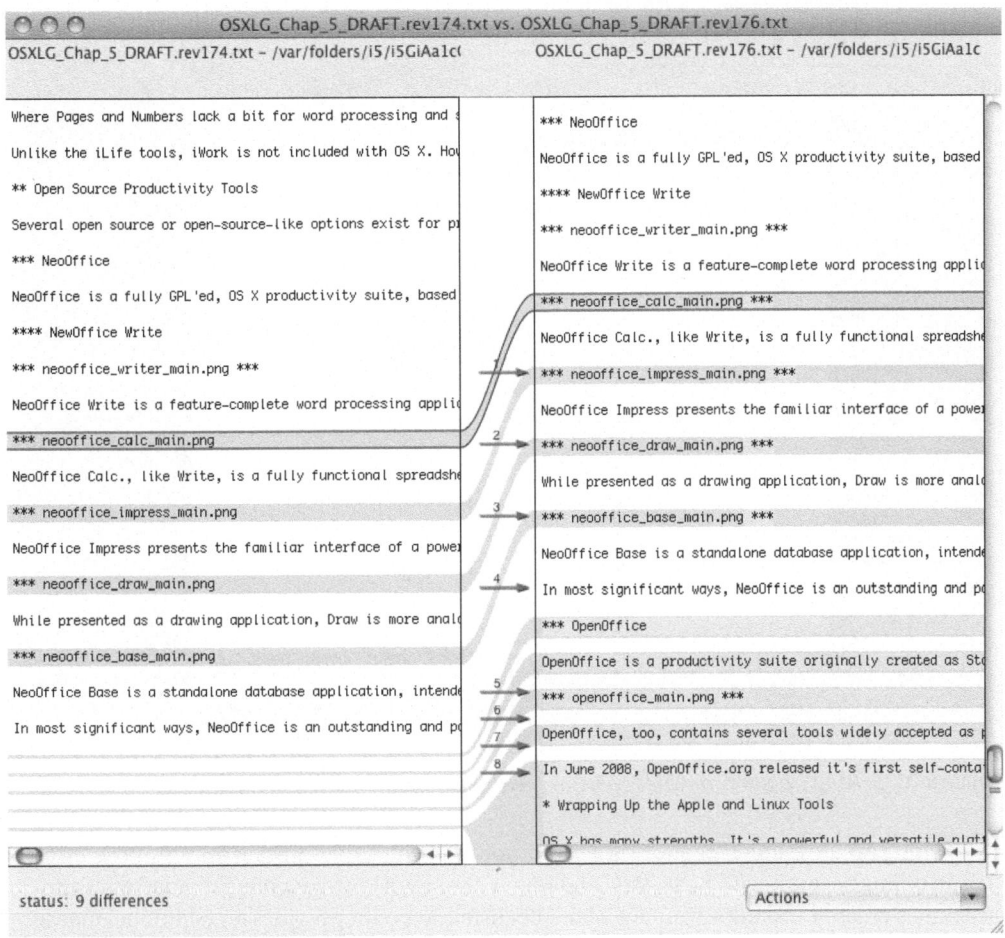

Figure 8-34. *Viewing differences between file commits in Versions*

One of the features of Versions that clearly distinguishes it from other front-end Subversion tools is clear the first time you open the client. The main interface, as shown in Figure 8-35, provides the option to create a free online repository via Beanstalk.

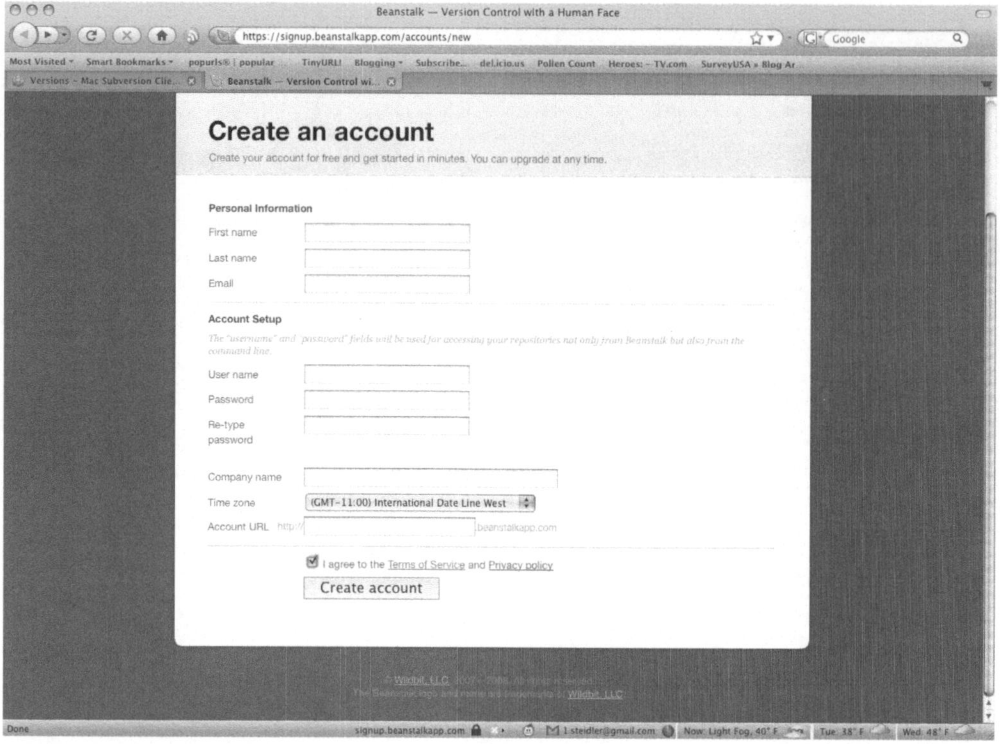

Figure 8-35. *Setting up a free online repository with Versions*

Setting up an online repository is a pretty painless process, requiring only that you establish an online account with Beanstalk, and follow the simple instructions provided once the account is created. Taking advantage of the Beanstalk account provides an additional measure of code security, since the files are stored off-site. Committing, checking out, and viewing files in a Beanstalk repository with Versions is no different from taking those same actions on locally stored files. The drawbacks to the free Beanstalk accounts are the limits of 20MB storage and three developers.

Versions provides access to the full set of Subversion subcommands and options. With the additional bonus of an online Beanstalk repository, it's a tool you'll certainly want to consider when looking at GUI front ends for your Subversion installation.

RapidSVN

Another GUI Subversion tool for Mac OS X is RapidSVN. It's available in .dmg image form at http://rapidsvn.tigris.org/.

Like Versions, RapidSVN uses bookmarks to create a new repository or to connect to an existing repository. As shown in Figure 8-36, creating a bookmark to a repository in RapidSVN requires only that you configure the URL for the repository. This can be an online repository or a local version.

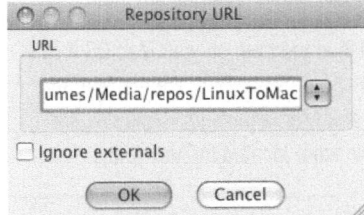

Figure 8-36. *Creating a repository bookmark in RapidSVN*

As with other GUI Subversion tools, the repository is browsable in a single RapidSVN window, as shown in Figure 8-37.

Name ▼	Revision	Rep. Rev.	Author	Status	Prop
Revisions	266	266	tony		
16506_ch05.doc	177	177	tony		
16506_ch05_artwo...	175	175	tony		
16506_ch06.doc	198	198	tony		
16506_ch07.doc	232	232	tony		
16506ch02_FP.doc	160	160	tony		
16506ch04.doc	145	145	tony		
16506ch_1-1_unix.	148	148	tony		
16506ch_1-1_unix..	150	150	tony		
advanced_network...	67	67	tony		
bash_profile.png	67	67	tony		
ch_1-unix_history....	46	46	tony		
Ch_2-Links.txt	54	54	tony		
Ch_2-Notes.txt	53	53	tony		
chapter_3_images....	105	105	tony		
disk_util-osx_driv...	70	70	tony		

RapidSVN – file:///Volumes/Media/repos/LinuxToMac

▼ 🖥 Bookmarks
  ▼ file:///Volumes/Media/repos/L
    ▶ Revisions

Ready

Figure 8-37. *Browsing the repository in RapidSVN*

The RapidSVN Preferences window allows you to configure the various tools used to take actions on the files controlled by Subversion. As shown in Figure 8-38, these include the Diff tool, the Merge tool, and the editor. The Preferences window also provides general configuration options and options for authentication.

> **Note** As is the case in Linux, you can check whether a specific tool is in the path on your Mac OS X system. To do so, simply open a Console window and enter the command `which [tool]`. If the tool is in the path, its location will be returned in the command line. To find the Diff and Merge tools for RapidSVN, for example, I executed the `which` command, which showed that both tools were located in `/usr/bin`.

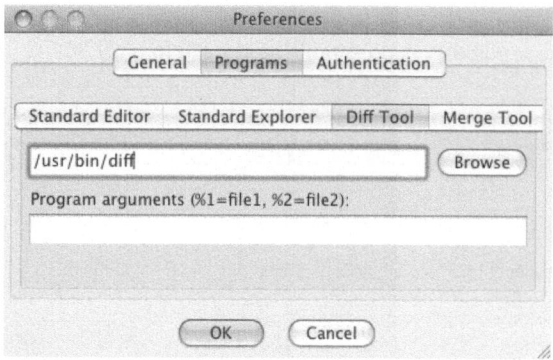

Figure 8-38. *Configuring the RapidSVN preferences*

Like Versions, RapidSVN provides the full set of Subversion tools for version control. However, one of the primary differences between the Versions and RapidSVN applications is the location of these tools. Versions places the most commonly used tools on the toolbar in the main window. RapidSVN places those tools in a context menu launched by right-clicking a file.

Managing Changes with Git

Subversion has the current buzz, but it's not the only version control system for Mac OS X. Git is a scalable, distributed version control system for Linux that installs easily in Mac OS X.

While Git is a powerful version control tool, its real power is in a distributed environment serving many developers. Within the open source community, Git is used in projects as diverse as Linux kernel development, Wine, and X.Org. Like Subversion, Git uses the copy-modify-merge versioning model, allowing users to create local copies of files, and then managing concurrent changes at the time of check-in to the repository. Other Git features include the following:

Git protocol: This is an efficient network protocol created specifically for Git. Users can also optionally use the HTTP protocol to check out and commit files.

Scalability: Git is designed with large projects in mind. It scales quickly and easily to accommodate ever-growing project demands.

UNIX tool approach: Git makes full use of the UNIX philosophy of many small tools that do one thing right. As a collection of these tools written in C, Git provides nearly unlimited flexibility for developers.

Cryptographic history authentication: Git histories are stored in a way that prevents those histories from being changed. This ensures the integrity of the file version histories.

The source code for Git is available at `http://git.or.cz/`. A Mac OS X `.dmg` image is available at `http://code.google.com/p/git-osx-installer/downloads/list?can=3`, as is the `OpenInGitGUI` front-end zip file.

To build and install Git from the source code package, execute the following commands:

```
$ tar zxvf git-1.6.0.4.tar.gz
$ cd git-1.6.0.4
$ ./configure
$ make && sudo make install
```

To install from the `.dmg` image, double-click the image file to mount the image, double-click the installer package, and follow the prompts.

Like Subversion, the command set for Git is deep. The command syntax is as follows:

```
git [--version] [--exec-path[=GIT_EXEC_PATH]] [-p|--paginate|--no-pager] [--bare]
[--git-dir=GIT_DIR] [--work-tree=GIT_WORK_TREE] [--help] COMMAND [ARGS]
```

The most common Git commands are listed in Table 8-8.

Table 8-8. *Common Git Commands*

Command	Description
add	Adds file contents to the index
bisect	Finds the change that introduced a bug by binary search
branch	Lists, creates, or deletes branches
checkout	Checks out a branch or paths to the working tree
clone	Clones a repository into a new directory
commit	Records changes to the repository
diff	Shows changes between commits, commit and working tree, and so on
fetch	Downloads objects and references from another repository
grep	Prints lines matching a pattern
init	Creates an empty Git repository or reinitializes an existing one
log	Shows commit logs
merge	Joins two or more development histories together
mv	Moves or renames a file, a directory, or a symlink
pull	Fetches from and merges with another repository or a local branch
push	Updates remote references along with associated objects
rebase	Forward-ports local commits to the updated upstream head
reset	Resets the current HEAD to the specified state

Continued

Table 8-8. *Continued*

Command	Description
rm	Removes files from the working tree and from the index
show	Shows various types of objects
status	Shows the working tree status
tag	Creates, lists, deletes, or verifies a tag object signed with GnuPG

Summary

Right out of the box, Mac OS X provides a complete environment for developers. It starts with the inclusion of several programming languages, focused both on object-oriented programming and on scripting. From C to Objective-C to Perl, Python, and Java—developers will find those language choices to be nearly complete.

Mac OS X also provides a rich development and debugging environment in Xcode. It's powerful and flexible, with all the features developers have come to expect in a modern IDE. And, as the tool used in the development of Mac OS X itself, Xcode is put to the test every day by Apple.

Finally, Mac OS X provides several great options for source control. While Mac OS X developers may install nearly any open source revision control tool, the system includes Subversion, currently one of the most popular code control tools. And if you're looking to make full use of Subversion without the learning curve required for the command-line tool, several GUI options are available. Versions and RapidSVN are two of those options for GUI-based source and code control with Subversion.

In short, if you've cut your programming teeth in the open source world, you'll find a lot of familiar ground in Mac OS X, and most of the tools provided require no further modification of your system.

CHAPTER 9

■■■

Hybridizing Your System

We've spent quite a bit of time trying to raise the comfort factor in making a transition from Linux to Mac OS X. It's clear that much of what can be done on one system can be done on another, although the path to similar tasks may vary. The systems share a common ancestor, after all, in UNIX. BSD *is* UNIX. Mac OS X is based on BSD, although it also contains quite a bit of proprietary code. And Linux is really a close cousin. BSD can run Linux applications, provided the optional Linux emulation layer is selected as an install component. Linux, however, can't run BSD applications. Add to that basic differences in binary formats, and it's not always clear how a specific tool or process will translate from one platform to the other.

As a result, it's not always evident how these robust platforms can be unified to bring the best of all worlds into a single system. For example, how can we tie the multimedia capabilities of Mac OS X to the strong network infrastructure of BSD and the complete configurability and flexibility of Linux? That would be the ideal, certainly. It's tough to get to that point without some details on the similarities and differences between the systems—the strengths and weaknesses, really. Once you have that knowledge, it becomes much clearer how to best fit the pieces together to meet your needs. With that understanding, it's much easier to adjust your system to meet your work flow.

In this chapter, we'll start by focusing on those similarities and differences, comparing BSD and Linux. From there, you'll be able to bridge any gap in your knowledge, as a Linux geek, regarding BSD, the basis of Mac OS X. Then we'll move on to the details to sharpen the resolution of your mental picture of Mac OS X as it relates to both other operating systems. In other words, we'll start the final chapter of this book with a definitive picture of all three systems and how they can coexist to best meet your needs.

Beyond that initial detailed comparison, we'll dig into some of the serious nuts and bolts of Mac OS X, spending some time on the task that a true Linux geek loves: kernel customization and compilation. It is possible to do. Darwin is BSD, as you know, and kernel building is as cherished a rite of passage for most hard-core BSD users as it is for Linux geeks. Personally, I would make the case that BSD users are doing kernel customization at a higher rate than Linux users these days, or that maybe neither are doing as much as used to be necessary. Most popular Linux distributions have become popular because of their ease of use—most stuff works most of the time. And many of the kernel tools are more deeply submerged in the systems than they've ever been. Short of the thrill of the chase, there's little incentive to expend the sweat when the effort might not measurably improve the system. The kernel-building skills that used to be necessary with Linux have been pushed aside by increasingly slick distributions. But maybe that's just my roots showing. If you're looking to optimize and hybridize the system for your needs, kernel configuration could be an important task.

In order to make the most of your Mac OS X system in the same way you've made the most of your Linux system, you will probably also need to add some Linux and BSD tools. That may present a challenge or two, but it's a challenge you can meet. We'll spend a bit of time in this chapter walking through the process of porting Linux and BSD applications to Mac OS X. With some effort, that should fill some of the cross-operating system potholes you may run over in the transition from Linux to Mac OS X. Remember that Mac OS X, like Linux, has a full complement of development tools, which will aid in porting and compiling Linux apps.

Finally, we'll look at how to run those desktop environments in Mac OS X that you've come to know and love in Linux. We'll walk through the process of installing and configuring both GNOME and KDE in Mac OS X.

How BSD and Linux Differ

In order to hybridize your Mac OS X system, it's important to understand the differences between BSD and Linux. One of the primary differences is in how each type of system starts up. In this regard, Mac OS X is similar to BSD, while Linux employs a method that relies on runlevels. Another difference is in the licensing for BSD and Linux. But before we get to those issues, we need to look at the basic distinction between a distribution and an operating system.

In order to simplify the following discussions a bit, we'll look at the various BSD versions (FreeBSD, OpenBSD, and NetBSD) as a single entity. We'll also view the various Linux distributions as one system. Some would argue that it's not entirely accurate to make such a statement, as they have some differences. But the similarities between BSD versions and between Linux versions make an argument that focuses on the differences a bit pedantic for our purposes.

Distribution vs. Operating System

The Linux model has become very familiar in the computing world. A Linux kernel is coded and tested by the communtiy, and then approved for release by Linus Torvalds. The testing and development of the individual tools used in the system occur outside the kernel testing. Linux distribution creators then package the kernel with a full set of tools, both for the system and for users. There are literally dozens of these packages—Linux distributions—to serve any number of user needs. Some provide commercial support for a fee. Most rely on community support for noncommercial use. In other words, Linux is a kernel included in collections of applications called *distributions*.

BSD is a full operating system that includes both the kernel and the userland tools. All elements of the system are under the control of the primary BSD developers, whether the particular flavor of BSD is NetBSD, OpenBSD, or FreeBSD. (As mentioned, Mac OS X is based on the latter: FreeBSD.) Because BSD is a true operating system, the BSD engineers can view the system as a whole, decreasing the possibility of incompatibilities among parts of the system.

Runlevels and System Startup

Think back to Chapter 1's initial discussion of the origins of UNIX and its place in the roots of BSD and Mac OS X. You'll recall that BSD is a direct fork of UNIX, created by students at UCB. That fork took shape beginning in the late 1970s, with BSD development proceeding in a path parallel to that of UNIX. As BSD development continued through version 4.2, UNIX development moved into System V (SysV).

Later, in the early 1990s, Linux would take on the SysV model in many ways. One of those ways was its implementation of *runlevels*, an important feature of both SysV and BSD. Briefly, the general concept of runlevels goes something like this: a runlevel determines the processes that are started. In most SysV systems, runlevel 0 shuts down the system; that is, it devolves to a state where no processes are running. On the other hand, runlevel 5 (depending on the Linux distribution) is full multiuser mode, with an X-based login and a graphical environment. Clearly, runlevel 5 requires many more processes than runlevel 0 or runlevel 1, which is single-user mode.

In a SysV system, the runlevel-related instructions for init—the mother of all processes—are provided in /etc/inittab. This file defines the processes to be initiated in each of the runlevels, as well as the starting runlevel of the system itself. The init and telinit commands move the system from one runlevel to another.

Runlevel-related services in SysV systems are generally located in /etc/rc.d /init.d/, although this varies a bit by distribution. These files may be either actual executable files or symlinks to files in another path on the system. In either case, they'll be kicked off at system start by rc (the run command), which is launched by init. Table 9-1 lists the runlevels in various Linux distributions.

Table 9-1. *Runlevels in Various Linux Distributions*

Runlevel	Features	Distributions
0	Halt	Fedora, SUSE, Slackware, Gentoo, Debian
1	Single user	Fedora, SUSE, Slackware, Gentoo, Debian
2	Full multiuser, no networking	Fedora, SUSE, Slackware, Gentoo
	Full multiuser with display manager	Debian
3	Full multiuser, console only	Fedora, SUSE, Slackware
	Full multiuser with display manager	Gentoo, Debian
4	Unused, user-defined	Fedora, SUSE
	Full multiuser with display manager	Slackware, Debian
	Aliased to runlevel 3	Gentoo
5	Full multiuser with display manager	Fedora, SUSE, Debian
	Unused, user-defined	Slackware, Gentoo
6	Reboot	Fedora, SUSE, Slackware, Gentoo, Debian

Note Despite its basis in Debian, Ubuntu doesn't follow the typical Debian runlevel structure. Ubuntu utilizes Upstart, a replacement for the /sbin/init daemon. Upstart starts and stops services based on events. Services can be respawned if they die unexpectedly or separate from their parent processes. Upstart was designed by Canonical specifically for use in Ubuntu.

In short, SysV systems, including Linux, define and launch groups of processes and services known as runlevels, as defined in the `/etc/inittab` file. This is not the case with BSD systems.

BSD doesn't use the `/etc/inittab` file to determine runlevels. Instead, BSD systems use `/etc/ttys` to boot the system into multiuser command-line mode or multiuser graphical mode. The `/etc/ttys` file generally establishes nine virtual terminals, with the GUI residing on tty8, accessible by pressing Alt+F8.

Rather than using `telinit` to move the system to runlevel 6 (reboot), as is the case in SysV systems, BSD systems simply use the `reboot` or `shutdown -r` command. Entering `shutdown` and pressing Enter when prompted will move the system into single-user mode. Typing `exit` in single-user mode will return the system to multiuser mode. While these commands are indicative of a BSD system, they do work on Linux systems, as well. However, unlike BSD, they work with `telinit` to move the system between runlevels.

Linux system startup varies from startup in BSD systems, as well. In Linux systems, the various runlevels are supported by an associated subdirectory on the system. `/etc/init.d` contains a full complement of startup scripts to start various services and applications. Most Linux systems also have an `/etc/rc.d` directory, which contains symlinks to actual scripts in the `/etc/init.d` directory. In the `/etc/rc.d` directory, the symlink names start either with S (for a startup script) or K (for a kill script), followed by a number. When the system starts, it finds all the S scripts in `/etc/rc.d`, and then works through them in numerical order to execute the appropriate `/etc/init.d` scripts. This process is also applied when shutting down the system, using the K scripts.

In BSD systems, all system startup scripts reside in `/etc/rc.d`, and scripts for third-party applications reside in `/usr/local/etc/rc.d`. Startup and shutdown scripts are controlled by another set of scripts in `/etc`. The names of these scripts begin with rc. Bootup services are defined and configured in `/etc/rc.conf`.

To summarize, Linux uses `telinit` to move between runlevels, as defined by `/etc/inittab`. BSD uses `/etc/ttys` to open `ttys`, and the `reboot` or `shutdown` command to start or stop the system. Linux uses startup scripts in `/etc/init.d` via order-named symlinks in `/etc/rc.d/init.d` to start and stop services at bootup and shutdown. BSD defines its startup services in `/etc/rc.conf`, using rc-named scripts in `/etc/rc.d` to start these services at bootup.

Licensing

Linux, as you know, is released under the GPL. This license aims to prevent closed source software. Any application developed and released under the GPL—original or derivative—must be accompanied by the source code for that application, as well as a notice of the terms of the license. The BSD license, on the other hand, is far less restrictive.

All-binary BSD releases are allowed. No source code is required for these releases, whether they are original or derivative. Many systems developers, especially those building commercial applications, find the BSD license to be a much better fit. It's a particularly good fit for small, single-purpose embedded systems.

The differences betwen Linux and BSD in runlevels, startup, and licensing are fundamental. Also, recall that Ethernet interfaces in BSD use a different naming convention than those of Linux, such as en0 in BSD versus eth0 in Linux.

Kernel Customization and Compilation

Nearly every true Linux geek has customized and compiled a kernel. It's possible to do that with Mac OS X as well, although it's not nearly as useful as in Linux.

You can build a standard XNU kernel in Mac OS X, or build one of a few alternate kernel types. As mentioned in Chapter 2, XNU is the kernel at the heart of Mac OS X, and it was also the basis of the NeXTStep system.

The standard XNU kernel will function in exactly the same way as the kernel originally installed on your system. This is considered a RELEASE kernel type. It's possible to explicitly specify a RELEASE kernel when building, although when no additional options are provided during the build process, RELEASE is the default build type. The following kernel configurations are also possible:

- DEBUG and DEBUG_TRACE provide debug and trace symbols.

- RELEASE_TRACE provides the trace function.

Note PROFILE is also available as a kernel configuration. However, it's currently reserved for future use and mapped to the RELEASE build type.

The XNU kernel build itself in Mac OS X is pretty straightforward. It doesn't require much time or configuration of the kernel code itself. In fact, the kernel build is the easiest and shortest part of the process. The element of the process that's time- and resource-consuming is initially setting up your system with all the tools necessary for a kernel build. You will need to download, install, and configure several packages before you'll be able to build an XNU kernel of your own for your Mac OS X system.

Setting Up the Build Environment

All the tools necessary for building a Mac OS X kernel are available from http://www.opensource.apple.com/darwinsource/. Many of the tools listed will require your acceptance of the user license agreement. You'll also need to be registered and signed in to the Apple Developer Connection. Once those steps are completed, download the following individual packages from the list. These tools will be named with the current version number, but for our purposes, you can disregard the version numbers for now.

- bootstrap_cmds

- Libstreams

- kext_tools

- IOKitUser

- cctools

- xnu

These are .tar.gz files. Put these tools in a known directory—perhaps one you created in an easily accessed location specifically for this purpose—and untar the files:

```
cd [your directory]
for i in *.tar*; do \
    tar zxvf $i; \
done;
rm -f *.tar.gz
```

Note If you're downloading the kernel-building files with Safari, it may automatically uncompress the files for you, leaving only the .tar files. In that case, your tar command will not require the z option.

Next, you'll need to ensure that /usr/local/bin is in your $PATH variable. In Mac OS X 10.5, PATH is defined by /etc/paths and /etc/paths.d/. You can make sure that /usr/local/bin is listed in one of these files with the following command:

```
$ echo $PATH
```

If /usr/local/bin isn't listed, add it as a single new line in /etc/paths.

When the file is modified, you can close the terminal window, or use the source command to load the new version:

```
$ source ~/.bash_profile
```

Next, change into the bootstrap_cmds directory:

```
$ cd bootstrap_cmds-[version]
```

This directory contains a tool you'll need to build from source, using gcc, in order to build the kernel.

```
$ cd relpath.tproj
$ gcc -o relpath relpath.c
```

The relpath binary will be located in your current directory. Copy it to the build path noted in the .bash_profile file:

```
$ sudo cp relpath /usr/local/bin
```

Now, install Libstreams:

```
$ cd Libstreams-[version]
$ make && sudo make install
```

Note When building the Libstreams tools, you may get an error message related to the man pages. This won't affect the tools themselves.

Next, change into the directory containing `cctools` in the kernel build tools directory you created. Once there, you'll need to copy a specific header file into a system library directory, as follows:

```
$ cp /usr/include/ar.h ./include
```

You'll also need to modify the makefile in the top level of the `cctools-[version]` directory. Edit the line containing `COMMON_SUBDIRS`, including any wrapped elements, to read as follows:

```
COMMON_SUBDIRS = libstuff libmacho misc
```

Now, you can build the tools with the following command:

```
$ make RC_OS=macos
```

Then copy the tool you just built to the appropriate system directory:

```
$ sudo cp misc/seg_hack.NEW /usr/local/bin/seg_hack
```

You'll also need to build another tool from the `cctools` package and move some additional libraries on the system:

```
$ cd ld
$ make RC_OS=macos kld_build
$ sudo cp static_kld/libkld.a /usr/local/lib
$ sudo ranlib /usr/local/lib/libkld.a
```

Next, we'll move on to the `IOKitUser` and `kext_tools`. First, create a new directory on your system:

```
$ sudo mkdir -p \
/System/Library/Frameworks/IOKit.framework/Versions/A/\
PrivateHeaders/kext
```

Then change into the new directory.

```
$ cd /System/Library/Frameworks/IOKit.framework
```

Create a symlink for the `PrivateHeaders` directory in the current directory:

```
$ sudo ln -s Versions/A/PrivateHeaders PrivateHeaders
```

Now, copy the header files from your uncompressed and untarred `IOKitUser` directory into the `PrivateHeader/kext` directory.

```
$ sudo cp [path to the IOKitUser directory]/IOKitUser-[version]/\
kext.subproj/*.h PrivateHeaders/kext
```

Next, build the `kextsymboltool` from source and copy it into the `PATH`.

```
$ gcc -o kextsymboltool kextsymboltool.c -I../cctools-[version]/include
$ sudo cp kextsymboltool /usr/local/bin
```

That completes the prebuild configuration for your system. Now, we can move on to the full kernel build.

■**Note** The kernel-building files may require rebuilding and reconfiguration as versions of the individual tools are updated. However, that will be the only time rebuilding and reconfiguration are required. The general build environment you set up should need to be created only once.

Building the Kernel

After the multiple steps required to set up the build environment, building the kernel itself seems like a breeze.

Uncompress and untar the xnu kernel source:

```
$ tar zxvf [path to the kernel source]/xnu-[version].tar.gz
$ cd xnu-[version]
$ source SETUP/setup.sh
$ make exporthdrs
$ make all
```

■**Note** If you're using csh, the source command should be source SETUP/setup.csh instead.

When the build process is complete, you'll find a freshly built XNU Mach kernel in the xnu-[*version*] directory at BUILD/obj/RELEASE_I386/.

As I noted earlier, it's possible to build alternative kernels for Mac OS X. This is accomplished at the final make stage, using one of the several options:

```
$ make KERNEL_CONFIGS=all
```

or

```
$ make KERNEL_CONFIGS=DEBUG
```

or

```
$ make KERNEL_CONFIGS=DEBUG_TRACE
```

or

```
$ make KERNEL_CONFIGS=RELEASE_TRACE
```

As mentioned, building without the KERNEL_CONFIGS option builds a RELEASE kernel, as does building with the PROFILE option (currently).

As you've seen, just as with Linux, it is possible to build a new XNU kernel for Mac OS X from source.

Porting UNIX Apps to the Mac

While we're in the realm of the hard-core Linux user, let's take a few minutes to talk about the process of porting applications from other UNIX and UNIX-like platforms to Mac OS X. Bringing new applications from UNIX to Mac OS X may be of interest to in-house app developers, open source developers, commercial UNIX developers, and others. These developers may want to take advantage of the Cocoa look and feel of Mac OS X applications, moving them away from a reliance on X11 or X.Org.

Why Port?

First, it's important to remember the roots of Mac OS X. BSD, the Mach kernel, and NeXTStep each played an important role in the history and development of Mac OS X. These are BSD or BSD-based systems.

In large part, Mac OS X is based on 4.4BSD Lite, with most of the utilities and libraries ported from FreeBSD. It also includes some code derived from NetBSD. Aside from the Apple documentation, the BSD documentation is likely to be your best source of information and troubleshooting tips as you begin to port UNIX applications to Mac OS X.

Mac OS X also relies heavily on the general design philosophy used to create the Mach microkernel and the original design efforts of Carnegie Mellon Unversity. While Apple has moved the Mach kernel a considerable distance from its roots, Carnegie Mellon's underlying theories regarding microkernels and their implementation still hold true. This is good background information to have when moving applications from another UNIX platform to Mac OS X.

The look and feel of Mac OS X is, in no small measure, indebted to NeXTStep. Mac OS X has grown considerably since the acquisition of NeXT by Apple in 1997, but the core technologies that came with the purchase still drive its development. In particular, the Cocoa APIs, some significant advances in how Apple views the kernel space, and filesystem advances are directly attributable to the work done at NeXT.

Those ancestral roots of Mac OS X, aside from providing interesting insight into the operating system, also supply the starting point for the evolution of many of the hallmark Mac OS X functions and features.

It's also important to bear in mind that Mac OS X is *not* an open source operating system. While it relies on Darwin, an open source project, much of the code that interacts with Darwin is the sole property of Apple. Much of the operating system's functionality is controlled by the fact that it's embedded into Mac OS X. That has two critical implications for developers porting applications to the Mac:

- It necessitates a better-than-average understanding of the operation of Mac OS X; in particular, the interaction of Mac OS X with Darwin.

- It has strong implications for licensing. As a developer (especially if you've been an open source developer to this point), you'll need to make some decisions about the licensing for the code you're porting to Mac OS X if you hold the copyright on the code.

That said, market share for Apple products has continued on an upward swing for the past several years. Some would attribute that to the "halo effect" of the iPod—the belief that it's the iPod that continues to bring new users to the Apple family of products.

Some would also attribute the positive market share movement to the general Apple philosophy that both its hardware and software should "just work." To a large extent, that's true. That philosophy has made it possible to bring many to computing who might otherwise be intimidated by the technology. Both the very young and the very old, for example, seem to feel a higher level of confidence when using the Mac. This has helped to lock Apple into a core group of users who will never even consider moving to another computing platform.

Some might also believe that the increasing market share is the result of crafty and intelligent marketing. Apple's "1984," "Think Different," and "I'm a Mac" campaigns are universally recognized for their power in branding the Mac platform and the resulting ability to draw new users into the Apple fold.

Still others take a more pragmatic view of Apple's success, crediting the overall stability of the platform to Apple's complete control over both hardware and its core software. Apple developers have a known hardware platform to which they develop. There are no surprises "in the field," where other companies creating operating systems find the bulk of their problems. There are no third-party graphics cards or the necessary drivers, for example, to stir into the development mix. I/O operations of all types are determined by a known hardware base, an approach that makes the Macintosh platform extremely reliable and predictable.

All these things may be true. All certainly have something to do with the increasing market share of the Apple platform. But what, in the end, does that increase have to do with porting applications from a UNIX platform to the Mac? If you're a commercial developer, it means a new and growing avenue for income.

In general, creating applications for Mac OS X will open even more opportunities as the market share of the platform continues to grow. Whether those applications are targeted to business or consumers, Mac users are accustomed to paying for the efforts of developers. That's a bit different environment than that in which many Linux developers have found themselves. Some Linux developers subsist on salaries or hourly wages, paid for in-house Linux- and UNIX-related work, rather than relying directly on payment for software development. The licensing of many Linux and UNIX applications sets up just such a scenario.

While direct compensation for UNIX work is more common than such payments for Linux work, the slice of the market pie controlled by UNIX is likely to decrease in coming years, as Linux development continues apace. It's much easier for new companies to leverage an open source platform than to pay considerable licensing fees for either UNIX or Windows. So, two of the three market slices from which developers can reasonably expect to draw an income for their efforts—Windows and UNIX—are shrinking, while the Apple slice continues to grow each year across a wide range of environments. While neither of those other two slices is likely to go away completely in the forseeable future, the income opportunities do continue to decrease.

Note With the introduction of Apple's App Store, an entirely new income avenue opened up for developers. To the tune of more than 10,000 applications, software created by individual developers, by small and medium development houses, and by large companies has found a strong niche on Apple's iPhone. Many small development houses, in particular, have come into a windfall since the App Store opening. In some cases, more revenue was generated in a single year (often at 99 cents per download) than in the entire combined history of the company prior to that event—more income derived from a single application than all combined income prior. That makes a pretty compelling case to consider moving your existing applications (especially those that might find a useful home on a mobile device) to the general Macintosh platform.

Income expectations aside, most developers take a real pride in the widespread use of software they've created. You don't create these applications in a vacuum or completely for your own purposes. Like the efforts of a carpenter, an automobile worker, or any other profession in which skilled people leverage tools to create a tangible product, there's a real sense of satisfaction in standing back and watching that product put to use in solving problems in the real world. While it's fundamental economics that everyone makes something, sells something, or services something, it's a fundamental fact of human nature that solving problems for a large pool of users is a very gratifying activity. That pool of users continues to grow on the Macintosh platform, as do the opportunities for the personal and professional satisfaction of a growing number of developers.

So, where to start in porting applications from UNIX to Mac OS X? That depends, in part, on the type of application you're moving from one platform to the other. Here, I'll provide the basics and a starting point for porting applications from UNIX and UNIX-like platforms. the Apple Developer Connection's documentation (`http://developer.apple.com/`) provides all the fine details you'll need to port your applications.

Good Practice

Darwin, as a BSD-derivative, is a prime potential platform for command-line applications. Not only do most command-line applications function well in Darwin, but the users in the environment in which those applications will be used are pretty fluent in their use. Mac OS X users who rely on the command line are, for the most part, converted or parallel UNIX users. They understand the ins and outs, and they're generally pretty proficient in using single tools in combination to maximize their power and efficiency. In other words, users for whom Mac OS X command-line tools will have some appeal understand the UNIX idea of tools doing a single job well.

Note Apple's design philosophy clearly states that users should never need to resort to the command line in order to perform any task for which a GUI is provided (see the Apple Human Interface Guidelines at `http://developer.apple.com/DOCUMENTATION/UserExperience/Conceptual/AppleHIGuidelines/ index.html#//apple_ref/doc/uid/20000957`). However, the very structure of that statement makes it clear that not all tools for the Mac will be based in a GUI.

On the other hand, applications that utilize a GUI will, of course, provide a bit more of a challenge to port from UNIX to Mac OS X. Differences in libraries will clearly stand as the largest issue in porting from UNIX to Mac OS X. (That alone makes another good case for understanding the lineage of Mac OS X.) Depending on the basis of the original application, moving its basic functionality into the graphical framework of Mac OS X may be a challenge, although not an insurmountable one.

With the preceding in mind, here are two general good practice guidelines for porting UNIX apps:

Command line, then GUI: As a general rule, Apple recommends that users porting applications from UNIX to Mac OS X port first to the command line, then to the GUI. In other words, understanding and separating the underlying functionality from the user-facing tools will provide the shortest path to a successful port.

Don't reinvent the wheel: As always, it's important to avoid "reinventing the wheel." Before you start down the path to port an application, make sure a similar application hasn't already been ported for Mac OS X. Investigating the Fink, MacPorts, and Darwin software libraries can save developers from the potentially expensive and exhausting process of duplicating an existing port.

Installing the Development Environment

In order to port your application to Mac OS X, you'll need first to ensure that the development system you'll be working on contains the BSD subsystem. This is an easy matter of checking the /Library/Receipts directory for a BSD.pkg file. This has been installed by default since Mac OS X 10.4, so it's imperative to check only on systems with prior versions of Mac OS X.

You'll also need to become familiar with the Mac OS X Terminal application, which shouldn't be too difficult for anyone comfortable with the terminal in UNIX or Linux. Terminal.app is located in /Applications/Utilities. As shown in Figure 9-1, Terminal.app is a tabbed and themeable terminal. To customize the Terminal application, open it and select Termninal ➤ Preferences from the menu bar. Several color and font schemes are available in the Settings tab. You can also create window groups, which are single window interfaces containing tabs with predefined contents. All in all, the transition to Terminal.app from a standard UNIX terminal application should be pretty seamless.

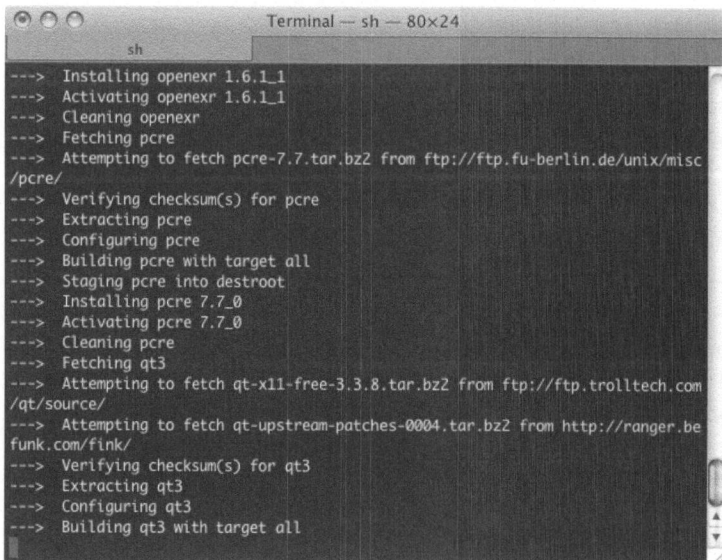

Figure 9-1. *Mac OS X Terminal application*

In order to port your application from UNIX to Mac OS X, you'll also need to install the Mac OS X developer tools on the system, if you haven't already done so. Instructions for installing these tools are provided in Chapter 4. Among those tools are Xcode, the Apple IDE; Interface Builder, the Apple tool for creating the GUI for your application (see Figure 9-2); FileMerge to compare and merge files and directories (see Figure 9-3); and PackageMaker for building Mac OS X packages (see Figure 9-4). These tools are provided on the Mac OS X installation DVD. You'll find them on your system at [`Boot Volume`]/Developer/Applications (Xcode and Interface Builder) or [`Boot Volume`]/Developer/Applications/Utilities (FileMerge and PackageMaker).

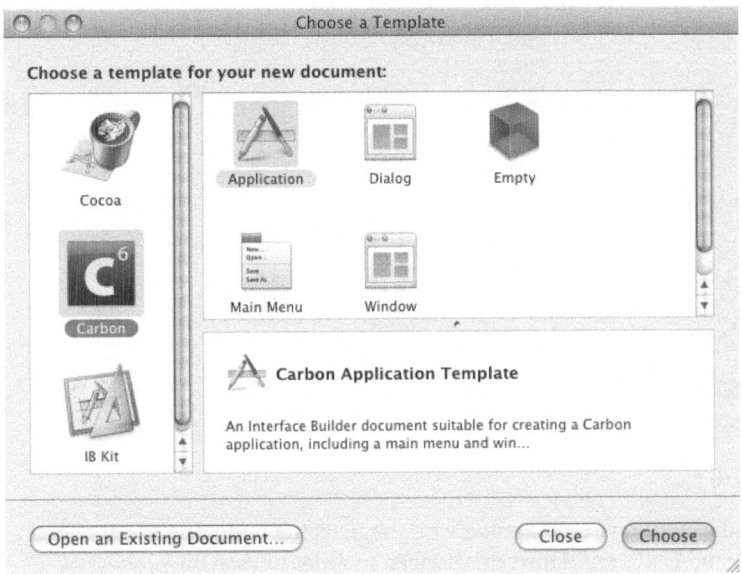

Figure 9-2. *Xcode Interface Builder*

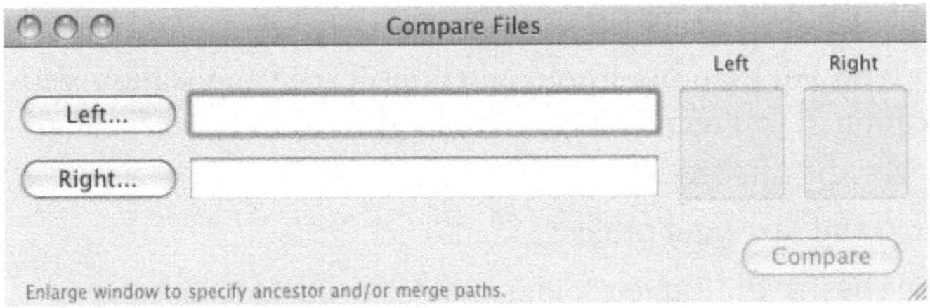

Figure 9-3. *Xcode FileMerge*

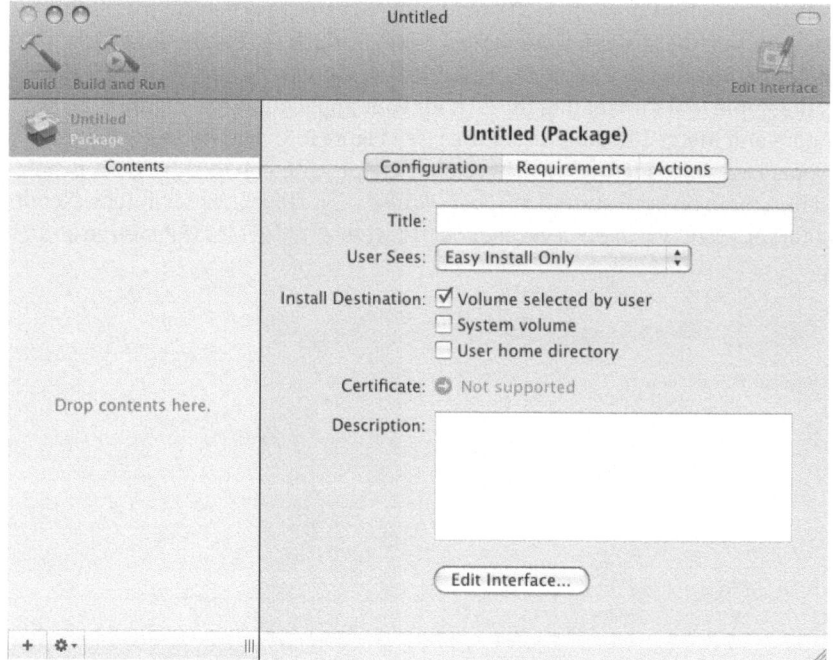

Figure 9-4. *Xcode PackageMaker*

Creating Makefiles

If you're a Linux or UNIX developer, you're familiar with the makefile build process. It's the time-honored path of all good UNIX and Linux developers. In order to ease the process of porting applications to Mac OS X, and to avoid an increased learning curve, you'll probably want to continue that tradition with your own applications. Fortunately, Xcode plays well with makefiles. Here's the procedure for creating makefiles:

1. Launch Xcode and choose File ➤ New Project.

2. Select the targeted project type. For example, if your end project is an application, you might select Cocòa Application. If you're building a command-line utility, select Standard Tool.

3. Follow the prompts to name and save your project.

4. Open the disclosure triangle beside the Targets folder and delete any default targets that may exist.

5. Select Project ➤ New Target to open the window shown in Figure 9-5.

6. Select External Target from the list, and then follow the prompts to name that target. When completed, a target icon with the name you just gave it appears in the Targets pane of the open Xcode window.

7. Double-click the new target. You'll see a new window with the build information for this target similar to Figure 9-6.

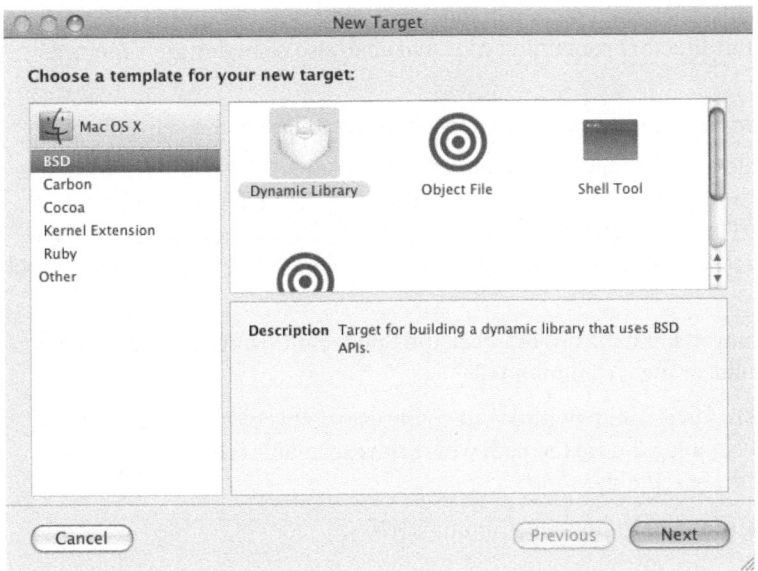

Figure 9-5. *Creating a new target*

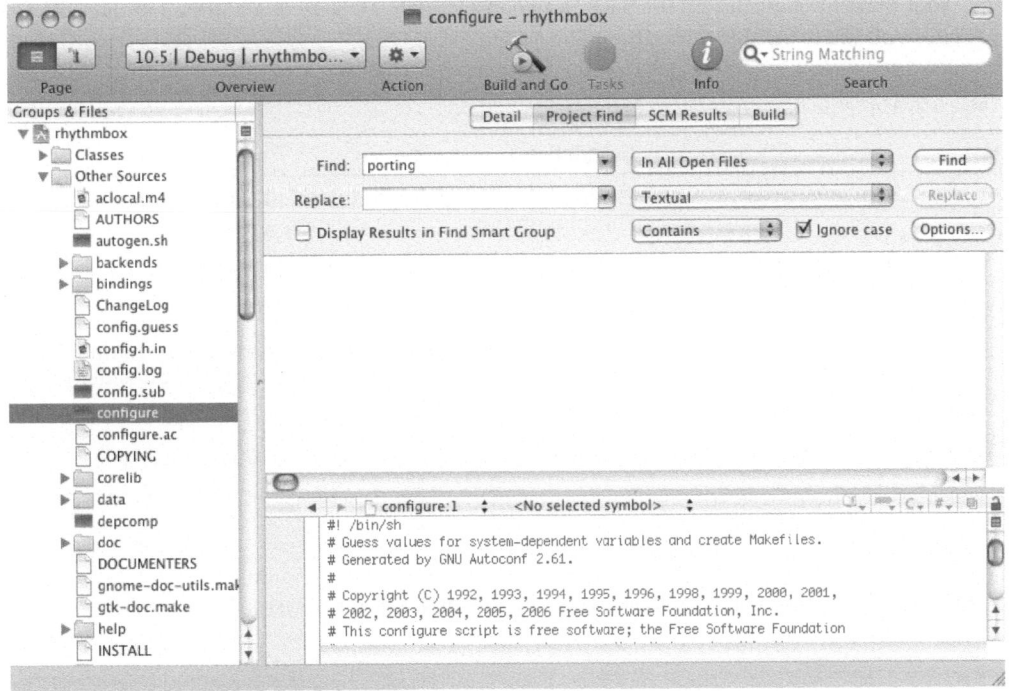

Figure 9-6. *Source code in the Xcode tool*

8. In the Custom Build Command section of the target inspector, change the Directory field to point to the directory containing your makefile, also changing any other settings as needed.

9. Change the active target to your new target by choosing Project ➤ Set Active Target.

10. Add the source files to the project by opening the disclosure triangle beside the Source folder in the left side of the project window and dragging the folder containing the sources from the Finder into that Source folder in Xcode. Xcode should now copy the files. Xcode will recursively find all of the files in that folder. Delete any files that should not be included.

11. When you are ready to build the project, click the Build and Go button in the toolbar, select Build ➤ Build, or press Command+B.

12. Once the project has been built, point Xcode to the executable by choosing Project ➤ New Custom Executable. Choose the path where the executable is located, and then add the name of the executable.

13. Run the resulting program by pressing Command+R.

This should get you started in bringing your application into the native build environment of Mac OS X.

Beginning with Mac OS X 10.5 (Leopard), the default compiler is GCC 4. Most Linux and UNIX users will be familiar with GCC 4.

Your makefile can contain the flags shown in Table 9-2. Unlike most other compiler flags, which are added to `CFLAGS`, these should be added to `LDFLAGS`.

Table 9-2. *Makefile Flags (Added to LDFLAGS)*

Flag	Description
`-bundle`	Produces a Mach-O bundle format file, used for creating loadable plug-ins
`-bundle_loader executable`	Specifies which executable will load a plug-in
`-dynamiclib`	Produces a Mach-O dynamic shared library
`-flat_namespace`	Creates a single-level namespace, contrary to the normal Mac convention of two-level namespaces (not recommended)
`-framework framework`	Links the executable being built against the listed framework
`-mmacosx-version-min version`	Specifies the targeted Mac operating system version

Note Mac OS X uses linked libraries like any other UNIX-based operating system.

Installing Linux Desktop Environments on the Mac

If you've been a Linux user for a while, you've probably landed on a preferred desktop environment. The desktop wars in Linux can be almost as vociferous as those between vi and emacs users. It's a good thing, really, that users feel strongly about their own preferences. Both major desktop environments, GNOME and KDE, have some real advantages, depending on your style of work.

And though the native look and feel of Mac OS X is one of the primary reasons many come to the platform, it's possible that you'll still want to use some of your favorite Linux applications, and do so within your chosen desktop environment.

Remember that Mac OS X is a BSD-like UNIX system, so many of those tools you've come to rely on in Linux will be available in Mac OS X as well, generally via MacPorts or Fink. You'll find that both KDE and GNOME are available for Mac OS X, although some functionality may be a bit limited. Here, we'll look at how to install these two popular Linux desktop environments on your Mac OS X system.

Note The full experience with Linux desktop environments will also require `xquartz-2.3.2`, available as a release candidate from `http://xquartz.macosforge.org/`. This version reintroduced full-screen support. A version for Mac OS X 10.6 (Snow Leopard) will also include full-screen support.

Installing GNOME

As the default desktop environment of several of the most popular Linux distributions (Ubuntu and Fedora, in particular), GNOME has been the desktop on which many users have cut their Linux teeth. But GNOME is more than just a desktop. It's also a development platform and a large project to coordinate the efforts of developers working on GNOME components. For Mac OS X, GNOME is available via the usual port systems, including MacPorts and Fink.

Installing GNOME using MacPorts is much the same as you've seen with the other MacPorts installations. In the case of GNOME, the following command will install the `gnome-desktop` package:

```
$ sudo port install gnome
```

In this case, gnome is an alias (or *metaport*) for the `gnome-desktop` package. This package provides the core libraries and icons for the GNOME desktop. This command will install all the base files necessary to run GNOME on a Mac OS X system.

Additionally, some system variables will need to be set in order for the desktop to operate properly:

```
XDG_DATA_DIRS
/opt/local/share
XDG_DATA_HOME
/opt/local/share
```

```
XDG_CONFIG_DIRS
/opt/local/etc/xdg
ESPEAKER
localhost
```

These variables will be set in the ~/.xinitrc files, as in the following example, which enables GNOME using any X11 and uses GNOME's built-in window manager, Metacity:

```
# make sure X11 is MacPorts and /usr/local aware
PATH=$PATH:/opt/local/bin:/opt/local/sbin:/usr/local/bin
export PATH

# make the freedesktop menu entries work
export XDG_DATA_DIRS=/opt/local/share
export XDG_DATA_HOME=/opt/local/share
export XDG_CONFIG_DIRS=/opt/local/etc/xdg

# enable sound
export ESPEAKER=localhost

# use GNOME's window manager
exec metacity &

# start GNOME
exec gnome-session
```

For users who have chosen Fink as their port system on Mac OS X, the following command will install GNOME:

```
$ fink install gnome
```

After GNOME is installed, run it within Mac OS X by executing this command:

```
$ gnome-session &
```

You can also make some modifications to ~/.xinitrc in order to run the GNOME desktop at login. Adding the following line will start the GNOME desktop at login:

```
exec gnome-session
```

Adding this line directs GNOME to use the D-Bus interprocess communication system:

```
exec dbus-launch gnome-session
```

■**Note** Originally developed by Red Hat, Desktop Bus, or D-Bus, is a daemon designed to facilitate communication between running processes. Applications taking advantage of D-Bus register with the service and are provided with a facility to look up the other services registered with the daemon. Users can run several D-Bus instances, or *channels*. These channels will always include a system channel, intended to communicate between inquiring processes and the Hardware Abstraction Layer (HAL), and a private channel for each user logged in to the system. D-Bus works with a low-latency, low-overhead protocol. It's also easy for developers to implement and is easily wrapped by other systems. For those reasons, D-Bus is quickly being adopted across the computing world.

Installing KDE

K Desktop Environment (KDE) is an increasingly popular environment for Linux users. Several Linux distributions install KDE as the default desktop environment. Based on the Qt toolkit, KDE is also an umbrella project for other applications intended to fit easily within the KDE environment. These projects include KOffice, K3b, Amarok, and others. These tools are so closely tied to the KDE libraries that they would be nonfunctional without them. In other words, in order to use many of the KDE-guided GUI-based tools, it's necessary to have KDE installed on the system. They don't function well—or in some cases, at all—as stand-alone tools.

KDE's original license limited its use to free operating systems, effectively ruling out using it on Mac OS X. Recent versions are released under a revised licensing agreement that allows the use of KDE in all environments. That change made it possible for developers to begin porting KDE for use in Mac OS X. KDE is now available as a stand-alone .dmg installer from http://mac.kde.org/?id=download, and as a port in both MacPorts and Fink.

Installing from mac.kde.org

The mac.kde.org site makes both full and individual packages available in a variety of download formats. The individual .dmg files are available for direct download, as are BitTorrent versions of both, an "everything" package, and the individual components of the KDE system.

The everything package for KDE is a 3GB file—a substantial download even on a fast connection. Fortunately, the BitTorrent versions are well seeded, and the network is active. The BitTorrent download on my machine took just over two hours. Figure 9-7 shows the first KDE installer screen.

Figure 9-7. *Beginning KDE installation from mac.kde.org*

When the download is complete, open the kde-mac folder and double-click the kde.mpkg file, as shown in Figure 9-8. Though the directory contains a full list of .pkg files, they will be installed in the proper order by the kde.pkg file. Table 9-3 lists the software tools included in the package.

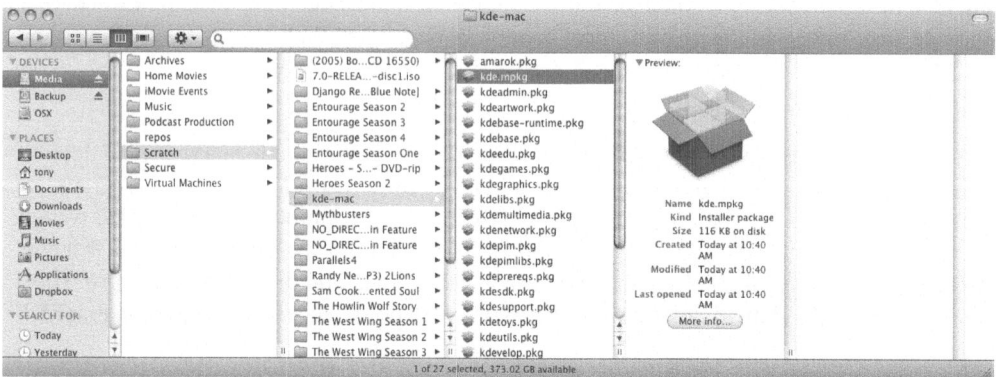

Figure 9-8. *Contents of the kde-mac folder*

Table 9-3. *Software Included with the KDE Desktop Installation*

Software	Description
Amarok	A KDE-based music management system
KDE Education	A package of several educational applications, which are designed with the special interface needs of young children in mind
KDE Games	A full range of games, including arcade, card, dice, logic, and strategy games
KDE PIM	A KDE-based personal information management application
KDE Toys	A package of amusement applications
KDevelop	A KDE-based IDE, supporting plug-ins and project management; directly supports C++, Ruby, and PHP development and version control with CVS, Subversion, Perforce, and Clearcase
KDE WebDev	A full kit of tools for web development, including Quanta, KImageMapEditor, KXSL Debug, and Kallery
KOffice	An integrated office suite for KDE that includes word processing, spreadsheet, presentation, and other office applications
KTorrent	A KDE BitTorrent application

As the underlying toolkit for KDE is Qt, that package is installed first, as shown in Figure 9-9, even before the base KDE packages. The individual package installations follow, including the base package and the included applications.

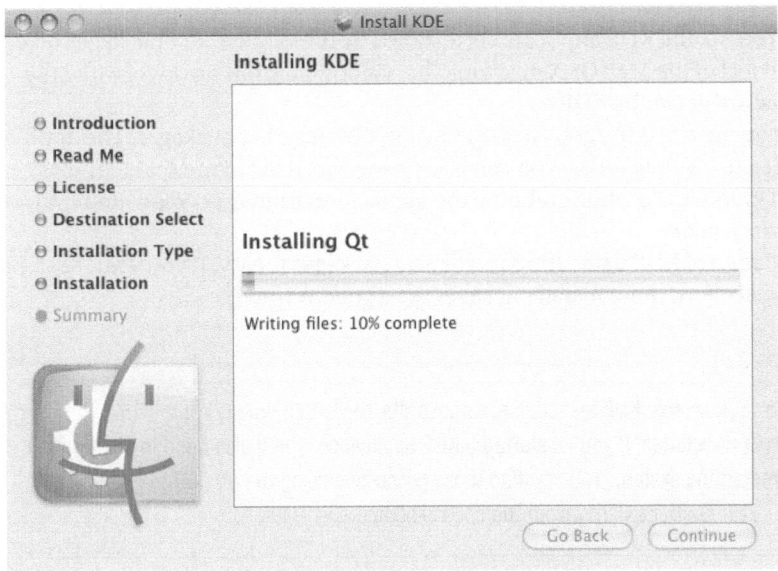

Figure 9-9. *Installing the underlying Qt libraries for KDE*

At the time of this writing, two issues existed with this package installation:

- A reboot is required in order for KDE to use D-Bus. Most of the KDE applications will not work without this piece.

- A postinstallation error that prevents a good installation can be avoided by issuing a command-line instruction. Change into the directory to which the KDE packages have been downloaded and unzipped, and then enter the following command from the command line:

```
$ chmod a+x *.pkg/Contents/Resources/postflight
```

It's not readily apparent when KDE is running, short of opening an application. A quick check from the command line will show something like the following:

```
Cerebellum:opt tony$ ps xa | grep kde
  392   ??  S      0:00.62 /opt/kde4-deps/bin/dbus-daemon --nofork --session
18252   ??  Ss     0:00.21 kdeinit4: kdeinit4 Running...
18253   ??  S      0:00.25 /opt/kde4/lib/kde4/libexec/klauncher
18277   ??  S      0:00.07 kdeinit4: kdeinit4: kio_file file
 local:/Users/tony/Library/Preferences/KDE/socket-
Cerebellum.local/klauncherJ18253.slave-socket
local:/Users/tony/Library/Preferences/KDE/socket-
Cerebellum.local/akregatorR18227.slave-socket
18570 s000  R+     0:00.01 grep kde
```

As shown in Figure 9-10, the KDE applications installed by the mac.kde.org packages take on part of the look and feel of the Mac OS X desktop. The window controls are Mac, while the contents of the window are drawn by KDE.

KDE applications are installed in /opt/kde4/bin by the KDE installer packages. The applications can be launched using the Finder. You can also create shortcuts to the Applications directory by pressing Option+Cmd while grabbing the application from /opt/kde4/ and dragging it to the Applications folder.

Overall, the installation of KDE using the mac.kde.org packages is easy. If you want to install KDE with minimal effort, these install packages are a good way to go.

Note To uninstall the mac.kde.org KDE installation, remove the /opt/bin/kde4, /opt/bin/kde4-devel, and /opt/qt4 directories. If you've started a KDE application, you'll also need to kill the individual KDE processes or restart the system. You can find those processes using the ps xa | grep kde command. Then execute kill [*process id*] from the command line.

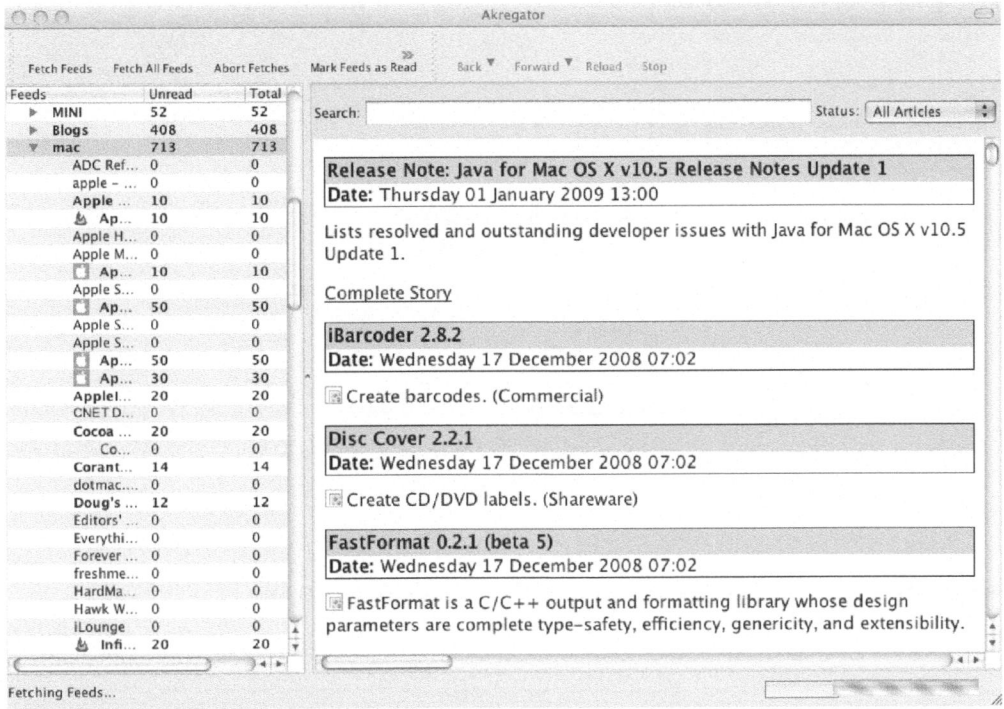

Figure 9-10. *Running Akregator, the KDE RSS aggregator in Mac OS X*

Installing KDE Using MacPorts

KDE can also be installed in Mac OS X using the MacPorts system. In a terminal window, issue this command:

```
$ sudo port install kde
```

The default port package is KDE3. As with the mac.kde.org package installation, qt3 will install first, followed by kdelibs, kdebase, kdenetwork, and the other pieces of the desktop environment. This is a large build, so don't panic if it takes quite a while.

When the build is complete, the KDE applications will be installed in the /opt/local/bin directory. Among those applications are Konqueror, the KDE browser (see Figure 9-11), and Kate, the KDE text editor (see Figure 9-12).

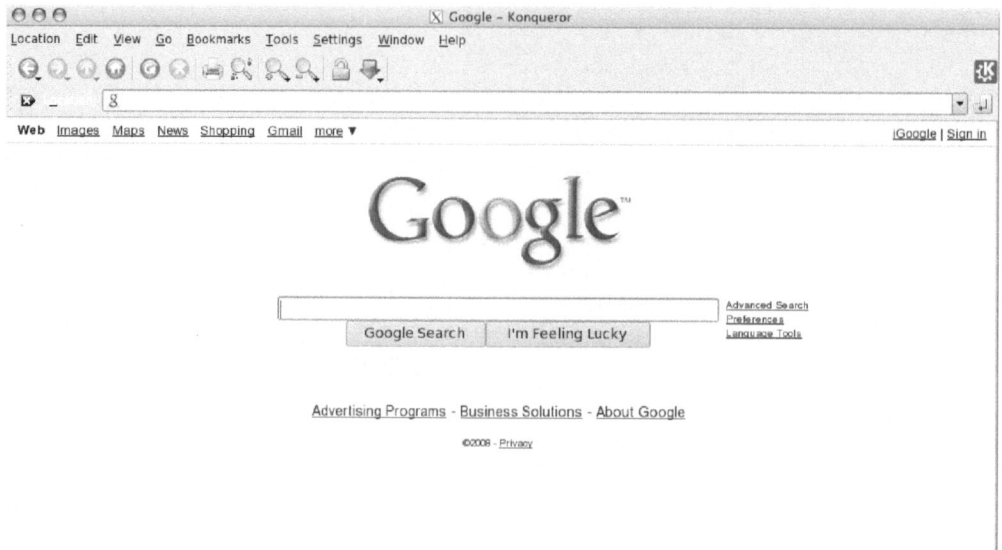

Figure 9-11. *Konqueror, the KDE browser and file manager, in Mac OS X*

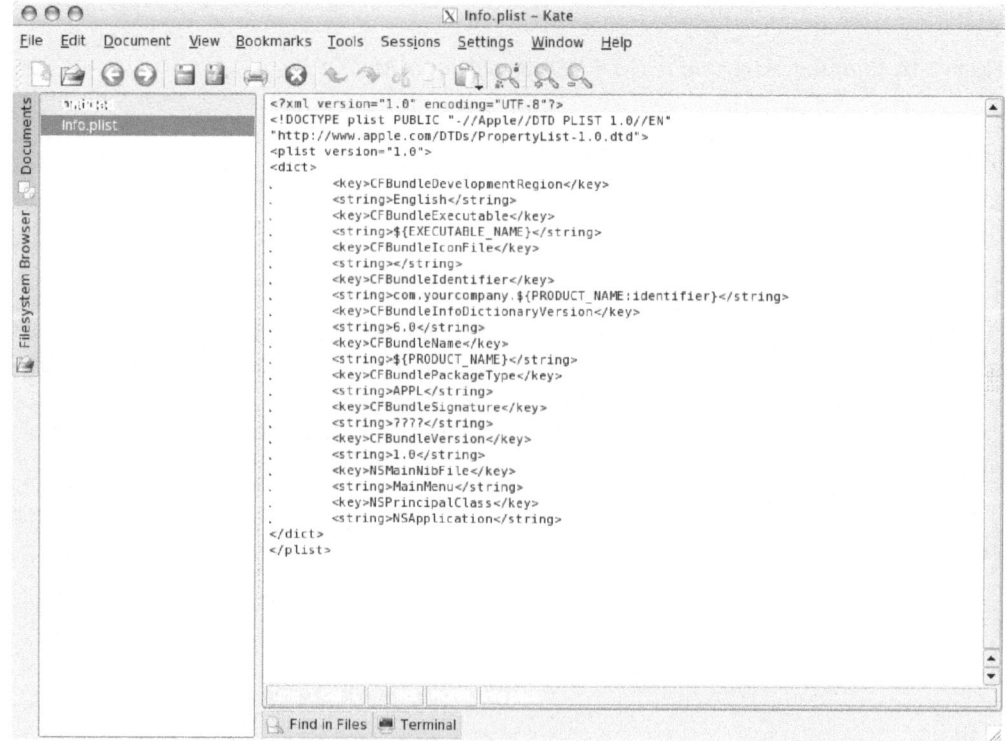

Figure 9-12. *Kate, the KDE text editor, in Mac OS X*

The other basic applications include KWrite from the KOffice suite; Konsole, the KDE console application; and many others. Additional packages can be installed using the port system. These include the full KOffice package, among others. Figure 9-13 shows KSpread, the KOffice spreadsheet application, running in Mac OS X. A list of KDE application ports is available on the MacPorts site at `http://macports.org/`.

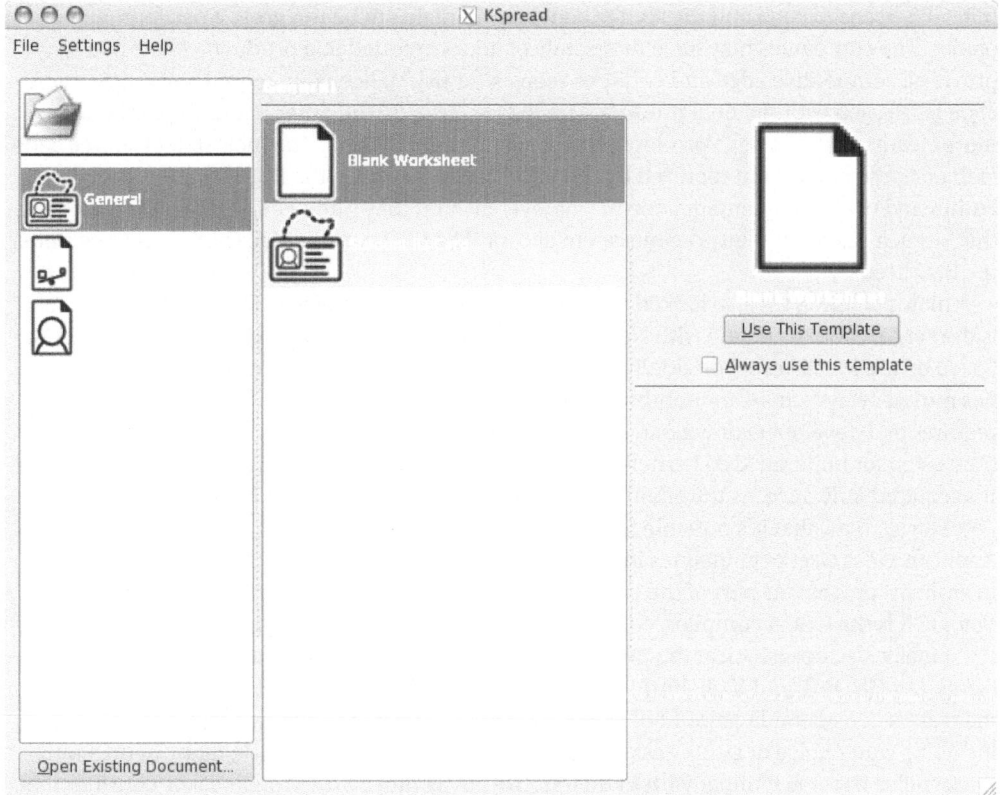

Figure 9-13. *KSpread, the KOffice spreadsheet application, in Mac OS X*

Summary

In this chapter, we looked at some of the ways to utilize the best of the Linux, BSD and Mac OS X worlds, combining them into a hybridized system that takes full advantage of the strengths of each system. They're all robust systems with great strengths and some weaknesses. By better understanding those strengths and weaknesses, it's possible to customize and use Mac OS X in a way that best suits your particular computing tasks and style.

To make the mental adjustment from Linux to the BSD-based Mac OS X, we first looked at the differences between Linux and BSD. Some real differences exist in the implementation of runlevels between the two systems. In fact, longtime users of either system might not recognize the concept of runlevels that exists on the other system. Linux uses `rc` scripts, `init`, and `telinit` to establish runlevels 0 through 6. These runlevels are sets of services, if you will, that determine the functionality of the system. Unlike Linux, BSD simply uses the `reboot` and `shutdown` commands to change the running state of the system.

Significant differences also exist in the licensing of Linux and BSD. Linux, licensed under the GPL, focuses sharply on source code, requiring the inclusion of source code with any system or application released under the GPL. This is a model that can be difficult for business, especially those businesses in highly competitive spaces. Many corporate legal departments find GPL-licensed code and the source code requirements to be too great a risk for their companies. The companies may have thousands of hours invested in a product—effort that may provide a competitive edge and could be seen as "at risk" if licensing requires that the source code is released with the final product. The BSD license, on the other hand, focuses much more clearly on the use of a product rather than the source code. The inclusion of source code with an application is not required by the BSD license. In effect, the BSD license allows both author and user to implement code in whatever fashion they find necessary. This is a model that's much easier for many businesses to accept. The BSD code in Mac OS X is released under the BSD license.

In this chapter, we also looked at the process of rebuilding Mac OS X's XNU kernel. This is the kernel code that came with NeXTStep when it was acquired by Apple in the mid-1990s. Based on the Mach kernel originally developed at Carnegie Mellon University, the XNU kernel has moved away from its monolithic roots. The process of building the kernel for Mac OS X requires that developers download some additional code tools. In fact, you saw that the first-time setup for building XNU kernels for Mac OS X is likely to be the longest part of the process. It's required only once, as the environment then exists for subsequent builds.

You also saw that it's possible to port applications created for BSD and Linux to Mac OS X. Apple provides a set of guidelines in its developer area online (`http://developer.apple.com/`) to ease this process. As part of the porting process, you found that the default compiler for Mac OS X is the GCC 4 compiler, complete with a full set of compilation options.

Finally, we took a look at the process for installing the most popular Linux desktop environments: GNOME and KDE. Both are available via the MacPorts and Fink systems. While it may take a considerable amount of time to download and install all the necessary packages, installing your choice of Linux desktop environment will allow you to use many of the Linux tools you've become familiar with in their native environment. You might easily consider that the ultimate system hybridization.

Index

You Need the Companion eBook

Your purchase of this book entitles you to buy the companion PDF-version eBook for only $10. Take the weightless companion with you anywhere.

We believe this Apress title will prove so indispensable that you'll want to carry it with you everywhere, which is why we are offering the companion eBook (in PDF format) for $10 to customers who purchase this book now. Convenient and fully searchable, the PDF version of any content-rich, page-heavy Apress book makes a valuable addition to your programming library. You can easily find and copy code—or perform examples by quickly toggling between instructions and the application. Even simultaneously tackling a donut, diet soda, and complex code becomes simplified with hands-free eBooks!

Once you purchase your book, getting the $10 companion eBook is simple:

❶ Visit **www.apress.com/promo/tendollars/**.

❷ Complete a basic registration form to receive a randomly generated question about this title.

❸ Answer the question correctly in 60 seconds, and you will receive a promotional code to redeem for the $10.00 eBook.

THE EXPERT'S VOICE™

2855 TELEGRAPH AVENUE | SUITE 600 | BERKELEY, CA 94705

Offer valid through 7/09.